The Accidental Taxonomist

Heather Hedden

Information Today, Inc.

Medford, New Jersey

First Printing, 2016

The Accidental Taxonomist, Second Edition

Copyright © 2016 by Heather Hedden

Library of Congress Cataloging-in-Publication Data

Names: Hedden, Heather.
Title: The accidental taxonomist / Heather Hedden.
Description: Second edition. | Medford, New Jersey : Information Today, Inc.,
    [2016] | Includes bibliographical references and index.
Identifiers: LCCN 2016002968 | ISBN 9781573875288
Subjects: LCSH: Information organization. | Classification. | Indexing. | Subject
    headings. | Cross references (Information retrieval) | Thesauri.
Classification: LCC Z666.5 .H43 2016 | DDC 025—dc23
LC record available at http://lccn.loc.gov/2016002968

Printed and bound in the United States of America

President and CEO: Thomas H. Hogan, Sr.
Editor-in-Chief and Publisher: John B. Bryans
Associate Editor: Beverly M. Michaels
Production Manager: Tiffany Chamenko
Marketing Coordinator: Rob Colding
Indexer: Kathleen Rocheleau
Cover Designer: Ashlee Caruolo

Composition by Amnet Systems

www.infotoday.com

Contents

Chapter 10: Taxonomy Planning, Design, and Creation 315

Chapter 11: Taxonomy Implementation and Evolution 349

Chapter 12: Taxonomy Work and the Profession 383

Figures and Tables

Foreword

Organizing electronic content using metadata fields with controlled vocabularies has at least a 50-year history. It's the story of how we got from expensive, rarely used time-shared databases to the almost ubiquitous web where anyone can "look it up" anywhere, anytime. The work of tagging content has always been done by an army of indexers, more geeks than librarians, working in more of a cottage industry than a factory. All were accidental information scientists with backgrounds in business, medicine, law, the humanities, and maybe sometimes library but rarely computer science.

Some people may think that the content in Heather Hedden's practical compendium is "old wine in a new bottle," but somebody had to write this stuff down. True, librarians have been doing cataloging, classification, and subject indexing for a long time, long before electronic content became a format to manage. But meaningfully adapting appropriate practices from library science and communicating them in a form that can be effectively used by a broad interdisciplinary audience is the major accomplishment of this book.

Taxonomies to support content indexing and finding could be tied to the history of database systems that included processable text information. At first these databases were electronic versions of abstracting and indexing services offered as very expensive, time-share online services (e.g., Dialog), later as subscription CD-ROM databases, and most recently as various types of web-mediated services. In the early days, two disciplines dominated the online services—medicine and law. Medical informatics was heavily subsidized by governments (especially in the United States) after World War II, and legal information (e.g., LexisNexis) was valuable enough to be paid for by large corporations who were the clients of large law firms. Medical Subject Headings (MeSH) was introduced by the National Library of Medicine in 1960. Its precursor was the subject headings of *Index Medicus*, which date from 1940. Medical "subjects" are one of the taxonomy gold standards. They include taxonomies for the human body, taxonomies for conditions and treatments, taxonomies for medical practice settings, etc.

The iterations of digital environments over the past 50 years have had major impacts on what would be considered effective and efficient information organization strategies. In the era of expensive, time-share online services, taxonomies needed to enable especially precise retrieval because every minute and every citation to an information source had a significant cost associated with it. End users, such as business managers, were typically not allowed to execute their own searches. This was an era of intermediated searching. The online searcher (often a librarian) was a highly trained gatekeeper and often a subject matter expert him- or herself.

With CD-ROMs the costs of online access were eliminated. But the content organization schemes had to be changed to work on these self-contained platforms. The web changed this again, at first replacing content organization with the power of web search engines (Google, Yahoo!, Altavista, etc.); global taxonomies, such as the DMOZ Open Directory Project; and very importantly, online shopping. Search engines transformed us into a "look it up" culture. Shopping online has taught everyone how to do Boolean searching, these days referred to as search refining.

The current era of the semantic web is proving to be a further watershed, because its underpinnings are the identification of named entities—people, organizations, locations, events, products, topics, and the like—when they occur in the content on the web. The first-generation web enabled the observation and boosting of content relevance based simply on its access and use. The semantic web is enabling the identification of relationships among all types of named entities and the presentation of information based on these relationships. Simply put, the semantic web is based on the organizing power of faceted taxonomy.

Inside the organization, the relatively new current expectation is that information should be as findable and linkable as on the public web. Enterprise applications are more and more becoming web services that happen to be within the organizational firewall. Employees expect there to be

- a single place for internal information delivery

- a view of information across different business silos

- easy access to others across different business groups to foster collaboration

- a trusted location for conducting day-to-day activities

As taxonomy becomes a ubiquitous part of the organizational information ecosystem, there is more and more demand from organizations for people who have the skills to integrate taxonomies into enterprise applications. But what exactly does creating and maintaining taxonomies entail, and where are you going to find the appropriate expertise to competently undertake these tasks? While this is a great time to be a taxonomy consultant, one measure of the success of one of our engagements is whether a taxonomy editor has been identified or hired to be the central point of contact for taxonomy maintenance. Hence, you may find yourself becoming an "accidental taxonomist."

This book is an excellent primer for the novice who finds him- or herself assigned (or volunteering for) the task of creating and maintaining a taxonomy. The book should also serve as a "bible" for the expert (I have a copy on my shelf). It answers these key questions I am frequently asked:

- What is a taxonomy?

- Who are taxonomists?

- How do you create, maintain, and use a taxonomy?

- Where can you find taxonomy tools?

This edition is a comprehensive revision, notably updating screen-shots of websites, renewing the section on taxonomy software, and adding information about two important new taxonomy standards: ISO 25964 (*Thesauri and Interoperability with Other Vocabularies*) and SKOS (*Simple Knowledge Organization System*), a W3C recommendation.

As a consultant, I am a proponent of keeping things as simple as possible. *The Accidental Taxonomist* is a very useful resource for me to share with my clients and prospects. It is full of information about the various considerations related to content organization and is one of the best sources for guidance on best practices for addressing them.

—Joseph Busch

Joseph Busch is an authority in the field of information science and a frequent speaker at conferences on metadata and taxonomy. Prior to founding Taxonomy Strategies, a consulting firm that guides organizations in improving information capture, preservation, search, retrieval, and governance, he was vice president for Infoware at Metacode Technologies and the Getty Trust's program manager for Standards and Research Databases. He is a past president of the Association for Information Science and Technology (ASIS&T) and a member of the Dublin Core Metadata Initiative Executive Committee.

Acknowledgments

The field of taxonomies is broad and multidisciplined, and thus no single taxonomist-author could comprehensively cover the subject without getting input and insights from others with different experiences. I am very grateful to the colleagues of mine who have contributed to this book. I especially want to acknowledge the very thorough review of the first edition of my book by two expert reviewers, Lynda Moulton and Alice Redmond-Neal, who voluntarily took time out of their busy schedules to meticulously go through every chapter. In addition to providing suggestions for better wordings and corrections to any inaccurate generalizations and assumptions, they each contributed some additional bits of information and insights from their own experience that I incorporated. Additional expert review on certain sections and chapters came from Margot Diltz and Tom Reamy.

I want to give a big thank you to my friend and indexing colleague Jean Jesensky for giving my book its initial read-through for clarity. Thanks also go to the taxonomy consultants I interviewed and the other taxonomists who completed my online surveys. For the second edition, I am grateful to Enterprise Knowledge for letting me log into their SharePoint 2013 account so that I could experiment with the Term Store and take a screenshot.

This book would not have been possible without the hard work of the staff of Information Today, Inc., especially John Bryans, who encouraged me to write both the first and second editions. John and his team helped make the first edition a success, leading to seven printings, and ably supported my many book signings in the years that followed its release.

In addition to those who helped directly with this book, I wish to acknowledge all those who contributed indirectly, such as by teaching or mentoring me or by giving me opportunities. My primary mentors in the area of controlled vocabularies and taxonomies were my manager at what was then Information Access Company (now Cengage Learning), Margot Diltz, and consultant Jessica Milstead. Through Gale's partnership with Synaptica, I also received feedback on my early vocabulary work from Trish Yancey. A later mentor was Joseph Busch, from whom I learned more about taxonomy implementation, including taxonomy testing and governance. I also appreciate the demo access that various taxonomy software vendors set up for me to experiment with the various products. Even the students I taught in my online courses helped me indirectly by asking questions, which I realized needed to be addressed. So I also thank Kris Liberman for giving me the opportunity to teach numerous sessions of my taxonomies workshop through the continuing education program of Simmons College School of Library and Information Science.

Finally, thanks go to my husband, Tom, also a freelancer, who had to work more to help financially support us during the year I wrote the first edition, as I was taking on less consulting work, and also for proofreading selected passages of my second edition.

About the Website
www.accidental-taxonomist.com

The Accidental Taxonomist mentions a number of websites throughout. These include examples of online taxonomies, software vendor sites, and useful reference sites. These websites are all listed in Appendix D. To facilitate quick access to these resources, a website with links to all these related sites can be found at www.accidental-taxonomist.com. Furthermore, the links will be maintained and updated on the website as needed over time, and new sources may be added. Please email your comments, changes, and suggested additions to the author at heather@hedden.net.

Disclaimer

Neither the publisher nor the author makes any claim as to the results that may be obtained through the use of this webpage or of any of the internet resources it references or links to. Neither the publisher nor the author will be held liable for any results, or lack thereof, obtained by the use of this page or any of its links; for any third-party charges; or for any hardware, software, or other problems that may occur as the result of using it. This webpage is subject to change or discontinuation without notice at the discretion of the publisher and author.

Preface to the Second Edition

When I published the first edition of *The Accidental Taxonomist*, I knew that changes would be needed within a couple of years, mostly to reflect the changes in thesaurus management software vendors, as software is a volatile industry characterized by new companies, acquisitions, and some vendors going out of business. It was also expected that the website examples, given as screenshots in the book, would change. As it turned out, the changes were more widespread than anticipated. I ended up replacing all screenshots and adding some new ones (totaling 44), since even existing software vendors or websites had updated their user interfaces. More than half of the various website URLs found throughout the book also had to be updated.

In the area of software, what I did not anticipate was that software changes have gone beyond just who the vendors are and what features vendors have added. There have also been some notable trends, such as in the adoption of Semantic Web standards, the convergence of taxonomy and ontology support, and more web-based, cloud/software-as-a-service offerings. Thus, in addition to adding more software vendors (and removing a few), I have also added a short section summarizing all of these software trends.

Also with respect to software, the first edition made no mention of SharePoint, since SharePoint 2010, the first version to support taxonomies, came out the same year my book did. So this new edition includes some discussion of managing taxonomies in SharePoint. There is not the space here to go into all the details, so I explore specific topics, such as managing polyhierarchy in SharePoint, on my blog, also called The Accidental Taxonomist.

The standards have changed too. ANSI/NISO Z39.19 2005 *Guidelines for the Construction, Format, and Management of Monolingual Controlled Vocabularies* was reaffirmed in 2010, but more significantly ISO 2788 *Guidelines for the Establishment and Development of Monolingual Thesauri* and 5964 *Guidelines for the Establishment and Development of Multilingual Thesauri* have been replaced by ISO 25964 *Thesauri and Interoperability with Other Vocabularies*, Part 1 in 2011 and Part 2 in 2013. This is not merely a reorganization of parts. The changes also comprise new content in the area of interoperability, including the exchange of taxonomy data and mappings between vocabularies. Now ANSI/NISO Z39.19 is coming due for a new version, but it is a long process. With an eye to a wider international audience, in this edition I cite the ISO standard along with the ANSI/NISO standard whenever relevant.

In addition to the change in the ISO thesaurus standard, there is also a change involving the wider adoption of other kinds of standards, most significantly those associated with the Semantic Web. Although development had begun earlier, the World Wide Web Consortium (W3C) formally released the SKOS (Simple Knowledge Organization System) standard only in August 2009, when I was busy finalizing my manuscript for the first edition, before the extent of the eventual adoption of SKOS was still unknown. Now it is quite common for taxonomy management software to follow the SKOS specifications of concept modeling and taxonomy output. So, more attention to SKOS is given in this edition.

Another trend, which was already underway at the time I wrote my first edition, but which I simply did not bother to consider in detail, is the convergence of metadata and taxonomy. So, I have added a short section on the topic. I needed the intervening years to actually work in areas where taxonomies and metadata meet, whether through consulting or in a department called Metadata Standards and Services, before I felt I could say something original on the subject.

As for the people who do taxonomy work, the accidental taxonomists, I conducted a new survey, which has shown that their backgrounds remain as diverse as they were when surveyed six years prior, but there are new stories and examples of how people got involved in this type of work and what they like about it. Meanwhile, the opportunities for taxonomists continue to grow. I executed the exact same search for jobs in fall of 2009 and again in fall of 2015, on the job board aggregator Indeed.com, and found the numbers of currently posted openings had significantly increased.

Although I considered myself quite experienced with various taxonomies at the time I wrote the first edition, I have continued to gain additional taxonomy work experience since, so here and there throughout the book I have added information based on further reflection. Thus, in the chapter on planning and designing a taxonomy, I have added some advice regarding designating facets for enterprise taxonomies, questions to ask during stakeholder interviews, how to conduct stakeholder workshops, and methods of testing taxonomies

I had also started writing my blog the year after the first edition, but the blog post topics are not the same as the additions to this book. The Accidental Taxonomist blog allows me to explore tangents in more detail, and this book is already longer than needs to be!

Taxonomies are interesting in that some things about them are fundamental and do not change, such as the notion of a concept, its varied names, its hierarchical and nonhierarchical relationships with other concepts. But, as anything related to information technology, there are things about taxonomies that do change, such as how they are managed, implemented, and utilized. Thus, it is not only the varied subject matter that makes taxonomy work interesting, but also the various implementations and opportunities to take advantage of in new technologies, such as those related to the Semantic Web and Linked Open Data. Although this new edition addresses these topics, my ongoing blog will cover further considerations in such areas.

Introduction

After reading a case study of an enterprise taxonomy in which corporate research librarians were charged with the task of building the taxonomy,[1] it occurred to me that many people who get involved in creating taxonomies do so by accident. Even if this case study is not typical, it illustrates the point: The growing interest in taxonomies means that the people being asked to create taxonomies may not have done that work before, may not have sufficient training, and/or may not even have thought of pursuing such work before they were asked to. This hypothesis was borne out by responses to an online questionnaire I wrote, in which taxonomists explained how they got into the field.

Most of us first became familiar with the term *taxonomy* in high-school biology when the concept was used in reference to the classification and naming of plants and animals. If you did not pursue a career in biology, you probably did not give the concept any further thought for quite some time after that. Although the term is also used to refer to nomenclature and classification of concepts in other academic disciplines, only since the late 1990s has it been understood to mean information organization in general. Taxonomy in this sense includes controlled vocabularies for document indexing and retrieval, subject categories in content management systems, navigation labels and categories in website information architecture, and standardized terminology within a corporate knowledge base. In some of these areas, such as websites, the application of taxonomy is relatively new, coinciding with the newer adoption of the term *taxonomy*. Other areas, such as controlled vocabularies and thesauri used in periodical indexing and literature retrieval, have been around for decades. Their publishers may continue to refer to a "controlled vocabulary," an "authority file," or a "thesaurus," even though the newer usage of the term *taxonomy* is also used for these purposes.

Today there are many meanings of the word *taxonomy*, which can complicate any research into the term. Although the original meaning, the *study* of classification, is rarely used, the term *taxonomy* continues to be used to designate classification systems of things. Originally used for the classification of things in nature, the term spread from the sciences to the social sciences and thus came to be used also for the classification of concepts. (One better-known example of such taxonomies is the Taxonomy of Educational Objectives, also known as Bloom's Taxonomy.) Despite the recent popularity of the term *taxonomy* for generic knowledge organization, the majority of books and scholarly articles on taxonomies in print today are still about highly specific classification systems in the sciences or social sciences. The taxonomists of those systems are experts in their academic disciplines rather than librarians or information architects.

Even as a generic system of knowledge organization, the term *taxonomy* presently has two different common usages. One meaning of taxonomy, reflecting the earlier usage for the classification of living organisms, is a hierarchical classification of things or concepts in what may be considered a tree structure. Terms within the taxonomy each have a "parent," or broader term, and a "child," or narrower term, unless the terms are at the very top or bottom levels of the taxonomy. Another, even more recent, usage of the term *taxonomy* is to refer to any controlled vocabulary of terms for a subject area domain or a specific purpose. The terms may or may not be arranged in a hierarchy, and they may or may not have even more complex relationships between each other. Thus the term *taxonomy* has taken on a broader meaning that encompasses all of the following: specific subject glossaries, controlled vocabularies, information thesauri, and ontologies. Each of these will be explained in further detail in Chapter 1. For the purposes of this book, this second, broader definition of taxonomy is used. It is the simplest term, and it corresponds to the word taxonomist.

As the word taxonomy has different meanings, so does the designation of a taxonomist. It can still refer to a biologist who specializes in the field of naming and classifying organisms. The majority of people with the title of "taxonomist" today, however, are information specialists, librarians, or information architects and are not likely to be subject matter experts. They deal with taxonomies in the broader definition of knowledge organization systems (not limited to hierarchical trees of terms). They may be creators of controlled vocabularies, thesauri, metadata schemes, or website categorization systems. "Taxonomist" is a more practical and catchy job title than "controlled vocabulary editor," "thesaurus creator," or "nomenclature manager."

Yet for the scope of this book, taxonomists are not limited to people who have the word taxonomy or taxonomist within their job title. There are other job titles for essentially the same tasks, such as vocabulary developer, technical categorization analyst, and information classification specialist. There are many people who work on taxonomies as only one of several job responsibilities, whether as corporate librarians, information architects, or knowledge managers. Finally, there are those who serve in the role of taxonomist temporarily on a project, returning to other duties after completing the taxonomy.

In sum, a taxonomist is someone who creates or edits taxonomies, either singly or as part of a team of taxonomists, and taxonomies are defined as any knowledge organization system (controlled vocabulary, synonym ring, thesaurus, hierarchical term tree, or ontology) used to support information/content findability, discovery, and access. This taxonomy work may be an ongoing job responsibility or a temporary project, and it may be a primary job responsibility or a secondary responsibility. These people and those who are interested in getting into such work are the primary audience of this book.

There is no undergraduate major or graduate degree in taxonomy and no department, program, concentration, or certificate in the field. Thus, people do not choose to be taxonomists when they decide what they want to study. Furthermore, the majority of graduate schools and programs of information science or library and information science do not have even a single course devoted to creating taxonomies (although it is often a topic within a course).[2] Therefore, even people with an education in information science are probably not thinking of working as a taxonomist. For this reason, too, we can say that many taxonomists become so by chance or by "accident."

Unlike working as a reference librarian or corporate librarian, working as a taxonomist does not usually require a degree in library and information science (although it is often preferred). For this reason, too, people with varied educational backgrounds may accidentally find themselves working as taxonomists. In fact, according to the results of an online survey of taxonomists in May 2015, just about half had a master of library science (MLS) or master of library and information science (MLIS) degree. (The full survey questions and answers are reproduced in Appendix A of this book.)

Information taxonomies are relatively new and growing in terms of their applications. New web interactive technologies make taxonomies more usable and user friendly, and the exponential growth of electronic data increasingly calls for new means of organizing and accessing information. Since information taxonomies have been getting attention only since the late 1990s or around 2000, any experienced professional who is getting into taxonomies is doing so somewhat accidentally. As for entry-level taxonomy positions for the new MLIS or MIS graduate, I have yet to see such a position posted.

As for my story, although I came to developing corporate taxonomies via work on controlled vocabularies for periodical database indexing, I did come to the field of controlled vocabularies quite accidentally. I had started my career in writing and editing and then responded to a job notice for an abstractor at the computer magazine publisher Ziff Communications, not realizing that Ziff, at the time, owned a large periodical-indexing division called Information Access Company. It turned out that the abstractors did the indexing and other metadata application as well, so after an intensive employee training on indexing, I got my first exposure to controlled vocabularies.

After indexing for a couple of years, I decided to move onward and upward into the controlled vocabulary management group and soon forgot about abstracting. But I never completely gave up writing, as the production of this book will attest. When my position was eliminated in early 2004 and I had to look for new work, I had difficulty finding a job in a profession that I didn't know what to call. My previous title had been "controlled vocabulary editor," but, alas, I found nothing by that name on the job board sites. Although publishers of aggregate periodical indexes are few and far between, it turned out that similar skills were in demand by large companies to organize and retrieve their internal documents. I then discovered *taxonomy* and *taxonomists* and realized that I could call what I had been doing for the previous 10 years "taxonomy work." With my prior taxonomist experience, I soon landed new taxonomy contract work and then, with that additional experience, a series of full-time taxonomist positions in addition to periods of independent consulting.

While taxonomy may no longer be the latest, hottest topic, as it was around 2000, it has moved beyond being a buzzword to become a topic of more stable interest. The following illustrate the sustained interest in taxonomies:

- An online discussion group dedicated to taxonomies, Taxonomy Community of Practice (groups.yahoo .com/group/TaxoCoP), has grown to 1,250 members, while a corresponding LinkedIn group has grown to 3,330 members.

- A two-day annual conference dedicated to taxonomies, Taxonomy Boot Camp (www.taxonomybootcamp. com), has been growing since its inception in 2005. Registrations increased 28 percent from 229 in 2014 to 292 in 2015.[3] A show of hands at the opening session of the 2015 conference indicated that close to 90 percent were attending Taxonomy Boot Camp for the first time.[4]

- The terms *taxonomy* and *taxonomies* are appearing in increasing numbers of posted job descriptions. A search on those words in job descriptions on Monster.com found increased usage, from 160 hits for the month of April 2008 to over 1,000 for the month of October 2015.

Although there are numerous articles and conference presentations on information taxonomies, books dedicated to the subject are rare. There have been several good books published on thesaurus construction in recent decades. While these might serve as useful guides for the practicing taxonomist, thesaurus construction books do not sufficiently cover other kinds of taxonomies, such as enterprise and website taxonomies, and issues of automated indexing and search. The more recent books on taxonomies, on the other hand, are focused on enterprise taxonomies or take a more project management perspective on taxonomy creation. These may be good books for the manager or executive who is considering a taxonomy project, but they lack sufficient depth to instruct the practicing taxonomist, who needs advice on how to handle various situations in working with the taxonomy terms themselves.

What was missing, in my view, was a practical book for the person actually creating and editing the terms within a taxonomy—a resource for practicing taxonomists designed to go beyond the introductory level. Introductory information on taxonomy creation abounds in articles, conference workshops, Taxonomy Boot Camp, and a few graduate school or continuing education courses. I teach such a continuing education course myself and have been asked by prospective students about offering an intermediate or advanced course, as nothing of that kind exists. Rather than teach a second course—an ongoing commitment—I decided to write this book.

That is not to say that *The Accidental Taxonomist* is purely at an advanced level. It is still appropriate for beginning taxonomists and includes all the content of my introductory course on creating taxonomies and controlled vocabularies. The currently practicing taxonomist will also find useful information, as additional content has been included based on various presentations and articles I have written over the past two years and on some more recent research.

Because there are many different kinds of taxonomies—for human and automated indexing, for literature retrieval and website information categorization, for consumers and internal enterprises—a taxonomist's experience in creating one kind of taxonomy is not necessarily sufficient preparation for working on a different kind of taxonomy. Thus, the book also serves the purpose of cross-training existing taxonomists for different kinds of taxonomy projects. If we want to carry the label of *taxonomist* and move from one job to another, then a broader understanding of the types of work and issues involved is needed.

The book aims to explain what you need to know to be a good taxonomist rather than how to create a taxonomy, step by step. Therefore the chapters are arranged in order of importance in terms of what you need to know, rather than in the project sequence for building a taxonomy. Chapters 1 and 2 provide background on taxonomies and taxonomists. Chapters 3 and 4 present the basics of term and relationship creation in accordance with the ANSI/NISO Z39.19 and ISO 25964 standards, which may serve as a review for experienced taxonomists but is fundamental for the new taxonomist. Chapter 5 provides practical information on the various taxonomy management software available. While some software tools have come and gone, others have been around for a long time and have staying power.

The following four chapters move beyond the basics to focus on particular issues for different types of taxonomies. Chapter 6 deals with creating taxonomies or thesauri used by human indexers, whereas Chapter 7 discusses the issues involved with creating taxonomies used in automated indexing, auto-categorization, or automated search. Chapter 8 examines various taxonomy structures, and Chapter 9 presents various display options.

Chapter 10 turns to broader issues of taxonomy planning and design, which often involve the taxonomist, and Chapter 11 deals with ongoing taxonomy work, such as the maintenance, merging, and translating of taxonomies. Finally, Chapter 12 returns the focus to the taxonomist: the nature of the work, what kind of work exists, and training and resources available.

As an aside, the quotations that lead off each chapter were proposed mottos for the Taxonomy Community of Practice discussion group (groups.yahoo.com/neo/groups/taxocop/info), suggested by its various members in January 2009. (The quotation for Chapter 1 was the winning motto.)

I hope the book will prove not just informative but practical and useful as well. While it covers most of what you need to know to create taxonomies, it does not address every detail. For additional specific instructions, I highly recommend consulting the ANSI/NISO Z39.19 standard, *Guidelines for the Construction, Format, and Management of Monolingual Controlled Vocabularies*, which is available free of charge. It offers a wealth of information, although it is really too much for the newcomer to taxonomies to digest. That's where *The Accidental Taxonomist* comes in, and in addition, the book includes coverage of additional types of taxonomies and taxonomy features not addressed in the standard.

Endnotes

1. Wendi Pohs, "Taxonomy and Classification Resources Should Sit on Development Teams," *Semantics in Practice Blog*, March 27, 2010, accessed December 20, 2015, wendipohs.blogspot.com/2010/03/taxonomy-and-classification-resources.html

2. Review of the course catalogs on the websites of the 58 academic programs listed in the directory of the American Library Association's "Alphabetical List of Institutions With ALA-Accredited Programs," accessed December 20, 2015, http://www.ala.org/accreditedprograms/directory

3. Taxonomy Boot Camp conference registration numbers provided by Information Today Inc. These numbers do not include an additional 50 or so speakers and exhibitors.

4. Conference chair Michael Crandall asked attendees at the opening session on November 2, 2015 if this was their first time attending, and he estimated that 90 percent of the attendees raised their hands.

Chapter 1

What Are Taxonomies?

Taxonomies? That's classified information.
—Jordan Cassel

The first step in discussing the role and work of the taxonomist is to clarify what a taxonomy is. Even if you already have some understanding of the concept, there are multiple meanings and various types of taxonomies that require further explanation. The descriptions provided here are not strict definitions, and the range of knowledge organization systems should be thought of as a spectrum.

Definitions and Types of Taxonomies

The word *taxonomy* comes from the Greek *taxis*, meaning arrangement or order, and *nomos*, meaning law or science. For present-day information management, the term *taxonomy* is used both in the narrow sense, to mean a hierarchical classification or categorization system, and in the broad sense, in reference to any means of organizing concepts of knowledge. Some professionals do not even like to use the term, contending that it is too often ambiguous and frequently misused. Yet it has gained sufficient popularity, and a practical alternative term does not seem to exist. In this book, taxonomy will be used in its broader meaning and not limited to hierarchical structures.

In the broader sense, a taxonomy may also be referred to as a *knowledge organization system* or *knowledge organization structure*. This designation sometimes appears in scholarly discussions of the

1

field, in course titles at graduate schools of library and information science, and in reference to standards. The designation *knowledge organization system* was first used by the Networked Knowledge Organization Systems Working Group at its initial meeting at the Association for Computing Machinery Digital Libraries Conference in Pittsburgh, Pennsylvania, in 1998. Gail Hodge further expanded on it in an article in 2000 for the Digital Library Federation Council on Library and Information Resources. In Hodge's words,

> the term *knowledge organization systems* is intended to encompass all types of schemes for organizing information and promoting knowledge management. Knowledge organization systems include classification schemes that organize materials at a general level (such as books on a shelf), subject headings that provide more detailed access, and authority files that control variant versions of key information (such as geographic names and personal names). They also include less-traditional schemes, such as semantic networks and ontologies.[1]

Although she does not mention taxonomies per se in this paragraph, Hodge goes on to list the various types of knowledge organization systems, which include the following:[2]

1. Term lists (authority files, glossaries, dictionaries, and gazetteers)

2. Classifications and categories (subject headings, classification schemes, taxonomies, and categorization schemes)

3. Relationship lists (thesauri, semantic networks, and ontologies)

The designation *knowledge organization system* has not caught on in the business world, perhaps due partially to its length. We are therefore not likely to hear of a *knowledge organization system manager/editor*, but rather just a taxonomist. The designation *knowledge organization system* may be receiving wider recognition, though, with increasing adoption of the World Wide Web Consortium's recommended framework for representing these various controlled vocabularies, which is called Simple Knowledge Organization System (SKOS).

While this book uses the term *taxonomy* broadly (as a synonym for knowledge organization system), most of our discussion focuses on taxonomies that have at least some form of structure or relationship among the terms (types 2 and 3 in Hodge's list) rather than mere term lists. Indeed, people do not usually call a simple term list a taxonomy. Let us turn now to definitions and explanations of some of these different kinds of knowledge organization systems or taxonomies.

Controlled Vocabularies

The term *controlled vocabulary* may cover any kind of knowledge organization system, with the possible exclusion of highly structured semantic networks or ontologies. At a minimum, a controlled vocabulary is simply a restricted list of words or terms for some specialized purpose, usually for indexing, labeling, or categorizing. It is "controlled" because only terms from the list may be used for the subject area covered. If used by more than one person, it is also controlled in the sense that there is control over who may add terms to the list and when and how they may do it. The list may grow, but only under defined policies.

The objective of a controlled vocabulary is to ensure consistency in the application of index terms, tags, or labels to avoid ambiguity and the overlooking of information if the "wrong" search term is used. When implemented in search or browse systems, the controlled vocabulary can help guide the user to where the desired information is. While controlled vocabularies are most often used in indexing or tagging, they are also used in technical writing to ensure the use of consistent language. This latter task of writing or creating content is not, however, part of *organizing* information. Because controlled vocabulary has this broader usage when applied to content creation, not merely information organization, the term *controlled vocabulary* should not be used as a synonym for knowledge organization system.

Most controlled vocabularies feature a *See or Use* type of cross-reference system, directing the user from one or more "nonpreferred" terms to the designated "preferred" term. Only if a controlled vocabulary is very small and easily browsed, as on a single page, might such cross-referencing be unnecessary.

In certain controlled vocabularies, there could be a set of synonyms for each concept, with none of them designated as the preferred term (akin to having equivalent double posts in a back-of-the-book index instead of *See* references). This type of arrangement is known as a *synonym ring* or a *synset* because all synonyms are equal and can be expressed in a circular ring of interrelationships. An example of a synonym ring, as illustrated in Figure 1.1, is the series of terms *applications, software, computer programs*, and *tools*. Synonym rings may be used when the browsable list of terms or entries is not displayed to the user and when the user merely accesses the terms via a search box. If the synonyms are used behind the scenes with a search engine and never displayed as a browsable list for the user, the distinction between preferred and nonpreferred terms is thus moot. Though these types of controlled vocabularies are quite common, they are often invisible to the user, so the terminology (synonym ring and synset) is not widely known.

Sometimes controlled vocabularies are referred to as *authority files*, especially if they contain just named entities. Named entities are proper-noun terms, such as specific person names, place names, company names, organization names, product names, and names of published works. These also require control for consistent formats, use of abbreviations, spelling, and so forth.

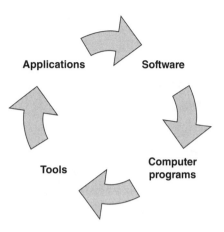

Figure 1.1 Example of terms in a synonym ring

Controlled vocabularies may or may not have relationships among their terms. Simple controlled vocabularies, such as a temporary offline list created by an indexer to ensure consistent indexing or a synonym ring used behind the scenes in a search, do not have any structured relationships other than preferred and nonpreferred terms. Other controlled vocabularies may have broader/narrower and related term relationships and still be called controlled vocabularies rather than thesauri or taxonomies. This is often the case at periodical and reference index publishers, such as Gale (a part of Cengage Learning), EBSCO, and ProQuest, which maintain controlled vocabularies for use in their periodical indexes. In some cases, the publisher maintains multiple kinds of controlled vocabularies, some being more structured than others, and controlled vocabulary is the more generic designation for all of these.

Hierarchical Taxonomies

When we think of taxonomy, hierarchical classification systems are what typically come to mind. However, as explained in the previous section, we are using a broader definition of taxonomy that encompasses all kinds of knowledge organization systems. So taxonomies that are structured as hierarchies will be referred to specifically as *hierarchical taxonomies.*

A hierarchical taxonomy is a kind of controlled vocabulary in which each term is connected to a designated broader term (unless it is the top-level term) and one or more narrower terms (unless it is the bottom-level term), and all the terms are organized into a single large hierarchical structure. Taxonomy in this case could apply to a single hierarchy or a limited set of hierarchies. This type of structure is often referred to as a *tree*, with a trunk, main branches, and more and more smaller branches off the main branches. Actually, if the taxonomy is displayed as a tree, it is an upside-down tree, with multiple smaller branches for narrower terms lower down on the page or screen. Another way to describe such structure is a taxonomy with *nested categories.* The expression *to drill down* is often used to describe how a user navigates down through the branches. An example of an excerpt from a hierarchical taxonomy appears in Figure 1.2.

The classic example of a hierarchical taxonomy is the Linnaean taxonomy (named after Carolus Linnaeus) of biological organisms, with the hierarchical top-down structure: kingdom, phylum, class, order, family, genus, and species. Hierarchical taxonomies are also common in geospatial classification, as for regions, countries, provinces, and cities. While hierarchical taxonomies tend to be used mostly for generic things or concepts, they can also be used for proper nouns that naturally fall into a hierarchy, such as place names, product names, government agency names, or corporate department names.

The structure of a hierarchical taxonomy often reflects an organization of nested categories. Some hierarchical taxonomies permit a term to have multiple broader terms, thus appearing in multiple places in the taxonomy, whereas other hierarchical taxonomies do not permit this "polyhierarchy" structure. Hierarchical taxonomies may or may not make use of nonpreferred terms. Finally,

Top Level Headings	Leisure and culture
Business and industry	. Arts and entertainment venues
Economics and finance	. . Museums and galleries
Education and skills	. Children's activities
Employment, jobs and careers	. Culture and creativity
Environment	. . Architecture
Government, politics and public	. . Crafts
administration	. . Heritage
Health, well-being and care	. . Literature
Housing	. . Music
Information and communication	. . Performing arts
International affairs and defence	. . Visual arts
Leisure and culture	. Entertainment and events
Life in the community	. Gambling and lotteries
People and organisations	. Hobbies and interests
Public order, justice and rights	. Parks and gardens
Science, technology and innovation	. Sports and recreation
Transport and infrastructure	. . Team sports
Leisure and culture	. . . Cricket
	. . . Football
	. . . Rugby
	. . Water sports
	. . Winter sports
	. Sports and recreation facilities
	. Tourism
	. . Passports and visas
	. Young people's activities

Figure 1.2 Terms in an expandable hierarchical taxonomy;
top categories (left) and the expansion of one category (right), from
the Abridged Integrated Public Sector Vocabulary, Version 2.00
(www.esd.org.uk/standards/ipsv)

nonhierarchical related term relationships may exist but usually are not present in such hierarchical taxonomies.

In contrast to the other types of taxonomies described subsequently in this chapter and this book, the hierarchical taxonomy is actually not a defined type of taxonomy. Rather, it is my designation for the narrower, standard definition of taxonomy: "A collection of controlled vocabulary terms organized into a hierarchical structure."[3] It is a kind of taxonomy that is commonly seen in countless real-world applications. And it is the type of taxonomy that the accidental taxonomist is probably most likely to create.

While in some contexts a faceted taxonomy may be considered different from a hierarchical taxonomy, faceted taxonomies, at the high level, are variants of hierarchical taxonomies that are implemented and used in a special way. Faceted taxonomies, like other hierarchical taxonomies, are intended to be browsed by the end user, starting from the top down. A facet is like a hierarchy, and the facet name is like the top-level term in a hierarchy. Relationships between terms that are other than hierarchical are optional and less common. Facets are explained in the section on Retrieval Support later in this chapter and are discussed in much more detail in Chapter 8.

Alpha-Numeric Classification Systems

Classification systems that utilize numeric, alphabetical, or alpha-numeric codes along with the descriptive terms are a type of hierarchical taxonomy. Examples include the Dewey Decimal Classification system and the Library of Congress Classification System for cataloging books. Other well-known examples of hierarchical taxonomies are the Standard Industrial Classification (SIC) and North American Industrial Classification Systems (NAICS) codes for classifying industries. There are classification systems from the United Nations and international agencies, such as the United Nations Statistics Division's classification for activities, products, and expenditure purposes, and the International Press Telecommunications Council's (IPTC) NewsCodes.

Classification systems, however, are not used exactly the same way as purely topical taxonomies. The conceptual idea is to "classify" documents, or put them into "classes," preferably in only one place. (In the case of classification of physical objects—for the purpose of shelving books, for example—there can be only one place.) Classes are like metadata for the document: They tell what class the document belongs in. They are not for topics discussed in the documents or what the document is all about; that is the purpose of indexing. A document could receive topical indexing from a taxonomy that is supplemental to its classification.

Furthermore, numeric code-based systems are not flexible and cannot easily be changed. It is not usually practical to insert additional codes into the scheme, unless perhaps the system allows for one additional hierarchical level. Because these systems are relatively unchanging, they don't need to be created or updated often, and their applications are somewhat limited. Thus, most of the subject areas that could use classification systems already have them, and they don't need changing. And those subject areas that don't have them are not suitable for them. What this means is that there is not much work for taxonomists in the area of classification systems.

Thesauri

The classic meaning of a *thesaurus* is *a kind of dictionary*, such as *Roget's*, that contains synonyms or alternate expressions (and possibly even antonyms) for each term entry. A thesaurus for information management and retrieval shares this characteristic of listing similar terms at each controlled vocabulary term entry. The difference is that a dictionary-thesaurus includes all the associated terms that *could potentially* be used in place of the term entry in various contexts; the user (often a writer) needs to consider the specific context in each case because in certain contexts some of the alternate terms would not be appropriate. The information retrieval thesaurus, on the other hand, is designed for use in *all* contexts within the domain of content covered, regardless of any specific term usage or document. The synonyms or near synonyms must therefore be suitably equivalent in *all* circumstances. An information retrieval thesaurus must clearly specify which terms can be used as synonyms (used from), which are more specific (narrower terms), which are broader terms, and which are merely related terms.

A thesaurus, therefore, is a more structured type of controlled vocabulary that provides information about each term and its relationships to other terms within the same thesaurus. The leadings standards that provide guidance for creating such thesauri are the following:

- International Organization for Standardization (www. iso.org/iso/catalogue_ics) ISO 25964. *Information and documentation - Thesauri and interoperability with other vocabularies*

  Part 1 (2011): *Thesauri for information retrieval*

  www.iso.org/obp/ui/#iso:std:iso:25964:-1:ed-1:v1:en

  Part 2 (2013): *Interoperability with other vocabularies*

  www.iso.org/obp/ui/#iso:std:iso:25964:-2:ed-1:v1:en

These have also been adopted by the British Standards Institute as BS ISO 25964-1:2011 and BS ISO 25964-2:2013.

- American National Standards Institute and National Information Standards Organization (www.niso.org); ANSI/NISO Z39.19 2005 (R2010): *Guidelines for the Construction, Format, and Management of Monolingual Controlled Vocabularies*

  www.niso.org/standards/z39-19-2005

Although the ANSI/NISO standard refers to "controlled vocabularies," a vocabulary created in accordance with these guidelines is usually called a thesaurus.

The standards explain in detail the three types of relationships in a thesaurus: hierarchical (broader term/narrower term), associative (related term), and equivalence (use/used for). Additional information about a term, such as a *scope note*, may be included to clarify usage. An example of a term and its details from a thesaurus is shown in Figure 1.3. The consensus is that if a controlled vocabulary includes both broader/narrower and related term relationships between terms, along with nonpreferred terms that redirect to the accepted term, then it is called a thesaurus.

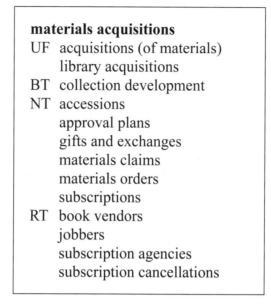

materials acquisitions
UF acquisitions (of materials)
     library acquisitions
BT collection development
NT accessions
     approval plans
     gifts and exchanges
     materials claims
     materials orders
     subscriptions
RT book vendors
     jobbers
     subscription agencies
     subscription cancellations

Figure 1.3 A term in the *ASIS&T Thesaurus* with its various
relationships to other terms (BT: broader term; NT: narrower term;
RT: related term; UF: used from)[4]

In comparing a thesaurus with a hierarchical taxonomy, a thesaurus typically includes the features of a taxonomy plus the additional feature of associative relationships, for a greater degree of structural complexity. However, while all terms must belong to a limited number of hierarchies within a hierarchical taxonomy, this is not a strict requirement for a thesaurus. Although most thesaurus entries will list a broader and/or a narrower term, such relationships are not necessarily required for every term. If there is no appropriate broader term, that relationship may be omitted. In a thesaurus, the focus is more on the individual terms than on the top-down structure. Thus a thesaurus might include multiple small hierarchies, comprising as few as two or three terms, without the strong overarching tree structure typical of a hierarchical taxonomy.

If you had to force all the terms in a thesaurus into a single hierarchical tree, some of the hierarchical relationships would probably be imperfect. Thesaurus guidelines, however, mandate that each term's hierarchical relationships be accurate and valid. In addition, having multiple broader terms for an entry is never a problem in a thesaurus, whereas such "polyhierarchies" may be prohibited in a given hierarchical taxonomy. Some thesauri do in fact have a significant hierarchical structure, and thus the distinction between a hierarchical taxonomy and a thesaurus may be blurred. Finally, recursive retrieval by a broader term (explained in Chapter 9) is not as common in a thesaurus as in a hierarchical taxonomy.

The greater detail and information contained in a thesaurus, compared with a simple controlled vocabulary or a hierarchical taxonomy, aids the user (whether the indexer or the searcher) in finding the most appropriate term more easily. A thesaurus structure is especially useful for a relatively large controlled vocabulary that involves human indexing and/or supports a term list display that the end user (searcher) can browse. In contrast to a hierarchical taxonomy, which is designed for user navigation from the top down, a thesaurus with multiple means of access can more easily contain a greater number of terms. Thus, a thesaurus may be able to support more granular (specific) and extensive indexing than a simple hierarchical taxonomy can, especially if the hierarchical taxonomy lacks nonpreferred terms. As thesauri explain relationships among terms, they are more common in specialized subject areas, where the purpose is not merely to aid the user in finding information but also to aid the user in obtaining a better understanding of the terminology. In some cases, thesauri have even been published and printed as stand-alone works, separate from any indexed content.

Examples of thesauri include the Getty Art & Architecture Thesaurus (getty.edu/research/tools/vocabularies/aat), the ERIC (Education Resources Information Center) Thesaurus for education research (eric.ed.gov), and the NASA Thesaurus of aeronautics and space terminology (www.sti.nasa.gov/thesvol1.pdf). The periodical and reference index publisher ProQuest also refers to its topical controlled vocabulary as a thesaurus.

Ontologies

An ontology can be considered a type of taxonomy with even more complex relationships between terms than in a thesaurus. Actually, an ontology is more than that; it aims to describe a domain of knowledge, a subject area, by both its terms (called *individuals* or *instances*) and their relationships and thus supports inferencing. This objective of a more complex and complete representation of knowledge stems from the etymology of the word *ontology*, which originally meant the study of the nature of being or existence. Tom Gruber provides a current definition of ontology:

> An ontology defines a set of representational primitives with which to model a domain of knowledge or discourse. … ontology can be viewed as a level of abstraction of data models, analogous to hierarchical and relational models.[5]

The relationships between terms within an ontology are not limited to broader/narrower and related. Rather, there can be any number of domain-specific types of relationship pairs, such as owns/belongs to, produces/is produced by, and has members/is a member of. The creator of the ontology also creates these relationship types. Thus, not only do the terms have meanings, but also the relationships themselves have meanings. Relationships with meanings are called semantic relationships.

The terms within an ontology not only have simple descriptions, such as scope notes in a thesaurus, but are also accompanied by specific attributes in a more structured format, such as properties, features, characteristics, or parameters. The terms also have assigned classes, which the ontologist defines, as an additional kind of classification. All of these components of an ontology—semantic

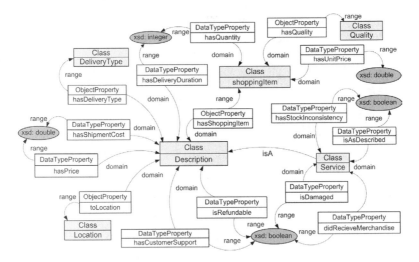

Figure 1.4 Example of a domain ontology dealing with
retail management (reproduced with permission of the creators,
Murat Sensoy and Pinar Yolum)[6]

relationships, attributes (for each of the terms/instances), and
classes—contribute to making an ontology a richer source of information than a mere hierarchical taxonomy or thesaurus. A sche-
matic representation of part of an ontology dealing with retail
management appears in Figure 1.4.

While not considered standards, there are guidelines of specifications for constructing ontologies in machine-readable format
for the web, which has become the most common implementation
of this type of taxonomy. The World Wide Web Consortium (W3C)
has published the RDF (resource description framework) Schema
and the Web Ontology Language (OWL) recommendation. There is
also a presentation format for ontologies called Topic Maps, which
is the set of ISO 13250 standards (six parts). Topic Maps are implemented more in Europe than in North America. A looser structure of knowledge organization that does not attempt to adhere to
such guidelines might be called a semantic network instead of an
actual ontology.

Ontologies are suitable for any subject area, but a significant percentage of those currently published have been in the biological sciences, such as the Gene Ontology, Protein Ontology, Systems Biology Ontology, and Purdue Ontology for Pharmaceutical Engineering. It is an interesting irony that taxonomies, which got their start in biological classification, are now widely used for any form of knowledge, while ontologies, which originally applied to the broad scope of existence, are now used most often in the field of biology. As other scientists find a need to express more complex relationships among terms in their disciplines, the spread of ontologies to other subject areas, however, will likely increase. There is also a growing importance of ontologies in semantic search engine deployment in specialized industries, and building ontologies could be a growth area for experienced taxonomists. In 2009, a new organization for supporting ontologies, the International Association for Ontology and Its Applications (www.iaoa.org), was founded.

The designation given to a knowledge organization system— controlled vocabulary, taxonomy, thesaurus, ontology, and so on— depends largely on the complexity of the structure, but complexity is not the only factor to be considered. As all these designations have ambiguous meanings, the choice of what to call a set of terms also depends on what is most clear and understandable to the contributors, stakeholders, or end users. Depending on the display of the knowledge organization system, the end users may not even need to know what it is called. The confusion in terminology is why we default to using the single designation of taxonomy in most contexts.

Taxonomies and Metadata

There is significant overlap between taxonomy and metadata. Metadata, sometimes called "data about data," is all the recorded, structured information about a content item, such as a document, digital asset (such as a video or image file), or webpage. Taxonomies (or more generally, controlled vocabularies) are often, but not always, metadata. And much, but not all, of metadata utilizes controlled vocabularies.

A content repository has a metadata schema, which may follow a suggested standard, such as Dublin Core Metadata Elements or MARC (Machine-Readable Cataloging), which is useful if the content is shared among different organizations; or it may have a customized metadata schema, which is more practical for managing metadata within an organization. A metadata schema comprises both the defined set of metadata elements or fields and the rules for each of those fields. Fields get filled or "populated" with specific values as appropriate for each individual content item.

Different types of metadata serve different purposes. The National Information Standards Organization (NISO) defines three kinds of metadata: descriptive, structural, and administrative. Descriptive metadata includes information on what a resource is about, expressed in keywords or short descriptions; and also includes other descriptive information that could be used to look up and retrieve the item, such as title, author, and document type. Structural metadata describes features of the resource, such as pagination or size. Administrative metadata describes information needed to manage a resource, such as its creation date, access rights, intellectual property rights, and archival preservation information. There are other methods besides NISO for classifying metadata types, but most methods distinguish between metadata for managing content and metadata for aiding in search or discovery and retrieval of content.

Taxonomy as Part of Metadata

Taxonomies, or controlled vocabularies in general, are associated with the descriptive type of metadata, for two reasons. First, taxonomists, by the nature of their work, are focused on the goal of descriptive metadata, which is to help users find content. Second, descriptive metadata tends to use controlled vocabularies more than other types of metadata. While administrative or structural metadata may require controlled lists of terms to populate some of its fields, a controlled "list" is not necessarily a controlled "vocabulary."

Regardless of the type of metadata, (descriptive, structural, or administrative), a specific metadata field may either allow free text or require the user to select from a controlled list of options. A controlled vocabulary is, of course, a type of controlled list. It would be incorrect, however, to call all controlled lists "controlled vocabularies." For example, the controlled list for a metadata field may consist of just a pair of values, such as *yes* or *no, male* or *female*, or *new* or *used*, or it may consist of just three or four values, such as *small, medium*, and *large*. These types of lists are not controlled vocabularies, because part of the definition of a controlled vocabulary is that a term is designated for a concept. In the preceding examples, there is not really any question of what word or term to use for each concept in the list of two or three. We don't even use the word "term" but rather "value" to refer to the choices in short controlled lists. There is no rule, however, as to the number of values a list must have before it is considered a controlled vocabulary. Rather, the defining feature of a controlled vocabulary is that concept-naming decisions need to be made when developing the list. Therefore, the list of 50 states of the United States by itself is not a controlled vocabulary, just a list, because there is no question of what to call them, whereas a list of just 15 "activity types" would likely be a controlled vocabulary, because names for those activities require research and consideration before a choice can be made from among various alternatives.

Controlled vocabularies of any size, including hierarchical taxonomies, may be used to support one or more descriptive metadata fields, especially a field that is called Subject, Topic, or Descriptor. A taxonomist is not necessarily responsible for all metadata, so he or she needs to work in collaboration with a metadata architect, metadata librarian, or content architect, especially in the blurred area of responsibility between short controlled vocabularies and long controlled lists. In addition to determining the metadata fields and their values, other decisions need to be made: whether assigning/tagging values from a specific metadata field is required or optional, whether a metadata field may hold only one value or can permit multiple values, and whether the field will be displayed in the user interface for end-user search-and-retrieval purposes.

Taxonomy That Is Not Metadata

If a taxonomy is implemented in a way that the terms, unlike other metadata, are *not* attached to a content item, then the taxonomy might not be part of metadata. If a taxonomy is implemented to support dynamic auto-indexing or search, and executed "on the fly," rather than being permanently attached to a record, then it is not metadata. While we have already stated that a hierarchical navigation design is not necessarily a taxonomy, in some cases a navigation scheme could be a taxonomy and may not be metadata. If a navigation scheme were designed as a taxonomy and taxonomy terms were hyperlinked to content, with some terms indirectly linked to more than one content item (such as through an intermediate navigation page), then the taxonomy terms would not necessarily be metadata.

Applications and Purposes of Taxonomies

As we have seen from the various definitions, there are different kinds of taxonomies or controlled vocabularies, based on their complexity. However, complexity is only one way to classify taxonomies. A more practical approach is to categorize them by their application and use. While a particular taxonomy can certainly serve multiple functions, there tends to be a certain emphasis in its design, use, and purposes. As such, each taxonomy serves primarily one of the following three functions, although there certainly can be combinations of the different types:

1. Indexing support

2. Retrieval support

3. Organization and navigation support

Indexing Support

For indexing or cataloging support, a taxonomy, better known as a controlled vocabulary in this context, is a list of agreed-on terms for the human indexing or cataloging of multiple documents and/ or for indexing performed by multiple indexers, to ensure consistency. If multiple documents, especially by different authors, will be indexed over time, the indexer is apt to forget exactly which index terms were assigned and perhaps inadvertently use different synonyms when the same topic comes up in a different document. Similarly, different indexers will also choose different index terms for the same topic if not forced to use a controlled vocabulary.

Thus, the taxonomy's initial purpose is to serve the people doing the indexing, although a second, equally important purpose is to serve the end users, who, of course, benefit from consistently indexed content and may also have access to the taxonomy. This type of controlled vocabulary is used for cataloging entire works and for indexes to periodical articles, image files, database records, multivolume printed works, webpages, and so on. Because indexers must always choose the most accurate terms, they often use a more structured thesaurus type of controlled vocabulary. The broader, narrower, and related term relationships guide the indexer to the best term, and scope notes further clarify ambiguous terms. Named entities are often indexed, too, and these are managed in an authority file. An authority file lacks the interterm relationships of a thesaurus but may have many synonymous nonpreferred terms for each preferred term, such as variations on an individual's name.

Controlled vocabularies for indexing support have been around the longest, and their format may be electronic or print. Such controlled vocabularies are used by reference and periodical article database publishers, including Gale (a part of Cengage Learning), EBSCO, and ProQuest, in more specialized subject databases, such as Chemical Abstracts and PsycINFO. And they are also used in the internal documents of large companies, especially those in the sciences. The fact that some of these controlled vocabularies are offered for sale/license illustrates the fact that they serve the purpose of indexing and not just specific content retrieval.

While controlled vocabularies for indexing are quite widespread, those that are publicly available on the web are limited and tend to be those published by public agencies. You may search or browse them, and in some cases, you may also access linked content. Library of Congress Subject Headings and Medical Subject Headings are two such examples.

Library of Congress Subject Headings (LCSH) (authorities.loc. gov) contains both subjects and names and covers all subject areas. LCSH was originally established for cataloging library materials but has also been adopted by various publishers for indexing articles. The terms are called *authorities*, as in authority file, even those that are not named entities. The purpose of the website is to aid catalogers of library materials in finding the approved subject heading in the Library of Congress controlled vocabulary. It is not aimed at the end user looking for a book, although consistently cataloged books will, of course, benefit the user. The subject headings can be searched and the results browsed alphabetically. Nonpreferred terms are included in the alphabetical list along with preferred terms. Nonpreferred terms are prefaced by a button labeled References, which provides a cross-reference to the preferred term. Preferred terms are called *authorized headings* (see Figure 1.5).

Medical Subject Headings (MeSH) (www.nlm.nih.gov/mesh/ MBrowser.html) is the thesaurus of the US National Library of Medicine, which is considered the authority for medical terms. Users can search terms, or they can browse by selecting the button

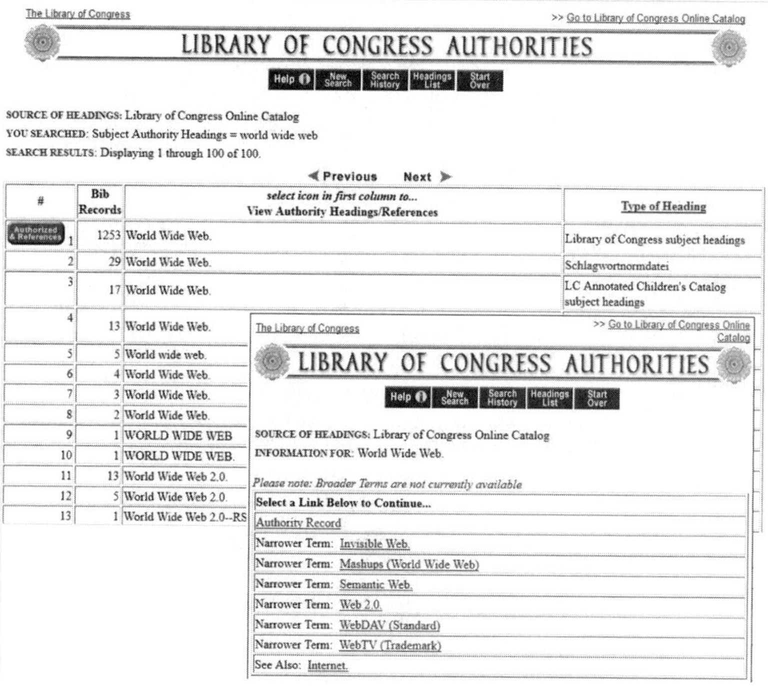

Figure 1.5 Two successive screenshots from Library of Congress Subject Headings, searching on the term *World Wide Web* and displaying its details

Navigate from Tree Top. The browse display is hierarchical rather than alphabetical. Clicking once on a term expands the tree and reveals its narrower terms; double-clicking on a term displays its details (see Figure 1.6).

Other examples of thesauri that aid indexing and are publicly available include the ERIC Thesaurus (eric.ed.gov), sponsored by the Institute of Education Sciences of the US Department of Education, and the various controlled vocabularies of the Getty Research Institute of the J. Paul Getty Trust: the Getty Art & Architecture Thesaurus, Getty Thesaurus of Geographic Names, Cultural Objects Name Authority, and Union List of Artist Names (getty.edu/research/tools/vocabularies).

MeSH Heading	Arm Injuries
Tree Number	C26.088
Annotation	GEN or unspecified; consider also / inj with specific bones of arm; also available are FOREARM INJURIES; HAND INJURIES; FINGER INJURIES; WRIST INJURIES & many specific organ/fract precoords
Scope Note	General or unspecified injuries involving the arm.
Entry Term	Injuries, Arm
Allowable Qualifiers	BL CF CI CL CN CO DH DI DT EC EH EM EN EP ET GE HI IM ME MI MO NU PA PC PP PS PX RA RH RI RT SU TH UR US VE VI
Entry Version	ARM INJ
Date of Entry	19990101
Unique ID	D001134

MeSH Tree Structures

Wounds and Injuries [C26]
       Abdominal Injuries [C26.017] +
       Amputation, Traumatic [C26.062]
  ▶ Arm Injuries [C26.088]
               Forearm Injuries [C26.088.268] +
               Humeral Fractures [C26.088.390]
               Shoulder Dislocation [C26.088.666]
               Shoulder Fractures [C26.088.749]
               Tennis Elbow [C26.088.890]
               Wrist Injuries [C26.088.906]
       Asphyxia [C26.103]
       Athletic Injuries [C26.115]
       Back Injuries [C26.117] +

Figure 1.6 Two screenshots from Medical Subject Headings, showing the term record and location in the tree structure for the selected term *arm injuries*

Retrieval Support

A taxonomy that serves indexing also serves end-user retrieval. Searchers benefit from nonpreferred terms, as their search terms may be different from the terms used to index the document. For example, a user may type in **doctors** for articles that are about physicians. Users can also take advantage of broader and narrower term relationships or hierarchies to broaden or narrow their search. These relationships, and also the related term relationships, may suggest to users other possible terms of interest. In such cases, the end-user searcher will be seeing an explicit representation of the taxonomy for navigation.

There are also taxonomies designed to aid search retrieval without supporting human indexing. These taxonomies are typically mapping tables of terms and their synonyms/variants designed to aid online retrieval. These might be synonym rings or synsets, especially if the terms are not even displayed to the user, or if there is a display, it may designate preferred terms.

Depending on the user interface display, there may or may not be a hierarchical structure to the taxonomy. A hierarchical arrangement allows users to browse and locate narrower (more specific) subjects of interest. Thus, users find out what is included in the taxonomy and what is not, saving themselves the trouble of repeatedly typing in terms that yield no results. Users may also find related subjects of interest by browsing the hierarchies.

These types of controlled vocabularies are often used with website search engines, enterprise search systems (used internally within a large organization), online databases, and large commercial directories (such as online "yellow pages" or classified ads). The format is always electronic, and a form of automated indexing is usually involved.

Examples of taxonomies aiding retrieval include Verizon SuperPages's yellow pages directory site (www.superpages.com/yellowpages) and the Amazon.com ecommerce site's "Shop by Department" categories (www.amazon.com/gp/site-directory), as shown in Figure 1.7.

While a hierarchy can be selected for browsing in each, the synonyms in the case of Verizon SuperPages and the related subject links in the case of Amazon.com are not displayed to the user, although the links are evident in the display of results.

Faceted Taxonomies for Retrieval Support

One way to better serve specifically the retrieval of data is to construct a controlled vocabulary that is divided into multiple subsets, lists of terms of different types representing different aspects of information. These aspects are often called *facets*, and this type of

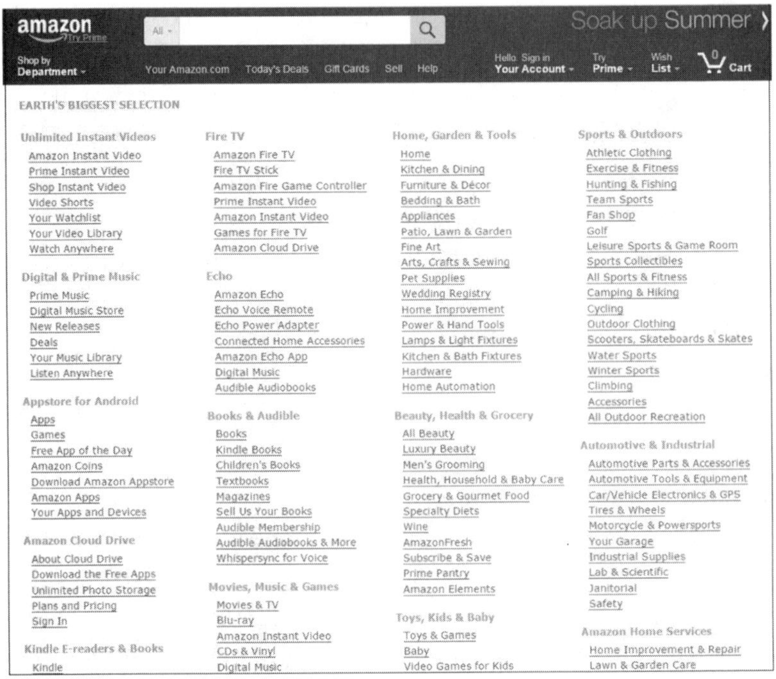

Figure 1.7 Top-level taxonomy of Amazon.com

controlled vocabulary is therefore called a *faceted taxonomy*. Examples of facets might be people, places, events, products, and laws. Facets can also reflect metadata other than subject categories, such as document type, author, and audience. The search interface for a faceted taxonomy is designed for the user to search on a selected combination of multiple facets.

Faceted taxonomies are commonly used for online databases and ecommerce sites, such as the shoe-retailing site Shoebuy.com. In Shoebuy's (www.shoebuy.com) advanced search, the facets are Category, Size, Width, Brand, Color, Price Range, and, additionally for women's shoes, Heel (height). Another example of a faceted browse interface can be found on the Microbial Life Education Resources site (serc.carleton.edu/microbelife/resources), where

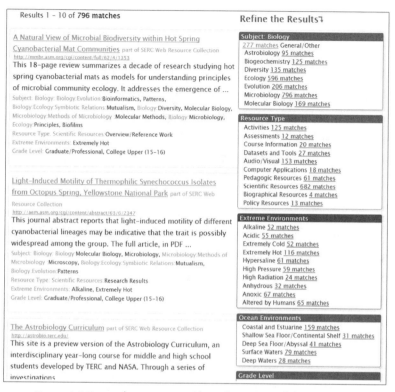

Figure 1.8 Faceted taxonomy in the right margin of the Microbial Life Education Resources search site

facets are Subject, Resource Type, Extreme Environments, Ocean Environments, and Grade Level (Figure 1.8).

Faceted taxonomies, or *faceted browse* systems, make use of the electronic format. Depending on the size of the vocabulary in each facet, these taxonomies may or may not make use of synonyms and may or may not have hierarchies within them. Some facets can be quite small. Facets are discussed in more detail in Chapter 8.

Organization and Navigation Support

A taxonomy, as a hierarchy, can provide a categorization or classification system for things or for information. For the organization of information, we often see taxonomies applied in website information architecture (structural design), online information services, intranet content organization, and corporate content management systems. In such websites or enterprise taxonomies, the emphasis is on classification and guided user navigation rather than on search and retrieval of specific information. *Navigation* means finding one's way around, whereas *retrieval* means going after specific information. The taxonomy for a website is a lot like a table of contents, organized by topic. It can be reflected in the navigational menu and in the site map. As such, it might be called a *navigational taxonomy*. These types of taxonomies tend to be relatively small and can coexist with additional, more detailed taxonomies elsewhere on the website.

An example of navigational website taxonomy that is present in both the site map and the navigational menu can be found on the Information Architecture Institute site map (iainstitute.org/en/site-map.php), where the top-level categories of the taxonomy and the navigation are Member Services, IA Network, Learning IA, and About Us (Figure 1.9).

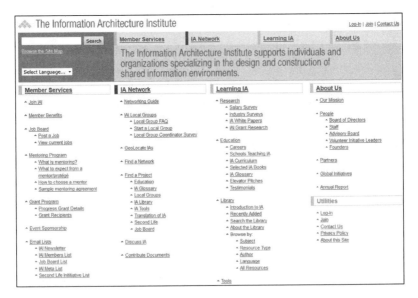

Figure 1.9 The Information Architecture Institute site map, a navigational taxonomy

Another example of a navigational taxonomy can be found on the MyFlorida.com site map (www.myflorida.com/taxonomy), where the top-level categories of the taxonomy, which also are the main navigation menu items, are Visitor, Floridian, Government, and Business. It is interesting to note that the file name for this site-map page has been named taxonomy.

Taxonomies can serve in the navigation of enterprise taxonomies. Enterprise taxonomies can be very large, but the top levels typically demonstrate some form of information organization for the enterprise. The purpose of this hierarchical organization is then not merely to retrieve documents but also to help users better understand the organization of the enterprise and its intranet and thus make better use of it.

It is open to dispute whether a website navigation structure can actually be called a "taxonomy," even if it is well designed. A taxonomy, as a form of a controlled vocabulary, serves the purpose of indexing, classifying, or categorizing. It is a system in which a single term can be reused to index or classify more than one item, document, or webpage. In a website navigation structure, on the other hand, a menu label or site-map entry points/links to only a single webpage. This is a significant difference. The website navigation label needs to match or fit only a specific page. A taxonomy term, on the other hand, needs to be applicable to multiple, slightly different content items. Furthermore, website navigation labels are sometimes deliberately worded so as to intrigue or entice a user to visit a certain page within the site, rather than purely to inform or guide users. Finally, the hierarchical relationship and structure of a navigation structure reflect a custom experience, and make no attempt to follow standard conventions for hierarchical taxonomic relationships (explained in Chapter 4).

So, rather than considering every multilevel website navigation hierarchy as a kind of taxonomy, it would be more apt to look into how to make some taxonomies (that serve for indexing multiple content items) serve a second purpose of providing or influencing a website's hierarchical navigation structure, in cases when a unifying hierarchical structure is desired. This could be the case for enterprise taxonomies, especially if they are implemented both in a content management system and on an intranet and/or public website.

Taxonomies for License

Although the primary objective of this book is to provide instruction on building taxonomies, it is not always necessary to build an entire taxonomy from scratch. Some or all of a taxonomy could be acquired from another source. While taxonomies for enterprises and content management systems should definitely be custom-created, a taxonomy for the indexing of documents or files in a given subject area could be purchased or licensed. Furthermore, taxonomies for license not only serve the purposes of indexing and content retrieval but may also provide an outline of a domain of knowledge. Many subject areas are already covered by existing published taxonomies. There are generic taxonomies for geographic places, industry types, product types, and so forth. In addition, lists of named entities are available from various sources. You might consider licensing an external taxonomy if the right taxonomy already exists and if creating one from scratch would be too great a task due to size, specialty subject area, and limited time. A licensed controlled vocabulary could be used for merely a single facet or for part of a larger set of taxonomies.

Taxonomies or controlled vocabularies that are available for license come from all kinds of sources: government agencies, professional associations, other nonprofit organizations, and a few commercial enterprises. Governmental published taxonomies available for license (or even free without a license) include LCSH, Library of Congress Thesaurus for Graphic Materials, MeSH, USDA National Agricultural Library Thesaurus, and the United Kingdom's Integrated Public Sector Vocabulary. The Getty Research Institute (part of the J. Paul Getty Trust) is a reputable nonprofit provider of controlled vocabularies, including the Art & Architecture Thesaurus, Getty Thesaurus of Geographic Names, and Union List of Artist Names. The leading commercial vendor of prebuilt taxonomies, WAND Inc. (www.wand.com), specializes in taxonomies in products and services. Some database publishers, such as Gale, a part of Cengage Learning, which created taxonomies initially as part of their own products, may also license these taxonomies alone (not a part of their content products).

The largest directory of taxonomies and thesauri available for use is Taxonomy Warehouse (www.taxonomywarehouse.com). The list is maintained by the taxonomy software vendor Synaptica. The database includes hundreds of taxonomies, including most of those mentioned previously. Some are simple controlled vocabularies or glossaries, but others are full-featured thesauri. Although some are hosted on the web, the data files (usually in CSV or XML formats) can be obtained for most of them. Figure 1.10 shows the information that Taxonomy Warehouse provides for a specific taxonomy. A single publisher may also offer numerous taxonomies on different subjects.

With the growing demand for tagging images, there are also an increasing number of "keyword lists" for photographers. Many of these are, in fact, hierarchical and faceted taxonomies. But since they usually do not include nonpreferred terms, they are rather simple taxonomies, despite the fact that some of them are very large (10,000 or 20,000 terms). Prices for these lists are relatively inexpensive compared with some of the commercial thesauri available, and some of the smaller keyword lists are free. A directory of these, called "Photography Keyword Lists & Free Keywording Resources for Lightroom," is available on the website of one keyword-list vendor, Photo-Keywords (www.photo-keywords.com/keywording-resources.php), which is targeted especially at freelance professional photographers.

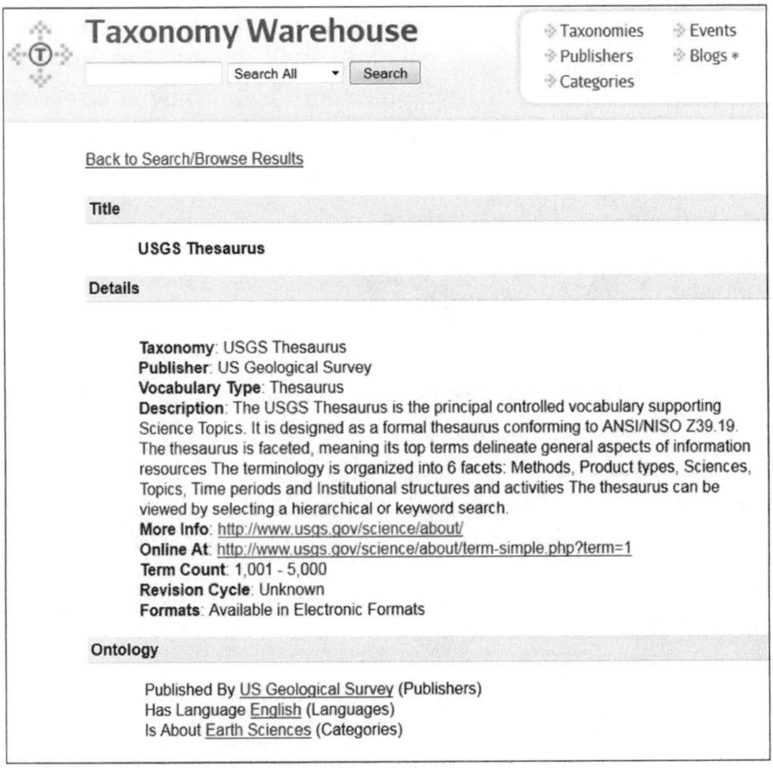

Figure 1.10 Example display of information for a single taxonomy offered through the Taxonomy Warehouse

Formats may vary, but typically, taxonomies or thesauri that are made available for other uses are formatted in some form of XML, whereby all terms, relationships, nonpreferred terms, scope notes, and so forth are retained when they are imported into other taxonomy management systems. The use of XML and other interoperable taxonomy formats is described in greater detail in Chapter 11. The photography keyword lists are available in Excel or text files, in a format that allows them to be easily imported into photo management software, especially Adobe Lightroom, while maintaining the hierarchy.

If you acquire a taxonomy, however, you will likely want to modify or enhance it for your own needs, and in any case it will require some maintenance over time. The following example case demonstrates how a generic taxonomy, taken as is, may not be ideal. A large-scale historical digitization project that coded early American election results used the Getty Thesaurus of Geographic Names. Even though the thesaurus includes historical place names, it was still found to be insufficient for the project's needs. It does not include all the towns and boroughs that were named in the elections project, and does not indicate exactly when various historical names were used or when boundaries were redrawn.

Licensing agreements may allow use of a taxonomy without a fee in some cases, but may prohibit for-profit use or require statements referring to the original copyright holder. If the taxonomy is treated as a published copyrighted work, whether free or for a fee, then there will also be restrictions on making changes to it.

A number of free controlled vocabularies, such as the Getty vocabularies, follow the model of Linked Open Data (LOD) and the Open Data Commons Attribution License, which allows modification of the vocabulary but require attribution to the original source. The Getty vocabularies website provides sample forms of attribution statements, such as: "This [title or report or article or dataset] contains information from Art & Architecture Thesaurus (AAT) which is made available under the ODC Attribution License."[7]

The policy for using and modifying MeSH is as follows:

> If the use is not personal, (1) the U.S. National Library of Medicine must be identified as the creator, maintainer, and provider of the data; (2) the version of the data must be clearly stated by MeSH year, e.g., 1997 MeSH; and (3) if any modification is made in the content of the file, this must be stated, along with a description of the modifications.[8]

Often you will want to make changes to the acquired taxonomy, so make sure the license permits changes. Also be aware that you are responsible for continued updating. Licensed taxonomies, both those that prohibit and those that permit changes, typically offer updates through an annual subscription. A solid understanding of how to create terms and relationships, as discussed in Chapters 3 and 4, is still necessary to manage prebuilt taxonomies. Therefore, acquiring a taxonomy from an external source does not eliminate the need for a taxonomist. Starting with a prebuilt taxonomy, though, can save time and make things much easier for the less experienced taxonomist. You can follow examples of term formats and relationships as you build out the taxonomy further.

History of Taxonomies

Taxonomies are both new and old. "Both librarians and indexers were doing 'taxonomy' long before it became a hot topic in the 1990s," wrote taxonomy trainer Jean Graef of the Montague Institute.[9]

Taxonomies in Cataloging and Indexing

The earliest taxonomies were for classification, such as for organisms or for books, but each item could only go in one place in the taxonomy. For example, a book gets a single call number for its location on the shelf. In the field of library science, by the end of the 19th century, more practical taxonomies emerged that supported supplemental descriptive cataloging, which is not limited to one descriptive term per book. The leading controlled vocabularies for cataloging books have been the American Library Association Subject Headings (1895), Library of Congress Subject Headings (LCSH) (1898), and the Sears List, published originally as the List of Subject Headings for Small Public Libraries (1923).

These were simple controlled vocabularies lacking broader/ narrower and related term relationships. LCSH used *See also* references for every kind of relationship and began to introduce broader term, narrower term, and related term references only in 1985.[10]

LCSH, back when it was still in its simpler form, was adopted by various periodical index publishers for the indexing of articles from multiple newspapers, magazines, and journals. These publishers included the H.W. Wilson Company (since acquired by EBSCO), which dated back to the start of LCSH, and Information Access Company (acquired by Gale, now a part of Cengage Learning) and ABI Inform (now ProQuest) in the 1970s. Cengage's and ProQuest's controlled vocabularies have diverged from LCSH over the years based on the work of their taxonomists.

Meanwhile, professional societies developed their own controlled vocabularies for indexing periodical literature in their fields since at least the early 1900s. These included the American Chemical Society's Chemical Abstracts Service founded in 1907. The word *thesaurus* was first used to refer to a controlled vocabulary for information retrieval purposes by Peter Luhn at IBM in 1957. Early published thesauri included the Department of Defense's *ASTIA Descriptors* in 1960 and the American Institute of Chemical Engineers' *Chemical Engineering Thesaurus* in 1961.[11] Standard thesaurus relationships emerged over time, and guidelines were developed that reinforced them, including UNESCO's 1967 guidelines, which formed the basis of the ISO 2788 standard of 1986[12] (superseded by ISO 25964 in 2011). Since the 1960s, various companies, government agencies, and professional associations have published dozens of specialized thesauri. In 1972, the new company Dialog began offering the first publicly available online research service, providing access to multiple bibliographic citation databases indexed with controlled vocabularies.

Corporate Taxonomies

Up through the 1980s, however, taxonomy (thesaurus) development was mostly limited to large index or literature-retrieval database publishers, a few large companies, especially in the sciences (such as DuPont), and government agencies. The companies and government agencies that developed taxonomies did so mostly within specific subject areas. Taxonomies for an entire organization, that is, enterprise-wide taxonomies, first began to appear in the late 1970s, but their adoption was limited. According to taxonomy and knowledge management consultant Lynda Moulton, it was not so much a lack of interest but simply the limitations of software tools at the time that hindered a wider adoption of enterprise taxonomies. Moulton recalls teaching a number of thesaurus construction workshops during 1982–1984, attended by librarians and indexers from such companies as Liberty Mutual, John Hancock, Fidelity, MITRE, and Digital Equipment Corp.[13]

Contemporary library automation began to emerge in the late 1970s and systems for "special libraries" (corporate libraries and information management) as early as 1980. Although dedicated taxonomy management systems had not yet appeared on the market, these earlier systems included taxonomy management features. These included BiblioTech by Comstow Information Services (acquired by Inmagic in 1999, and since 2014 part of Lucidea), which was first installed at Polaroid in 1981, and TechLib, released in 1984, which was built on BASIS (acquired by OpenText in 1998). Comstow held a number of workshops that were devoted to thesaurus development for corporate libraries in the early 1980s.[14]

It was only in the late 1990s that a broader interest in taxonomies, and the corresponding tools to support them, developed. For example, the taxonomy consultancy Earley Information Science started working on classification, categorization, and metadata projects (essentially taxonomy, but not called that yet) to help their clients make the most out of the Lotus Notes application, by build-ing classification structures, forms, and navigation. In 1998, IBM introduced its Lotus Discovery Service, which "really called out the need for a taxonomy," according to Seth Earley, so he and other consultants at the time provided services in creating taxonomies for Lotus Notes.[15]

The Growth of Enterprise and Web Taxonomies

The emergence and growth of the web in 1990s was a major con-tributing factor in the growing interest in taxonomies, for sev-eral reasons. The web enabled smaller publishers to offer online information services. Companies started developing intranets that quickly expanded in size and required better navigation and search. "With the growth of the internet, there was a lot of interest in building to improve search results," explained Synapse Corp. (now Synaptica LLC) co-founder Trish Yancey regarding the start of the company.[16] The proliferation of search engines, and then site search or enterprise search, also led to an interest in taxono-mies as it became apparent that search alone was not sufficient. According to Jean Graef, "Taxonomy became hot when IT real-ized that search engines by themselves couldn't solve the whole retrieval problem."[17]

Finally, attention to site design and navigation through the new field of information architecture also put value on taxonomies. Indexer, information architect, and taxonomist Fred Leise wrote, "As the field of information architecture and the influence of Louis Rosenfeld's and Peter Morville's *Information Architecture for the World Wide Web* grew, the knowledge of library science-related information, such as faceted browsing classifications and the use of synonym rings as search improvements, spread more widely."[18]

The growing interest in taxonomies in the 1980s and 1990s was also reflected in the growth of taxonomy management software. Software for creating and maintaining taxonomies was originally developed internally within the few large organizations that had already developed taxonomies. In 1980 Comstow released Biblio-Tech, its fully integrated library system for corporate and government libraries, which included a module for thesaurus creation, fully integrated with the cataloging and indexing module. Battelle Columbus Laboratory released similar functionality in TechLib soon after.[19]

In the mid-1980s commercial PC software for thesaurus creation became available, including the desktop tools MultiTes, Term Tree, and TCS (later a part of WebChoir). Of these, only MultiTes is still offered today. Larger-scale client–server systems became available in the 1990s, reflecting the growing demand. Synapse Corp. had developed software to maintain taxonomies it was creating for others as a consulting service but soon found a market for the software itself and began selling the Synaptica taxonomy management system, the first commercial, web-based thesaurus management software, in 1999. Similarly, Access Innovations had been offering indexing services since 1978 but then found demand for its taxonomy management tool and has commercially offered its Data Harmony Thesaurus Master since 1998. Wordmap, another taxonomy software vendor, was founded in 1998. Content management systems and enterprise search solutions, which only really entered the market in the 1990s, have also begun to offer taxonomy management components or features.

The 1990s also saw the establishment of commercial vendors of taxonomies, including Synapse Corp. and WAND, both of which were founded in 1995, and the automatic taxonomy generator company Intellisophic in 1999.

The rise of the term *taxonomy* paralleled this growing interest in taxonomies. Former taxonomy consultant Ron Daniel got his start in the field working for the Department of Energy on its thesaurus. He recounts how, around 1997, it was starting to use the word *taxonomy* interchangeably with *thesaurus* and another term that hasn't become quite as popular, *synonymy*.[20] Earley recalls starting to use the word *taxonomy* with clients around 1996 or 1997. Moulton recalls the adoption of the term *taxonomy* as follows:

> Throughout my professional career, first as a technical librarian, then as a software developer and consultant, the operative terminology for my work was thesaurus.
>
> ... I first heard the term taxonomy applied to "organization maps," in the early 1990s. ... In the late 1990s I began to see the term "taxonomy" routinely used to describe "terminology maps," "topical hierarchies," and "terminology relationships." Before long, taxonomy became the de facto label for topical navigation schemes on commercial websites that had a focus on text content retrieval. ... At some point I recognized that the term "thesaurus" was not understood by IT and business management professionals. So, about 2000, I adopted taxonomy to cover any controlled vocabulary being developed or applied in any indexing, metadata management or retrieval situation. ... To this day, I use thesaurus and taxonomy interchangeably depending on which word will most likely resonate with my audience.[21]

Our online survey completed by 148 taxonomists in May 2015 also confirmed the relatively later adoption of the term *taxonomy*. Whereas 26 (17.6 percent) of the respondents had been involved in taxonomy work as we define it (taxonomies, controlled vocabularies, metadata for classification or tagging, thesauri, or authority files) for more than 15 years, only 11 (7.5 percent of the total) reported that their work was specifically called "taxonomy" as long ago as 2000 (15 years prior to the survey). Going back 20 years or more (1995 or earlier), 18 respondents, or 12.2 percent, claim to have already been in the field, but only 2 of them said it was called "taxonomy" then. (See Appendix A, Questions 2 and 3.)

Another way to track the growth in the popularity of taxonomies is to track the mention of taxonomies in periodical literature, especially in business and trade journals. While many of these articles may be about specific subject taxonomies, rather than information taxonomies in general, searching on the plural word *taxonomies*, rather than *taxonomy*, focuses the results more on the creation of generic information taxonomies. Looking at Gale's Business Collection subscription database on InfoTrac for the word *taxonomies* in titles and full text shows a marked increase from 1998 to 2002 and then a steadier occurrence in subsequent years, except for a spike in 2010, as shown in Table 1.1. Business Index covers 3000–4000 magazines, journals, newsletters, industry reports, and newswires.[22] "Taxonomies" is not a subject term in the Gale databases, but rather the slightly broader "controlled vocabularies" is used.

The turning point came around 2000. In the summary of the European Business Information Conference (EBIC) conference in 2000, Tom Koulopoulos, president of the Delphi Group and renowned writer and public speaker on knowledge management, declared, "Taxonomies are chic." Since then taxonomies have been a popular topic in conference presentations and workshops. The Montague Institute held its first taxonomy roundtable in 2000. A significant number of taxonomies had become available publicly (usually for licensing), so in 2001 Synapse Corp. (now Synaptica, LLC) launched its Taxonomy Warehouse website directory of taxonomies. Taxonomy consultant Marcia Morante recalled as follows:

> The year 2000 was probably the very beginning of the commercial taxonomy wave. That was the year that I started with Sageware, and we still had to do a lot of explanation. But by that time, there were definitely a few companies whose business was built around taxonomies.[23]

Table 1.1 Number of periodical articles about taxonomies
in Gale's Business Collection database on InfoTrac

Year	"taxonomies" in article titles	"taxonomies" in article text	"controlled vocabularies" Subject
1998	0	6	0
1999	0	16	0
2000	3	92	0
2001	6	111	0
2002	8	231	0
2003	8	180	0
2004	14	208	0
2005	7	204	0
2006	5	200	1
2007	7	206	9
2008	4	214	8
2009	6	217	10
2010	10	365	15
2011	8	159	6
2012	6	192	5
2013	3	169	4
2014	4	206	31

Although newer buzzwords, such as *folksonomy, social network-ing*, and *Web 2.0*, superseded *taxonomy* in their usage in the 2000s, a sustained interest in taxonomy and taxonomists continues. Search industry analyst Steve Arnold analyzed web traffic on Google from 2002 to 2008 on the term *taxonomy* and found it continuing to remain strong, stronger than *CMS* (content management systems). He concluded that "taxonomy is a specialist concept that seems to be moving into the mainstream."[24]

Endnotes

1. Gale Hodge, *Systems of Knowledge Organization for Digital Libraries: Beyond Traditional Authority Files* (Washington, DC: The Digital Library Federation Council on Library and Information Resources, 2000), 1, accessed December 20, 2015, www.clir.org/pubs/reports/pub91/pub91.pdf

2. Ibid., 4–7.

3. National Institute of Standards Organization, ANSI/NISO Z39.19-2005 (R2010) *Guidelines for Construction, Format, and Management of Monolingual Controlled Vocabularies* (Bethesda, MD: NISO Press, 2010), 166.

4. Alice Redmond-Neal and Marjorie M. K. Hlava, eds., *ASIS&T Thesaurus of Information Science, Technology, and Librarianship*, 3rd ed. (Medford, NJ: Information Today, 2005).

5. Tom Gruber, "Ontology," accessed December 20, 2015, tomgruber.org/writing/ontology-definition-2007.htm

6. This image, reprinted with permission of the authors, first appeared in Murat Sensoy and Pinar Yolum, "Ontology-Based Service Representation and Selection," *IEEE Transactions on Knowledge and Data Engineering* 19, no. 8 (2007). It is also available at mas.cmpe.boun.edu.tr/project/AgentBasedSemanticWebServices.htm

7. Patricia A. Harpring (Managing Editor of the Getty Vocabulary Program, Getty Research Institute), email to author, January 13, 2016.

8. MeSH Memorandum of Understanding, accessed December 20, 2015, www.nlm.nih.gov/mesh/termscon.html

9. Jean Graef, email to author, November 21, 2008.

10. Alva Stone, "The LCSH: A Brief History of the Library of Congress Subject Headings, and Introduction to the Centennial Essays," *Cataloging & Classification Quarterly* 29, no. 1–2 (2000): 1.

11. Jean Aitchison and Stella Dextre Clarke, "The Thesaurus: A Historical Viewpoint with a Look to the Future," in *The Thesaurus: Review, Renaissance, and Revision*, eds. Sandra K. Roe and Alan R. Thomas (Binghamton, NY: Haworth Press Inc., 2004), 7.

12. Ibid., 8.

13. Lynda Moulton, telephone interview with the author, October 19, 2009.

14. Lynda Moulton, email to author, October 19, 2009.

15. Seth Earley, telephone interview with author, November 22, 2008.

16. Kimberly S. Johnson, "International Information Provider Buys Franktown, Colo., Taxonomy Company," *Denver Post*, June 30, 2005.

17. Jean Graef, email to author, November 21, 2008.

18. Fred Leise, email to author, December 2, 2008.

19. Lynda Moulton, email to author, October 19, 2009.

20. Ron Daniel, telephone interview with author, December 1, 2008.

21. Lynda Moulton, email to author, November 9, 2009.

22. Gale/Cengage Learning Database Title Lists, solutions.cengage.com/Gale/Database-Title-Lists, updated June 30, 2015. A count of titles without an end date. Titles are added and dropped over the years, so an exact title count for a span of years is not possible.

23. Marcia Morante, email to author, November 21, 2008.

24. Steve Arnold, "Taxonomy: Silver Bullet or Shallow Puddle," *Beyond Search* blog, September 27, 2008, accessed December 20, 2015, arnoldit.com/wordpress/2008/09/27/taxonomy-silver-bullet-or-shallow-puddle

Chapter 2

Who Are Taxonomists?

Taxonomists: Classy people.
—Harry A. Pape

Taxonomists, as we define them, are people who work on taxonomies. Just as there are various kinds of taxonomies, there are various kinds of taxonomists. Among those who identify themselves as taxonomists, taxonomy work is as likely to be their secondary job responsibility as it is a primary one. Although most people who work on taxonomies are employed full time, there are also a significant number who are independent contractors and consultants. As for when taxonomists entered this field of work, the times are roughly evenly distributed over the past 15 years or so, with 4–6 years of work in taxonomies being the most common two-year range of experience by a small margin.

These characteristics of taxonomists—and the others described in this chapter—come from our own online survey conducted in May 2015, comprising 14 multiple-choice and four open-response questions. All quotes in this chapter are taken from that survey unless noted otherwise (in an endnote). Self-described taxonomists were solicited as survey participants from among members of several taxonomy-related LinkedIn and Yahoo groups, and a total of 150 people responded. The complete survey and multiple-choice results, along with the names of the online groups contacted, is in Appendix A. A slightly larger survey of 184 self-described taxonomists conducted by Patrick Lambe in mid-2009, which is also cited in this chapter, shows similar responses to the same kinds of questions.[1]

Backgrounds of Taxonomists

Taxonomists have varied backgrounds. The largest number have training or experience in library science, about half of today's taxonomists. In our survey, 54.4 percent (81 out of 149) of the self-described taxonomists have an MLS or MLIS degree, and 30.3 percent chose "librarian" out of a list of 13 options to describe their prior professional background. (This question did *not* allow multiple answers, so more taxonomists likely had some library experience but did not consider it their primary background.) The primary professional backgrounds of the others included the following: 11.4 percent each for "Knowledge management" and "Content management/Web content/Content strategy," 9.1 percent for "Software/IT," 6.1 percent for Indexing, 5.3 percent for "User experience/Information architecture," and an equal number at 4.5 percent for each of "Records management," "Project management," and "Writing, editing, or publishing." Additionally, five respondents came to taxonomy work directly from being students. (Most taxonomist positions, though, are not entry level.) These statistics correlate with Lambe's survey finding that 46 percent of taxonomists hold an MLIS, master of information management, or master of knowledge management. Another informal survey of taxonomists, by a simple show of hands at a general session at the Taxonomy Boot Camp conference attended by this author in 2007, indicated that approximately half of the attendees had a background in library and information science. Most others had business or technology backgrounds.

Library Science and Cataloging

Although there is no certificate or degree in taxonomy creation, the degree programs that provide the best preparation for this kind of work are the MLS or MLIS. These programs typically have courses on knowledge organization and classification in general; some also offer a course more focused on thesauri, controlled vocabularies, and taxonomies. Nevertheless, although 54.4 percent survey respondents said they had an MLS or MLIS degree, fewer reported having taken courses on taxonomies. Only 14.8 percent (22 out of 149 respondents) of taxonomists had been in some kind of concentration or specialty program that was specifically taxonomy-related, 16.1 percent had taken two or more college/university courses on taxonomy-related subjects, and 5.4 percent reported taking only one such course. Indeed, a number of the taxonomists with an MLS or MLIS degree reported that their only specific training in taxonomy or classification was on the job. Those who reported taking college courses on taxonomy/thesaurus creation, which was their initial source of interest in the subject, often sought out taxonomy work later. These nonaccidental taxonomists are still in the minority, though.

While some MLS/MLIS graduates had already taken an interest in taxonomies and thesauri as students, others came to the field through other work. Cataloging and metadata design are common prior career paths to taxonomy work. In our survey of taxonomists, we asked them how they first got started doing taxonomy work. Several of their responses refer to cataloging:

- "I was working as a cataloger when a taxonomy job opened up at my company and I applied. ... I learned on the job."

- "I have been a cataloger and indexer for decades, but my first taxonomy work was a request for a group of librarians to develop a topical taxonomy for website content."

- "I was asked to provide a metadata structure for a library of compliance training materials."

- "I had worked with controlled vocabularies in other contexts (esp. museum cataloging)."

- "Through designing a cataloging system."

The activity of cataloging is actually more similar to indexing than it is to taxonomy design and creation, although catalog design is similar to taxonomy design.

Knowledge Management and Content Management

Taxonomy development and implementation for internal enterprise purposes (as opposed to external-facing information or retrieval services) come under the broader field of knowledge management (KM). So knowledge management is another logical background for individuals who move on into the specialty of taxonomies, and 15 of 132 survey respondents (11.4 percent) said that knowledge management was their primary background. An often quoted definition for knowledge management comes from the Gartner Group in 1998:

> Knowledge management is a discipline that promotes an integrated approach to identifying, capturing, evaluating, retrieving, and sharing all of an enterprise's information assets. These assets may include databases, documents, policies, procedures, and previously un-captured expertise and experience in individual workers.[2]

Taxonomies often play a role in identifying and retrieving information assets, although they are insufficient for uncaptured expertise or knowledge. Survey respondents with a background in knowledge management explained how they got involved in taxonomies:

- "It was part of my first knowledge management portal project."

- "I was invited by an ex-colleague to help on a project at his new employer, based on my knowledge of the industry and my work on knowledge management."

- "In an interview for a KM job my future boss asked if I was comfortable handling the company's taxonomies. I said

yes, sure. Of course. As soon as I walked out, I quickly
Googled 'define: taxonomy'."

- "I was working in knowledge management and found a
major gap in the taxonomy awareness and competencies
portion of KM implementations. I revisited my initial
library science training and built a body of work that
eventually resulted in my book *Organising Knowledge*."
—Patrick Lambe

Unlike library/information science, however, degree programs
in knowledge management are extremely rare, although there
are occasional single courses offered on the subject, especially in
library/information science schools and in business schools.

Content management, in contrast to the broader field of knowledge management, is specifically focused on managing the life
cycle of content items, typically digital files, and this is usually done
within a content management system (CMS). Thus in one sense,
the scope of information handled in content management is limited. In another sense, though, content management goes beyond
knowledge management, which focuses on internal information.
Content management may deal with third-party content and may
deal with content that is published for external users. Taxonomies are very suitable for facilitating content management, and
many content management systems now support the integration
of taxonomies, in addition to basic metadata. Survey respondents
who had a prior background in content management, whether
internal (enterprise content management) or external publication (web content management), explained how they got involved
in taxonomies:

- "I was an archivist that got an out-of-school internship in
content management."

- "To help our clients implement useful document and
content management solutions."

- "Organizing content in the Drupal content management system."

- "Starting as a web content manager, as my need to better control the content and improve users e-commerce experience I found myself needing to develop taxonomies for improved navigation as well as dynamically serving up the right related content."

Digital asset management (DAM) is essentially a subspecialization within content management that deals with rich-media content assets, such as images, video, audio, and other multimedia content. Specific to these kinds of assets is the additional process of managing digital rights and permissions. DAM was not listed as option in the survey, but three respondents entered it in the comments field as their background. Explanations of DAM backgrounds of survey respondents included the following:

- "Working on digital asset management for photo assets in a creative environment."

- "Photographer and Digital Asset Manager."

- "I worked for an online photo company and as part of that work I developed and maintained the controlled vocabulary."

- "Assistant in a film archive."

Information Technology

Professionals with a more technical background in software, information technology, or database development may also end up working on taxonomies. Those with an information technology background tend to have prior experience in one or more of the following: information management, software development, search engine software, information/database management software, or text analytics. Survey respondents explained a background in search as follows:

- "[Got started in taxonomies] as part of maintaining a government website's search engine."

- "I was researching new search terminology for the company I am currently working for then I was later transferred to the taxonomy department to better relate our multiple search structures with our product taxonomy."

A background in information/database management software was reflected in the following survey responses:

- "I started in the mid- to late '90s developing a customized Filemaker Pro template to allow picking from a hierarchical value list to create a list of keywords that were then inserted into the File Info of Photoshop files (using the International Press Telecommunications Council metadata standard)."

- "I'm the developer of open source tool to manage taxonomies and other formal representations of the knowledge."

- "I have developed an information system for the Austrian Integrated Monitoring, handling soil-, species- and other taxonomies."

Consultant Jim Wessely is an example of a taxonomist with a background in text analytics. Wessely described his early work as "computational research in text analytics and auto-classification in a very large research facility." He said, "In '98 I realized that I needed to create taxonomies so that I had organized structures to which I could auto-categorize content."

Some taxonomists have both a software/IT and a library/information science background. This combination of skills makes them especially suited for taxonomy work and its technical implementations. Jean Graef of the Montague Institute, which provides taxonomy and knowledge management training, explained her role as follows:

> I'm in the business of covering gaps between corporate information cultures and technologies. ... I got interested

in it when I realized that there was an opportunity for a boundary-spanner like me to help bridge the gap between the way IT staff viewed taxonomy (a browsable hierarchy on a website), the way librarians viewed it (a subject index to a collection of books), and the way editors viewed it (a topical hierarchy at the beginning of a book and a topic index at the back). ... The technologists didn't understand how to create semantic relationships, and librarians and indexers didn't understand how to translate their semantic structures and skills into internet-based technologies.[3]

Taxonomy consultant Marcia Morante also had a combined background of library science training and work experience with software companies. She wrote as follows:

Although I have an MS in library and information science, I never worked in a library. All of my jobs out of graduate school were with search engine companies. Two of them are no longer in business or were bought out—Infodata and Information Dimensions. Several are still around: Fulcrum (taken over by a company that was taken over by OpenText), Verity, and Autonomy. In those days, the focus was on text searching (Boolean and/or "natural language") and very little on metadata. However, given my educational background, controlled vocabularies were never far from my mind.[4]

Ontologies, because of their data modeling aspect, tend to be designed by people with a more technical background. Ontologies also appeal to those who are interested in the web development aspect of the semantic web. Math or logic (philosophy) backgrounds are also suitable for ontology work, as relations in ontologies are sometimes based on set theory.[5]

Indexing

Indexing is another common background for taxonomists. While cataloging is done on the material or document level and follows prescribed rules, indexing is done on an article, page, or even paragraph level and thus involves greater subject analysis and gives greater decision-making power to the individual indexer. Periodical article indexing or other "database" indexing typically requires the indexer to look up terms in a controlled vocabulary and assign each document one or more such terms that best describe the document's content. These controlled vocabularies need to be maintained and updated. It is natural that those who have used controlled vocabularies for indexing might transition into the role of managing the controlled vocabularies.

Another kind of indexing is involved in creating indexes at the back of books. Although indexers of books generally do not use controlled vocabularies, some of the skills used in creating indexes and taxonomies are similar, so book indexers, too, may be attracted to taxonomy work. Relevant skills include the following:

- Deciding what is important and likely to be looked up

- Deciding how best to word a concept

- Structuring hierarchical relations among terms, as main entries and subentries in a book index, or as broader and narrower terms in a taxonomy

- Determining variant terms, as double-posts or *See* references in a book index or as nonpreferred terms (used for) in a taxonomy

- Creating related term relationships, as *See also* relationships in a book index or associative relationships in a taxonomy

The majority of book indexers work as freelancers, and a considerable amount of taxonomy work can also be done on a freelance/

contract basis. Taxonomists who previously worked as indexers recounted the transition as follows:

- "I started by doing indexing; I indexed three books. Then, I was able to get corporate library work that included some taxonomy assignments."

- "Got a job as an indexer and after a few years took over the controlled vocabulary creation and maintenance."

- "Got hired into a Fortune 500 company on the basis of my indexing background, as they knew they needed a taxonomist for their data governance organization."

When people with a background in indexing move into taxonomy work, they usually start out working on taxonomies that support human indexing, as just described. They then may move on to work on other kinds of taxonomies.

Information Architecture/User Experience
Skill in taxonomy is increasingly being required of information architects, the professionals who design the structure and navigation for websites or intranets, especially large and complicated ones, and the user interfaces of online information retrieval systems. Information architecture focuses on the structure and organization of content, leaving graphic design to the artistically talented. Information architect–taxonomists generally work on organization/navigation types of taxonomies rather than those supporting indexing or search retrieval, but a few have branched out to work on retrieval support taxonomies especially when a search engine is integrated into a website.

The first information architects, in fact, had backgrounds in library and information science, and some graduate programs of library and information science now offer courses in information architecture. In more recent years, however, there has been a slight shift in the profession toward an emphasis on user-experience and user-centered design, reflecting an overall increase in interest in user-experience design.[6] Thus the most qualified information architects now combine expertise in information organization/ design with a focus on serving user needs.

Several taxonomists with a user-experience or information architecture background explained how they got into taxonomies:

- "As I started in web design, it became a natural step in my process to make information more findable."

- "By accident, designing portals."

- "Trying to improve the user experience; they are using shared drives and folders."

- "When I moved from 'Business Analysis' to Information Architecture, I learned about content modeling and hence taxonomies. I started it with a simple blog, and gradually planned ecommerce…"

Today the word *taxonomies* often appears in job descriptions for positions in information architecture or user-experience design, although this would typically refer to small navigation taxonomies, and the role of taxonomy could still be relatively small in these roles.

Subject Matter Experts

Another possible route to taxonomy work—less common now than it used to be—is for a taxonomist to start out as a subject area specialist, such as a scientist or healthcare industry professional. Knowing a subject area very well is an important qualification for building a technical-subject taxonomy. Those with subject matter expertise background explained how they got into taxonomy work:

- "Years ago, working with an internal proprietary research which was comprehensively indexed by subject."

- "I was a subject matter expert for a search engine creating web content and taxonomy categories and a

position opened internally for a taxonomy manager, I
applied and got the job."

- "I worked for a contractor for the National Institute
  of Diabetes, Digestive Diseases, and Kidney/Urologic
  Diseases (NIDDK)—they had three separate vocabularies/
  authority lists (one for each of the three disease areas) and
  I offered to merge them, to help searchers find what they
  needed more easily."

An interesting story is that of Marti Heyman, currently a knowledge manager at Deloitte. She explained how she got into indexing/
taxonomy work with a scientific background (a BS in chemistry),
accidentally moved into a different subject area, and then realized
that she enjoyed the taxonomy work in general, regardless of the
subject area:

> I started using and developing controlled vocabularies
> in corporate settings in 1991 when I joined DuPont's
> Indexing and Abstracting Group. ... As a former poly-
> mer chemistry researcher at DuPont, I was one of a few
> indexers responsible for the indexing and abstracting of
> said polymer chemistry research reports.
>
> However, I made the mistake of many junior staff, and
> I actually took vacation, thus missing a critical meet-
> ing. Of course, during that meeting the senior staff
> resolved how they would reduce the significant backlog
> of research materials about electronic materials. Their
> solution was simple: assign the work to the junior staff
> member not present at the meeting! ... Well, it was obvi-
> ous I was closer to being technically qualified to index
> these reports than any of the agricultural science or life
> science folks, so I went off to do my best. What I quickly
> discovered was that given a basic understanding of

physics and mathematics, one really could do a pretty decent job indexing and abstracting these technical reports by using the technical thesaurus as the knowledge map to the company's view and understanding of the domain. I was floored and I was hooked; truly an accidental taxonomist.

Actually, a BS degree may not be sufficient to pursue a high-level career in taxonomy management. Heyman went on to earn both an MLIS and an MBA later in her career.

Taxonomists with expertise in a particular subject area more often work on the larger taxonomies for indexing or retrieval support and especially on more complex thesauri. Ontologists are also typically subject matter experts, with perhaps some additional background in linguistics.

Accidental Taxonomists

Many taxonomists have come to their work not by applying for a taxonomy job but because a need arose within an organization where they were working in another capacity. Responsibilities were redefined, or what started out as a single project eventually became a job. Occasionally a taxonomy job is created because an individual sees a need and pursues an initiative. Some of these accidental taxonomists explained in our survey how they got into the profession:

- "I began in technical customer support, moved into crisis/outage management and as part of that knowledge management and program management, which eventually lead into information architecture and web architecture. It's been a very organic process." —Allan Grohe

- "Learned myself some HTML in the '90s that translated to volunteering to build the first web portal for performing arts resources at NYPL for the Performing Arts." —Barbara McGlamery

- "I was hired to write copy, was quickly promoted to an editor position and then was later assigned to taxonomy projects, something I had never really heard of before being assigned to the initial project."

- "I applied for a job in Context Management and it turned out that my main work will be taxonomy consulting and taxonomy maintenance."

- "I fell into the specialty. Starting as a web content manager, as my need to better control the content and improve users e-commerce experience I found myself needing to develop taxonomies for improved navigation as well as dynamically serving up the right related content. I discovered that taxonomies are just a natural way of thinking for me."

- "The library inherited a SharePoint site which tried to organize content in a hierarchical page format. Since then, it has evolved to a searchable database. During the course of that evolution, the role and power of tagging and taxonomy became very clear."

- "Was put in charge of a content team that manages millions of pieces of UGC [user-generated content], we needed a way to organize our content so we just started creating taxonomies."

Taxonomy work, especially when it involves building a new taxonomy rather than ongoing maintenance, is very often project-oriented work. Thus, the project might pull in additional people for a temporary period. Some of these people then return to their previous duties, others may end up staying on with taxonomy maintenance duties added to their job description, while still others truly enjoy the experience and their new skills and seek out such jobs and projects in the future.

Taxonomist Skills

The main task of a taxonomist is to create taxonomies, namely, the terms and their structured relationships or categories. Although the next chapters will address this in detail, let us first consider the basic skills required of a taxonomist. The skills discussed here are based on this author's own experience rather than on any job descriptions.

Familiarity with the principles of knowledge organization structures. The core skill of a taxonomist is to have a solid understanding of the relationships between terms—broader/narrower, related, and equivalent—and to implement these relationships accurately and consistently according to standards and best practices.

Analytical skills. Survey results and feedback from users or potential users must be analyzed to determine user needs and how they should be met. Content must be analyzed to determine what concepts should make up the taxonomy. Concepts themselves need to be analyzed in terms of meanings and usage to determine whether a given concept is better left as one or broken into two. Writing rules for taxonomy terms in an auto-categorization system also requires analytical skills.

Organization/categorization skills. The taxonomist needs to determine how concepts, subjects, or entities are to be classified or categorized for creating hierarchical relationships. It is worth noting that organizing concepts is not necessarily the same as organizing things or one's environment—even a person with a messy desk can work as a taxonomist.

Language skills. Taxonomies deal with words and phrases. A solid understanding of grammar is important to ensure that terms are created in a consistent style and relationships between terms are correctly constructed. Strong language skills also aid the taxonomist in compiling comprehensive lists of synonyms as nonpreferred terms. Thus, there is a creative language component to taxonomy work.

Research skills. Taxonomists often need to research the meanings and usage of terms to make the proper term choices, determine their scopes, and relate them correctly to other terms.

Search skills. Taxonomies usually support searching, so it is imperative that the taxonomist be a capable online searcher in order to understand the taxonomy's implementation and use. The taxonomist should be familiar with both the basic and the advanced features common in online search systems and search engines, including complex Boolean searching, wildcards, and truncation. It may also be important for a taxonomist to know how to manipulate search results. Although searchers of all levels use taxonomies, the taxonomist needs to fulfill the expectations of the advanced searcher. Taxonomists also need search skills to conduct research on potential terms, as previously mentioned.

Technical skills. While taxonomists do not need to be software developers, they must have competence in using different kinds of software. Basic skills in using a spreadsheet program are fundamental as it is common to create simple taxonomies this way. Taxonomists should also have experience using various database management systems as taxonomies, metadata, and content are organized and stored in some form of a database structure. Taxonomists should have experience with (or be able to learn quickly and independently) at least one taxonomy/thesaurus management software program. Basic familiarity with XML, and possibly also RDF and OWL tagging formats, is highly desirable. Experience with specific content management systems, document management systems, and/or enterprise search systems is desirable and sometimes requested but not always necessary.

Subject matter expertise. Depending on the position, specific subject matter knowledge may or may not be required. For publicly accessed taxonomies, it is usually not necessary. For internally used taxonomies, however, especially in the fields of pharmaceuticals, healthcare, financial services, legal services, science, and engineering, subject matter knowledge is important.

Attention to detail. Taxonomy work requires accuracy and consistency in creating terms. For example, capitalization and abbreviations should be consistent. Some taxonomy tools do not even have a spell-checker, so careful checking on the part of the taxonomist is required.

Attention to user needs. While a taxonomist need not be a professional in the area of user experience, an understanding of user needs, expectations, and behaviors in the online environment is very valuable, so some exposure to the field of user-centered design is helpful. The taxonomist might have input into the design of the search/browse user interface.

Ability to work independently. In many cases an organization has only one taxonomist, and a taxonomist may report to someone who does not know taxonomies very well. Thus, the taxonomist needs to be able to make decisions independently, set priorities, determine requirements, and plan timetables.

Ability to work with diverse people. The taxonomist will likely need to work with those in other specialties: software developers, interface designers, and product or project managers. If the taxonomy will be used for an external product or service, then the taxonomist may also need to work with people in marketing, sales, or customer support.

Adaptability and flexibility. Taxonomy projects are often somewhat unpredictable, and they vary greatly. The taxonomist may have to work on the draft taxonomies received in various formats and may have to submit taxonomy deliverables in different formats for different stakeholders or customers. This is especially the case when serving external clients.

Communication skills. Taxonomists need to write down the policies and procedures involved in creating the taxonomy and the instructions for its use. Additionally, taxonomists may contribute to user documentation. Taxonomists also need to be able to communicate well orally with different groups in order to convey the purpose, function, and best use of the taxonomy. It may be necessary to explain the purpose and function of a taxonomy to a large group, so presentation skills are also needed. As taxonomies are generally not widely understood, good communication skills are important.

Related Duties

Although the primary task of a taxonomist is creating terms and their relationships, there are numerous additional related responsibilities. The extent to which the taxonomist is involved in the following tasks depends on the type of taxonomy, its implementation, and the project management:

- Project planning
- Researching concepts and names
- Developing and documenting policies
- Taxonomy use/search testing
- Indexing support or supervision
- Interface design
- Metadata design

If available at the time, taxonomists are often included in the planning process, even if others make project and market decisions. All kinds of taxonomies require some degree of user studies or research in order to guide the design of the taxonomy, and taxonomists are often involved at this stage. The main reason for not including a taxonomist in designing and implementing user studies would be simply because that person may not have been hired or assigned to the project yet.

Creating taxonomy terms involves some research to scope and define the terms and their relationships. Certain terms, especially named entity terms, may have additional attributes that require further research—for example, latitude and longitude coordinates for place names, headquarters location for company names, birth dates for person names, and various specifications for products.

As the taxonomy is developed, those involved in the project will be called on to make decisions and refine policies. As a result, the taxonomist must document the taxonomy creation policies in order to guide future development and use of the taxonomy. The taxonomist will also likely need to develop and document policies for the continued maintenance of the taxonomy. In addition to policies, if the project relies on an internally developed or customized taxonomy management system, the taxonomist may need to document the basic procedures for creating terms and relationships. The taxonomist might even be asked to perform user testing of taxonomy management software.

After a taxonomy is created, it needs to be tested. Taxonomists typically perform at least some of the testing themselves, especially if it involves sample searches rather than site navigation. A navigational taxonomy, however, should also be tested by sample user groups. Evaluating the user test results, and possibly setting up the user tests in the first place, is the role of the taxonomist.

The taxonomist will undoubtedly also get involved, to an extent, in any indexing that uses the taxonomy. If there is human indexing, then the taxonomist may perform some sample test indexing and will probably be responsible for writing the indexing guidelines. The taxonomist may train and monitor indexers and will need to check indexers' work, adjusting the taxonomy to improve accurate use. Even if the indexers have a supervisor to train them and check their work, the taxonomist needs to inform indexers of new and changed terms and to solicit their suggestions for new terms. If the taxonomy is used in a form of automated indexing or auto-categorization, the taxonomist is involved, but in a different way. Tasks may include writing rules for rules-based auto-categorization or selecting sample training documents for fine-tuning an algorithm-based auto-categorization system. Chapters 6 and 7 cover these related indexing tasks in detail.

A taxonomy is usually a part of something larger, and whatever that something is, the taxonomist may work on it as well. In many cases, the taxonomy is integrated into a web interface. In such implementations, the taxonomist needs to evaluate the interface and provide input into its design.

In content management, document management, or records management systems, taxonomies provide input into certain metadata fields, so the taxonomist may also be involved in defining the overall metadata architecture. Patrick Lambe analyzed how members of the largest online taxonomy community described themselves in their introductions (367 self-reports in introductions from April 2005 to September 2009 on the Taxonomy Community of Practice Yahoo! group) and found that "metadata work" was the biggest area of application for taxonomy, with "findability/discovery/search" coming in second.[7] In other words, metadata work is not merely related to taxonomy work; the two are often inseparable. There are a number of books on the topic of metadata, significantly more than on taxonomies, so there is no need to discuss metadata design at any length in this book.

Employment of Taxonomists

According to our survey, a bigger section of taxonomists (44 percent, or 65 out of 149 respondents) are employees in organizations that use taxonomies primarily internally, for their website, or in ecommerce. Another 20 percent are employees of organizations that incorporate taxonomies into a marketed information product or information service (information providers, software vendors, etc.), and 12 percent are employees of companies or agencies that provide taxonomy services or custom taxonomies to clients. The rest, about 25 percent, are self-employed as business owners, independent consultants, or freelancers.

There has been no significant change in this distribution of taxonomist employment in recent years, as similar results came from the same survey we conducted seven years prior. In Lambe's survey of 184 taxonomists, aside from the taxonomists who are independent contractors, consultants, or involved in the professional services industry (26 percent), leading sectors employing taxonomists are publishing news and media (13 percent), information and communications technology (13 percent), government (9 percent), education (7 percent), and finance/banking (5 percent).[8] We will look at where taxonomists are employed in this section and address the nature of freelance and consulting work in Chapter 12.

Where Taxonomists Work

Full-time and temporary taxonomists are employed by the following kinds of organizations, with the sectors that employ more taxonomists listed toward the top:

- Large corporations in any industry
- Government agencies
- Publishers and the media industry
- Information providers and database vendors
- Online marketing and advertising services
- Retailers in ecommerce
- Agencies and consultancies
- Taxonomy software vendors and taxonomy vendors
- Nongovernmental organizations and membership associations

In addition, people who would not consider themselves taxonomists but who occasionally work on taxonomies as a secondary activity work in

- libraries

- museums and

- academic institutions

Let's examine each of these sectors more closely. Specific companies that are mentioned in the following paragraphs are primarily based on a review of LinkedIn member profiles: current employers of individuals who have *taxonomist* or *taxonomy* in their job title with that employer. Additional employers come from job postings for taxonomist jobs.

Large Corporations

Taxonomists may work in any industry as long as the company is large enough to have significant information management needs. In many such companies, though, there is likely only a single taxonomist on staff. The taxonomies in these industries, which are often enterprise taxonomies, contribute to content management or document management systems and are primarily for internal use. If the company has a knowledge management team, this is where the taxonomist might belong, but a taxonomist might also be a part of other departments, such as research/corporate library, information technology (IT), or even documentation.

Large companies that have taxonomists on staff include financial services, such as Fidelity Investments, Franklin Templeton, Goldman Sachs, JP Morgan Chase, and Morgan Stanley; insurance companies, such as Allstate, AIG, and GEICO; technology companies, such as Apple, Cisco Systems, Dell, Google, Hewlett-Packard, IBM, Intel, Microsoft, and Oracle; biotechnology and pharmaceutical companies, such as AstraZeneca and PerkinElmer; consulting companies, such as Deloitte, and Ernst & Young; and other manufacturing and industrial companies, such as Caterpillar, the Clorox Company, ConocoPhillips, and Lockheed Martin.

Government Agencies

Government agencies and legislative offices manage massive amounts of information, and many state and federal agencies employ someone in a taxonomist role. The taxonomies in these agencies organize information both for internal access and for public access via the web. Examples of US agencies that employ taxonomists are the Department of State, the Federal Aviation Administration, the General Services Administration, and the National Air and Space Administration (NASA). The US federal government also outsources some taxonomy and related services, so a number of taxonomists work for government contractors. For some federal government jobs, a security clearance is a requirement, even for a contractor. Large international agencies, such as the United Nations and the World Bank, also employ taxonomists.

Publishers and the Media Industry

Companies in the broadly defined publishing and media industries, which have vast amounts of content that need to be managed, are also common employers of taxonomists. Publishers of some newspapers and periodicals, such as the *New York Times*, have long employed taxonomists to create and maintain their own thesauri, used by their own indexers to support retrieval of their articles or other content. Examples of other publishers that have taxonomists on staff include the children's book publisher Scholastic; textbook publishers Cengage Learning, McGraw-Hill, and Pearson; and the magazine publisher the National Geographic Society.

As other forms of content, such as images, sound recordings, and video, are digitized, media companies involved in television, film, and image publishing have also begun to employ taxonomists. These include the companies A&E Networks (including History.com),

Disney ABC Television Group, Gannett, HBO, Netflix, and Martha Stewart Living Omnimedia. Additionally, vendors of stock photos and images, such as Getty Images and Corbis, make use of taxonomists.

Information Providers and Database Vendors

A separate class of publishers is the online information vendors that index published content, usually from multiple sources, for databases sold primarily to libraries and researchers and sometimes to consumers over the web. In this type of publishing, taxonomies are part of the information product/service being marketed. Since information retrieval is their core business, these companies may have not just one taxonomist (more likely called a thesaurus editor or controlled vocabulary editor) but a staff of several. Traditional information vendors that have employed taxonomists for decades include EBSCO, Gale (a part of Cengage Learning), and ProQuest. In addition to these companies, vendors of more specialized subjects that also have staff taxonomists include Bloomberg BNA, LexisNexis, McGraw-Hill Financial, and Thomson Reuters.

Some professional associations and nonprofit organizations publish specialized, academic, or technical information databases, such as the American Psychological Association (PsycINFO) and the American Chemical Society (Chemical Abstracts). Their taxonomists need to be subject matter experts as well.

Newer information websites, which are advertising-supported, that have enough rich content to benefit from hiring taxonomists include recipe websites, such as Allrecipes.com, various consumer health information websites, and the student note-sharing website StudyMode.

Online Marketing and Advertising Services

A new kind of online service that has been recruiting taxonomists is the dot-com startup specializing in niche information—often in business-to-business marketing and web advertising services. Those that have hired taxonomists include Adchemy, Dex Media, Groupon, OwnerIQ, and YP.

Retailers and Ecommerce

Both traditional retailers and online-only retailers use taxonomies to categorize the products on their websites to help customers find what they want to purchase. The internal organization of products is also useful to the employees, especially of the large retailers. Retail companies with taxonomists on staff include Best Buy, Guitar Center, Home Depot, JCPenney, Lowes, Office Depot, Sears, Staples, and Target. Online-only vendors that employ taxonomists include Amazon.com and Zappos.com. Nontraditional online marketplace providers where taxonomists work include eBay, Etsy, and Tradesy. Some companies, such as Sears and Amazon, employ multiple taxonomists.

Agencies and Consultancies

There is a continuum of different kinds of agencies and consultancies dedicated to helping clients organize and present information. Some are medium to large management consultancies that include knowledge management consulting and taxonomy consulting within knowledge management. Smaller consultancies might specialize in knowledge management or even taxonomies. While some web design and user-experience firms have little interest in taxonomies, other information architecture and design agencies that serve clients with especially large website projects employ information architects specializing in taxonomies. Some consultancies also hire taxonomists as contractors on a project basis.

Taxonomy Software and Taxonomy Vendors

Some automatic-indexing software includes integrated taxonomies, so software companies may employ or contract taxonomists to build generic and possibly customized taxonomies. Some taxonomists also work for companies that develop vertical-market search software. Vendors of taxonomy or thesaurus software, such as Access Innovations (Data Harmony), SmartLogic, and Synaptica, also have taxonomists on staff to provide taxonomy development/consulting services for their software clients.

Although taxonomy vendors are a natural employer for taxonomists, there are very few such enterprises. They comprise the companies, organizations, and government agencies mentioned among the sources of licensed taxonomies in Chapter 1, such as the Library of Congress, National Library of Medicine, Getty Research Institute, and WAND. Depending on whether they are creating new taxonomies or merely maintaining existing ones, these organizations may have one to several taxonomists on staff.

Organizations and Associations

Nongovernmental or nonprofit organizations and membership associations with a lot of information to manage may also employ taxonomists. The information being organized may be for internal use or for public use, but most typically it involves resources for the association's members, such as subscription periodical articles, newsletter articles, conference presentations and proceedings, and industry guidelines and policies. Examples of associations that currently employ taxonomists include Financial Accounting Standards Board, IEEE, the National Fire Protection Association, the Project Management Institute, and SAE International.

Libraries, Museums, and Academic Institutions

While repositories of knowledge might seem like the most natural kind of employer for taxonomists, this is not necessarily the case, simply because taxonomies in some form have already existed for decades and creating new ones is not necessary. Libraries have the Library of Congress Subject Headings (LCSH) and the Sears List of

Subject Headings. Museums often use the *Revised Nomenclature for Museum Cataloging* by James R. Blackaby.

The trend we are seeing, however, is that libraries and museums are digitizing their collections (especially smaller, special collections), putting them into databases, and making them accessible in various electronic formats, including the web. Smaller, more specialized collections both require and permit taxonomies different from the traditional cataloging vocabularies, and web access similarly changes the parameters for retrieval. Academic libraries in particular have numerous small, special collections, each of which would benefit from its own taxonomy rather than fitting into a general vocabulary, such as LCSH. Thus, librarians and museum archivists find themselves (accidentally perhaps) taking on taxonomy projects. For libraries, this work typically falls under the responsibility of "technical services."

In addition, some of the larger academic libraries employ taxonomists, particularly if the institution has its own publications or has created its own online information service to serve students, faculty, and researchers. An example is Harvard Business School's Baker Library, which has engaged in taxonomy projects.

Job Titles

Employed taxonomists work under various job titles. The simple, one-word title *taxonomist* is common, although more common are two-word titles with the word *taxonomist* in them. There are also many titles containing the word *taxonomy*, but there are many people involved in taxonomy work whose job titles do not refer to taxonomy.

From our 2015 survey of such people, only a quarter of the 130 respondents reported a job title that included *taxonomy* or *taxonomist*, a smaller percentage than the 37.3 percent who reported that taxonomy work was their primary job responsibility. For a further breakdown of terms in the survey respondents' titles, 21 had *taxonomist* (9 were just *taxonomist*, and 12 *taxonomist* with another word or two), 11 had *taxonomy,* 11 had *information architect* or *user experience,* 9 had *content,* 7 had *knowledge,* 6 had *metadata,* 5 had *information* other than *information architect,* 4 had *ontologist* or *ontology,* and 3 had *search.* Another common term was *consultant,* which appeared in 13 job titles.

The following job titles have appeared in LinkedIn member profiles[9] and responses to our survey question "What is your job title?," (survey responses marked by an asterisk):

- Advanced Taxonomist

- Assistant Taxonomist

- Associate Data Taxonomist

- Associate Taxonomist

- Business Taxonomist

- Chief Taxonomist

- Consulting Taxonomist

- Content Taxonomist

- Corporate Taxonomist*

- Enterprise Taxonomist*

- Information Taxonomist

- Junior Taxonomist

- Knowledge Sharing Taxonomist

- Legal Taxonomist

- Nomenclature Taxonomist

- Product Taxonomist

- Senior Data Cloud Taxonomist

- Senior Lead Taxonomist

- Senior Taxonomist*

- Site Taxonomist—eCommerce

- Taxonomist Consultant

- Web Taxonomist

There are also many titles that combine the word *taxonomist* with another title. These may include the word "and," an ampersand, or a slash, with *taxonomist* coming either first or second. Following is a list of titles that have been combined with that of *taxonomist*:

- Browse Developer (Browse Developer & Taxonomist*)

- Business Analyst

- Business Semantics Lead

- Cataloger

- Classification Specialist

- Content Architect

- Content Editor

- Content Information Manager

- Content Manager

- Content Specialist

- Content Taxonomist & Curator

- Data Analyst

- Data Curator

- Human Factors Engineer (Taxonomist/Human Factors Engineer*)

- Indexer (Indexer and Taxonomist*)

- Information Analyst

- Information Architect

- Knowledge Editor

- Librarian (Taxonomist/Librarian*)
- Library Director
- Metadata Manager
- Product Manager
- Program Manager
- Project Manager
- Search & Portal Team Lead
- Search Analyst
- Search Specialist
- Senior Digital Asset Manager
- Senior Information Manager
- Technical Librarian
- User Experience Architect

Titles with the word *taxonomy* in them are about twice as common as those with the word *taxonomist*. They include the following:

- Analyst, Product Taxonomy
- Archivist/Taxonomy Librarian
- Chief Taxonomy and Experience Officer*
- Library and Taxonomy Manager
- Managing Editor, Science & Taxonomy
- Metadata & Taxonomy Analyst
- Product Taxonomy Specialist
- Search & Taxonomy Analyst
- Search & Taxonomy Specialist
- Search/Taxonomy Manager

- Senior Business Analyst—Taxonomy & Classification
- Senior Search & Taxonomy Analyst
- Senior Taxonomy & Search Consultant
- Senior Taxonomy Analyst*
- Senior Taxonomy Specialist*
- Structured Data/Taxonomy Specialist
- Taxonomy & Indexing Manager
- Taxonomy & Knowledge Manager
- Taxonomy & Publishing Manager
- Taxonomy Analyst
- Taxonomy and Metadata Analyst*
- Taxonomy and Metadata Specialist
- Taxonomy and Search Analyst
- Taxonomy Architect
- Taxonomy Associate
- Taxonomy Consultant
- Taxonomy Data Specialist
- Taxonomy Developer
- Taxonomy Development Manager*
- Taxonomy Editor
- Taxonomy Manager*
- Taxonomy Program Manager
- Taxonomy Specialist*
- Taxonomy Supervisor

As taxonomy has become the responsibility of a department and not just an individual in an organization, it is increasingly common to find titles of managers and directors with the word *taxonomy* in them. These include the following:

- Assistant Director, Content and Taxonomy
- Director of Records and Information Systems
- Director of Taxonomy
- Director of Taxonomy and Metadata*
- Director, Content Taxonomy
- Director, Taxonomy & Search
- Manager, Search and Taxonomy
- Manager, Search, Taxonomy & Data Governance
- Manager, Taxonomy & Hierarchy
- Manager, Taxonomy & Systems
- Manager, Taxonomy and Metadata Services Group*
- Manager, Taxonomy and Metadata Solutions
- Manager, Taxonomy Production
- Senior Manager, Taxonomy and Search

There are also many jobs in which taxonomy development and management is a significant responsibility, but whose titles do not contain the word *taxonomist* or *taxonomy*. These include the following:

- Category Analyst
- Content Librarian*
- Content Manager*
- Content Strategist*
- Data Architect

- Director, Research & Knowledge Services*
- Enterprise Information Architect*
- Experience Architect*
- Indexed Content Manager*
- Information Architect*
- Knowledge Architect*
- Knowledge Management Analyst*
- Knowledge Manager*
- Knowledge Sharing Business Analyst*
- Knowledge Sharing Strategy Specialist*
- Manager, Content and Collaboration Services*
- Online Content Analyst*
- Ontologist*
- Ontology Engineer*
- Principal Program Manager, Information Standards, User Engagement
- Product Ontology Linguist*
- Search Editor*
- Search Metadata Technical Specialist*
- Search Vocabulary Specialist*
- Senior Knowledge Management Consultant*
- Senior Manager, Metadata Services*
- Senior Metadata Librarian*
- Technical Information Specialist
- UX Consultant*
- UX Researcher*
- Vocabulary Editor

Even though the word *taxonomy* occurs more frequently than the word *taxonomist* in job titles, we will continue to refer in this book to taxonomists because it is the simplest one-word designation.

Endnotes

1. Patrick Lambe, "Taxonomists: Evolving or Extinct? The Future of Taxonomy Work," presentation delivered at the Taxonomy Boot Camp conference, San Jose, CA, November 19, 2009.

2. Bryan Duhon, "It's All in Our Heads," *Inform* 12, no. 8 (September): 10.

3. Jean Graef, email to author, November 21, 2008.

4. Marcia Morante, email to author, November 21, 2008.

5. Irene Pappas, email to author, July 29, 2009.

6. The relative growth in interest in "user-experience design" compared with decline in "information architecture" over the period of 2005–2015 is evidenced by Google Trends topic and search-term comparisons and by Gale's periodical database keyword search result count comparisons.

7. Patrick Lambe, "Taxonomists: Evolving or Extinct? The Future of Taxonomy Work," presentation delivered at the Taxonomy Boot Camp conference, San Jose, CA, November 19, 2009.

8. Ibid.

9. Job titles are based primarily on the current Title field (not in the self-described professional headlines) of several hundred LinkedIn member profiles identified with "taxonomy" or "taxonomist" in keyword searches conducted in July and August 2015.

Chapter 3

Creating Terms

Taxonomies: Not as boring as you think.
—Seth Earley

While different kinds of taxonomies may have different structures and different kinds of relationships between terms, they are all made up of terms. Therefore, we will begin our discussion on creating taxonomies with the details of how to create terms.

Concepts and Terms

Just as there are various types of taxonomies, so are there various designations for the terms—the controlled and defined words or phrases that make up the taxonomy. Fundamentally, a taxonomy comprises distinct *concepts*, which are things or ideas; a *term*, on the other hand, is a label for a concept, and a single concept may be described by multiple, somewhat synonymous terms.

Although in a very simple hierarchical taxonomy you may decide to have just a single term per concept, most controlled vocabularies accommodate multiple terms for each concept. In a synonym ring or synset type of taxonomy, all the terms for a concept have equal standing. In other taxonomies, however, the taxonomist designates a single term as preferred, and the rest are nonpreferred terms, which serve as cross-references pointing to the preferred term. Even in the case of a synonym ring, each concept needs to have a single name, at least for internal administration purposes, although it does not matter so much what name it is.

You may find any of the following designations used to refer to terms or components of a taxonomy.

A *concept* is a thing, idea, or shared understanding of something. A set of synonymous terms could describe it. It is therefore the combination of both a preferred term and its various nonpreferred terms, if any, or all the linked synonyms within a synonym ring. Nevertheless, a concept has to be called something, so if there are also nonpreferred terms, the concept is typically referred to by its preferred term name (a convention that may lead to confusion between a concept and its label), even though every concept is more than just a term. A concept may also be called any one of the following:

- Node: A concept as expressed within a hierarchical taxonomy. If a hierarchy is like a tree, then the nodes are places where new branches or leaves connect. A node may refer to the preferred term alone, especially if there are no nonpreferred terms, or to the preferred term plus its nonpreferred terms.

- Object: A concept especially in an object-oriented database structure. An object comprises any nonpreferred terms and also their definition, notes, and any other attributes. Information on relationships to other terms/ objects may be part of an object as well.

- Individual: A concept in an ontology.

- Entity: Sometimes used for a concept in an ontology or semantic network.

- Instance: May refer to (1) an individual in an ontology; (2) a named entity as it relates to a broader topical term, in an instance-type of broader/narrower relationship; or (3) the most specific concept at the narrowest, bottom level of a taxonomy.

- (Term) Cluster: A concept that comprises multiple equivalent terms.

- Wordset: A concept that comprises multiple equivalent terms.

- Taxon: A concept usually only in biological taxonomies.

A *term* is a label for a concept—the most common, generic designation, which can be in any controlled vocabulary. It can refer to any kind of term, both preferred terms and nonpreferred terms. However, it sometimes refers to just the preferred term, so the designation may be somewhat ambiguous in practice. Other designations for terms, used to avoid ambiguity, include Vocabulary term and Subject term.

A *term record* is the complete information regarding a term, especially as stored and displayed in taxonomy management or indexing software. It includes all of a term's relationships, notes, categories, and any additional attributes, along with administrative information, such as approval status, creation, and modification dates, in other words, the metadata for a single term. Not all of these details need to be included, though, for it to be called a term record. Since most taxonomy management software is based on some kind of database management software, a term record is thus a database record. A term record may also be called *term details.*

A *preferred term* is the official displayed word or phrase for the concept. Nonpreferred terms are the various synonyms, variants, or other sufficiently equivalent words or phrases used as cross-references pointing to the preferred term. Other names for a preferred term include the following:

- Descriptor: A preferred term, especially when nonpreferred terms are called nondescriptors
- Subject descriptor: A preferred term, especially one that is a subject or common noun, not a named entity or proper noun
- Authorized term: A preferred term, especially if nonpreferred terms are called unauthorized terms
- Node name: A preferred term when the designation "node" is used for concepts—this is more often an internal, rather than an end user, designation

A number of other designations often used in taxonomies are ambiguous, as they might refer either to concepts or to preferred terms. These include the following:

- Categories
- Subjects
- Subject areas
- Topics

As there are many ways to refer to the terms or concepts in a taxonomy, one of the first tasks in creating a new taxonomy is to decide what to call its components. It is not unusual to use one designation internally, because it appears logical to you, the taxonomist, or to the software developers responsible for the search software or the user interface, and it also appears logical to display a different designation in the user interface because it makes sense to the end users. Indeed, you might even need to create a mini controlled vocabulary to describe the taxonomy. At the very least, a glossary is helpful. In the following pages and chapters, we will refer to concepts and terms specifically and to preferred terms only when needed.

In creating terms, the taxonomist actually has two tasks:

1. Identify the concepts that make up the taxonomy.
2. Choose the preferred terms for each of the concepts.

Identifying Concepts

Deciding what concepts should go into a taxonomy involves gathering information on what *could* be included and then further evaluating these concepts to decide what *should* be included. In gathering information, the taxonomist should use two sources:

1. Documents/files representing the content to be searched with the taxonomy

2. People, including the taxonomy owners, subject matter experts, and sample users

Content as a Source of Concepts

Obviously, the primary source for concepts should be the content or material that will be indexed or categorized with the taxonomy. These materials could be almost anything: articles, reports, book chapters or sections, white papers, product specifications, brochures, transcripts, legal documents, website or intranet pages, image files, video files, presentation files, and so forth. The taxonomist's task is to look for significant concepts contained in or associated with these documents. Reading the full texts is neither practical nor even always possible, as in the case of multimedia files. Rather, the taxonomist should look for concepts within any of the following text sources that may be associated with the documents or files:

- Titles of the documents or articles
- Subdocument-level section headings
- Abstracts or summaries
- Image or illustration captions
- Website navigation menu labels, site maps, and web-page titles
- Tables of contents and chapter names in longer documents
- Items within directory listings, especially products, names, and so on
- Existing metadata (keywords, titles, short descriptions)

There could also be significant concepts that are mentioned only within the body of a text, but a quick skim of the lead paragraph and the lead sentences of additional paragraphs should be sufficient for identifying these concepts. Additional sources for a content audit specifically for enterprise taxonomies are listed in Chapter 10.

To keep track of the potential concepts at this stage, it is probably easiest to enter them into a spreadsheet table (such as Excel), along with information pertaining to the concept and its source. Of course, to record them, you will need to name the concepts, so even at this stage, each concept requires some sort of term. The term you choose at this point is not final, and you can change it later. Usually the term used in the content text is sufficient unless it is vague and needs clarification. Writing down two or three terms for a concept, separated by slashes, is also fine.

There are different methodologies for recording the concepts at this stage of taxonomy preparation, sometimes referred to as a content audit or a content inventory. There could be a new row for each concept, with the source document noted in one of the columns, as illustrated in Figure 3.1.

Alternatively, there could be a new row for each source file with multiple concepts, as found in each source file, recorded in one of the columns, as illustrated in Figure 3.2. This latter method might be preferred if you want to make sure you include every source page/document.

	A	B	C	D	E
1	Concept	Source	Variants	Category	Notes
2	DVD Players	http://shop.onl	DVD recorders, Digital	Consumer Electronics	
3	Televisions	http://shop.onl	TV sets	Consumer Electronics	
4	Stereos	http://shop.onl	Home audio	Consumer Electronics	home, not car
5	Laptops	http://shop.onl	Notebook computers	Computers	

Figure 3.1 Example of how a spreadsheet can be set up for a content audit, with a unique row for each concept

	A	B	C	D	E	F
1	URL/Location	Format	Type	Terms	Audience	Notes
2	http://shop.onl	HTML	Product data	DVD players, Television, Stereo	customers	
3	http://shop.onl	HTML	Product data	Laptops, Monitors, Keyboards,	customers	
4	http://shop.onl	PDF	Press release	Technology partnership, Marke	public, investors	

Figure 3.2 Example of how a spreadsheet can be set up for a content audit, with a unique row for each source file or document

If the content to be indexed is in the form of a stream of incoming files, such as periodical articles, then only a sample of the content can be analyzed for concepts. This is better described as a content survey than an audit. If, on the other hand, the content is relatively stable, as on a website, then ideally you should conduct a complete content inventory, as long as the number of pages is not too many to look at individually (hundreds instead of thousands of pages). If the number of pages is too great, you should still conduct an audit of representative pages. In the case of a complete content inventory, such as of a website or intranet, it is best to record the unique file name and directory in the first column of the table and then enter concepts into a subsequent column, thus ensuring that every page, or at least every representative page type, is inventoried. In addition to a concept and its source file, other information to record may include additional synonyms for the concept, content type, file format, and audience. Although the focus at this stage is the concepts, if additional synonymous terms for the same concept are evident, you should definitely note them for future use in building the taxonomy.

The task at this point closely resembles descriptive indexing or cataloging. In a sense, you are test indexing the content to see what concepts might be useful for indexing. This approach makes most sense if you are preparing a taxonomy primarily for indexing a collection of documents or files. If, on the other hand, the taxonomy is to organize a website or intranet, support a search engine or content management system, or otherwise constitute an enterprise taxonomy, then you need to be more liberal in collecting concepts. For these purposes, you are not indexing documents, rather you are gathering all concepts of potential interest, which you will weed through later.

There are also automated methods for extracting candidate terms from sample content. Simple text analytics programs can generate lists of nouns or noun phrases occurring in the text; many programs will also sort those terms by frequency. An example of keyword extraction tool is AlchemyLanguage API, a web-based service from AlchemyAPI (www.alchemyapi.com), an IBM company, which offers monthly subscriptions. There are also several free online term extraction tools, but these can only analyze one document at a time. These include TerMine from the National Centre for Text Mining at the University of Manchester, United Kingdom (www.nactem.ac.uk/software/termine/), Terminology Extraction by Translated Labs (labs.translated.net/terminology-extraction), and Term Extraction by fivefilters.org. Most programmers can also write scripts to extract single words, although extracting useful phrase terms, as these other applications can do, is more complicated. With the right tools, unstructured text can quickly produce useful lists of candidate terms.[1]

If the content already has metadata, there are additional software tools that are useful for extracting the metadata. For example, some taxonomists have used Metalogix (www.metalogix.com) for this purpose. It is designed to support migration of content to the latest version of SharePoint, but its inventory feature captures a lot of metadata that can be useful for analyzing the content.[2]

People as a Source of Concepts

The various people who contribute ideas for the concepts within the taxonomy usually include the owner or manager of the taxonomy, subject matter experts, users or test users, and finally you, the taxonomist.

The owner, manager, or sponsor of the taxonomy (who may be a product manager, project manager, or executive in an organization) often has a significant stake in the taxonomy and may want to suggest at least some concepts, based on the person's understanding of strategic or business needs and the search database design or perceived customer or user needs. These suggestions are more likely to be the top-level concepts in a hierarchical taxonomy but often include other miscellaneous sample terms. Concept suggestions from the taxonomy owner are welcome, but usually the taxonomist should decide the term names.

If a specialty subject area is to be covered, subject matter experts should also be consulted to ensure that all the basic concepts within that subject area are included, although these experts are of greater importance during the stage of determining term names rather than concepts. For a hierarchical taxonomy, subject matter experts can recommend the inclusion of concepts that would fill in any gaps in the hierarchy.

Users are an important source of ideas for taxonomy concepts. If the taxonomy is part of a product or service marketed to external clients or is part of an external website, then you can pose questions pertaining to the taxonomy to focus groups or test-market users. If the taxonomy is for internal use, as an enterprise taxonomy, then you should conduct interviews to find out the needs of employees of various departments who will contribute to and search for the content. Usually some form of online searching has already been taking place before a taxonomy comes along. Search engine logs of user queries and feedback forms can provide ideas for concepts in both general and specific terms.

Finally, you, the taxonomist, can contribute concepts to be included in the taxonomy. Especially if the taxonomy is general in nature, you may rely on your general knowledge. If you have built hierarchies or facets before, you can draw on your previous experience. If charged to build a hierarchical taxonomy, for example, on news categories, industries, or occupations, you can establish a good basic structure on your own, especially if you are familiar with well-known classification systems in these areas, such as industry SIC or NAICS codes. In some cases, it is better to start out with your own ideas of concepts before consulting outside reference sources, lest the outside sources influence you too much.

Evaluating Concept Inclusion

Inevitably, there will be more concepts than practical for a taxonomy, especially when including concepts gathered from a content audit. A potential concept should become a term only if the following questions can be answered affirmatively.

1. *Is the concept within the intended subject area scope of the taxonomy?*

A taxonomy needs to have a defined subject area scope; otherwise, it can get out of hand. This is especially the case for a hierarchical taxonomy because hierarchies work best when confined to a specific area. This contrasts with an alphabetical back-of-the-book index, which can easily accommodate off-topic entries.

2. *Is the concept important and something users are likely to look up?*

Trivial subjects should not be included. Any analysis of document content will reveal numerous concepts that are relatively insignificant. If these concepts do not come up in user studies or interviews, then you can probably omit them.

3. *Is there enough information on the concept?*

Just because a concept appears in the text does not mean that it should be indexed. A given concept may come up only once and with little substantive information about it. This is another reason a taxonomy or a human-created index provides more useful information than a mere keyword search. If creating a taxonomy for periodical-types of content (i.e., if new content is added over time), you also need to determine whether there will be recurring future occurrences of the concept. Will there be a sufficient number of documents on the topic over time? For websites, a content survey thus needs to be large enough so that you can recognize whether a given concept is indeed rare or may appear more frequently.

4. *Do users want and expect the concept to be covered?*
If a concept appears only marginally in the content and user questionnaires and search logs never reveal any interest in that concept, then perhaps it should not be included in the taxonomy. Conversely, a marginally covered concept that is repeatedly a topic of interest among users should be included in the taxonomy as long as there is at least some content or anticipated content on the topic.

Choosing the Preferred Term

Unless the taxonomy is of the synonym ring type, the taxonomist must select a preferred term to describe each concept; the other possible terms for a concept can then become nonpreferred terms. In general, the preferred term should reflect the language of the taxonomy's users. If you decide to include a concept in the taxonomy but are not ready to finalize its preferred term name, you may still enter a temporary term name into the taxonomy as a *candidate term*. Most commercial taxonomy management software supports the designation of candidate versus approved terms. Candidate terms cannot be used for indexing, and the software flags them as requiring further review.

Choosing among Synonyms

Selecting the preferred term often involves choosing between two or more synonyms, such as the following:

> **doctors** vs. **physicians**
> **movies** vs. **motion pictures**
> **cars** vs. **automobiles**

In choosing the preferred term from two or more synonyms, the taxonomist needs to consider the following:

1. *The wording the intended users will most likely look up.*
   This is especially the case in a displayed, browsable

taxonomy. For example, if the users are the general public, they are more likely to look up **doctors** than **physicians**. Healthcare professionals, on the other hand, will more likely look up **physicians**.

2. *The subject focus or scope of the taxonomy and its indexed content.* The content and scope are closely related to audience. For example, if the scope is travel services, then **cars** is probably more appropriate than **automobiles**. If, instead, the focus is on selling vehicle parts, then **automobiles** is likely the more appropriate term.

3. *Enforcing an organizational/enterprise controlled vocabulary.* This consideration applies especially if the taxonomy is for internal use or is a public agency taxonomy. For example, an intranet for a company may require the term **employee development** instead of **employee training**.

4. *Conforming to academic, cultural, political, or trade/industry standards.* This includes taking into consideration cultural sensitivities and what is "politically correct." For example, it has become more common to use the term **Middle East** instead of **Near East**. If a taxonomy has a scholarly or academic focus, then the preferred terms will reflect those accepted by the discipline.

5. *Consistency in style throughout the taxonomy.* A taxonomy should use a similar level of wording throughout, either informal or formal/technical, to make it more predictable for the user. For example, names of occupations should be either consistently formal, such as **physicians**, **attorneys**, and **law enforcement officers**, or consistently informal, such as **doctors**, **lawyers**, and **police officers**, but not a mixture of both levels.

6. *The wording of terms within the documents/content indexed by the taxonomy.* This will depend, of course, on

the degree of consistency within the body of content. If the content has multiple authors, then wording is likely to be inconsistent in some areas. Where it is consistent, though, the content can be a guide for choosing the preferred term, but as just mentioned, this factor is secondary to the needs and expectations of the users.

The relative importance of these different criteria will vary, but in general, the wording that is most likely to be looked up by the intended users/audience—in other words, the preferred language of the taxonomy's target population—should take precedence over the other criteria.

Choosing among Near Synonyms

At times, the taxonomist needs to choose which of two similar, but not synonymous, concepts will be the preferred and the nonpreferred. When two concepts have overlapping meaning, maintaining a distinction may be important for the nuances within a specialized subject area, but it is often not practical when it comes to indexing and organizing content. Without clear distinctions between concepts, users may become confused, and content will not be consistently indexed, whether by humans or by auto-categorization methods. Examples of closely related terms, which might require the taxonomist to select one as nonpreferred, include the following:

> **foreign policy** vs. **international relations**
> **colleges and universities** vs. **higher education**
> **books** vs. **literature**

Naturally if the taxonomy has a narrow focus and there is a significant volume of content on each related subject, then perhaps the two concepts should be maintained as distinct terms. Both **foreign policy** and **international relations** could exist as separate terms in a single taxonomy focused on international affairs, both **colleges and universities** and **higher education** could exist as terms in a taxonomy focused on education, and both **books** and

literature could exist in a taxonomy focused on the humanities. However, even with specialized content, maintaining accurate indexing quality would require a great deal of effort (see Chapter 6), so it may still be simpler to choose one term as preferred and the other as nonpreferred. If the taxonomy does include terms with overlapping meaning, it tends to work best if they are used in different facets. For example, **colleges and universities** could be in an institutions/organizations facet while **higher education** could be in a topic/subject facet.

A similar dilemma arises in choosing between different grammatical forms of a word, such as terms describing a topic or an action. For example, see the following:

> **contracts** vs. **contracting**
> **investments** vs. **investing**
> **manufacturers** vs. **manufacturing**

Even in a specialized taxonomy, it is nearly impossible to maintain the distinction between two single-word terms differentiated only by their morphological form, and the taxonomist must choose one over the other. Again, a possible exception would be in a faceted taxonomy. For example, **contracts** could be in a subject facet while **contracting** could be in an actions facet, but the indexing would need to follow clearly written rules and policies in order to distinguish the two. In any case, terms within the same hierarchy should adhere to the same morphological form for consistency of style. Determining the overall style is the taxonomist's decision but may require input from other people.

Sources for Preferred Term Choice

Content is the primary source for concepts, but not necessarily for preferred term names. If the content is consistent and the same terms appear throughout the content to be indexed, then the terms from the content should be primary candidates for the preferred term names. Far too often, however, term usage is inconsistent within a diverse collection of content, and the taxonomist needs to rely on other sources in choosing the preferred terms.

While content is the determining factor in choosing concepts, in general people play a more important role in determining the preferred terms. You should consult subject matter experts, if available, to choose the preferred term for any specialized or technical concepts. The experts understand the terminology better and can advise you on the most appropriate term for specific circumstances and audiences. Taxonomy owners or sponsors play less of a role in determining term names than they do in suggesting some of the top-level concepts, but in certain circumstances, their input into the choice of preferred term names is important. This is particularly the case for internal nomenclature used in enterprise taxonomy.

User expectations and needs are also very important in settling on the preferred term for each concept. Access to information on user expectations varies greatly depending on the type of taxonomy and its use. If the taxonomy is to be part of an information product or service that offers licenses or subscriptions, then the company's marketing department will likely conduct user studies, and the taxonomist may be only marginally involved in designing these studies. If the taxonomy is to be implemented primarily on a website that is freely accessed by the public, then the user-experience or user-centered design staff will likely be the ones conducting user research, and the involvement of the taxonomist in this research will depend on the degree to which the taxonomist is integrated into the user-experience team.

If the taxonomy is part of an internal content management system, document management system, or intranet, then the users are internal employees. This means that the marketing department will not bother to research user needs, thus leaving more of this responsibility to the taxonomist. On the other hand, gathering information from users who are employees is much easier in a practical sense because the users are identifiable and can be contacted.

Nevertheless, in a taxonomy of hundreds or thousands of terms, it is not always feasible to gather user opinions regarding the preferred term for every concept. Gathering input from potential users and other stakeholders will be discussed in more detail in Chapter 9.

External Sources for Preferred Terms

Finally, there are external published sources that can provide valuable input in determining your preferred terms. These include industry standards, specialized glossaries, and the publications or websites of regulatory agencies and trade and professional organizations. Especially interesting are other existing taxonomies or controlled vocabularies. You may utilize those taxonomies that are publicly accessible, but only on a term-by-term basis if you do not have a license. In some cases, it is also possible to purchase a license to an entire taxonomy, as described in Chapter 1, which allows you to use as much of the taxonomy as you wish.

Publicly available taxonomies or controlled vocabularies for browsing include the Library of Congress Subject Headings (LCSH), Library of Congress Thesaurus for Graphic Materials, and those of government agencies, such as NASA, the US Department of Education (ERIC Thesaurus), the National Agricultural Library, and the National Library of Medicine. United Nations agencies maintain multilingual thesauri, such as the UNESCO Thesaurus. A longer list of online thesauri is available on the Online Thesauri and Authority Files page of the American Society for Indexing website (www.asindexing.org/about-indexing/thesauri/online-thesauri-and-authority-files).

There are other sources for determining the preferred term for a named entity (person, company, organization, creative work, place, etc.). These include the Library of Congress Name Authorities (along with the LCSH, part of the Library of Congress Authorities), government websites, and the websites of companies or organizations. For the correct forms of names of people in current events, you can consult websites of reputable newspapers. Finally, for names that have variant forms or spellings, checking the total number of results from a Google search on each variation, restricted by language (English), will indicate which form or spelling is the most common. You will also need to develop consistent policies for certain kinds of names; for example, whether to spell out, abbreviate, or omit company designators in company names.

Term Format

When it comes to the format of the terms, there are guidelines in the published taxonomy standards. ANSI/NISO Z39.19-2005 (2010) *Guidelines for the Construction, Format, and Management of Monolingual Controlled Vocabularies* addresses the issue of single words versus multiword terms (section 6.3); grammatical forms of terms (section 6.4); singular and plural nouns (section 6.5); abbreviations, slang and jargon, popular or scientific names, foreign or loan words, and variations in spelling (section 6.6); capitalization (section 6.7); and compound terms (section 7).[3] Rather than repeat the entire contents of ANSI/NISO Z39.19, we will discuss only some of the points of formatting here. It is important to remember that these standards are guidelines only, and there can certainly be flexibility in their application, especially for an internally used taxonomy.

Lowercase or initial capitals, but not title caps. Although the guidelines recommend all lowercase, initial capitalization is also common. Using title capitalization, however, could cause confusion between proper nouns and generic terms. For example, **Business services** or **business services** are both fine, but not **Business Services**. There is a tendency to use initial capitalization for terms in hierarchical taxonomies to represent a view of hierarchical category labels, whereas all lowercase terms more commonly appear in less hierarchical thesauri or controlled vocabularies. (Examples in this book demonstrate both styles.)

Single words or multiword terms. The preferred length of terms will largely be determined by your software system, the user interface, and what makes sense for usability. Except for proper nouns, which must appear in complete form regardless of length, terms are usually one to four words long.

Nouns or noun phrases. Terms are usually nouns or adjective plus noun phrases. Prepositional phrases are acceptable if they are commonly phrased concepts, such as **prisoners of war**. Terms may be verbal nouns, such as **teaching**, but not verbs, such as **teach**. Adjectives alone, such as **educational**, are generally not used except in a faceted taxonomy in which a feature or characteristic is a facet, in which case the facet comprises a short list of adjectives, such as a list of colors. Adjectives can also serve as subdivisions in precoordinated indexing, discussed at the end of this chapter.

Common nouns or proper nouns. Common nouns and proper nouns (named entities or unique entities) may be kept separate in individual taxonomies or authority files, or they may be integrated so as to link proper nouns (narrower terms) to their corresponding common-noun terms, such as **Golden Gate Bridge** and **bridges**.

Countable nouns. Countable nouns used as terms are in the plural when possible in order to reflect the fact that there are multiple records indexed or multiple occurrences of the topic in the content. However, abstract concepts, substances, and collective nouns are not plural, and neither are body parts, according to the standards. For example, preferred formats are **hospitals, healthcare**, and **ear**. Be aware that countable and noncountable forms of some nouns have slightly different meanings, such as **finance** and **finances**. Both are correct forms, depending on the meaning required, and taxonomy management software should support this distinction.

Parenthetical qualifiers. There are different ways to handle multiple concepts in a taxonomy that have the same term name, also known as homographs. Usually parenthetical qualifiers are an option for disambiguation, although certain software systems may preclude this. An example is **French (language)** and **French** (**people**). It may not even be necessary to have parentheses in both of the terms. For example, you might have **walnut (wood)** and **walnuts**; **walnuts** in the plural is unambiguous and must mean the nuts, whereas **walnut** in the singular might be ambiguous. The form of the qualifier could be of the subject *domain*, as in **Saturn (astronomy)** and **Saturn (mythology)**, or of the term *category*, as in **Saturn (planet)** and **Saturn (god)**. Choose a single format, either domain or category, and stay consistent with it. Do not use parentheses to modify a term with an inverted qualifying adjective, though, such as **schools (elementary)**. Instead, **elementary schools** is the preferred format.

Acronyms, if well known. Use an acronym instead of a spelled out form if the acronym is better known. For example, **DNA** is preferred over **Deoxyribonucleic acid**. Be sure that the acronym is not ambiguous: If the scope of the taxonomy is broad, **CDs** could mean either compact discs or certificates of deposit, in which case you should use the full form as the preferred term.

No term inversions. Inverted terms with a noun followed by an adjective, such as **loans, commercial**, were common in controlled vocabularies in printed formats and in the older LCSH used in physical card catalogs because they aided the user when alphabetical browsing was the only option. Now that taxonomies exist in electronic formats and users can search them in addition to browsing them, these awkward inversions are no longer necessary. Thus, **commercial loans** would be the preferred term. If you know that there will also be a browse option for the taxonomy, then you may include inverted terms as nonpreferred terms, but avoid them as preferred terms in all cases.

Precoordinated Terms

When coming up with concepts, especially from analyzing content sources, it may be difficult to discern whether a complex idea should be expressed as a single concept or a combination of two or more concepts. Take, for example, the idea of foreign relations between the United States and Mexico. This could be a single term:

United States–Mexican relations

It could be two terms:

United States foreign relations AND **Mexico**

And it could also be three terms:

United States AND **Mexico** AND **International relations**

The terms shown in these examples are all combinations of two or more concepts and are called precoordinated terms. Precoordinated means that two or more concepts are put together (i.e., coordinated) prior (thus *pre-*) to indexing and searching. Other examples of precoordinated terms include the following:

> **Hispanic actors** instead of the separate concepts
> **Hispanics** and **actors**
> **software testing** instead of **software** and **product testing**
> **sales force training** instead of **sales force** and **employee training**
> **plastic motor vehicle parts** instead of **plastic parts** and **motor vehicles**

Sometimes precoordinated terms are very obvious, with the word *and* joining two concepts to create one term. This format appears in LCSH and other thesauri based on it, but the standards today discourage this practice. Examples are as follows:

> **business and politics**
> **computers and children**

Another kind of precoordination of terms involves a main heading term and a subdivision term that limits the scope of the main heading. In this case, the two terms remain distinct but are tied together and used in combination, both at the indexing stage and in retrieval. This is the format used in the LCSH and in other cataloging systems, and it is still commonly used in catalogs of library materials. An example is as follows:

Massachusetts—History

This type of structured indexing or second-level indexing is discussed further in Chapter 6.

Advantages of Precoordination

The justification for creating a precoordinated term is that if the scope of the content provides sufficient coverage of the combined concept and the audience is sufficiently interested in the concept, precoordination makes it easier for the users to find that specific information. Use of a precoordinated term retrieves content about the combined concept more reliably than merely combining the terms at the search stage, which is referred to as *postcoordination*. Postcoordination, even if done correctly, as in Boolean searching, may not always retrieve the desired results, as the following examples illustrate.

Precoordinated term: **Hispanic writers**
Postcoordinated alternative: **Hispanics** and **writers**
But this could also retrieve content about **writers who write about Hispanics.**

Precoordinated term: **Russian foreign policy**
Postcoordinated alternative: **Russia** and **foreign policy**
But this could also retrieve content about **foreign policy toward Russia.**

Precoordinated term: **software testing**
Postcoordinated alternative: **software** and **product testing**
But this could also retrieve content about **software used for testing various products.**

If the content being indexed is very limited and consistent in its type and focus, then such unpredictable results from Boolean-type searching are less likely, and postcoordination is fine. If, however, the content is varied, there is a greater chance of unreliable results with postcoordinated searching. Thus, a broad scope of content benefits from precoordination to avoid ambiguity. Precoordinated terms are also common, though, in specialized subject taxonomies, where there are a greater number of narrower, specific topics. Finally, precoordination is desirable when users are likely to employ a high level of phrase searching to target specific complex topics—in other words, subject expert users.

Considerations in Precoordination

Precoordinated terms do have their disadvantages, however. Using precoordinated terms requires a larger, more complex taxonomy, which then requires more time and effort—and consequently cost—to maintain. The user, whether a human indexer or end-user searcher, may not expect precoordinated terms and thus may overlook them or may use them inconsistently. Thus, it is more difficult to index content correctly with a larger, more complex taxonomy comprising precoordinated terms.

You are not as likely to create precoordinated terms for a taxonomy accessed through a faceted search/browse, as facets naturally enable postcoordination. This does not mean that a faceted taxonomy should never contain precoordinated terms. Rather, any precoordinated terms would likely be limited to certain subject areas. For example, if you have a *place* facet of geographical names, then you would probably not also include *place names* as a precoordinated term. Furthermore, a small, simple taxonomy, which faceted taxonomies usually are, is simply less likely to have precoordinated terms. A website navigation taxonomy can be an exception: although relatively small, it may be describing very specific and often precoordinated concepts, such as **meeting room reservations policy**.

In conclusion, you should consider creating precoordinated terms whenever

- postcoordination cannot reliably retrieve the desired content of a subject of relative importance

- the subject area is focused and thus deep, as in a relatively specialized controlled vocabulary

- there is a significant amount of anticipated content for the precoordinated concept

- the types of documents making up the content vary greatly, a factor that contributes to unreliable results with postcoordinated searching and

- you are creating a hierarchical navigation taxonomy

Notes and Attributes

As mentioned previously, a concept is more than just a term. It comprises a preferred term and its equivalent nonpreferred term(s) with a single definition and possibly additional information. Depending on how you manage the taxonomy, the concept's definition may be merely implied, or you may write it down and store it with the concept. Supplemental information pertaining to the concept, such as notes regarding its use, foreign language equivalent preferred terms (in a bilingual or multilingual taxonomy), and designated concept types or categories, is also sometimes stored with the concept and might also be searchable.

Scope Notes and Other Term Notes

Except in technical subjects, it is best to avoid dictionary-type definitions of concepts in taxonomies. Usually users of a taxonomy understand the meaning of its concepts, so including obvious definitions is a waste of everyone's time. Furthermore, copyright law prohibits you from copying a definition found in a published dictionary, so trying to think up original definitions for each concept would require additional effort.

What may be necessary, however, is a note of clarification as to the use of the concept, or more precisely its preferred term, within the context of the taxonomy. As this refers to the term's scope of usage, this note is commonly called a *scope note* (often abbreviated as SN). Scope notes serve any one of the following purposes:

1. To restrict or expand the application of a term

2. To distinguish between terms of overlapping meaning (the terms involved may have reciprocal notes)

3. To provide advice on term usage

The following two examples illustrate different ways in which a scope note can restrict the use of a term:

From the ProQuest Controlled Vocabulary:
inequality
SN: Socioeconomic disparity stemming from racial, cultural, or social bias

From the NASA Thesaurus:
analyzers
SN: Excludes devices for performing mathematical analysis

The following example from the NASA Thesaurus illustrates how a pair of reciprocal scope notes distinguishes between terms of overlapping meaning:

aramid fiber composites
SN: Aramid fiber utilization in composites. For properties of aramid fibers themselves use "aramid fibers."

aramid fibers
SN: Properties of aramid fibers themselves. For aramid fiber utilization in composites use "aramid fiber composites."

The following example, taken from the ERIC Thesaurus, illustrates advice on term usage:

school organization
SN: Do not confuse with "School District Reorganization."

A scope note ought to be viewable to all: the taxonomy editors, any human indexers, and the end users. Keep scope notes concise to facilitate quick reading by the user and to save space in the user interface display. Keep in mind that users may not have the patience to read the notes, however, or may not even know that scope notes exist, so do not use a scope note as the only means to disambiguate otherwise identical terms or homographs. Also, at some point in the future, the taxonomy could be implemented in a different user search interface or a third-party vendor's interface that does not support scope note display. For this reason, too, you cannot rely on scope notes to clarify ambiguity. What is more critical, though, is that human indexers have access to the scope notes for correct, consistent indexing.

Although scope notes will most likely be accessible to the users, you may also choose to create other kinds of term notes that are not necessary for the end user and will display only in the taxonomist and indexer interfaces. These would include notes pertaining to the history of a term, such as a change from a previous preferred term name, or the splitting or merging of concepts. It may also be desirable to include a field noting the source of the term. The source can be a reference to a periodical article, another thesaurus, or even web usage according to search engine (such as Google) results. A source note can refer to the concept and/or to the preferred term name.

Notes can be summarized as follows:

- If term notes are included, not all concepts need notes (except perhaps in a technical subject thesaurus).

- Notes should be concise.

- There may be multiple types of notes serving various purposes (scope, history, source, etc.).

- Notes may be intended for the end user, indexer, or other taxonomists. You can designate different levels of access for different note types.

Descriptive Attributes

If you are maintaining the taxonomy in a kind of database system and each concept is a database record, it is technically very simple to store various types of additional information for each concept or preferred term. Thus, the taxonomy not only serves to retrieve indexed files or documents but also organizes relatively static data for each concept. This structure makes most sense for named entity (proper noun) types of terms, such as people, companies, organizations, brand-name products, places, laws, and events. Examples of possible extended attributes for various kinds of concepts include the following:

- Named persons: birth date, occupation/title, affiliation, address

- Companies: industry code(s), headquarters location, ticker symbol

- Places: latitude and longitude

- Events: dates, location

The values for the extended attributes themselves should be restricted if possible. For example, you might have a controlled vocabulary of cities for company headquarters location and a standard format for entering dates and latitude/longitude. If the search interface supports it, end users can then limit searches according to the extended attributes, thus providing a more powerful means to execute and narrow a search. Most commercial thesaurus management software offers the ability to store some additional data with each concept, under various labels: attributes, additional data, term characteristics, term info, and so forth. In the user interface, the information may have various labels, depending on the term type.

Administrative Attributes

Finally, a concept or term can be assigned various administrative attributes, including identifier numbers, approval status, and creation/update of data. Supporting such data is a standard feature in commercial taxonomy/thesaurus management software. If your organization is developing software for taxonomy maintenance internally, you should ensure that it supports administrative attributes.

In some cases, assigning each concept a unique *identifier number* allows you to easily manage multiple taxonomies in which the same term name may occur more than once. It also provides an added measure of security when changing term names. Multidigit numeric identifiers may be assigned sequentially to denote the order in which the concepts or terms were added.

A *term approval status* attribute is an important feature. It allows the taxonomist to create a candidate term and then research it further for possible modification or even elimination before allowing it to go live. This feature is especially practical for a taxonomy that is in active use for indexing. Term approval may also be an issue if there are junior-level taxonomy editors whose additions of new terms need approval from a taxonomy manager.

Standard administrative statistics that any taxonomy management software ought to record include each term's creation date, date last modified, and the user ID/initials of the taxonomist who made the changes. It is often useful to be able to call up or determine how many terms you modified within the past week or month. For example, you may want to review a batch of work you did recently, such as offline batch spell checking, in cases where the thesaurus software lacks a spell-checker.

Considering the various notes and attributes that a taxonomy term may have, we see how taxonomy and metadata can come full circle. While a taxonomy or controlled vocabulary provides descriptive metadata for a file or document, a single term in the taxonomy can itself be described by a large amount of metadata.

Endnotes

1. Lynda Moulton, email to author, November 9, 2009.

2. Layne Foit, Taxonomy Community of Practice group post, "Subject: Content Inventory tools—Mac or PC," November 15, 2007, accessed December 20, 2015, https://groups.yahoo.com/neo/groups/TaxoCoP/conversations/topics/2341

3. National Institute of Standards Organization, *ANSI/NISO Z39.19-2005 (R2010) Guidelines for Construction, Format, and Management of Monolingual Controlled Vocabularies* (Bethesda, MD: NISO Press, 2010), accessed December 20, 2015, www.niso.org/apps/group_public/download.php/12591/z39-19-2005r2010.pdf

Chapter 4

Creating Relationships

A day without taxonomies is not found.
                                        —Jared Spool

What makes a taxonomy more useful than a mere term list or glossary is the presence of relationships between its terms. Relationships between pairs of terms are bidirectional (reciprocal). Broadly speaking there are three kinds of relationships:

1. Equivalence: between preferred and nonpreferred terms

2. Hierarchical: between broader and narrower terms

3. Associative: between related terms

The most basic controlled vocabularies and authority files have at least the equivalence relationship. Classification and categorization schemes, thesauri, and nearly all taxonomies have hierarchical relationships and usually (but not necessarily) associative relationships as well. Thesauri, ontologies, and semantic networks additionally have associative relationships. Thesauri have all three kinds, but ontologies may lack the equivalence relationship. In fact, the kinds of relationships in a given knowledge organization system are often the defining feature. (Decisions regarding which kinds of relationships to include and what kind of knowledge organization system to have are covered in Chapter 10.) Even if you have decided that your taxonomy will include all three kinds of relationships, it is not required that every single term have all three kinds. Each individual relationship should provide some value or purpose. Although hierarchical taxonomies have hierarchical relationships for all terms, a thesaurus might not. It is unusual, however, for a term in a taxonomy or thesaurus to have no relationships to other terms. Such a term is called an *orphan*. An individual taxonomy's policy may specify whether orphan terms are permitted.

Relationship types are often denoted by labels, with their corresponding abbreviations or codes, between pairs of terms or preceding the various related terms for a selected term. The following is a list of the most common such labels, although you may choose a different designation in each case:

- Equivalence: USE/UF (use/use[d] for)
- Hierarchical: BT/NT (broader term/narrower term)
- Associative: RT (related term)

All relationships are reciprocal, meaning that they function in both directions between a pair of terms. For example, *Term A* has a relationship with *Term B*, and *Term B* has a relationship with *Term A*. Depending on the relationship type, the relationships may or may not be identical in both directions. If the relationship is not identical in both directions, it is asymmetrical. The equivalence and hierarchical relationship types are asymmetrical. If the relationship is the same in both directions, it is symmetrical. The default associative relationship type is symmetrical.

Equivalence Relationships and Nonpreferred Terms

An important feature of controlled vocabularies, except for those that are small enough to browse through on a single page, is to have synonymous or equivalent nonpreferred terms pointing, as a kind of cross-reference relationship, to the desired preferred terms. These guide the searcher, either visibly or invisibly, to the preferred term that is linked to the content. The equivalent nonpreferred terms also support the indexing, whether manual or automatic.

As we have seen in the previous chapter, concepts and preferred terms may have various designations. Not surprisingly, the same is true of nonpreferred terms. You do not have to call them nonpreferred terms but can take your pick from the following list:

Aliases
Alternate labels
Alternate terms
Altlabels
Entry terms
Equivalent terms
Lead-in terms
Nondescriptors
Nonpostable terms
Nonpreferred terms
NPT
See references
Use for terms
Use references
Used for terms
Variant terms
Variants

Additionally, you might run across the following designations for nonpreferred terms, but you should avoid using them due to ambiguity:

- Synonyms. However, nonpreferred terms are not just synonyms.

- Keywords. However, a keyword can also mean a significant term used for indexing or searching that is not in the taxonomy.

- Cross-references. However, cross-references can mean either *See* references or *See also* references, the latter being an associative relationship rather than a nonpreferred term.

"Alternate label" is the designation used in the SKOS guidelines of the World Wide Web Consortium for vocabularies for the Semantic Web (explained in more detail in later chapters). As SKOS is becoming a more common model in newer taxonomy management systems, the designation alternate label is seen more.

When it comes to the style and format of nonpreferred terms, you have more freedom than when creating preferred terms. After all, there is no need to maintain consistency in style, as you are trying to anticipate all the possible formats of terms that users might possibly search for or enter.

The Equivalence Relationship

When compiling nonpreferred terms that refer to a preferred term, it may not seem as though you are creating a relationship, because a preferred term and a nonpreferred term do not have the same standing in the controlled vocabulary. In fact, it might have been perfectly logical to address nonpreferred terms in Chapter 3. However, thesaurus standards describe equivalence as a kind of relationship, thesaurus management software handles nonpreferred terms as relationship types, and thesauri usually display them as relationship types. Other vocabulary or ontology management software that is not specifically for thesauri, especially that which is SKOS based, would not treat equivalence as a relationship. Such software manages vocabulary as concepts rather than having a set of terms that can be either preferred or nonpreferred. It is important, though, to understand the thesaurus approach.

The notion of equivalence does not imply that the terms have to be equal or that they are synonyms. First, it is the concepts, not the terms themselves, that are equivalent. Second, the two terms merely need to be sufficiently similar with respect to the content being indexed that trying to maintain them as distinct terms would lead to too much redundancy, ambiguity, and confusion, and thus for the purpose of indexing the content, they should be treated as the same.

The equivalence relationship between a preferred term and a nonpreferred term is asymmetrical. Thus, a different label for the relationship is used depending on the direction. A nonpreferred term instructs the indexer or searcher to *use* a preferred term, whereas a preferred term is *used for* a nonpreferred term. The expression of the relationship is "nonpreferred term use preferred term," and the reciprocal is "preferred term use(d) for nonpreferred term." (There is no difference between *use for* and *used for*.) In standard thesaurus notation, the relationship is represented by USE/UF. For example, see the following:

> inundations   floods
>   USE **floods**   UF **inundations**

As the taxonomist, you may choose to use a different name for your equivalence relationship, such as *see* and *seen from*, if that makes more sense to your users.

Typically, multiple nonpreferred terms refer to a single preferred term. In other words, a preferred term may have multiple nonpreferred terms, as in the following example:

> **Oil and gas industry**
>   UF **Oil and gas industries**
>   UF **Oil companies**
>   UF **Oil industry**
>   UF **Oil producers**
>   UF **Petroleum companies**
>   UF **Petroleum industry**
>   UF **Petroleum sector**

In the other direction, each nonpreferred term typically refers to only a single preferred term; that is, there are no multiple *use* references. However, this is not always the case. Some thesauri permit a one-to-many *use* reference, whereby a nonpreferred term may refer to two (but no more) preferred terms under certain conditions. Typically in this situation, the nonpreferred term would be a precoordinated type of term, and the two preferred terms would be the constituent terms coming from breaking apart this precoordinated term. Both preferred terms must be used in combination, in both indexing and in searching, to achieve the desired results. In other words, there is an implied AND, not OR, combination of the two preferred terms. For example, see the following:

> folk drama
>> USE **drama** AND **folk culture**

To convey the concept of **folk drama**, the indexer must assign both the term **drama** and the term **folk culture** to the document, and to properly retrieve documents on folk drama, the searcher must enter both the terms **drama** and **folk culture**. This multiple *use* relationship is often known as *used for and* or *used for plus*. It appears only in more structured thesauri, not in simple taxonomies, and the nonpreferred terms must display to both the indexers and the end users. The multiple *use* relationship occurs in many traditional printed-only thesauri, but not all electronic/database-driven controlled vocabularies support this feature. You might choose to allow for multiple *use* relationships if you have decided to create a controlled vocabulary with few or no precoordinated terms, or if the content available on a particular precoordinated concept is rather minimal, yet research indicates that users want to search with the precoordinated term.

Types of Nonpreferred Terms

The most typical kind of nonpreferred terms are synonyms, but there are many other types as well. Table 4.1 lists the various kinds of nonpreferred terms and an example of each. (The actual choice of preferred term in most of these sample pairs is arbitrary.)

Near Synonyms

Near synonyms, also called quasi-synonyms, can be tricky, and your choice to use a given nonpreferred term will depend on the scope

Table 4.1 Types of nonpreferred terms

Type of Nonpreferred Term	Example
synonyms	**cars** USE **automobiles**
near-synonyms	**junior high schools** USE **middle schools**
variant spellings	**defence** USE **defense**
lexical variants	**hair loss** USE **baldness**
foreign language terms	**Luftwaffe** USE **German Air Force**
acronyms/spelled out forms	**UN** USE **United Nations**
scientific/technical names	**neoplasms** USE **cancer**
phrase variations	**buses, school** USE **school buses**
antonyms	**misbehavior** USE **behavior**
narrower terms	**hand drills** USE **hand tools**

of the content. In the example in the table, using **middle schools** for **junior high schools** (or vice versa) will be fine in most cases, but not for a thesaurus dedicated to the field of education, where the nuanced differences are important. In other cases, two terms may be synonymous only within a limited scope, and if that is the scope of the thesaurus, then there is no problem. The following example of nonpreferred terms may or may not be acceptable depending on the content:

> aviation
>> UF **flight**
>> UF **flying**

The terms **flight** and **flying** are acceptable as equivalent terms for **aviation** if the content or database is focused on careers, skills, industries, services, engineering, and so on, but they are not acceptable as nonpreferred terms in a broader, general-interest database that may contain information on birds. When trying to determine whether a term will work as a nonpreferred term, ask yourself this: Given the scope of the content covered, can the preferred term *always* be used to mean this nonpreferred term?

Variant Spellings

Spelling variations may include British/US spellings and acceptable variations that you would find in a dictionary. Avoid including incorrect spellings as nonpreferred terms unless they (1) are common, (2) unambiguously have the meaning of the preferred term, and (3) are not displayed to the end user so as not to be confusing. Incorrect spellings as nonpreferred terms are more common for proper nouns.

Foreign Language Terms

Foreign language terms are typically used for native-language names of organizational or corporate entities or for rare cases of foreign words that are sometimes used in English discourse (such as **sharia** USE **Islamic law**), if not chosen as the preferred term in the first place. Foreign organizational names are usually nonpreferred terms only in the case of Latin-script-based languages (French or German, for example, but not Russian, Arabic, or Chinese). Otherwise, transliterations would be necessary, and then even more variations would come into play. In a bilingual or multilingual taxonomy, the different language terms are *not* treated as nonpreferred terms but rather have a specially designated foreign language relationship. Each language's preferred term then has additional nonpreferred terms in its own respective language.

Acronyms

Acronyms, if used as nonpreferred terms, need to be unambiguous. Therefore, you need to take into consideration the scope of the taxonomy and content. For example, **CDs** can refer to either compact discs or certificates of deposit, so for a general news/information service, such an acronym should not be used as a nonpreferred term and without some kind of qualifier.

Phrase Inversions

Phrase inversions typically involve putting an adjective after a noun. Only add them if you expect them to display in a browsable alphabetical list to the user, either the end user or the indexer. Otherwise, there is no need for them. Browsable alphabetical (as opposed to hierarchical) displays are more common for indexers than for end users. It is rare for end-use displays to consist of alphabetical lists of terms that are not proper nouns, unless the thesaurus is published in print form.

If phrase inversions are used, they should begin with a word that is likely to be looked up for the concept. They may be an inversion of the preferred term or an inversion of nonpreferred term, such as **pants, dress** USE **trousers** (in addition to **dress pants** USE **trousers**). Avoid creating phrase inversions as nonpreferred terms for prominent preferred terms that have multiple narrower terms. For example, you should not create **industry, computer** USE **computer industry**, since **industry** is likely a term in the taxonomy with numerous narrower terms. If users choose to look up the word **industry** first, they will find specific industries listed as narrower terms, which is easier to browse than a list of inverted nonpreferred terms.

Antonyms

Antonyms generally work as nonpreferred terms for concepts that are limited to characteristics or attributes. Examples include the following pairs: **rigidity/flexibility**, **softness/hardness**, **obedience/disobedience**, and **literacy/illiteracy**.

Narrower Terms

Narrower or more specific terms (discussed in detail in the next section, Hierarchical Relationships) can be acceptable as nonpreferred terms for their corresponding broader preferred terms. The broader term can logically be used for the narrower concept that it includes. This is known as *upward posting* or *generic posting* and is done when there is too little content on the narrower subject to justify the term, but there is reason to believe that people will look it up. On the indexing side, if a document discusses a very specific topic for which there is no preferred term in the taxonomy, such as **tidal power energy**, then the corresponding broader term of **alternative energy** should be used to index it. On the user search side, narrower terms may be used as nonpreferred terms only if the relationship is displayed so that the user is made aware of the fact, as in **tidal power energy** USE **alternative energy**. Otherwise, if a search on **tidal power energy** retrieved documents on all forms of alternative energy, the majority of which were not about tidal power, the user would end up with many undesired results to sift through and would assume the search was not functioning properly. If the end-user interface does not support the display of nonpreferred terms pointing to preferred terms, it may be possible to designate the nonpreferred term for indexing use only and not for end-user application. Otherwise, you should generally avoid upward posting except in unique circumstances when documented search behavior seems to warrant it.

In any case, if you designate narrower terms as nonpreferred terms, do so with discretion. Often a narrower concept is narrower to more than one broader preferred term, which would result in an unintended *used for and* or *used for plus* relationship. Furthermore, many end-user search interfaces will offer the additional option to search by keyword (words or phrases *not* in the taxonomy, but rather in the titles or texts) anyway. If such keywords were nonpreferred terms to a broader preferred term, then instead of getting the desired results through a keyword search, the user would get a much larger set of results, including many undesired records that match the broader term. Finally, you will want to consider narrower concepts as candidates for preferred terms if sufficient usage over time warrants it. If, however, such narrower terms were labeled as nonpreferred terms, then their frequency in keyword searches may not (easily) be tracked, and it would not be clear whether there was sufficient usage to reclassify a given term as a preferred term.

How Many Nonpreferred Terms to Create

Since each preferred term can have multiple nonpreferred terms, you may wonder how many nonpreferred terms to create for each. Considerations include whether the nonpreferred terms will be used for indexing only or also for end-user retrieval, whether the indexing is by humans or automated, whether the end user can browse the taxonomy or has access to a search box, and whether and how a search system matches entered keywords to taxonomy terms.

Nonpreferred terms may be displayed to the user or may not actually be displayed but function in the background to match a user-entered term to the preferred term. The user can be either the indexer or the end-user/searcher. In a controlled vocabulary that is implemented online, it is common to have the nonpreferred terms visible to the indexer but not to the end user. If there is a desire to educate the user on what the preferred term is, however, then nonpreferred terms, along with their corresponding preferred terms, would be displayed. This is especially common in academic thesauri.

If the taxonomy is small and easily browsable within a single page or through pull-down/drop-down term lists, then nonpreferred terms may not be needed for the user search and may only be implemented on the indexing side (whether human or automated), if at all. This may be the case for term lists in the examples of the Shoebuy.com and the Microbial Life Education Resources sites mentioned in Chapter 1.

If users can input search strings into a search box (instead of or in addition to browsing the taxonomy), more nonpreferred terms are needed because the users cannot see the terms to choose from and must guess what the search terms should be. Keep in mind that whenever a search box exists alongside a browsable taxonomy, a significant number of end users will ignore the taxonomy display and simply use the search box.

Even if the taxonomy is displayed for browsing, the type of display may affect the need for certain nonpreferred terms. Taxonomies that are displayed for end-user browsing may be arranged hierarchically, alphabetically, or both, although alphabetical arrangement is less common. Typically, only the alphabetical arrangements of taxonomies can logically show nonpreferred terms interspersed among the preferred terms; it is simply not practical to intersperse nonpreferred terms within a hierarchical display. If a browsable alphabetical display is the only means of accessing the taxonomy, then you may omit nonpreferred terms that are very close alphabetically with their corresponding preferred terms. This is because the user would find the preferred term in that part of the alphabetical display anyway if searching for the same start of a nonpreferred variant. An example of alphabetically close nonpreferred terms is as follows:

> **ethnic groups**
>> UF **ethnic minorities**
>> UF **ethnicities**

In a taxonomy that is displayed alphabetically only, you would not need these two nonpreferred terms, **ethnic minorities** and **ethnicities**. If a search box were present, though, the additional nonpreferred terms would be quite useful.

How the search feature within the taxonomy functions is also an important factor in determining the need for types of nonpreferred terms. At the simplest level, taxonomy search can be a word or phrase search to match search strings exactly against taxonomy terms. If a search system was programmed to match user-entered keywords or phrases with taxonomy terms and then to present the user with multiple matching taxonomy terms from which to select, then these keywords or phrases may not be needed as nonpreferred terms. The keywords would need to be somewhat unique, however, to be effective in this way. For example, if the user entered **nonverbal learning**, the matched term **nonverbal learning disorder** would be retrieved, which was probably the desired result. However, if the user entered **United States**, not only would the preferred term **United States of America** be retrieved, but so would the names of dozens of US federal agencies and companies. In this case, finding the desired term within the list of retrieved terms would be time-consuming. It would be preferable simply to designate **United States** as a nonpreferred term for **United States of America**, to take precedence over any partial term phrase matching.

More sophisticated search within the taxonomy utilizes tables, rules, and algorithms so as to retrieve equivalent singular/plural variations, terms with multiple words in them in any order, and possibly grammatical stemming (such as –ing and –ed endings). This is sometimes referred to as "smart search." If smart search is available, then nonpreferred terms for such variations are not needed. For example, a smart search on the phrase "children's diseases" will retrieve the taxonomy terms of **Diseases in children** (a nonpreferred term for Pediatric diseases), so it is not necessary to add "children's diseases" as an additional nonpreferred term. If you have access to the search feature, it is a good idea to test a smart search of the potential nonpreferred term in the taxonomy if there is any question regarding the need to add it.

If indexing is being done automatically, a greater number of nonpreferred terms might be needed to facilitate automatic matching of appropriate words and phrases in the various texts, depending on the method of automatic indexing used. Chapter 7 covers automated indexing in detail.

Finally, the nature of the end users may affect the need for nonpreferred terms. A narrow, limited, and uniform group of users, such as members of a certain profession, is likely to look up concepts consistently and thus not need many nonpreferred terms. The general public, on the other hand, is very diverse in the ways they think of concepts, so numerous nonpreferred terms are needed in order to serve everyone.

In summary, a greater number of nonpreferred terms are needed in the following circumstances:

- Users can look up content via a search box.

- Taxonomy search is not "smart" and does not employ grammatical stemming.

- Automated indexing, which matches terms to words and phrases in text, is involved.

- The users are diverse.

Even for a relatively static taxonomy, the number of nonpreferred terms should be permitted to grow as needed. The taxonomist cannot be expected to fully anticipate all nonpreferred term needs from the beginning.

A final note of caution regarding nonpreferred terms: You should not rely on a dictionary-type thesaurus, such as *Roget's*, to suggest equivalent terms. Not only is it limited in that it contains only individual words, not phrases (and only a minority of the words are nouns), but because it serves a very different purpose. It provides all the *possible* equivalent words for a given entry term, and the appropriateness of any given equivalent would depend on the specific context. Nonpreferred terms, on the other hand, must be equivalent in *all* circumstances of usage for the preferred term. For example, in *Roget's Thesaurus*, a synonym for **performer** is **player**. However, players are not always performers, so in a taxonomy, **players** is not an acceptable nonpreferred term for **performers**.

Hierarchical Relationships

The presence of hierarchical relationships among terms is what makes a simple controlled vocabulary into what is best known as a

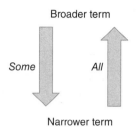

Figure 4.1 Hierarchical relationship characteristics

taxonomy. Hierarchical relationships indicate subordination among concepts. Subordinate concepts are members, parts, examples, or instances of a broader concept, class, or category. The presence of a hierarchy facilitates the navigation of the taxonomy and the location of a concept or clarifies the scope of a concept in relation to others.

The hierarchical relationship, like the equivalence relationship, is asymmetrical, or directional; that is, the relationship is not the same in each direction between a pair of terms. According to the standards for controlled vocabularies, a hierarchical relationship pair consists of a broader term and a narrower term. *All* members of a narrower term's category must be contained within the broader term, but a broader term is not limited to containing the members of a single narrower term. Thus, only *some* members of a broader term constitute the members of a given narrower term. The diagram in Figure 4.1 illustrates this directional relationship.

As the hierarchical relationship is asymmetrical, a different label for the relationship is used depending on the direction. A broader term refers to its narrower term with the label NT, and a narrower term refers to its broader term with the label BT. The expression of the relationships is "broader term NT narrower term" and "narrower term BT broader term." For example, with the terms **fruits** and **apples**, all apples are fruits but only some fruits are apples.

fruits	**apples**
NT **apples**	BT **fruits**

The all/some rule for creating hierarchical relationships ensures that a user navigating from a broader term down to a narrower term will find content that is indeed completely within, yet more specific than, the broader term. Similarly, if navigating from a narrower term up to a broader term, the user will find content that includes all of the narrower term and more. The following example of a hierarchical relationship is incorrect:

> **breakfast dishes**
>   NT **egg dishes**

Although egg dishes are most often for breakfast, they are not *always* for breakfast.

Adhering to the all/some rule also supports inclusive retrieval results of multiple narrower terms. A nested approach to retrieval allows a user to select a term that has narrower terms and retrieve not only content that was indexed with the selected term but also all content that was indexed with each of its narrower terms. This feature, sometimes called *recursive retrieval*, may or may not be desired in the search interface, and you, as the taxonomist, may not know whether the taxonomy will ever be used this way. However, if you build hierarchical relationships correctly following the all/some rule, then there is no problem if recursive retrieval is implemented. (Recursive retrieval is discussed in more detail in Chapters 8 and 9.)

The designations BT and NT are the most common for the hierarchical relationship, but as the taxonomist, you can choose to use other labels for your hierarchical relationships, such as *parent* and *child*, if that makes more sense to your users or system developers. In accordance with the family metaphor, terms that share the same broader term are then called *siblings*. A child/narrower term in a sense "inherits" the additional broader meaning of its parent/broader terms, and it also may "inherit" certain properties, such as types of descriptive attributes (explained in Chapter 3), category or facet designations (explained in Chapter 8), and administrative and editorial policies.

Types of Hierarchical Relationships

Although determining whether a given concept is subordinate to another is often intuitive, sometimes it is not. To ensure that you create a hierarchical relationship only when appropriate, it helps to understand the different types. According to thesaurus standards, there are three kinds of hierarchical relationships:

1. Generic–specific

2. Instance

3. Whole–part

Generic–specific refers to a category or class and its members or more specific types. You can think of it as expressed by the wording *is, a,* or *are* in the following construction: "narrower term is a (kind of) broader term," or "narrower terms are a (kind of) broader term." Examples are as follows:

computers NT **laptops**	Laptops are a kind of computer.
financial services NT **investment services**	Investment services are a kind of financial service.
engineers NT **software engineers**	Software engineers are a kind of engineer.

If it is desirable to distinguish between the different types of hierarchical relationships in a taxonomy, the standard notation used here is BTG/NTG, which stands for broader term (generic)/narrower term (generic). Here is an example:

libraries
    NTG **academic libraries**
	academic libraries
	    BTG **libraries**

Instance refers to a unique named entity, a proper noun, which has a narrower term relationship to the class to which it belongs. Instances include named individuals, companies or organizations, brand-name products, specific geographic places, published works, laws, and so on. This relationship is not much different from the generic–specific type and also fits the "is a" phrase construction of "narrower term is a (kind of) broader term" or, more specifically, "narrower term is a specific instance of broader term." Examples are as follows:

national parks NT **Grand Canyon**	Grand Canyon is a specific instance of national parks.
children's writers NT **Rowling, J.K.**	J. K. Rowling is a specific instance of children's writers.
holidays NT **Thanksgiving**	Thanksgiving is a specific instance of holidays.

If you are distinguishing between the different types of hierarchical relationships, the standard notation used here is BTI/NTI, which stands for broader term (instance)/narrower term (instance). Here is an example:

automobiles NTI **Toyota Corolla**	**Toyota Corolla** BTI **automobiles**

In some organizational systems, however, named entities are kept in separate taxonomies or facets, in which case the *instance* hierarchical relationship cannot be created, as relationships between separate taxonomies may not be supported.

A *whole–part* relationship refers to something that is not more specific but rather is a part of a whole, where the part is the narrower term and the whole is the broader term. You can test the relationship by constructing a phrase with *is within* or *is a constituent part of:* "narrower term is within (the) broader term," or "narrower term is a constituent part of (the) broader term." The whole–part type of hierarchical relationship is much less common than the generic–specific type, as it occurs only within systems (including anatomical), organizations, geographic places, or disciplines/fields of study. Other kinds of whole–part relations, such as "nonpermanent placement in" (e.g., **automobiles** and **garages**) or "manufactured things" (e.g., **automobiles** and **automotive parts**), should be treated as associative and *not* hierarchical. Examples of whole–part hierarchical relationships are as follows:

US Congress NT **US Senate**	The US Senate is a part of the U.S. Congress.
Colorado NT **Denver**	Denver is within Colorado.
biology NT **marine biology**	Marine biology is a part of biology.

If you are distinguishing between the different types of hierarchical relationships, the standard notation used here is BTP/NTP, which stands for broader term (partitive)/narrower term (partitive). Here is an example:

digestive system
   NTP **stomach**
	stomach
	   BTP **digestive system**

In summary, to decide whether the relationship between a pair of terms is indeed hierarchical and not merely associative, remember to think of the concepts behind the terms, and then try formulating a sentence according to one of the following models:

- Narrower terms are a (kind of) broader term.

- Narrower term is a specific instance of broader terms.

- Narrower terms are a constituent part of (the) broader term.

- Narrower term is within (the) broader term.

If any one of these sentences holds true for a term pair in *all* cases, not merely sometimes or often, then the hierarchical relationship is valid.

Polyhierarchies

Sometimes a term may have more than one broader term. This is called a *polyhierarchy*, or multiple broader terms (MBT). Polyhierarchies may occur within each type of hierarchical relationship—generic–specific, instance, or whole–part—or may even be a combination of types. An example of a generic–specific polyhierarchy is as follows:

> **school librarians**
> BT **educators**
> BT **librarians**

An example of a whole–part polyhierarchy is as follows:

> **Egypt**
> BT **Africa**
> BT **Middle East**

Polyhierarchies can involve terms that are in the same larger hierarchical structure and share the same ultimate parent, as in the case of **light trucks** in Figure 4.2.

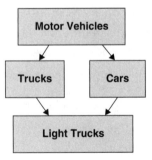

Figure 4.2 Polyhierarchy for the term *light trucks*

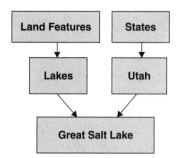

Figure 4.3 Polyhierarchy for the term *Great Salt Lake*

Polyhierarchies can also be based on two different methods of categorization, or in other words, two different hierarchical types. For example, **Great Salt Lake** is narrower to **lakes** as an instance and also narrower to **Utah** in a whole–part hierarchy, as illustrated in Figure 4.3.

When creating a polyhierarchy with two (or more) broader terms, make sure that none of these terms has a direct hierarchical relationship with the other, in which one is the broader term of the other. To use the parent–child metaphor, a term cannot be designated as a narrower term to both a parent term and a grandparent term. For example, the following pair of broader terms would be incorrect:

> **genetic engineering**
> > BT **biotechnology**
> > BT **technology**

Technology is already the broader term of **biotechnology**, so it should not also be an immediate broader term of **genetic engineering**.

Finally, remember that the all/some rule for hierarchical relationships applies to polyhierarchies. All members of a narrower term must belong within/be a part of each of its broader terms in a polyhierarchy, just as in a simple hierarchy.

Although the published thesaurus standards provide specific guidelines on when to create polyhierarchies, the ultimate determining factors for whether you create polyhierarchies are the user interface design and the technical capabilities of the search/browse software.

Associative Relationships

Associative relationships, also known as related term relationships, are created between terms in a taxonomy to provide the indexer or searcher with useful information. Often a related term associated with the original search term is in fact a better match to the concept that the user was trying to locate. In addition, a list of related terms can be useful information in itself because it outlines the subject area of a concept. Finally, related terms allow a searcher who is merely browsing a subject area to branch out and discover related topics of interest. The associative relationship functions in a similar manner to *See also* cross-references in a book-style index. Associative relationships are generally not used in simple hierarchical taxonomies, but they are a required feature of standard thesauri. Unlike hierarchical relationships, simple associative relations are symmetrically bidirectional by default. The standard designation of RT (related term) applies in either direction. For example, see the following:

Cameras	Photography
RT **Photography**	RT **Cameras**

Creating associative relationships is generally more subjective than creating hierarchical relationships. Not everyone shares the same belief as to what constitutes "related," although differences of opinion usually depend on context. The taxonomist's task is to determine whether the terms are conceptually related, regardless of the circumstances. Furthermore, rules for creating associative relationships are not as strict as for hierarchical relationships.

Associative relationships may exist between terms within the same hierarchy or between terms of different hierarchies.

Associative Relationships across Different Hierarchies

It is more common to create associative term relationships between terms belonging to different hierarchies than between sibling terms. This is because the sibling terms already have an implied similarity relationship by being siblings under the same broader term, and this relationship is usually clear in the display of the hierarchy. Since the purpose of the associative relationship is to inform the indexer/searcher that other terms exist, it is the associative relationship indicating related terms in *other* hierarchies that is most helpful. A different hierarchy in this case means that the terms do not share a broader (parent) term or a broader term of a broader term (grandparent). Whether they have a shared ultimate top term depends on the structure of the taxonomy. In the example in Figure 4.4, the two terms **engineering** and **engineers** are located in different hierarchies but are clearly related.

There are many circumstances when establishing an associative relationship between terms of different hierarchies is desirable. Table 4.2 lists various possibilities. This list is not exhaustive, and taxonomists are free to add other related term types.

An index or a thesaurus that is displayed only in an alphabetical browse, such as in print only, would not designate related terms (or *See also* cross-references) between terms that lie next to or very near each other in the alphabetical list, such as **physics** and **physicists**. However, if the users access the taxonomy via a search box, they

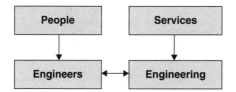

Figure 4.4 Associative relationship between terms in different hierarchies

Table 4.2 Types of associative relationships

Process and agent	**Research** RT **Researchers** **Researchers** RT **Research**
Process and counter-agent	**Infections** RT **Antibiotics** **Antibiotics** RT **Infections**
Action and property	**Environmental cleanup** RT **Pollution** **Pollution** RT **Environmental cleanup**
Action and product	**Programming** RT **Software** **Software** RT **Programming**
Action and target/patient	**Auto repair** RT **Automobiles** **Automobiles** RT **Auto repair**
Cause and effect	**Hurricanes** RT **Coastal flooding** **Coastal flooding** RT **Hurricanes**
Object and property	**Plastics** RT **Elasticity** **Elasticity** RT **Plastics**
Object and origins	**Petroleum** RT **Oil wells** **Oil wells** RT **Petroleum**
Raw material and product	**Timber** RT **Wood products** **Wood products** RT **Timber**
Discipline and practitioner	**Physics** RT **Physicists** **Physicists** RT **Physics**
Discipline and object/phenomenon	**Meteorology** RT **Weather** **Weather** RT **Meteorology**
Part and whole (which are not systems, geographic places, etc.)	**Office furniture** RT **Offices** **Offices** RT **Office furniture**

would not see such neighboring terms that are obviously related alphabetically. Therefore, in a searchable taxonomy, it is important to create the associative relationship consistently regardless of whether the terms begin with the same letters or words. Even if a browsable display version of the taxonomy exists, whenever a search box is also present, a significant percentage of users will choose to access the taxonomy via the search box rather than take advantage of the alphabetical browse.

Associative Relationships Within the Same Hierarchy

The associative relationship can be created between two terms that share the same broader term (known as siblings) and also have overlapping meaning or usage. In fact, according to thesaurus standards, the associative link is required under these circumstances. In the example in Figure 4.5, the two terms **local taxes** and **property taxes** both share the same broader term, **taxes**, so they are considered sibling terms to each other. They also both have overlapping meaning (inasmuch as local taxes are largely property taxes, and most property taxes are local).

Other examples of sibling terms with overlapping meaning that should have the associative relationship between them are as follows:

> **children's books** RT **picture books**
> **Middle East** RT **North Africa**
> **communications industry** RT **media industry**

For simplification and to avoid ambiguity, remember that in controlled vocabularies it might be preferable to combine concepts with overlapping meanings to create a single term. You may even have the word *and* within the term, such as **communications and media industry**. In general, it is better to avoid having pairs of terms for concepts if their meaning overlaps too greatly.

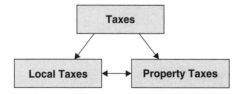

Figure 4.5 Associative relationship between sibling terms with overlapping meaning

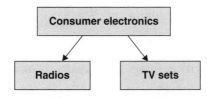

Figure 4.6 No associative relationship between sibling terms
with no overlapping meaning

If sibling terms do *not* have overlapping meaning (i.e., they are mutually exclusive), then the associative relationship is not required nor expected. It is not incorrect, according to standards, to have all sibling terms related, but since it is not necessary, in this case you should avoid creating such a relationship. Besides being a waste of the taxonomist's time, it creates needless information, which gets in the way of efficient thesaurus browsing. In the example in Figure 4.6, the two sibling terms **radios** and **TV sets** need not have an associated relationship created between them.

How Many Associative Relationships to Create

The extent to which you create associative relationships is, to a certain degree, a judgment call. It requires a keen sense of what would aid the user. Ask yourself if the searcher (or indexer) would get helpful information from a reminder that a particular term has a link to another term in the same general concept area. Keep in mind that the relationship needs to be close to being useful.

As with hierarchical relationships, you should create associative relationships between a term and its nearest relationships but not also to broader terms or narrower terms of those related terms. For example, suppose you have in a thesaurus the following two sets of terms and relationships:

computers
RT **computer peripherals**

computer peripherals
NT **keyboards**

NT **monitors**
NT **printers**

You should then *not* also have the following:

computers RT **keyboards**
computers RT **monitors**
computers RT **printers**

Similarly, you should not create associative relationships between all the related terms of a related term. For example, you may have **engineers** RT **engineering** and **engineering** RT **CAE software**, but you should *not* also have **engineers** RT **CAE software**. Of course, selected related terms of related terms may be related to each other, if appropriate. Unlike hierarchical relationships, a close circle or web of related terms *is* acceptable, as in the following example:

Germany
　RT **Germans**
　RT **German language**

Germans
　RT **German language**
　RT **Germany**

German language
　RT **Germans**
　RT **Germany**

If you are unsure whether two terms are closely enough related to have an RT relationship, ask yourself, "Would *most* of the people looking up the first term also be interested in information on the second term *most* of the time?" The answer should not be "only some people some of the time." For example, **Germany** RT **World War II** is *not* appropriate, despite an obviously close tie. Most people looking up Germany would be interested in issues other than World War II. The decision may depend on the scope of the content covered by the taxonomy, however. It might be acceptable to have an associative relationship between Germany and World War II in a specialized history resource.

Simple hierarchical taxonomies, especially those that are relatively small, may not have any associative relationships at all. However, creating just a few associative relationships is never a good compromise. A taxonomy should have either fully developed associative relationships or none at all—it should not go partway. It would be confusing or misleading to the user to find related terms only sporadically. The application of associative relationships should be logical and consistent for all types of terms.

Hierarchical/Associative Ambiguities

Despite the detailed nature of the taxonomy standards in distinguishing between hierarchical and associative relationships, there are still some gray areas, which various taxonomies may handle differently.

One area of ambiguity is the relationship between companies and their industries. While the generic–specific hierarchy is clear within industry groupings, opinions differ over whether to treat companies as instances of an industry. If you use the "is a" wording test, then a company is not an industry. For example, it is not correct to say, "Ford is an automobile industry." However, if the industry were named differently, then companies could be instances. For example, if the **automobile industry** were called **automobile companies** or **automobile manufacturers**, then the companies would be valid instances of such broader terms. Thus, if you want to display companies as instances of industries in your taxonomy, it would be better to name your industries with words ending in *companies, manufacturers, producers, providers,* or the like so that the relationships appear logical to the users. Otherwise, the relationship is associative.

A similar questionable area is whether members constitute narrower terms of the organization to which they are affiliated, as a whole–part relationship, since one can argue that the members are part of an organization. However, according to the ANSI/NISO Z39.19 guidelines, a whole–part hierarchical relationship exists when "one concept is inherently included in another, regardless of the context."[1] Applying this standard, it is clear that such a relationship is not hierarchical but rather associative, because membership status can change. If it is important to your taxonomy display to designate members as narrower terms to an organizational affiliation, you could do this through the instance rather than the whole–part relationship, provided that you use appropriate wording for the broader term organization. For example, instead of the organization **OPEC** having a narrower term relationship with its country members, which would be incorrect, you could use **OPEC countries** or **OPEC members** as the broader term, and then its member countries would be correctly linked as narrower terms. Needless to say, you probably do not want both terms—**OPEC** and **OPEC countries**—in your taxonomy, and maintaining both could be complex and confusing. So in most cases, the associative relationship is preferable for member–organization relationships.

Ambiguity can also occur when it is not clear whether terms of an apparently whole–part relationship are indeed within a "system." To qualify as a whole–part hierarchical relationship, the narrower term must be a constituent part of a broader term that comprises a *system*, which can be anatomical, administrative, political, or corporate. Whole–part constructions that are put together and can be taken apart again, such as **office furniture** and **offices** or **soccer goals** and **soccer fields**, are not hierarchical but associative. Since one may remove furniture from an office or soccer goals from a field, the inclusion is not inherent regardless of the context. Manufactured systems, however, can be more difficult to discern. A good example would be **automobile engines** and **automobiles**.

Some taxonomists will consider such a relationship to be hierarchical while others will consider it associative. In fact, the relationship depends on the context. If your content is an automobile user's manual, then the whole–part hierarchical relationship might be acceptable because the user of an automobile considers its parts to be a system. If, on the other hand, your content covers the automobile manufacturing industry, in which different automotive components are manufactured by different companies in different facilities and locations, then the relationship between **automobiles** and any automotive parts, including **automobile engines**, should be associative.

In all these ambiguous cases, the existence of more specific, semantic relationships would eliminate the ambiguity.

Semantic Variations for Relationships

You might wish to customize the relationships between certain terms by including more meaning than simply related or broader/narrower. *Semantic* refers to meaning, so more complex, customized relationships that have added meaning are often called semantic relationships. Commercial taxonomy/thesaurus software provides the ability to designate your own customized relationships to varying degrees. Although semantic relationships alone do not make an ontology, they are one of the key features that distinguish ontologies from other taxonomies.

Creating customized relationships in a taxonomy can result in an enhanced user experience. Semantic relationships between terms allow the user to access content in more ways, rather than just drilling down through a hierarchical tree or jumping across to related terms. If semantic relationships are implemented in a relational database, users can explore how different categories relate to each other and then access the desired content. For example, a movie database with semantic relationships among various types of terms (genres, themes, actors, producers, production companies, directors, countries, years, etc.) allows the user to obtain more customized retrieval results. These may include lists of actors who performed in certain genres in given years and countries, countries where certain subjects were the theme of movies in certain years, or production companies for which a given actor worked.

Even when you designate your own relationships, you should still base each one on a standard type: equivalent, hierarchical, or associative. Doing this will ensure that the relationships comply with standards and thus are logical. Additionally, most taxonomy software systems distinguish among the three different relationship types in their display, regardless of how you might customize the relationship names. Thus, for example, when generating a hierarchical display, the software knows to include relationships that are fundamentally hierarchical. Terms in a hierarchical relationship may branch out in a tree display. Therefore, most thesaurus software that supports semantic relationships requires that you choose a basic relationship type (equivalent, hierarchical, or associative) for any custom relationship.

When you define your own relationship types, they will still be reciprocal between the members of a pair of terms, that is, they will function in both directions. Users may approach the relationship from either term in a pair, and they need to link from one term to the other. Any customized semantic relationship is not, however, symmetrical. The only symmetrical relationship that exists is the generic associative type: the related term (RT). Customized relationships are inherently asymmetrical, or directional, as a consequence of the richer meaning they contain. You can compare this with relationships between people. For example, a generic associative relationship that is symmetrical is as follows: "Tom is related to David," and "David is related to Tom." A semantic version of this relationship might be as follows: "Tom is the uncle of David," and "David is the nephew of Tom." This relationship designation is not identical in both directions. Thus, when you create a new kind of semantic relationship, you need to give distinct names and abbreviation codes to the relationship in both directions.

When designating your own relationships, they need to be specific enough to convey the desired meaning but not so specific as to be restrictive. Remember, the relationship needs to apply to multiple term pairings, not just a single pair. You also want to limit the set of relationships so that you or other people editing the controlled vocabulary can easily keep track of what the relationship choices are and not overlook any when creating relationships between terms. Two or three kinds of relationships based on each of the RT and BT/NT types, for a total of four to six, are often sufficient, although complex databases use more.

Hierarchical Semantic Relationships

The following are sample variations based on the hierarchical (BT/NT) relationship. There is nothing standard about them; the all-caps codes are merely examples of relationship labels that have been created by taxonomists. Some are more general (closely following the standard variations of hierarchical types of relationships), and some are more specific.

Based on whole–part geographic:
Located in (LOC)/Contains Location (CONT)
> **Empire State Building** LOC **New York, NY**
> **New York, NY** CONT **Empire State Building**

Based on whole–part organizational:
Has parent organization (PAR)/Has suborganization (SUB)
> **Internal Revenue Service** PAR **Dept. of the Treasury**
> **Dept. of the Treasury** SUB **Internal Revenue Service**

Based on instance:
Is of the profession (PROF)/Has individuals (IND)
> **Smith, Joe** PROF **biomedical engineers**
> **biomedical engineers** IND **Smith, Joe**

Associative Semantic Relationships

Given the opportunity to customize relationships, you are more likely to customize associative relationships than hierarchical relationships. This is because there are so many kinds of associative relationships, such as those illustrated in Table 4.2. The following are sample variations based on the associative (RT) relationship. Again, there is nothing standard about them. The type and specificity of the relationship depend on the scope of the content indexed or tagged with the controlled vocabulary.

Produces the product (PRD)/Is manufactured by the company (COM)
Apple Inc. PRD **iPod**
iPod COM **Apple Inc.**

Has member affiliation with (AFF)/Has members (MEM)
Saudi Arabia AFF OPEC
OPEC MEM Saudi Arabia

For treating (TRE)/Can be treated with the drug (DRUG)
ACE inhibitors TRE hypertension
hypertension DRUG ACE inhibitors

Has patent (PAT)/Invented by (INV)
Smith, Joe PAT Patent #7,501,419
Patent #7,501,419 INV Smith, Joe

You may designate any code abbreviation you wish, as long as it is unique to the taxonomy. When creating the relationship names and their abbreviation codes, you should make them logical with respect to the type of term that follows the code in the expression, that is, the direction of the relationship "from–to."

The relationship names and codes will be visible to the taxonomists, indexers, and systems administrators but not necessarily to the end users. Semantic relationships can link various types of data in ways that are not obvious to the end user, functioning "under the hood." If the semantic relationships do in fact display to the end user, they should be designated by their full relationship names and not just the codes. Relationship names that will be displayed to the end users should be carefully chosen to be simple yet unambiguous, to make navigating the taxonomy as easy and user friendly as possible.

Semantic Equivalence Relationships

There are various situations in which you may want to distinguish between different kinds of nonpreferred terms. For example, you may want certain nonpreferred terms to display to the user and other nonpreferred terms (such as incorrect or misspelled terms) not to display. Thus, in addition to USE and UF, you might have something such as COR (Correct term) and CORF (Correct for), as in the following example.

Millenium COR **Millennium**
Millennium CORF **Millenium**

All the various equivalence relationships function as nonpreferred terms, but only those you designate with the standard USE will display, and those with COR will not display.

In these cases, a different relationship name allows you to manage the nonpreferred terms so that they are implemented only where and when appropriate. You might designate common abbreviations or acronyms this way, especially if the user can also search specifically by abbreviation or acronym. This can reduce ambiguity, especially for two-letter abbreviations, such as for states. Such standardized variants are also common in scientific fields. You might also use semantic equivalence relationships to give slang or jargon terms a designated status because this kind of nonpreferred term might be used only for certain audiences or in certain geographic regions or may change over time.

Sometimes specific kinds of nonpreferred terms are maintained for administrative purposes. Examples include a former or obsolete name for a term or the term name used by a third-party vendor or content provider's taxonomy. You might also want to have a nonpreferred term function on the indexing side but not on the end-user search side. As explained previously, a narrow concept can always be used as a nonpreferred term for its corresponding broader concept from the point of view of indexing, for it is logical to retrieve a document on a specific topic under the term for a slightly broader concept. However, it can be problematic on the search side to have a narrow concept function as a nonpreferred term, because a user who searches for a specific topic using the nonpreferred term would not be pleased to retrieve documents on other topics that merely share the same broader concept. You can solve this problem by designating a specific type of equivalence relationship that only operates on the indexing side. You could call it *USE-I* and *UF-I*, where *I* stands for indexing, and instruct the programmers to implement it only on the indexing side.

The SKOS framework for vocabularies for the semantic web specifies two kinds of nonpreferred terms by default: alternative labels and hidden labels. So if you use SKOS-based thesaurus management software and you need no more than two different types of nonpreferred terms, then the default will suffice, and there is no need to create additional semantic equivalence relationships. Furthermore, the SKOS framework does not manage nonpreferred terms as relationships,[2] so SKOS-based software may not even permit the creation of additional semantic equivalence relationships, rather only semantic hierarchical and associative relationships.

Endnotes

1. National Institute of Standards Organization, ANSI/NISO Z39.19-2005 (R2010) *Guidelines for Construction, Format, and Management of Monolingual Controlled Vocabularies* (Bethesda, MD: NISO Press, 2010), Section 8.3.3, page 49, accessed December 20, 2015, www.niso .org/apps/group_public/download.php/12591/z39-19-2005r2010.pdf

2. "Correspondence between ISO 25964 and SKOS/SKOS-XL Models," ISO TC46/SC9/WG8 working group for the ISO 25964 standard about Thesauri, December 11, 2013, accessed October 25, 2015, www.niso .org/schemas/iso25964/correspondencesSKOS

Chapter 5

Software for Taxonomy Creation and Management

Taxonomy, thesauri, ontology, oh my!
—Julie Martin

A simple controlled vocabulary, such as a synonym ring, or a small, unified hierarchical taxonomy that lacks nonpreferred terms, could be created on paper (or in Word or Excel). Creating and maintaining a more typical larger taxonomy or a more complex thesaurus, however, with equivalence, hierarchical, and associative relationships, and perhaps also scope notes and term attributes, requires a specialized kind of database software. In fact, the indexing thesaurus as we know it did not exist prior to the computer age of the late 1950s. Database software designed specifically for the creation and maintenance of thesauri originally existed primarily in the form of in-house custom-developed software used on mainframe or minicomputers. Commercial thesaurus development software for mainframes and minicomputers first appeared in the early 1980s, embedded in such products as BiblioTech (VAX/VMS), TechLib (IBM and VAX/VMS), and Cuadra STAR (AlphaMicro), which were the forerunners of current content management systems. These modules also provided early navigation frameworks for browsing content by exposing the thesaurus to users.[1] Later in the 1980s, a few single-user desktop thesaurus software packages were introduced. These were followed in the 1990s by client–server-based distributed thesaurus software systems and then web-based systems. Most recently, taxonomy management components have been incorporated into some content management and enterprise search software. Today all of the following software options exist:

1. "Homegrown" programs developed in-house, especially within large organizations

2. Software not designed for creating taxonomies

3. Single-user desktop thesaurus software

4. Larger-scale, multiuser client–server- or web-based thesaurus systems

5. Taxonomy creation and editing components of larger systems that focus on capabilities for searching, indexing, content management, or document management

6. Industry-specific (vertical market) software for creating classification structures

Our survey of taxonomists conducted in May 2015 asked broadly what kind of software they used for taxonomy work: "What software do you primarily use to work on taxonomies or other controlled vocabularies?" The largest number, although less than half, used commercial software that is not intended for taxonomy creation, such as generic database or spreadsheet software. About a quarter of those responding used internally developed software, and just under a quarter used commercial dedicated thesaurus/taxonomy/ontology management software. This is somewhat surprising, because in a similar survey in late 2008, users of commercial dedicated thesaurus/taxonomy/ontology management software were the largest group (37.5 percent), and use of other commercial software that is not intended for taxonomy creation came in third (18.8 percent), after use of internally developed thesaurus/taxonomy management systems (23.4 percent). A lesser but significant number of respondents used software in which taxonomy management is a component or module. The detailed breakdown from 141 respondents appears in Table 5.1.

Table 5.1 Survey responses for types of software used for working on taxonomies or other controlled vocabularies

Type of Software Used	Number	Percent
Commercial software that is not intended for taxonomy creation (such as a word processor, spreadsheet, or database management software)	43	30.5%
An internally developed thesaurus/taxonomy management system	36	25.5%
Commercial dedicated thesaurus/taxonomy/ ontology management software	32	22.7%
Commercial software, of which taxonomy management is a feature, module, or component	17	12.1%
Open-source dedicated thesaurus/taxonomy/ ontology management software	13	9.2%

Software Not Designed for Creating Taxonomies

The fact that the highest response category of surveyed taxonomists used software not designed to create taxonomies is significant, especially since the survey allowed for only a single answer. We might assume that software not intended for taxonomies is the primary software used by taxonomists working on small taxonomies. This is not necessarily the case, however, since in another survey question on taxonomy size, a majority of respondents indicated that they typically work on taxonomies of over 1,500 terms. Additionally, there are many taxonomists who create the first steps of a taxonomy in software not designed for a taxonomy and then expand and manage the taxonomy further in dedicated taxonomy management software.

Two types of software commonly used by taxonomists in the early stages of taxonomy development are (1) spreadsheet software, to record lists of terms within categories or facets, and (2) mind mapping, concept modeling, or ontology software, to develop a structure for a taxonomy. You may use one or both of these tools, depending on the nature of the taxonomy and the way you approach the project. Some people also use ontology software for designing taxonomies.

Spreadsheet Software

Although the assertion by one writer on taxonomies that "the vast majority of taxonomies are still created and maintained in Microsoft Excel"[2] is most likely an exaggeration (especially with respect to the *maintenance* of the taxonomies), the prevalence of this tool in taxonomy creation should not be underestimated. The accidental taxonomist is especially likely to use Excel, due to lack of experience with taxonomy software or perhaps due to lack of time, skills, or budget to evaluate different software alternatives. Even organizations intending to purchase taxonomy software or already owning such software often start building their taxonomies in Excel because it provides an easy way for various contributors, both in-house and external, including subject matter experts who might not be taxonomists, to quickly build up lists of terms and perhaps some simple hierarchy. When the taxonomy gets too complex or too big, such as when it contains several hundred terms, it is time to move it into taxonomy software.

If you are creating a small taxonomy, such as facets for browsing, or merely the start of what will eventually become a larger taxonomy, it is possible to represent each of various hierarchical levels or facets of the taxonomy through individual columns on a spreadsheet worksheet. The first column contains terms at the top level, the second column contains terms at the second level, and so on. For each term, its broader term (if any) is in the column to its left, and its narrower terms are in the column to its right. Each row is unique by its narrowest term (column filled in to the right). You may use a column to the far right for nonpreferred terms. Multiple nonpreferred terms should be kept in the same column and cell

	A	B	C	D	E	F
1	Level 1	Level 2	Level 3	Level 4	Level 5	Equivalent terms
2	Data center types					
3		Data center classes				
4			Single tenant enterprise data centers			Corporate data centers
5			Multi-tenant data centers			Mixed tenant data centers
6				Multi-tenant data center services		
7					Build to suit multi-tenant data centers	Powered shell data centers
8					Colocation centers	coloc;Hotels;Carrier hotels
9				Multi-tenant network connectivity		
10					Carrier-neutral data centers	Network-neutral data centers;Cloud neutral data centers
11					Non-neutral data centers	
12			Modular data centers			
13		Data center applications				
14			Systems of record data centers			
15			Monolithic data centers			
16			Cloud data centers			
17			Engineering data centers			
18			Small and medium business data centers			SMB data centers
19	Data cer	Data center applications				
20		Data center servers				
21			Data center server classes			
22				High-end servers		
23				Midrange servers		
24				Volume servers		
25			Data center server form factors			
26				Standalone servers		
27					Tower servers	Pedestal servers
28					Mid-tower servers	Mini-tower servers

taxonomy   Data Center resources   ⊕

Figure 5.1 Using Excel to create a five-level taxonomy

and may be separated by a delimiter, such as a semicolon. Another column can be used for notes.

Figure 5.1 illustrates how you might use Excel to indicate three levels of a taxonomy with columns compacted so that terms overlap, and narrower terms appear indented under their broader terms. This visual format is often desirable for sharing the draft taxonomy with stakeholders or subject matter experts for their review and input.

If there are multiple categories, hierarchies, or facets, you could create a separate Excel worksheet for each hierarchy or facet. Each worksheet can be saved as a CSV (comma-separated values) file, a format that can easily be imported into another system with relationships across rows preserved. As an import file, however, you might have to follow certain column-naming conventions, and typically all broader terms must be repeatedly filled in. There can be no blank cells to the left of a filled-in cell. Figure 5.2 illustrates the same taxonomy excerpt as in Figure 5.1 but with the broader terms

	A	B	C	D	E
1	Level 1	Level 2	Level 3	Level 4	Level 5
2	Data center types				
3	Data center types	Data center classes			
4	Data center types	Data center classes	Single tenant enterprise data centers		
5	Data center types	Data center classes	Multi-tenant data centers		
6	Data center types	Data center classes	Multi-tenant data centers	Multi-tenant data center services	
7	Data center types	Data center classes	Multi-tenant data centers	Multi-tenant data center services	Build to suit multi-tenant data centers
8	Data center types	Data center classes	Multi-tenant data centers	Multi-tenant data center services	Colocation centers
9	Data center types	Data center classes	Multi-tenant data centers	Multi-tenant network connectivity	
10	Data center types	Data center classes	Multi-tenant data centers	Multi-tenant network connectivity	Carrier-neutral data centers
11	Data center types	Data center classes	Multi-tenant data centers	Multi-tenant network connectivity	Non-neutral data centers
12	Data center types	Data center classes	Modular data centers		
13	Data center types	Data center applications			
14	Data center types	Data center applications	Systems of record data centers		
15	Data center types	Data center applications	Monolithic data centers		
16	Data center types	Data center applications	Cloud data centers		
17	Data center types	Data center applications	Engineering data centers		
18	Data center types	Data center applications	Small and medium business data centers		
19	Data center hardware	Data center applications			
20	Data center hardware	Data center servers			
21	Data center hardware	Data center servers	Data center server classes		
22	Data center hardware	Data center servers	Data center server classes	High-end servers	
23	Data center hardware	Data center servers	Data center server classes	Midrange servers	
24	Data center hardware	Data center servers	Data center server classes	Volume servers	
25	Data center hardware	Data center servers	Data center server form factors		
26	Data center hardware	Data center servers	Data center server form factors	Standalone servers	
27	Data center hardware	Data center servers	Data center server form factors	Standalone servers	Tower servers
28	Data center hardware	Data center servers	Data center server form factors	Standalone servers	Mid-tower servers

taxonomy | Data Centers resources | (+)

Figure 5.2 Using Excel to create a taxonomy for import

repeated, as may be required for importing. (The equivalent terms are still included but do not fit in this screenshot.)

There are a number of drawbacks to using a spreadsheet to create a taxonomy. There is the problem of scalability. If each top-level term has multiple narrower terms and each of these second-level terms has multiple narrower terms, then rather quickly it becomes difficult to visualize the complete hierarchy as higher-level terms become increasingly spaced apart. It may also become unwieldy to represent polyhierarchy, if large branches of the taxonomy need to be repeated. The spreadsheet format is also not adequate for nonpreferred terms. Even though multiple non-preferred terms can be included if separated by a delimiter, such as a semicolon or pipe, the fact that they must be confined to one cell for each preferred term results in the tendency for the taxonomist to be less than comprehensive in creating them. Finally, and perhaps most significantly, there is no enforcement of rules, such as term uniqueness, consistency, and relationship reciprocity. You could accidentally enter the same term twice (not intending a polyhierarchy), you could enter two variants of the same concept, you could enter a term as both preferred and nonpreferred, you could enter a term as nonpreferred for two different preferred terms, and, if you tried to add associative relationships, you might also name the related terms incorrectly. For these reasons, it's best to keep taxonomies in Excel small, so you can see what you have and not make incorrect duplications.

Mind Mapping, Concept Modeling, and Ontology Software

To capture more than just hierarchical relationships and include other relationships, categories, attributes, and so on, some taxonomists are now using mind mapping and other concept modeling software. A mind map is a diagram, used for brainstorming, visual thinking, or problem solving, that illustrates ideas, concepts, actions, and/or tasks and how they interrelate. Similar to mind maps and mind mapping software are concept maps and concept mapping software. There is not much distinction between the two, except that concepts maps are not necessarily as complex as mind maps. Concept maps are not as simple as flowcharts, however.

While hand-drawn mind maps have been in use for a long time, only recently have advanced graphics technologies enabled the development of mind mapping software. Now there are more than two dozen commercial and free and open source mind mapping software tools for Windows and Macintosh and a few for Linux.[3] Mind mapping software that taxonomists have used includes free tools, such as XMind (www.xmind.net), FreeMind from Source-Forge (freemind.sourceforge.net/wiki), and Cmap from the Florida Institute for Human & Machine Cognition (cmap.ihmc.us), and commercial software, such as TheBrain from TheBrain Technologies LP (www.thebrain.com), MindManager from Mindjet (www.mindjet.com), and VisiMap from Coco Systems Ltd. (www.visimap.com).[4] Depending on the tool, you can create polyhierarchical diagrams or different relationship types in mind maps, and usually

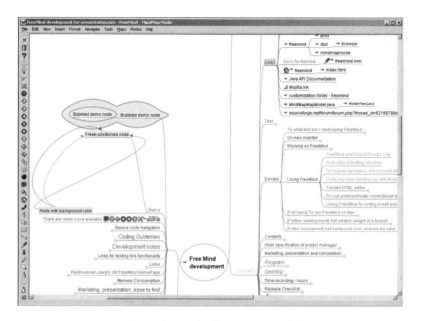

Figure 5.3 Mind map display in FreeMind (Source:
en.wikipedia.org/wiki/File:Freemind-0.9x_Screenshoot.png)

you can easily move concepts and branches. It may or may not be possible to export the output. Figure 5.3 is a screenshot of a mind map in FreeMind.

Using mind mapping or other concept modeling software is not an efficient or practical way to develop or manage a large taxonomy. Mind maps can become unwieldy and get too large to print. Nevertheless, visually minded taxonomists might find them a desirable way to put down and organize their initial ideas for a taxonomy. Other practical applications of mind mapping software are brainstorming taxonomy structures in a group or team setting and presenting a proposed taxonomy to an audience, especially at the early point in its creation, to sell the idea of the taxonomy to stakeholders.

Ontology-editing software, on the other hand, often both supports graphic representations of concept interrelationships and provides a means of managing a large number of concepts, along with their categories or attributes. Software for designing ontologies includes TopBraid Composer from TopQuadrant (www.topquadrant.com/tools/modeling-topbraid-composer-standard-edition) and the freeware Protégé (protege.stanford.edu). Compared with mind mapping software, dedicated ontology-editing software has a steeper learning curve, as it can have rather complex capabilities. Also, you may not as easily be able to generate graphic representations of hierarchical taxonomies in ontology editors. If the goal is to quickly get an initial graphic sketch of a budding taxonomy or to have a nice graphic representation of the start of a taxonomy for a presentation, then mind mapping software is more practical than ontology editors. Ontology editors, on the other hand, are compliant with standards for the semantic web, so they are a good option for generating web-based ontologies.

Dedicated Taxonomy Management Software

When it comes to building and managing a taxonomy, dedicated taxonomy/thesaurus management software should be the preferred choice. Whether what you are creating is called a taxonomy, a thesaurus, or a controlled vocabulary and whether the emphasis is on design and creation or management, the same kind of software is generally used. We will refer to all such full-featured software simply as taxonomy management software, even though all such software supports all standard thesaurus relationships. If a taxonomy is purely hierarchical and does not utilize related term relationships, then the related term feature of the software is simply not used.

Software Compliance with Standards

One important characteristic to consider when choosing software for building classification systems is whether it supports established standards. Taxonomists should be most interested in software that supports thesaurus standards, namely ANSI/NISO Z39.19 or ISO 25964, but there are other standards to be aware of.

SKOS has become more common as a standard governing taxonomy management software since it was officially released by the World Wide Web Consortium in 2009. It comprises specifications and working standards "to support the use of knowledge organization systems (KOS) such as thesauri, classification schemes, subject heading systems and taxonomies within the framework of the Semantic Web."[5] It is important to understand the distinction between the thesaurus design and construction guidelines contained in ANSI/NISO Z39.19 or ISO 25964, which describe, among other things, the characteristics of the relationships between terms; and the specifications or standards for the architecture, framework, and computer-readable structure of the controlled vocabulary, which is the focus of SKOS. The two different sets of standards thus complement each other, rather than being alternatives to each other.

ANSI/NISO Z39.19 or ISO 25964-1 are guidelines specifically for thesauri, whereas SKOS is a model for "knowledge organization systems" that are slightly more broadly defined than thesauri, to include taxonomies, vocabularies, ontologies, and so on, which do not necessarily have to conform to the stricter thesaurus rules. SKOS-based software thus may deliberately permit relationships or duplicate terms that are prohibited by ANSI/NISO Z39.19 or ISO 25964, in order to allow more flexible usage of the software. Ideally then, the SKOS-based software has administrative controls to let the user select which rules to enforce. For some people SKOS-compliance is most important, and for other people the support of thesaurus standards is most important.

In other areas, records management software, which also supports taxonomy creation, will likely follow records management standards, which include business activity classifications. This is specified in a different ISO standard, ISO 15489.

While you could build a simple hierarchical taxonomy in almost any "classification" tool, software for thesaurus management that meets the criteria listed in the following section is a wiser choice for many reasons. In addition to the various features that thesaurus software offers, the taxonomies created will be more adaptable and scalable for future enhancements, different implementations, export options, and merging with other vocabularies. The standards, ANSI/NISO Z39.19 (section 11.4) and ISO 25964-1 (section 14), also provide detailed thesaurus software requirements, so anyone developing software for thesaurus management should consult the relevant sections of either of those standards.

Taxonomy/Thesaurus Software Characteristics

The basic requirement of thesaurus software is to maintain terms, their associated relationships, and other attributes. As we have seen, the relationships are reciprocal between pairs of terms. By using thesaurus software, you create or edit the relationship in only one place. If you decide to rename or delete a term, the change will be reflected in all of the relationships of the term. Features for adding optional scope notes and user-defined classification categories are also standard in thesaurus software. In addition to meeting these requirements, most thesaurus software includes the following features: merging and subsuming terms, designating candidate and approved terms, indicating term creation date and modification date, permitting multiple hierarchies (polyhierarchies), disallowing illegal relationships (e.g., circular relationships), generating reports in different displays, and exporting taxonomies in platform-neutral file formats for use in other systems. When one is building a taxonomy, speed and ease are important. Therefore, most software permit adding successive relationships of the same type (nonpreferred terms, narrower terms, or broader terms) simply by hitting the *enter key*. You should consider the following characteristics when comparing various thesaurus software packages.

Taxonomy Display

Just as there are various formats to display a taxonomy or thesaurus to end users (described in Chapter 9) or to indexers, there are different display options in the user interface for the taxonomist who is editing the taxonomy. Typically thesaurus software provides the option of both alphabetical and hierarchical display views that the taxonomist may switch between, such as by using tabs. The alphabetical display may also have the option to include or exclude nonpreferred terms.

Related to how the software displays the taxonomy is how the software organizes a complex taxonomy. Additional types of displays may be available in a reporting feature. Thesaurus software products also differ in whether they create single isolated thesaurus files or multiple named hierarchies that can be linked to each other.

Term Display and Editing

Each taxonomy term has relationships and other details that can be individually displayed and edited. The various thesaurus software products differ in how term details are displayed, how the editing is done, and what additional term attributes are present. The process of creating terms and their relationships may be performed through various means: main menu selections, context menu selections, shortcut key combinations, other keyboard commands, toolbar buttons, and mouse drag and drop. Features that may or may not be present include single-step merging/subsuming terms, single-step moving of a branch (a term and all its narrower terms), and drag-and-drop adding of relationships.

Rules Enforcement

A thesaurus should follow the guidelines spelled out in Chapter 4 on term relationships. While it takes human thought to create relationships correctly, certain rules in the software can help, for example, by *not* permitting the following:

- Terms that are related to themselves

- Pairs of terms that have more than one kind of relationship between them (both associative and hierarchical, both equivalence and hierarchical, or both equivalence and associative)

- Terms that have a broader term that is narrower to a narrower term of the first term (circular references)

- Term names that duplicate within the same taxonomy but are not the same concept (not having the same term ID and functioning as a single term for indexing), unlike polyhierarchy

Software that is described as "thesaurus management software" or ANSI/NISO Z39.19 or ISO 25964 compliant can be expected to enforce these thesaurus rules. Software described as "vocabulary management," "taxonomy management," and merely "SKOS-compliant" does not necessarily enforce these rules, or at least not by default. Even so, it may be possible, often through administrative settings in the software, to set these rules, especially in software that claims to serve multiple purposes of managing taxonomies, thesauri, and other vocabularies.

Even if they are not actually "rules," the software should offer various quality checks or controls. For example, it should also be possible to identify for further scrutiny terms that lack any hierarchy (and may also associative relationships) with other terms, sometimes called "orphan terms." Actually permitting orphan terms is up to the policy of the specific taxonomy. Software controls may also be desired for permitting multiple *use* references or to control the use of polyhierarchy (none, only up to two broader terms, only within the same hierarchy, etc.).

Taxonomy Searching

Taxonomy search and navigation are important, not only for the end user of the implemented taxonomy but also for the creator of the taxonomy, who needs to know, for example, whether a given term already exists. You need the capability to search for terms in order to find appropriate terms with which to make relationships, to avoid inadvertently duplicating concepts, to make global changes on terms if a style policy changes, and so on. Different software tools vary in their list of options for searching.

Customization of Relationships and Attributes

The ability to define and customize relationships, types of notes, and categories of terms is important in making a thesaurus software product versatile and extensible. Although standard thesaurus relationships are limited to broader/narrower term, related term, and use/used for, you might also wish to create specific user-defined relationships, as described in the final section of Chapter 4. Thesaurus software varies in the degree to which it supports customizing relationships based on the three basic relationships (hierarchical, associative, and equivalent).

One of the benefits of thesaurus software, which is based on database management software, is that additional information can be assigned and stored with each term as a database record. A scope note is the most typical kind of such additional information, but there could be other kinds of notes as well, such as standardized industry codes for industry terms or birth/death dates for person name terms. Categories are often used in taxonomies to classify terms for end use, by source, or for any other purpose that you may have. Categorizing terms makes it easier to batch edit them and to designate terms for certain end-use search interface characteristics. Categories are explained in greater detail in Chapter 8.

Importing, Exporting, and Reports

In addition to building a taxonomy from scratch (i.e., manually typing in each term), you may want to take advantage of external lists of terms to import and incorporate into the taxonomy. Most often, these might be lists of names, organizations, or places, but they could also be legacy taxonomies, along with their relationships, for incorporation into a new system. Thus, the ability to import or batch load data is an important feature of a thesaurus software package.

Exporting the taxonomy into formats that can then be imported into other systems is crucial for thesaurus software. A taxonomy is not just something to look at but is to be used in the indexing/tagging of files, documents, or webpages and then by a final end user for search and retrieval of those documents and pages, often through one or more other software systems. Generic export formats for use in other systems include comma-separate values (CSV) and standard formats of XML (eXtensible Markup Language), such as the format followed by SKOS.

You will want software that can generate interim reports of various kinds to aid in the task of building the taxonomy. These could include lists of candidate terms, deleted terms, or orphan terms, in addition to taxonomy reports that include only certain specific data or relationships for each term. Occasionally a taxonomy is published for third-party use, in which case various outputs, including a printed document, might be desirable. These outputs are usually based on options in the report feature. Chapter 9 describes in detail the various kinds of taxonomy output displays.

Checklist for Comparing Features

The thesaurus software products mentioned in this chapter all have the characteristics just described, but they differ in some areas. Following is a list of variable features you may want to consider when comparing products:

- Interface design and ease of use

- Thesaurus relationship rules enforcement (by default or by settings)

- Speed (limited mouse clicks) in adding repeated terms and relationships

- Single-step creation of new terms and relationships

- Single-step branch (term and narrower terms) moving

- Drag-and-drop relationship adding

- User-defined relationships of all three types

- Multiple taxonomy display options in the user interface

- User-defined term notes

- User-defined term attributes

- Spell-checking

- Import and export formats

- Support for bilingual or multilingual taxonomies (equivalent preferred terms in more than one language; different character set displays)

Your specific user preferences and the nature of the taxonomy project will ultimately determine which software product you should choose.

Taxonomy/Thesaurus Software Resources

No complete or authoritative list of thesaurus software products exists, for various reasons, including the blurred definitions of *taxonomy* and *thesaurus*, the integration of thesaurus management capabilities into software with wider applications, the presence of both general and vertical market software, and the regionalism of vendors in Europe and other parts of the world. Most significantly, since the thesaurus software alone does not provide a solution to any information management and retrieval problem because taxonomy creation skills and expertise are also required, the market for such specialized software remains relatively limited. Thus, industry analysts do not see the need to follow the thesaurus software industry specifically as compared with more automated solutions, such as enterprise search and auto-categorization.

To complicate matters further, *taxonomy software* is a vague notion. Some auto-categorization or auto-classification software systems have gone further to develop technology for the automatic generation of simple taxonomies. Thus, taxonomy software today can include these automatic taxonomy creation systems and not just software to aid the human creation and editing of taxonomies. In fact, auto-categorization or auto-classification tools, whether they can actually generate taxonomies or merely make use of them, are now also included within the broader category of taxonomy software. The realm of taxonomy software may also extend to vendors of software that utilize text analytics or entity extraction to suggest terms. To further complicate matters, thesaurus software is not always called that. Some vendors prefer other names, such as *business semantics management software.*[6] If the software supports customized relationships, then it might be called ontology software.

The two most comprehensive lists of thesaurus management software (beyond this book and its website) are maintained on taxonomy resource websites that are owned, ironically, by software vendors. The vendors, Synaptica and Access Innovations, have both determined that the benefits of driving traffic to their product websites through a linked site on general taxonomy resources outweigh the risks of listing their competitors' names. Synaptica lists software products in the "Marketplace" category of the Taxonomy Warehouse site (www.taxonomywarehouse.com). Taxonomy Warehouse started out as a directory of taxonomies for license from third parties but has since grown to include additional taxonomy-related resources. Access Innovations has a very long list of products (and a few services) on the Thesaurus Software page of its TaxoBank resource website (http://www.taxobank.org/content/resources). The core of this directory was migrated over in 2013 from the Willpower Thesaurus software directory, which was created and managed by the independent consultant Leonard D. Will, starting in the mid-1990s.[7] Will's original list of 38 thesaurus management tools has grown to about 100 with the inclusion of related products and services, such as tools for text analytics and search.

Taxonomy Software Trends

Noticeable trends in taxonomy/thesaurus management software include a move toward web-based and especially cloud-based software-as-a-service (SaaS), more combinations of ontology and thesaurus management, more SKOS/RDF/Semantic Web framework software, and more plug-ins to SharePoint, content management systems, and search engines.

Synaptica pioneered web-based thesaurus management software when it introduced its product in 1995, when the web was still young, but now other vendors also offer web-based subscription software. Data Harmony Thesaurus Master from Access Innovations was originally only available in a Java-based, multiplatform client–server installation; later a web SaaS version was added. Access Innovations's president Marjorie Hlava has made the observation that "Increasingly our customers use the cloud version of the software."[8] Similarly, Semaphore and Wordmap started out as client–server only software and now have web or SaaS options. MultiTes, available as a single-user Windows desktop program since 1983, introduced a multiuser cloud version in 2013. Newer thesaurus management software products have been introduced that are solely web-based. These include PoolParty, introduced in 2009, TopBraid Enterprise Vocabulary Net (EVN), released in 2010, Coreon, released in 2014, and the free and open source software TemaTres and VocBench, which became available in the late 2000s. Web-based platforms have also led the trend in taxonomy read-only applications, which allow reviewers to browse, search, and possibly even comment on the taxonomy.

Taxonomy/thesaurus management software and ontology software used to be completely different products, typically available from different vendors for different purposes, but the trend recently has been for vendors to combine taxonomy and ontology management in a single software package, or to provide ontology management capabilities by means of extensions or add-on modules. Some ontologists might consider such software to be a "light" version, as compared with dedicated ontology management software.[9] The combination of features has its benefits, though. For example, an organization may have simple taxonomy requirements at first that later evolve to require a more complex ontology, especially as the users become more familiar with the ontology capabilities.

Supporting linked data and interoperability with Semantic Web content has become more important. Therefore, World Wide Web consortium (W3C) recommendations of RDF specifications, OWL, and the SKOS framework are being adopted more widely. The newer products PoolParty and TopBraid EVN are both built around SKOS models. Synaptica and Data Harmony Thesaurus Master have long been able to export to a SKOS and OWL schema, but it was only in 2013 that Data Harmony added user-defined fields to the SKOS export to include all fields in a term record. Additionally, in 2011 Synaptica introduced an Ontology Publishing Suite, to publish an ontology or part of an ontology to the web. SKOS is not necessarily an alternative standard to ANSI/NISO Z39.19, but rather a framework that can be followed in addition to ANSI/NISO Z39.19. While a software product typically follows one or the other, ideally it complies fully with both, and some products now do.

Plug-ins and connectors for search and content management are becoming more common. The most widespread tool for internal content management (even though it is not really a content management system) is SharePoint. Now almost all enterprise-level thesaurus management software products have methods to connect to SharePoint, whether through APIs, plug-ins, or dedicated "connector" modules. There are also increasing numbers of content management systems and search software products being supported by thesaurus management connections and APIs, with RESTful APIs in particular.

Single-User Desktop Thesaurus Software

Offerings in commercial, single-user desktop thesaurus software are extremely limited. There were a few more low-end products in the market in the past, as listed in the Willpower/TaxoBank thesaurus software directory, but because taxonomies are created for the needs of organizations, not individuals, the relatively small market of individual users could not support these inexpensive products. So now almost all commercial thesaurus software products are multiuser, either web hosted or client–server based, and marketed to organizations. This is not necessarily a problem for independent-contractor taxonomists, who are not expected to use their own software but rather have access to the software licensed by their clients.

The only native Mac OS taxonomy tool, Cognatrix from LGOSystems Pty. Ltd. (Australia), was pulled from the market in early 2014, due to installation issues with later versions of Mac OS. It is the intention of the vendor to revamp Cognatrix and release it again as an Apple App upon the release of a newer version of the Apple user interface.[10]

MultiTes

MultiTes Pro (www.multites.com), the flagship product of Multisystems, based in Miami, Florida, is the only lasting, commercially licensed, single-user, affordable desktop thesaurus management software. It has been on the market since 1983 and continues to be supported with periodic updates. Its price for a single user has not changed in a decade—in 2015 it remained at $295. Multiple-user packages are also available. In 2013 Multisystems introduced a multiuser subscription cloud-based version of the software called MultiTes Online.

MultiTes meets expected requirements described in the earlier section. Its major drawback is probably its user interface, which lacks a hierarchical display option, although hierarchical *reports* can be generated. The product was developed as thesaurus software, not taxonomy software, so a hierarchical view was not considered necessary. Taxonomists trained and experienced in thesaurus construction principles should not have difficulties using MultiTes, but novice taxonomists or subject matter experts who edit a taxonomy might consider the interface nonintuitive. In

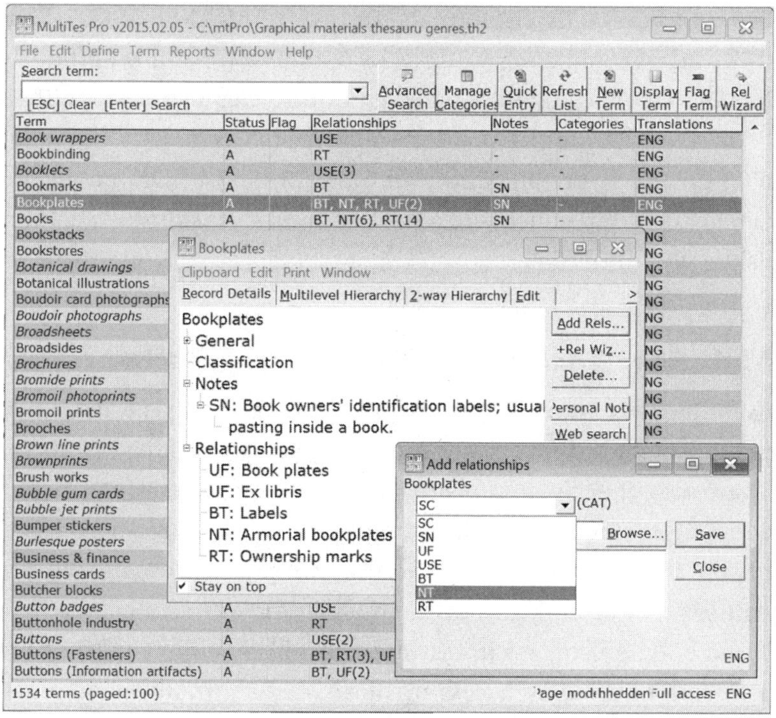

Figure 5.4 MultiTes taxonomy display with selected term details

MultiTes, the alphabetical thesaurus list takes up the entire window width, so viewing or editing term details involves clicking on the desired term and opening a pop-up window rather than using a screen pane/area (see Figure 5.4).

MultiTes's primary strengths include its full support for user-defined relationships, term notes, and term categories. It also supports multilingual thesauri. However, in addition to the need to generate a report in order to see the hierarchy, other drawbacks include the inability to subsume or merge terms in a single step, the inability to create relationships across multiple thesauri, and the lack of a spell-checker.

MultiTes accepts imported data as text only, either in a text file or pasted to a clipboard. The data must follow a specific format and cannot use tags. Export formats are text, HTML, XML, SKOS/RDF, RTF, and three different CSV layout options. Two add-on products for MultiTes facilitate web and enterprise deployment. MultiTes WDK (Web Deployment Kit) enables publication of a live MultiTes taxonomy on the internet/intranet. MultiTes EDK (Enterprise Deployment Kit) consists of a set of tools for transferring and publishing thesaurus data onto corporate servers.

Multiuser Taxonomy Management Software

Commercially available enterprise-level taxonomy or thesaurus management systems have been around only since the late 1990s. These are either client–server systems or web-based systems, which allow simultaneous work by multiple users, any number of whom can be remote. Thus, even if you do not purchase such software yourself, if you work as a taxonomy contractor or consultant, you could end up using such software, most likely remotely. There are also various levels of access privilege, ranging from full administrator to taxonomy-level administrator to taxonomy editor to read-only access. Certain configuration functions, such as customizing relationships, can be performed only in the administrative area or module. Companion software modules, add-ons, and custom integration allow these thesaurus management systems to be integrated with indexing systems and end-user search systems. These software systems may be supported with on-site custom integration and training services.

Free trials for these commercial systems may require a prospective customer request rather than a simple download from the website. Pricing varies but can be in the thousands or tens of thousands of dollars, and is based on the number of servers or the number of users or seats, the degree of support, installation and configuration services, and so on. Therefore, before making a purchase, you must carefully evaluate how a particular software system and any additional modules might best suit your organization's needs.

Dedicated, large-scale, general-use (not vertical market) thesaurus management systems include, but are limited to, the following (alphabetically): Coreon, Data Harmony Thesaurus Master, Mondeca Intelligent Topic Manager, PoolParty, Smartlogic Semaphore Ontology Editor, SoutronTHESAURUS, STAR/Thesaurus, Synaptica, TopBraid EVN, and Wordmap. Each of these products includes all the capabilities described in the earlier section Taxonomy Thesaurus Software Characteristics, unless noted otherwise. The short descriptions that follow are not meant to be complete lists of features. Individual software tools may also share features that are highlighted in the description of other tools. Software in which thesaurus management is integrated within a product that has other nonthesaurus capabilities is addressed in a later section.

Coreon

Coreon (www.coreon.com) is the newest entrant to the taxonomy software market, released in 2014 by the German-based company Coreon GmBH. *Coreon* stands for Content Repository Online. The company was founded in 2012 as a spin-off from ESTeam AB, a language technology software and services company based in Sweden. Coreon uniquely supports the combination of taxonomy management and terminology management. For example, the user can enter terms into a multilingual vocabulary in any language to obtain translations in either direction, and the software also complies with terminology standards. Coreon is currently the only commercial taxonomy management software that also supports *ISO* 30042:2008, also known as TermBase eXchange (TBX), for interchange of terminological data. Coreon is fully SKOS-compliant but at this time may not fully support thesaurus standards ANSI/NISO Z.39.19 or ISO 25964. Coreon's user interface is in English, with other language interfaces planned. It is available solely as SaaS.

Coreon displays term hierarchies by default, not in the traditional complete top-down expandable/collapsible tree structure, but rather by displaying the immediate broader and narrower terms, and from there the user can click on terms in either hierarchical direction, which makes more sense for the polyhierarchies that the software supports. The software also offers an interactive, animated representation of the taxonomy branches within the default term details window. Users have the option of creating semantic customized relationships for ontologies, and can also designate different kinds of nonpreferred terms. Coreon manages multilingual vocabularies with translations in all languages of the European Union plus Ukrainian and Russian, and plans to add Asian languages.[11] The software is a linguistically tuned variant of the Solr, search engine, which enables sophisticated search on the terms, such as grammatical stemming and word order changes. Coreon offers various levels of user access, including read-only to share a taxonomy with reviewers. Sample read-only taxonomies in Coreon are available for viewing on the company's website. Import and export formats are XML, ISO TBX, and SKOS.

Data Harmony Thesaurus Master

Data Harmony Thesaurus Master (www.dataharmony.com) has been commercially available from Access Innovations (Albuquerque, New Mexico) since 1998. Prior to that, the software had been developed and used only in-house for the indexing and taxonomy services that the company has been providing since 1978, especially for the scholarly publishing market. The software is available both in a multiplatform Java-based version (used on Windows, Mac, Solaris, and Linux) and as cloud service over the web. Client software allows remote access, but a single-user desktop version is also available. Another Data Harmony product is M.A.I. (Machine Aided Indexer), a partner tool for categorization described in Chapter 7. Thesaurus Master and M.A.I. are available as an integrated product called MAIstro, and additional software extensions are also available.

Thesaurus Master (screenshot in Figure 5.5) fully complies with thesaurus standards of ANSI/NISO Z.39.19 and ISO 25964 (Parts 1 and 2). Some of Thesaurus Master's additional features include a

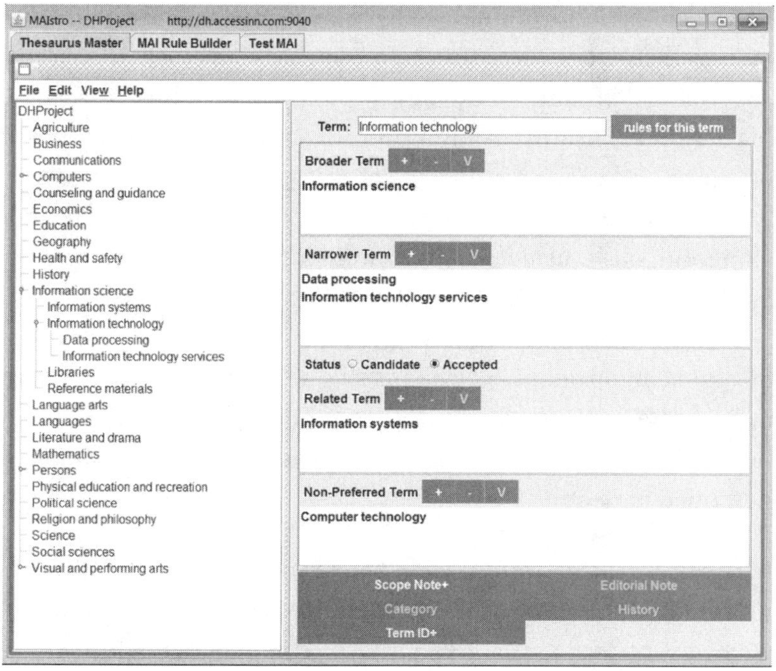

Figure 5.5 Data Harmony Thesaurus Master's split-screen display,
with the browsable taxonomy in the left pane and selected,
editable term details (term record) in the right pane

dynamic, expandable tree view, a drag-and-drop ability to move the
location of a term, support for all standard thesaurus display types,
support for "facet indicators" (node labels), user-defined notes fields,
the option to make all sibling terms automatically related terms to
each other, full multilingual display, and a collaboration feature for
adding comments to terms. The administrative module provides for
password-governed security and nine levels of user access. Import
formats include text, Word documents, XML, CSV, and MS Excel as
tab delimited. Export formats include XML, HTML, OWL, OWL2,
SKOS, Zthes, MARC (concise or expanded), and tab delimited. Export
options also allow for various display types, such as hierarchical, permuted, and alphabetical flat format. There are also connectors for
exporting to SharePoint and various content management systems.

Rather than add ontology-like capabilities to their thesaurus management tool, in 2016 Data Harmony released a separate stand-alone product, Ontology Master. Thus, while Thesaurus Master only permits customization of some relationships (based on the equivalence and associative types, but not the hierarchical type), Ontology Master, supports fully customized relationships, along with customized classes. Ontology Master also supports the guidelines of OWL, SKOS, and RDF Triples.

Data Harmony's parent company, Access Innovations, also offers off-the-shelf taxonomies, custom taxonomy creation, consulting, and search implementation. A machine-aided indexing product that integrates with Thesaurus Master or Ontology Master is described in Chapter 7.

Mondeca's Intelligent Topic Manager

Mondeca's Intelligent Topic Manager (ITM) was introduced in 2008 by Mondeca S.A., (www.mondeca.com), founded in 2000 and located in Paris, France. The company also sells automated indexing software, called Content Annotation Manager, and search software, called Semantic Search, which can be purchased together or separately. Mondeca products were developed as web-based software from the beginning and are available either installed locally on a web server or as SaaS, hosted either by Mondeca or by a cloud service such as Amazon Web Services. The user interface is available in both French and English versions.

ITM conforms to both SKOS vocabularies and OWL-standard ontologies, so in addition to supporting the creation of taxonomies, the same software enables the creation of ontologies. Accordingly, its features include support for both standard thesaurus relationships and customized relationships based on customized classes. Other term-editing features include drag and drop to move a term/change its relationships, a wizard to add multiple new terms at once, a graph visualization of relationships, and a search and read-only interface for nontaxonomist users to review the taxonomy. ITM supports multiple languages, with translations between terms, and allows for the use of Latin, Cyrillic, Arabic, and Chinese scripts. There is also the option for users to customize thesaurus management rules, such as whether to permit or prohibit polyhierarchies or terms having parents within the same or different hierarchies. So, while thesaurus creation in ITM does not have to be compliant with ISO 25964 thesaurus standards, it can be if the rules are set up to make it so.

ITM can import and export thesauri in formats of XLS, XML, RDF, SKOS, and Topic Maps. The software has connectors for Share-Point, search engines Solr and Elastic Search, and selected content management systems, such as Alfresco. Additionally, REST Web APIs support the integration of ITM with many other content management and search systems. The company also offers consulting services, including custom taxonomy development.

PoolParty

PoolParty (www.poolparty.biz) is a relatively new entrant to the taxonomy management software market, introduced by the Semantic Web Company in 2009. The software company, based in Vienna, Austria, was founded in 2004 as a spin-off from the services company punkt .netServices, which started in 1998. The user interface is available in English, German, French, Italian, or Slovak.

The core component of the PoolParty suite is the thesaurus management tool called PoolParty Thesaurus Server. PoolParty is available either as a web-based cloud service, for an annual subscription fee, or installed on premises on a Linux or Windows Server for a one-time license purchase. Under both license options, PoolParty is available in four tiers of features and modules: PoolParty Basic Server, PoolParty Advanced Server, PoolParty Enterprise Server, and PoolParty Semantic Integrator. Selected modules of a higher tier can also be purchased as add-ons to a lower tier. Figure 5.6 is a screenshot from PoolParty Thesaurus Server.

Basic features of all PoolParty products are multilingual support, support for multiple projects, term history (changes) information,

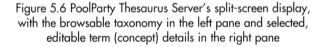

Figure 5.6 PoolParty Thesaurus Server's split-screen display,
with the browsable taxonomy in the left pane and selected,
editable term (concept) details in the right pane

a Visual Mapper for pie-chart visualization of terms and their relationships, an API for web access, and a Taxonomy Creator Web Part for SharePoint. PoolParty can import from and export to Excel and to various RDF formats, including OWL, and can also generate synonym reports suitable for import to SharePoint search and Google's Customized Search Engine (CSE). Alphabetical, detailed, and hierarchical thesaurus reports can also be generated. PoolParty supports standard thesaurus relationships, but in order to create customized relationships, along with classes, at least the PoolParty Advanced Server tier or the Ontology Manager add-on module for the Basic Server is required. Other Advanced Server or add-on module features include a taxonomy browser wiki front end, taxonomy mapping, SPARQL (database query) end points, and a linked data publishing front end.

According to the Semantic Web Company, what distinguishes PoolParty from other thesaurus management software is the ability to create linked-concept taxonomies/thesauri based on Semantic Web standards for both enterprises and organizations that want to publish open data. Its thesauri are fully compatible with the SKOS format, and the software utilizes Linked Open Data (LOD).

PoolParty Thesaurus Server is designed with considerations of ISO 25964 standards but does not enforce all rules by default. For example, the default settings prohibit circular relationships but merely flag duplicate terms or the use of two types of relationships (such as BT/NT and RT) between the same pair of terms, and this flagging occurs only after running a quality report, not when the term or relationship is first created. Users can change the default quality settings, to prohibit such relationships. There are eight different scenarios that can be set by the user to "ignore," "report," or "enforce." Thus before starting to use PoolParty, the settings should be adjusted from the defaults by a taxonomist who fully understands the relationships and desired rules.

Additional available modules include PowerTagging (for semi-automated indexing), Linked Data Management, Text Mining and Entity Extraction, and Semantic Search.

SAS Ontology Management

SAS Institute (www.sas.com), a major developer of business analytics software based in Cary, North Carolina, is better known for its text analytics products, especially Enterprise Content Categorization, which is described in Chapter 7, than for taxonomy management. Included in the text analytics suite is SAS Ontology Management, which is available as both a stand-alone product and integrated with SAS Enterprise Content Categorization. As with other SAS software, SAS Ontology Management is client–server software, which runs on Linux, other Unix, or Windows servers and Linux or Windows clients. An SQL database is also required.

SAS Ontology Management is generally used by companies already using other SAS software.

SAS Ontology Management was designed specifically for ontologies, so it uses ontology terminology (such as classes, slots, instances) that may be unfamiliar to the taxonomist. Although focused on ontologies, the software also manages and displays term hierarchies sufficiently and clearly manages nonpreferred terms (alternate terms), so it can also be used for simpler taxonomies and thesauri. For ontology management, though, it has a sophisticated support for classes, even including hierarchies of subclasses and attributes of classes. Features include full customization of classes, relationships, and attributes, an advanced search feature, multiple-user permission-level types for different projects, and batch find-and-replace. SAS Ontology Management import formats are XML and RDF/OWL, and XML is the only export format. The ontology management software can be integrated with the SAS auto-classification software, and there are APIs for connecting to content and search systems, including SharePoint, Oracle Endeca, and Documentum. Nevertheless, SAS Ontology Management does not appear to be widely used or marketed beyond existing SAS software customers.

Semaphore Ontology Editor

Semaphore is a suite of products offered by the London-based company Smartlogic Semaphore Ltd. (www.smartlogic.com) since 2006. The company also has a US subsidiary, Smartlogic Semaphore Inc., based in San Jose, California. The core product, Ontology Editor (previously called Ontology Manager), can be licensed and used separately or integrated with the rest of the suite. Semaphore products are web-based and are available either in an internally installed version or vendor hosted in a SaaS arrangement.

The Ontology Editor (Figure 5.7), despite its name, is also full-featured thesaurus software. In addition to supporting ontology standards (RDF/OWL), it also supports the ISO 25964 thesaurus

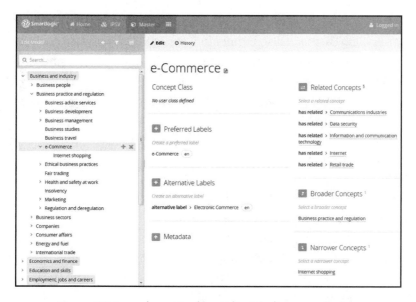

Figure 5.7 Semaphore Ontology Editor's split-screen display,
with the browsable taxonomy in the left pane and selected,
editable term details in the right pane

standard and ANSI/NISO Z39.19, so it is completely appropriate
for any taxonomy or thesaurus, in addition to ontologies. Features
include drag-and-drop capability to move terms and relationships;
the ability to protect imported vocabulary terms from changes,
while supporting the extension of such vocabularies with the addition of narrower terms; a task feature to manage workflow of such
things as pending and approved terms; and the support of URIs for
individual terms.

Optional additional modules include an ontology/taxonomy
mapping tool and an Ontology Review Tool that allows collabo-
rators view and search the ontology/taxonomy and to also submit
comments, without editing the terms, and a text mining tool for
text/fact extraction. A related auto-classification product, Classification Server, is described in Chapter 7.

Ontology Editor's import and export formats include Excel/
CSV and the various Semantic Web RDF XML standards, including

SKOS, Turtle (Terse RDF Triple Language), and N Triple (a subset of Turtle). There are also connectors available for SharePoint, Google Search Appliance, Apache Solr, OpenText, MarkLogic, and IBM Watson, in addition to a connector for the *Content Management Interoperability Services* (*CMIS*) open standard, which enables connection to any CMIS-compatible content management system.

STAR/Thesaurus

The thesaurus management software STAR/Thesaurus, offered by Vancouver-based Lucidea Corp. (lucidea.com), has been on the market since the late 1990s. It is one of a suite of Cuadra STAR brand software products for archives management, collections management, knowledge management, digital asset management, and records management. In 2008 Los Angeles-based Cuadra Associates was acquired by the Canadian company Sydney PLUS, and in 2013 Sydney Plus changed its name to Lucidea. Cuadra's market emphasis has been libraries, museums, archives, associations and societies, government agencies, and database publishers, but STAR/Thesaurus could certainly be used in any enterprise or application. STAR/Thesaurus can be purchased and used by itself or integrated into any of these other STAR software systems to provide vocabulary control for indexing and cataloging.

STAR/Thesaurus is multiuser client–server software that runs on Linux, Solaris, or Windows for the server and on Windows for the desktop client. Additionally, the product offers a web-based user interface for just displaying, browsing, and searching a thesaurus without editing it. While the product is priced per data-entry user, there is no charge for any number of browse users.

The software meets the ANSI/NISO Z39.19 guidelines for thesaurus management through its support of standard relationships and enforcement of various rules, such as no circular relationships. It supports customizable notes and term attribute fields. As for customizable relationship types, those can be created only on the administrator, server-side of the software. Import/export format options are tagged ASCII text and CSV. While an XML output is not a standard option, skilled administrators could convert a tagged text file to XML. The vendor Lucidea also offers services of custom importing from other formats.

Synaptica Knowledge Management System (KMS)

Synaptica (www.synaptica.com) is a web-services-enabled application accessible via a web browser from Synaptica, LLC, based in Denver, Colorado. It was the first web-based taxonomy management software when the product was commercially introduced in 1995. Licenses are available in annual or perpetual forms based on the number of users. Training services are also available. A separate indexing module, IMS (Indexing Management System), is also available. Despite being a relatively small company, Synaptica has a global reach with an office in the United Kingdom, additional sales affiliates in Europe, and partnerships in Singapore, Malaysia, and Australia.

The user interface of Synaptica offers alphabetical or hierarchical browsing, along with sophisticated term-searching options, and utilizes pop-up windows for selected term details, as shown in Figure 5.8.

Synaptica and the thesauri it helps create comply with ISO 25964 and ANSI/NISO Z39.19. Software features include a global term and relationships editor that can create a list of terms to edit, a side-by-side editing view, a drag-and-drop capability, a term subsume function, the ability to map between taxonomies, the ability to assign relationship weights (an added level of complexity more suited for ontologies than most taxonomies), custom category assignment, thesaurus replication/versioning, an independent search and browse utility for non-taxonomy editors, user-defined relationships, an interactive visualization tool with term nodes branching out, a dashboard with metrics and graphs to display thesaurus details, UTF-8 encoding for outputs on reports, and up to 12 gradations of permission levels. Import formats are CSV, text,

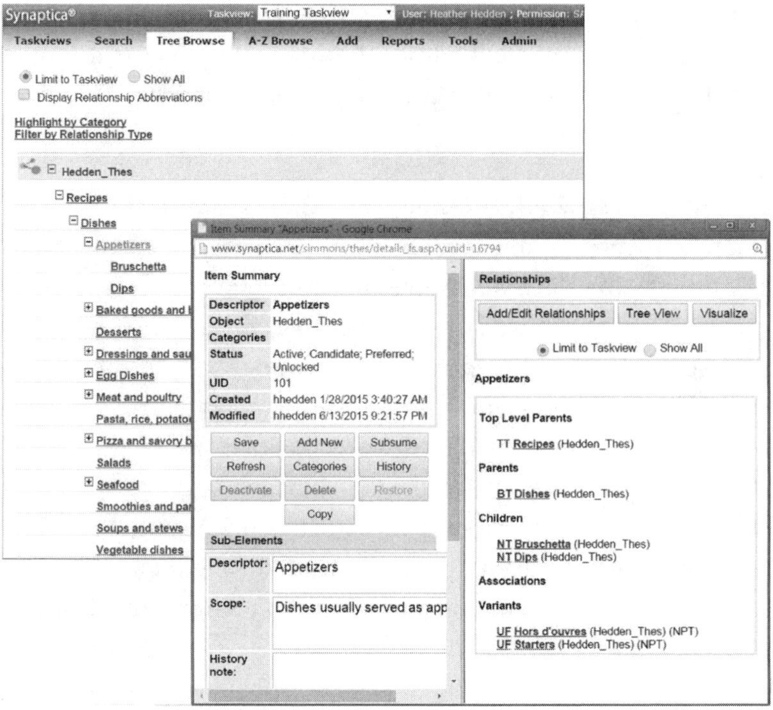

Figure 5.8 Synaptica's hierarchical taxonomy
display and selected term details

Excel, and XML (including schemas of Zthes, SKOS, and OWL). Export formats are CSV, HTML, Word, Excel, and XML (including schemas of Zthes, SKOS, SKOS-XL, and OWL). Synaptica also offers a SharePoint connector for direct importation of taxonomies into the SharePoint Term Store and also offers APIs for integration with other software systems. Additional products and services include automated indexing, faceted search based on Apache Solr, and knowledge audit and taxonomy development services.

TopBraid Enterprise Vocabulary Net

While some taxonomy/thesaurus management software vendors have added ontology support or modules to their products, TopQuadrant (www.topquadrant.com), founded in 2002 and based in Raleigh, North Carolina, has gone somewhat the other way. The company started with a complex, single-user ontology modeling software, TopBraid Composer, introduced in 2006, and then in 2010 it released a simpler and easier-to-use thesaurus management product, TopBraid EVN, to satisfy a wider market, which has now become the company's leading product. Not long after EVN was introduced, ontology creation capabilities (although not as complex as in TopBraid Composer) were added to EVN.

EVN is a multiuser software that runs on a Linux or Windows server, and users log in remotely from any operating system with any browser. So, while it is web-based for the users, EVN is not over-the-web SaaS. TopBraid EVN supports SKOS, including SKOS-XL standards, rather than ANSI/NISO Z39.19 or ISO 25964. Standard thesaurus rules, such as no circular relationships, are enforced, but the user can additionally define customized rules about data and metadata by means of a form.

In addition to supporting standard and customized relationships, classes, and term attributes or properties, EVN supports mapping/crosswalks between vocabularies, query-building tools for customized reports (in addition to standard reports), and a multifield search feature. One of the distinguishing features of EVN is taxonomy-editing workflow management, which involves the ability to keep sets of proposed changes in "working copies" that can be reviewed and reported on with no effect on the production copy until a user with the appropriate permissions puts it into production. The EVN user interface has the standard hierarchical taxonomy display in the left pane and then the details of a selected term in the right pane, but additionally a third pane further to the right displays the search functions, as shown in Figure 5.9.

Import and export formats include Excel/CSV (including exporting to the format of CSV for the SharePoint Term Store), XML (including importing from MultiTes's XML format), and RDF/OWL. TopQuadrant can also provide other customized formats.

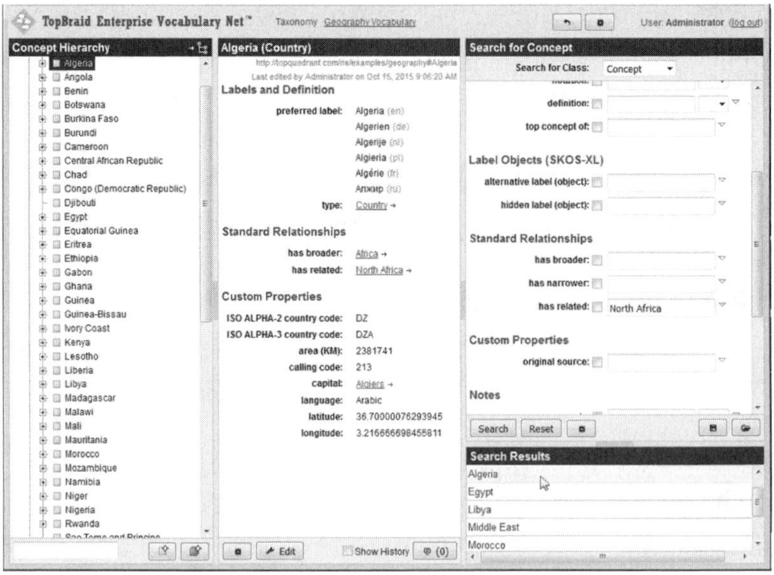

Figure 5.9 TopBraid Enterprise Vocabulary Net user interface with taxonomy hierarchy, term details, and search functions (Image credit: TopQuadrant, Inc.)

Integration with third-party applications can also be done with APIs, ideally documented RESTful APIs.

Related add-on modules available are TopBraid Vocabulary Explorer, a read-only version of EVN that allows stakeholders and subject manager experts to search and navigation of the taxonomy and add reviewer comments; TopBraid EVN Tagger, which supports indexing of content through a user interface that displays the context for both the content and vocabulary and AutoClassifier, and add-on auto-categorization tool to EVN Tagger. TopBraid also offers what it calls a JumpStart package, which is a development (nonproduction) copy for building a networked vocabulary management system for a proof-of-concept project at a significantly reduced price. Additional data management products from TopQuadrant are TopBraid Reference Data Manager, TopBraid Insight (for data warehousing), and TopBraid Live (a business applications server).

Wordmap

Wordmap (www.wordmap.com) was launched in 1998 by the UK company of the same name, and in 2007 the taxonomy consultancy Earley Information Science, Inc. (based outside of Boston, Massachusetts) acquired Wordmap Inc. as a wholly owned subsidiary. There are three versions of Wordmap: Wordmap Enterprise, Wordmap Express, and Wordmap skuDB. Wordmap Enterprise is an Oracle database client–server application, which runs on a Windows, Linux, or Solaris server, and is accessed by users through Windows or with a Java-based browser user interface. Since Wordmap Enterprise uses an Oracle database for its repository, a separate Oracle license is required. Wordmap Express, introduced in 2010, has all the features of Wordmap Enterprise but is additionally available as SaaS (cloud hosted), and it comes packaged with an Oracle Express repository that requires no extra license fee. Wordmap skuDB, introduced in 2014, is designed specifically for product taxonomies, enabling management of complex attributes for terms/product categories and integration with product information management (PIM) systems. Wordmap skuDB is available only as SaaS, and can additionally export taxonomies to HTML.

Wordmap's features include the ability to display two taxonomies side by side with drag and drop, support for creating customized attributes and relationships (and the ability to turn on or off the relationship name display), support for multilingual taxonomies with translation designations, the generation of many kinds of reports, and the ability to set user access/privileges at various levels, including the individual node level. Wordmap also has a feature for mapping different taxonomies to each other, which could be used, for example, in creating a unified enterprise taxonomy. One of the unusual aspects of Wordmap Enterprise or Express is its nomenclature (which is different in Wordmap skuDB), including the following:

Wordset = concept, node, object
Lead word = preferred term

Members = nonpreferred terms
Physical relationships = hierarchical (BT/NT) relationships
Nonphysical relationships = associative (RT) relationships

Import formats include text, CSV, Excel, and XML, and the export formats are CSV and XML. In addition, Wordmap offers connectors to export to Oracle Endeca and SharePoint and also import from SharePoint. Finally, custom direct application access to Wordmap taxonomies is available through a Java API. Wordmap also sells a separate auto-classification software module, Intelligent Text Classifier.

Free and Open Source Software

There are several free and open source offerings of thesaurus software. They tend to have their origins in academic projects in computer science, information science, or library science. In addition to being free, these applications tend to have the advantage of being able to run on multiple platforms and yet can be installed and used by a single user. The editing features may be a little less standard and thus less intuitive. Additionally, documentation tends to be less, and support may be lacking compared with commercial software. Some free offerings of the previous decade are no longer available. While these products do not have as many features as commercial software, they are worth considering for long-term experimentation (unlike commercial demo software, they have no time limit), for use in nonprofit or low-budget projects, or by anyone with a strong interest in working with open source software.

TemaTres

A popular open source freeware for creating taxonomies and thesauri is TemaTres (www.vocabularyserver.com), which has its origins in the Library and Information Science program of the University of Buenos Aires, Argentina. It has been used by various nonprofit organizations and government agencies, and many example thesauri are available on the TemaTres website. The software, which has been available since the mid-2000s, is being maintained and updated by its lead developer, Diego Ferreyra, with the latest version, TemaTres 2.1, released in early 2016. It is web-based, which means it requires a PHP, MySQL, and HTTP web server, so it may not be the configuration that any independent taxonomist would set up and install at home. A demo server is available to try out, though.

Features include support for all thesaurus relationships and customized relationships based on the standard types, non-preferred terms and hidden labels (a subtype of nonpreferred), user-defined notes, categories for terms, various search capabilities, various report options including quality reports such as for orphan terms, multilingual thesaurus support, mapping of relations between vocabularies, batch deleting of terms, support for polyhierarchy, and support for SPARQL end points. The user interface is available in Brazilian, Portuguese, Catalan, Chinese (Simplified), Dutch, English, French, Italian, and Spanish. Unlike many commercial taxonomy management software applications, there is no split screen or pop-up window feature, so it is not possible to view the expandable/collapsible taxonomy hierarchy and selected term details at the same time. Rather, term details display in a new webpage, and then you click the back button to view the hierarchy again.

TemaTres uses the SKOS model, and since version 1.5, released in 2012, it has been compatible with ISO 25964. An issue is that duplicate terms can be created, but are detected only when running a quality report , and thus it appears as if thesaurus rules are not enforced. Rules are indeed enforced if the terms are not duplicates, but in version 2.0 duplicates can still be created too easily.

Import formats include plain tagged text, tab-indented text, and SKOS XML. Export formats are text (hierarchical or alphabetical lists) and various XML formats, including SKOS-Core, Zthes, Topic

Maps, WordPress XML, Metadata Authority MADS, Dublin Core, VDEX, BS 8723, SiteMap, and SQL. Related tools include TemaTres-View to integrate vocabularies with any web form; TemaTres Keywords Distiller, a simple keyword extraction tool; TemaTres Visual Vocabulary, a graphical visualization of terms and their relationships; TemaTres Web Publisher; and Skoser, a search and navigation tool for SKOS RDF format files.

VocBench

VocBench (vocbench.uniroma2.it) is, according to its website, "a web-based, multilingual, editing and workflow tool that manages thesauri, authority lists and glossaries." It was developed originally for the management of the AGROVOC thesaurus of the Food and Agriculture Organization (FAO) of the United Nations as a joint project of FAO, which is based in Rome, Italy, and the Artificial Intelligence Research group at the University of Rome Tor Vergata. AGROVOC, which has over 32,000 concepts in 21 languages, had been in a relational database, but with VocBench, the thesaurus was converted to the SKOS-XL format for use with linked data and alignment with other public vocabularies. The Artificial Intelligence Research group also developed a semantic extension for the Mozilla Firefox browser called Semantic Turkey, which is the back end for VocBench. Like TemaTres, users of VocBench tend to be nonprofit organizations, including international organizations, government agencies, and research institutes.

Although "ontologies" is not in the official description, VocBench is definitely an ontology development tool, not just for taxonomies and thesauri, yet it is also suited for hierarchical taxonomies. Its user interface features the familiar expandable hierarchical tree in the left pane and selected term details in the right pane. Different types of term details are accessed on different tabs, so you don't see all of the term details together. For example, there is a separate tab for definition, for associated relationships (related terms and semantic relationships), for hierarchical relationships, for notes, and so on. There is even a tab for linked data "Alignments," which show the equivalent term in the vocabularies of other organizations, via live URLs linking to those organizations' thesaurus websites. Term links to Wikipedia pages is another implementation of linked data. Other features include a tracking of history of changes made; a SPARQL editing tool; and workflow states with multiple term statuses, including proposed, validated, published, and deprecated. Vocabularies can be imported as RDF, and the export format is SKOS-XL.

VocBench is web based, with web server requirements of Apache Tomcat, MySQL, and OWLIM installed on a Sesame2 server, but if you don't have your own web server, you can still try out VocBench with a sandbox account on an available, hosted cloud version. As open source software, the source code is also available for download. The software has been successfully tested for use in Safari, Chrome, Firefox, and Internet Explorer browsers. The user interface is available in numerous languages. The software is being actively maintained with updates made about twice a year. (Version 2.3 is the latest to date as of this writing.) A 100-page PDF user manual in English with numerous screenshots is available, and there is also a VocBench user discussion group as a Google group.

ThManager

ThManager (thmanager.sourceforge.net) was developed by the Advanced Information Systems Laboratory of the Computer Science and Systems Engineering Department of the University of Zaragoza and GeoSpatiumLab S.L., both in Zaragoza, Spain. The software is multiplatform, running on a Java Runtime Environment. The user interface is available in English or Spanish. The thesauri are fully SKOS compatible, but import and export formats are limited to only SKOS XML. Following the SKOS standard, ThManager supports multilingual thesauri, including different language scripts, such as Cyrillic and Greek.

The thesaurus viewer has the typically intuitive display of an expandable hierarchy tree in the left pane and details of a selected term in the right pane, but the user interface of the thesaurus editor has some weaknesses. Instead of leaving the SKOS model in the background, the user interface follows the SKOS model too closely, displaying broader, narrower, and related concept links to term IDs rather than to term names/labels. The user can click on a term ID to call up a new navigation window to see the term names, but this is an added step.

As is the case sometimes for freeware, ThManager is not updated frequently. It was last significantly updated in 2006. Even for Windows 7 the installation requires a "portable" version due to an installation bug, since TheManager was not tested for Windows 7, and funds for further development at the time of this writing were lacking.[12] There is adequate documentation in English, though, and technical support questions receive responses.

Protégé Ontology Editor

Protégé (protege.stanford.edu) is actually an open source ontology editor, not a thesaurus management program, and unlike some commercial thesaurus/ontology software, Protégé is designed specifically for ontology modeling and not for creating thesauri or taxonomies. Nevertheless, it is sometimes used by taxonomists and is reasonably well known in the broader field of vocabularies and knowledge organizations systems. There are workshops, conferences, training, and several discussion groups supporting the Protégé user community. Protégé was developed by the Stanford Center for Biomedical Informatics Research at the Stanford University School of Medicine in the early 1990s and is most often used by scholars to create scientific ontologies. It is available for Windows, Mac OSX, and Linux and can run on other platforms with a Java Runtime Environment.

As Protégé is an ontology editor (not a thesaurus editor), one of the main drawbacks is that it does not have a standard feature for the equivalence relationship. Some taxonomists have developed work-arounds, though, and thus have successfully implemented nonpreferred terms in Protégé-developed thesauri, but it takes extra effort to learn and implement such methods. Taxonomists have claimed Protégé to be powerful, but it is not necessarily user-friendly or intuitive.[13] An SKOS editor plug-in for Protégé (code.google.com/p/skoseditor) facilitates the creation of standard thesauri, but the SKOS editor currently available may not be for the latest version of Protégé.

Other Software with Taxonomy Management Components

Since taxonomies are used in combination with certain other functions—indexing, document management, or search—software systems designed for these other purposes may also include a taxonomy management component or module. Taxonomy management is sometimes, but not always, a feature of the following:

- Metadata or cataloging software, especially for archives and libraries

- Content management and document management systems

- Records management software

- Automatic indexing and enterprise search and discovery software

The taxonomy management features of such integrated systems, however, may not comply with the standards. So, the eventual usefulness of the taxonomy in a final application may be limited.

Library and Archive Management Software

Library or archive management software may include thesaurus management components, although this is not always the case since libraries and archives typically utilize existing controlled vocabularies or taxonomies (such as Library of Congress Subject Headings, Library of Congress Thesaurus for Graphic Materials, or the Getty Thesauri).

Corporate library-management software vendor Soutron Global (www.soutronglobal.com) headquartered in Encinitas, California, and its affiliate Soutron Ltd. (www.soutron.com) in the United Kingdom offer a thesaurus software product, SoutronTHESAURUS. SoutronTHESAURUS is web based, supporting an unlimited number of remote users, and is available either internally installed or in a vendor-hosted option in a SaaS arrangement. The software supports user-defined relationships (in addition to the standard relationship types), multilingual thesauri (including non-Western character sets), and the ability to merge terms. Multiple related taxonomies can be maintained within a single domain. Thesauri can be imported from XML and exported to XML or CSV. Although SoutronTHESAURUS can be purchased as a stand-alone product in addition to being integrated with the Soutron Library Management System, the company makes no effort to market the thesaurus management software separately, and there is almost no information about it on its websites.

Library and archive software Adlib (www.adlibsoft.com) is distinguished for its thesaurus management capability. Adlib is sold by the Axiell Group, a leading European software company for archives, libraries, and museums, with headquarters in Sweden, which acquired the British company Adlib Information Systems in 2013. Each of the products, Adlib Archive, Adlib Library, and Adlib Museums, has the added feature for creating and editing thesauri, which the software can then use for cataloging archive documents, library materials, or museum objects. The thesaurus management feature of Adlib supports hierarchical, associative, and equivalence relationships; scope notes; and multiple-language term translations. Adlib software is available in Dutch, French, and German user interfaces, in addition to English.

Content Management Systems

Content management systems (CMSs), a category that includes enterprise content management, web content management, and document management software, are a logical place for integrating taxonomies. Indeed, some CMS products do claim to have "taxonomy" features, but they may be rather rudimentary tagging systems. According to content management and taxonomy consultant Lynda Moulton, "It is not common for any content management systems to be tightly integrated with advanced thesaurus management capabilities."[14]

As with library systems, though, it is more common to import taxonomies into a CMS than to create them within such systems. In general, a CMS should be thought of not as a system for building and managing taxonomies, but rather as an application in which a taxonomy can, and perhaps should, be implemented. Vendors of taxonomy management systems often provide connectors, APIs, or custom integration services to implement taxonomies in various CMSs. If, however, an organization has acquired a taxonomy from a third party (including a custom-developed taxonomy from a consultancy) and does not own taxonomy management software, the ability to make minor updates to the taxonomy within the CMS is important. Since a CMS is less likely to support thesaurus standard rules, updates to the taxonomy need to be done with care. Additional issues involving a taxonomy in a CMS may include the support and display of multilevel hierarchies and support for polyhierarchy.

Records Management Software

Electronic records management software, which can be considered a form of a CMS, is an area with more potential for thesaurus management features. Records managers, the users of such software, tend to have a library and information science background and thus may already have a familiarity with taxonomies. Furthermore, thesaurus capabilities are included in government-recommended guidelines for records management software. Records management is important not only in the financial and legal industries but also for government agencies. The National Archives and Records Administration has endorsed the 2002 and 2007 editions of the US Department of Defense records management application (RMA) standard (DoD 5015.2 STD). Adherence to the standard is required for all defense agencies and strongly encouraged for all other federal agencies. Among the nonmandatory features, Section C6.2.9 Retrieval Assistance states, "RMAs should have additional search-and-retrieval features, such as full-text search, to assist the user in locating records. The search utility should include the capability to create, modify, or import additional thesauri."[15] British and Australian national standards for records management software have similar specifications.

Since the thesaurus management capabilities of records management systems are not always sufficient, there are third-party thesaurus/classification management software vendors focused specifically on RMAs. Two Australian vendors take the lead in this records and information management market.

Synercon Group, headquartered in Australia and with subsidiary offices in London and Los Angeles, offers a.k.a. (www.a-k-a.co, presented as "information governance" software). The a.k.a. software package supports the creation of taxonomies/thesauri in accordance with the thesaurus standard ISO 25964, record classification schemes in accordance with business activity classifications standard of ISO 15489, and record retention and disposal schedules in accordance with the DIRKS (Designing and Implementing Records Keeping System) methodology, also a part of ISO 15489. The software exports are in CSV and XML formats. There are custom integration tools and also a connector available for the HP TRIM Records Management System. A.k.a is Windows-based client–server software and requires a Microsoft SQL database. It can also be installed on a single PC.

Another Australian vendor, Active Classification Solutions (www. acs121.com), sells One-2-One, which is essentially Windows-based thesaurus software with additional features to support records management. It includes disposal maintenance features and connectors to integrate with electronic documents and records management systems, including Objective ECM, OpenText eDOCS DM, HP Trim, and HP Records Manager.

Data Management Software

Large database management systems, and the variations of data warehousing, master data management systems, and big data systems, may also make use of taxonomies, whether they are called that or not, and thus have taxonomy management capabilities. These include both general and vertical market-specific applications. For example, IBM's InfoSphere Master Data Management solution includes a Reference Data Management Hub feature. "Reference data" in IBM products means taxonomy or ontology.[16] Oracle offers taxonomy or thesaurus management within various vertical market software solutions, such as the Thesaurus Management System. (TMS). The Thesaurus Management System is part of the Oracle health science application suite, aimed particularly at managing data for the drug development process, and provides taxonomy management capabilities within the Oracle Data as a Service (DaaS) for Marketing product.

Microsoft SharePoint

In some respects, Microsoft SharePoint software is in a class by itself. Used widely by many organizations as their intranet platform, it was originally developed as client–server based collaboration software, but its features and utilization quickly evolved to allow its use as a basic document/content management system in organizations whose needs are not great enough or critical enough to require a dedicated document management system, content management system, or records management system. SharePoint, which is accessed by users via a web browser, is available both in client–server installations and SaaS, in the latter case as part of the Office 365 suite for businesses.

For its purposes as a content management system, SharePoint supports the assignment of metadata to documents or other files uploaded to SharePoint. Then other users can search or filter on the metadata terms to find the desired documents. Filtering on the metadata terms can be done either by sorting on selected metadata "columns" in a displayed table of documents within a single "library" or data list, or by selecting terms from within dynamically displayed facets (also called "refinements"), to limit search results.

While earlier versions of SharePoint allowed users to assign metadata to documents, with the release of SharePoint 2010 and its new Managed Metadata Service feature SharePoint also supports taxonomies for metadata. The managed metadata or taxonomies in SharePoint can have deep hierarchies, nonpreferred terms, and scope notes/definitions, and there is a type-ahead feature to match newly created terms against existing terms in the taxonomy. An added feature is custom sorting of the display order of terms. Taxonomies are maintained in a "Term Store" that can be shared on different SharePoint "sites" across the organization. (Managed Metadata Service and Term Store are essentially synonymous.) It is also possible to import a simple hierarchical taxonomy (without nonpreferred terms) into the Term Store as a CSV file. The ability to create and edit taxonomies in the Term Store requires administrative permissions, but the interface is easy to use. Figure 5.10 shows the editing of taxonomy terms in SharePoint's Term Store.

While SharePoint could be considered as a kind of content management system that supports the creation and editing of taxonomies within the software, the taxonomy management features are limited. As of SharePoint 2013, there is no enforcement of standard taxonomy rules, so it is possible to create circular relationships, duplicate terms, and so forth. For example, the same term could

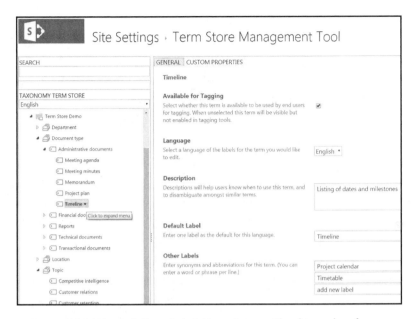

Figure 5.10 Microsoft SharePoint's Term Store, with a hierarchy of terms partially expanded, a term, "Timeline," selected, and that term's editable details in the right pane. Hovering over a selected term activates a down arrow that when clicked opens up a context menu to create a narrow term or perform other functions

be created as both a preferred term and a nonpreferred term to another preferred term. Polyhierarchy can be created, but requires the "Reuse Terms" function, whereas the default is to create two separate terms with the same name. Furthermore, polyhierarchy is only permitted across different taxonomy hierarchies or facets, whereas often it is desired for a term within a hierarchy or facet. Also, SharePoint does not support associative relationships, only hierarchical. Nevertheless, Share Point's Term Store feature is adequate for the creation of relatively small hierarchical or faceted taxonomies for the typical content management users of SharePoint (either a small- or medium-sized organization or just a department within a larger enterprise). If a large taxonomy is required, it's much better to create it in a dedicated thesaurus management software and then import it into SharePoint through the SharePoint connectors available from many thesaurus software vendors.

Taxonomies can be created in SharePoint, using either of two distinct implementations: (1) importing taxonomies into the Term Store, which enables the taxonomy terms to be used for manual tagging by SharePoint users who upload documents, and (2) integration of taxonomies into SharePoint search, which may additionally utilize third-party auto-categorization technologies, but does not have to. A comprehensive taxonomy with sufficient nonpreferred terms may achieve acceptable results without the addition of auto-categorization software, but auto-categorization technologies will significantly improve the accuracy of search results. SharePoint has a built-in search feature, which, if integrated with a taxonomy, supports dynamically displayed facets and their values, including any hierarchies within facets. These are shown in a left-hand margin "Refinement" pane, by which users may filter their search results. Without taxonomies, the Refinement pane shows only default metadata as facets, such as author, date, and tags of uncontrolled keywords.

The same taxonomy may be used in both the Term Store for manual tagging and column filters and in SharePoint Search and its resulting refinements. It is also possible to use different taxonomies, such as a small one for the Term Store and a larger one, with many nonpreferred terms, in SharePoint Search. When creating or importing a taxonomy in the Term Store, the taxonomist has the option of making the taxonomy available for SharePoint Search. Often organizations, which prefer to use auto-categorization and do minimal manual tagging, will utilize taxonomies for search only and not bother with the Term Store. A taxonomy created in dedicated thesaurus management software could be imported to the Term Store, SharePoint Search, or both.

Automated Indexing and Search Software

Like CMSs, automatic indexing/auto-categorization/enterprise search software may or may not have taxonomy support. Even when it does, it rarely includes full-featured thesaurus management capabilities. As the emphasis in these systems is on automated information retrieval, their components for taxonomy creation and management also tend to be automated or minimally manual, although there are some exceptions. Chapter 7 covers automated indexing software in more detail.

Integrated Systems Conclusions

The technology and features in the various integrated software systems discussed here are focused, not on taxonomy creation, but rather on one of the other areas of information management, search and discovery, automated indexing, records management, or web publishing. Thus the capabilities and ease of use of the taxonomy management features are generally inferior to those of dedicated thesaurus software and may vary greatly from one product to another since they are competing primarily in other areas. You should consider these other capabilities carefully with respect to your organization's requirements. Otherwise, you may be paying for features that you don't need or missing features that you do need or will need as your taxonomy and its application grow.

Endnotes

1. Lynda Moulton, email to author, October 28, 2009.
2. Darin Stewart, *Building Enterprise Taxonomies* (Portland, OR: Mokita Press, 2008), 137.
3. "List of Mind Mapping Software," Wikipedia, accessed October 24, 2015, en.wikipedia.org/wiki/List_of_concept-_and_mind-mapping_software
4. Postings to Taxonomy Community of Practice discussion group, "Subject: mind mapping software?" April 21–22 and July 10, 2009, groups.yahoo.com/neo/groups/TaxoCoP, and the additional suggestion of The Brain by Lynda Moulton, email to author, October 28, 2009.
5. Definition of SKOS from "SKOS Simple Knowledge Organization System - Home Page" on the World Wide Web Consortium (W3C) website, accessed October 19, 2015 www.w3.org/2004/02/skos, updated December 13, 2012.

6. Theresa Regli, "Taxonomy management, or BSM? It's all semantics," CMS Watch Trendwatch Blog, July 16, 2007, accessed December 20, 2015, www.cmswatch.com/ Trends/972-Taxonomy-management,-or-BSM?-It%E2%80%99s-allsemantics

7. The migration of the Willpower Thesaurus Software directory to the TaxoBank website is explained in a blog post by the author, "Taxonomy Software Directories," The Accidental Taxonomist Blog (April 11, 2014), accessed December 20, 2015, www.accidental-taxonomist.blogspot.com/2014/04/taxonomy-software-directories.html

8. Marjorie Hlava, email to author, January 23, 2015.

9. Ashleigh N. Faith, an ontologist, wrote "lightweight ontology is where most taxonomies are headed" to the discussion thread "Taxonomy management software in use" on the Taxonomy Community of Practice LinkedIn group, April 2015, accessed December 20, 2015, www.linkedin.com/groups/1750/1750-5978204693472489476

10. LGOSystems sales team, email to author, January 30, 2015.

11. Michael Wetzel (Managing Director, Coreon), email to author, October 26, 2015.

12. Jesús Barrera Francés, Project Manager, GeoSpatiumLab, email to author, October 22, 2015.

13. Postings to the Taxonomy Community of Practice discussion group, "subject "protégé," November 19–20, 2008, 20, 2008. finance.groups.yahoo.com/group/TaxoCoP

14. Lynda Moulton, email to author, May 29, 2009.

15. Department of Defense Directive 5015.02-STD: *Electronic Records Management Software Applications Design Criteria Standard* (April 25, 2007), 114, accessed December 20, 2015, www.dtic.mil/whs/directives/corres/pdf/501502std.pdf

16. Ralph Tamlyn, former chief taxonomist and IT architect at IBM, email to author, August 24, 2015.

Chapter 6

Taxonomies for Human Indexing

Taxonomies: Find what you really want.
                    —Mike Gardner

As explained in Chapter 1, support of indexing is one of the main purposes or applications of a taxonomy, with the other purposes being retrieval support and organization/navigation support. There are different methods of indexing, and you need to consider these differences when developing a taxonomy. The two fundamental kinds of indexing are human (or manual) and automated. This chapter will discuss issues pertaining to creating taxonomies for use by human indexers, and Chapter 7 will deal with particularities of taxonomies for automated indexing. Sometimes the same taxonomy will be used for both human and automated indexing, a situation that requires attention to many issues and possibly a few trade-offs.

What Is Human Indexing?

Before considering the issues involved in developing a taxonomy for human indexers, we need to have an understanding of who indexers are and what they do.

Tagging, Cataloging, Classifying, or Indexing

When we speak of human indexing with a taxonomy, we are referring to analyzing content and assigning appropriate descriptive terms selected from a taxonomy. Within a given organization, this process might not be called indexing but could be referred to as tagging, keywording, classifying, or cataloging. There are subtle differences in these designations.

Tagging, sometimes called *keywording*, by definition does not necessarily imply using a taxonomy (controlled vocabulary) but rather could involve creating new terms as desired with little or no authority control. However, since the designations of tagging and keywording are more familiar outside the library science profession and the term *indexing* has its own ambiguities, there are organizations that choose to call the process of assigning controlled vocabulary terms as tagging or keywording. What the process is called may also depend on who does it. While there are people with the job title "indexer," there are no "taggers" or "keyworders." Tagging or keywording, when described as such, is often done by people whose main job function is not indexing but rather something else, such as content creation or editing. The designations "tagging" and "keywording" imply a degree of simplicity, a task that can be done by someone without formal training in indexing. How simple it actually is depends on the content, the taxonomy, and the indexing policies. Tagging may also differ from indexing by including tags for additional metadata, such as date or source, and not just descriptive terms.[1]

Cataloging has a more specialized meaning and is generally restricted to the organization and description of library materials (both physical and digital), archive documents, and museum collections. Cataloging often involves assigning descriptive subject terms from a taxonomy (subject cataloging), but it also includes recording other metadata that may be bibliographic, may refer to source type and history, or may include a physical description (descriptive cataloging). Additionally, when cataloging physical materials, an important part of the task is classification, the assigning of a unique locator, such as a call number, to the material, because the material can have only one physical location (a shelf, file box, display case, room, etc.). Essentially there is overlap between cataloging and indexing. Cataloging often, but not always, includes subject indexing, but it also involves more. In any case, subject catalogers do utilize taxonomies, usually called authority files or thesauri.

Classification, which is not limited to physical library materials, means assigning an item to a class. Assigning organisms' names in a biological taxonomy or naming scientific or technical concepts and grouping them is also called classification. Classification is actually different from indexing or tagging in that an item can only go into one class. In classifying, you ask, "Where does this item go?" whereas in indexing, tagging, or subject cataloging, you ask, "What terms describe this item?"

Indexing really means to create an index, a list of terms, each of which indicates or points to (the original meaning of *index*) where to find information/content on a desired subject. Traditionally an index appears as a browsable, alphabetical list that you can run your index finger through. Of course, in the online environment, the browsable index may not always be displayed to the end user, but the process of indexing—that is, assigning index terms to content—may be the same.

Indexing With a Taxonomy

Indexing content that is diverse, often from multiple sources, and also spread out over time requires the use of a taxonomy (in the broad sense of a controlled vocabulary) in order to maintain consistency. Indexers may not remember exactly which index terms they chose for similar topics in the past, but a taxonomy ensures that their choices will be consistent. The use of a taxonomy also enables consistent indexing by multiple indexers who are needed when there is a large quantity of content or time-sensitive content. Consistent indexing is necessary to enable comprehensive retrieval on a given search term.

For indexing with a taxonomy, the taxonomist completes the taxonomy (although it will of course be subject to revision) prior to any indexing other than test indexing. Then the indexer (or indexers) uses the taxonomy by linking its predefined terms to the content. The indexing is usually performed using a software system that allows access to the taxonomy, through browsing or searching, validating the indexer's choice of terms while also connecting to the repository of content being indexed or at least to references (URLs, URIs, file paths, etc.) to the content items. The indexing software may or may not connect with the taxonomy management software. This kind of indexing is sometimes called database indexing because some form of database management system is used to correlate index terms with documents. Each indexable document or media file is treated as a distinct database record, which has index terms and other metadata in its various database record fields, and users query the database to obtain their search results.

This type of indexing typically deals with numerous documents, articles, files, or webpages, and each is usually indexed as a unit. Thus, index terms may be assigned to reflect the most important concepts or names in the document or file as a whole, rather than at a more granular paragraph or sentence level. A large document may be broken into defined sections. The indexer may be expected to index a certain number of documents or document-section records per hour.

The indexing of multiple documents with taxonomy terms results in a dynamically growing list of documents for each term. Typically, the end user is offered options for sorting the list of retrieved results, such as by date or relevancy. The option for relevancy opens the possibility that the indexer could "weight" the assigned index terms. When choosing a term from the taxonomy, the indexer may also be able to designate the term as *primary* or *secondary* (or *major* or *minor*) by means of a scroll menu or check box. Then, when an end user searches on a term from the taxonomy, the retrieved documents that were indexed with the term as *primary* will sort to the top of a relevancy-ranked list, above documents that were indexed with the term as *secondary*.

Database indexing, sometimes known as *open* indexing, differs in several ways from back-of-the-book indexing, which can be called *closed* indexing.[2] Book indexing is "closed" because the indexing comes to a close once all the pages have been analyzed and indexed. The index itself can be finalized and thus usually goes into print as part of the book. Closed indexing usually does not involve using a taxonomy/controlled vocabulary, and the indexer will try to come up with terms that reflect the language of the work. Open indexing, on the other hand, usually involves a taxonomy, and the indexer is challenged to translate from the author's choice of words to the preferred terms in the taxonomy. Book indexing also tends to be more granular, to the level of detail of paragraphs or even sentences, compared with open indexing, which takes place predominantly at the document level.

Who Are Indexers?

Indexers of open/database indexes, who are making use of taxonomies, vary in terms of their backgrounds, degree of training, and subject specialization. They could be taxonomists, information specialists, librarians (especially corporate librarians), or subject area specialists with an advanced degree in a specific field. Some organizations have taxonomist-indexers who take on a combination of taxonomy management and indexing tasks, while other organizations clearly split the roles. A large volume of indexing usually requires a number of dedicated indexers, however, and the largest commercial periodical database indexes have at times employed dozens of indexers. Since employers of full-time database indexers are few, they cannot expect their new-hire indexers to have previous indexing experience. Thus, these employers usually provide thorough on-the-job training for such indexers. Indexers might have a degree in the subject matter of the content being indexed or a general humanities or social sciences degree if they are indexing nonspecialized content. They may work in-house, or they may work remotely if the indexing system and taxonomy database support remote access.

If remote access is supported, then independent contractors may also be used. However, unlike closed indexing, which can involve a different indexer for each book, it is only practical to have open indexing done by freelancers if they are long-term, steady contractors. Indexing is less costly to the organization and more profitable to the indexer if speed and efficiency can be attained, which takes time and experience. There is a long learning curve, not only to become proficient in using an organization's unique indexing system but, more important, to become familiar with the terms in the taxonomy. An indexer who knows the most commonly used terms in a taxonomy spends less time navigating to desired terms and will also index more correctly. This can be an obstacle to new freelance indexers. Freelance indexing is profitable to the indexer who can work quickly, because contract indexing rates tend to pay per record (document/file) indexed rather than hourly. The rate for database indexing is comparable to the book indexing rate.[3] A document may comprise multiple pages, but unless the article is unusually long or scholarly, the depth of indexing and number of index terms assigned to a periodical-type article are similar to those assigned to a single page in a book.

For long-term, large-volume database indexing, some publishers have found it cost-effective to outsource to editorial service firms overseas, such as in India or the Philippines, which have staff with sufficient English language skills for the task. Detailed documentation and training need to be provided in these cases, where the publisher lacks direct contact with the indexer. Instead, the publisher needs to maintain close contact with the overseas indexing supervisor.

Finally, indexing is sometimes performed by people whose primary task is not indexing but rather some other content-related duty, such as writing, editing, or content management, especially if the quantity of indexing is not great enough to constitute a full-time job. Nevertheless, these people should be trained in the use of the organization's taxonomy, indexing techniques, and policies, with emphasis on the policies. Lack of training, which often happens with a supplemental task, will likely result in poor indexing.

When to Use Human Indexers

Automated indexing, described in Chapter 7, is becoming increasingly popular for large indexing projects. For most other situations, the greater accuracy provided by trained human indexers is more important than speed and volume. Humans can identify concepts, not just words or strings of words, and they can discern whether a concept is significant and worthy of being indexed. Obviously, they cannot index as quickly as automated systems, but if the volume of content is not overwhelming and indexing quality is of great importance, then human indexers are preferred. The following factors favor human indexers:

- A high emphasis on quality and accuracy in indexing and retrieval

- A manageable volume of documents

- The presence of nontext files for indexing (images, video, audio)

- Content that is varied in document types/formats and varied in subject areas (making it more difficult to "train" automated systems)

- A corporate culture that is more comfortable with hiring, training, and managing employees or contractors and/or developing its own human indexing software than with making a large financial investment in externally purchased technology

Scholarly, academic, scientific, medical, and sometimes legal documents are more likely to be indexed by human indexers as these are areas in which indexing accuracy takes precedence. Publishers, which are the creators of content, also tend to favor human indexing, since humans can easily index at the same time as they are editing or publishing a document. If the volume of content is relatively small, then human indexing is cost-effective for any subject area or industry. For indexing any nontext media, humans are needed to assign index terms, tags, or other metadata because automated indexing relies on text-based algorithms and analysis. Automatic image-recognition technologies have recently emerged, but they are quite rudimentary and can only suggest possible people, places, or topics, which still requires human review to be accurate and comprehensive. As multimedia is an increasingly significant form of content, the role of human indexers will remain significant.

Terms, Relationships, and Notes for Indexers

When creating a taxonomy for use by human indexers, you need to pay attention to certain issues with respect to terms, relationships between terms, and notes for terms.

Preferred and Nonpreferred Terms for Indexers

Although you should create preferred terms that are appropriate for end users, nonpreferred terms can take into consideration the indexers as well. In the rare cases of a taxonomy that will be viewed by the indexers only and not by end users (because they are accessing it only by a search box), you can consider the indexers' expectations for preferred terms, too. In such cases, factors to consider include whether indexers are subject matter experts, who expect certain concepts and preferred term names for them, or whether the indexers are generalists.

As for nonpreferred terms, certain kinds of terms are particularly helpful for human indexers. If the indexer will access an alphabetical list of terms that combines both nonpreferred and preferred terms (even if simply by means of truncated start-of-word searching), nonpreferred terms should begin with a word likely to be looked up alphabetically (i.e., a keyword). Consequently, inverted terms can be useful as nonpreferred terms, as in the following example:

libraries, public USE **public libraries**

If the indexer reads a document about public libraries, the first word that comes to the indexer's mind would likely be *libraries*. Therefore, the indexer types in *libraries*. Depending on the design of the indexing software, the indexer could retrieve the exact broader term of **libraries**, which could be expanded to reveal its narrower terms, a list of all terms with the word *libraries* within them, or a short list of terms that start with the word *libraries*. (The indexer may even have the option to choose the display type.) In the case where the more specific nonpreferred term **libraries, public** appears and the indexer selects it, the corresponding preferred term is applied to the document. Accessing the preferred term via the nonpreferred term can be more efficient, as a single-step action, than first selecting the broader term **libraries** and then calling up its term details screen to see what its narrower terms are.

If the end user can see the nonpreferred terms (which is less often the case in the hypertext environment), then there may be nonpreferred terms that you want the indexer but not the end users to see. Examples include inverted terms or older names of terms (names that are no longer used but are still familiar to indexers). In any case, a different kind of equivalence relationship would be appropriate, such as USE-I and UF-I, as discussed in Chapter 4. Another type of nonpreferred term that is useful specifically for indexers is what we might call a shortcut. It is an acronym, abbreviation, or code for a commonly used term that indexers understand within a term type, category, or facet but that is not suitable for end users or in automated indexing due to its potential ambiguity.

A good example of this would be a two-letter state or country abbreviation limited to geographic terms; for outside the geographic context, two letters, such as *ma*, would be ambiguous. A shortcut could also be an internal custom abbreviation for industry types, if there is a short list of industries, or action types, or any term limited to a vocabulary type. The purpose of these shortcut types of nonpreferred terms is to save the indexer keystrokes and make the indexing go faster. For example, there could be a facet for business actions, limited to around 50 to 60 terms, and each could have a three-letter shortcut code, such as **ACQ** for **acquisitions, divestitures & mergers**, **FRE** for **financial results & earning**s, **NPS** for **new products/services**, and **ORD** for **orders & contracts**. The idea is that the shortcuts should be easy to memorize by virtue of being logical and limited in number.

Term Relationship for Indexers

Relationships between terms, even if not as efficient as nonpreferred terms in directing the indexer to the best preferred term, are also very helpful for navigating a taxonomy. In addition to guiding indexers to the desired term, the set of relationships for a given term also provides the indexer with a better understanding of the intended meaning and scope of the term.

It is often the policy in indexing to use the most specific terms appropriate, and hierarchical relationships can guide the indexer to the most specific term. Only by means of hierarchical relationships or a hierarchical display can an indexer be certain which is the most specific term available. Additional broader terms may or may not be suitable for indexing the given content, but if they are, the indexer can also benefit from seeing these relationships.

Associative relationships are also highly useful to indexers, who otherwise might overlook the existence of an additional appropriate term—or perhaps what turns out to be a more appropriate term than the one first selected. This could be the case with related terms, such as a process and an agent, an action and a product, or a discipline and an object. For example, for a document about programming software, the indexer initially selects the product-type term **software** but then sees the related action term **programming** and realizes that indeed programming is the focus of the article so decides to select that term instead. Similarly, for an article about weather predictions, the indexer initially selects the object term **weather** but then sees the related discipline term of **meteorology** and recognizes it as the more appropriate term. For the benefit of indexers, associative relationships should be as comprehensive as practical. Chapter 4 discusses how many associative relationships to make.

Term Notes

As mentioned in Chapter 3, taxonomy terms may have short descriptive notes attached to them. Whether they are scope notes aimed at both end-use searchers and indexers or indexer notes visible only to the indexers, these notes are very useful to the indexers. Even if end users do not bother to look at scope notes, indexers who work daily with the taxonomy know where and how to view a term's notes. Thus, even though scope notes may be for dual audiences, the primary readers of scope notes tend to be the indexers.

Indexer notes, which are aimed only at indexers and thus displayed only to indexers, may be similar to scope notes in their content and style, or they may explain more. Often indexer notes focus on usage, with instructions from the taxonomist to the indexer on when or how to use the term in indexing. A typical usage note for indexers might be "Use a more specific term if possible" for a relatively broad term. Here is a specific example of an indexer note in a thesaurus that also uses scope notes, from the Gale/Cengage Learning controlled vocabulary:

> **African American churches**
> Indexer Notes: Use this term primarily for articles related to the church as an organization. For African American church buildings, please use this term and Church buildings.[4]

Although this explanation could certainly serve as a scope note, it may have been decided that such instructions were unnecessarily complex for the end-user searchers of this particular resource.

Indexer notes can also give brief explanatory information for a specific term that is not about scope or usage. This is particularly the case for a name of an organization or a technical or scholarly concept that is not widely known and therefore not likely familiar to an indexer but that would be the term chosen by the searcher who wanted to look up this topic. This information is certainly helpful, if not necessary, for the indexer, who cannot be expected to be thoroughly knowledgeable on all the topics to index, especially if the content is broad in scope.

In conclusion, when creating taxonomy terms for human indexers, it is best to have (1) supportive nonpreferred terms, including phrase inversions and shortcuts; (2) extensive relationships between terms; and (3) indexer-focused term notes for clarification.

Taxonomy Structure and Indexing Interface

If human indexers will use a taxonomy, then the broader taxonomy structure and display may include features of which human indexers can take advantage. Maintaining distinct vocabulary or authority files can make access to and usage of the vocabularies more logical to the indexers. Although not common, secondary-level subdivision terms, which allow more precise precoordination of concepts, could be supported. Additionally, how the taxonomy is displayed and how the indexer accesses it are matters of concern.

Distinct Vocabularies and Authority Files

The organization of terms into distinct subvocabularies, facets, or authority files can be helpful for indexers, especially in ensuring thoroughness of indexing. If the end-user interface breaks the taxonomy out into more than one vocabulary or facet (such as topics, organization names, industries, locations, and actions), then the indexer's view of the taxonomy should similarly be broken out into the same vocabularies or facets for a consistent perspective with that of end users. Even if the end user sees only a simple search box, there still should be term-type distinctions for the indexer. The segmentation of multiple different vocabularies makes it easier for the indexer to look up terms, especially in alphabetical browse lists and when named entities are involved.

Distinct vocabularies also aid in enforcing indexing policy to support consistent indexing. For example, an editorial policy might call for indexing individual names of people, places, companies, and organizations, but with a limit of four each per document, and might also require at least two topic terms, but no more than five, per document. Maintaining separate vocabulary files for each of these types makes it easier to meet the indexing criteria. Furthermore, customization of the indexing software could enforce the editorial policy.

Finally, by maintaining distinct vocabularies or authority files, you can also support distinct policies for maintaining each vocabulary and manage indexer involvement in that maintenance. For topical terms, for example, indexers may be required to use only the terms provided, but for named entities they might be permitted to enter new candidate terms and use them immediately for indexing prior to taxonomist approval. Some files in your taxonomy might permit this kind of overriding, while others would not. If you have human indexers and separate facets or vocabularies, you could conceivably support having more than one term with the same name, each in a distinct facet or vocabulary type. Examples are the term **French** in a language facet and **French** in a people or nationality facet, **churches** in a places or structures facet and **churches** in an organizations facet, or **mergers** in a topics facet and **mergers** in an events/business activities facet. Automated indexing would not necessarily make the correct distinction, but human indexers can.

Structured Indexing and Subdivisions

Some commercial periodical index databases, such as Gale Info-Trac and the Readers' Guide to Periodical Literature, support what is called structured indexing or second-level indexing, which is a form of precoordination. Structured indexing makes use of a secondary controlled vocabulary set of what are called subdivisions, which serve to narrow or qualify the main term for more refined retrieval results. Although sometimes called "subheadings," they should not be confused with narrower terms. At Gale, a part of Cengage Learning, they are known as "topical scope designators." In the Reader's Guide to Periodical Literature, they have been called "centered headings," because in the print version of the index, they display centered within the page. Structured indexing is also used in Library of Congress Subject Headings, so it is commonly seen in library online public access catalogs. An example is as follows:

Alzheimer's Disease—Diagnosis

The first term in the sequence, in this case **Alzheimer's Disease**, is called the heading, and the next term, **Diagnosis**, is the subdivision, because the content indexed with the heading is further "subdivided" based on various subdivision terms, which may include **treatment, demographics**, **genetic aspects**, **case studies**, and others. This is *not* the same as a broader term and a narrower term; **diagnosis** is *not* a narrower term for **Alzheimer's Disease**. Rather, a subdivision acts as a kind of modifier. Indexing policy may require that the indexer always use subdivisions for certain headings, unless the content is a general discussion of the topic so that main headings will display multiple subdivisions in the index. Subdivisions function in a similar manner to subentries in a back-of-the-book index, allowing the user to narrow a search result with prescribed taxonomy terms. Some systems support the use of third- and even fourth-level subdivisions, assuming there is sufficient material indexed at the second level. An example is as follows:

Massachusetts—History—Local

Subdivision terms, which in the two preceding examples are **Diagnosis**, **History**, and **Local**, are typically controlled vocabulary terms themselves, maintained in their own vocabulary lists. Thus, as a taxonomist, you might maintain a controlled vocabulary file of standard subdivisions. Typically, subdivisions are classified, and certain headings use certain subdivisions. For example, the subdivision **Diagnosis** is used only with headings that are types of diseases, but **History** could be used with places or any topics (including diseases).

Structured indexing can yield more precise retrieval results, but to be accurate, structured indexing requires human indexers. Thus, if you are making use of human indexers, you might consider implementing structured indexing. However, the indexing software and the end-user search interface need to be designed and developed to support structured indexing. A generic database management system with simple index-term fields would not be adequate for structured indexing.

Taxonomy Display and Access

How a taxonomy is displayed and how it can be searched are also important considerations for indexers, enabling them to find the terms they need quickly. Since the indexing interface may be designed even before there are any indexers, the taxonomist may be the one to provide input into the indexing interface design. Desired display features would include the following:

- A searchable alphabetical list of terms, displaying the section of the alphabet starting with a truncated search—it may have a toggle option to display both nonpreferred and preferred terms or to display preferred terms only

- The option to browse the hierarchical display of the taxonomy

- Hyperlinks leading from nonpreferred terms to their corresponding preferred terms

- Details of a selected preferred term (also called the term record), including all its relationships (BT, NT, RT) and notes, to display in a new window or pane

Indexers benefit from being able to browse terms alphabetically. A hierarchical display alone, which can guide a user to a more specific term of interest, may be less appropriate for indexers than it is for end-use searchers. End users might need guidance in coming up with concepts, whereas skilled indexers usually can identify the concepts to describe the content that they are indexing but often need references to the appropriate preferred terms. If the taxonomy is very small, however, and the entire hierarchy can fit on one browsable page/screen, then there is no need to have an alphabetical display in addition to the hierarchical display.

Efficient methods of searching for terms in the taxonomy should be made available to the indexer, including options for truncated or start-of-word searching and word-within-a-term-phrase searching. The indexing software interface should also be optimized for ease, speed, and accuracy in indexing. For example, common operations should have keyboard shortcuts and not always require the use of a mouse. If indexers have memorized certain index terms, they should be able to enter these into the index fields with validation, rather than being required to browse the taxonomy every time to pick a term. Of course, what methods are "efficient" varies with the individual. Different indexers may prefer different approaches, depending on their experience or cognitive style.

The term record, or the standard thesaurus display for details of a term, and the relationship abbreviations in particular may not make much sense for an end user, but for an indexer they provide clear and useful information. The display to the indexer may be quite similar to that displayed to the taxonomist. Following is an example of a term with its "details" that are useful for an indexer:

Water supply
    SN **The supply of public potable water**
    UF **Water utilities**
    UF **Water works**
    BT **Utilities**
    NT **Reservoirs**
    NT **Water mains**
    NT **Water towers**

When indexers are certain they have found the correct term, they add it to the record without further consideration, but if they are unsure of a term's appropriateness, they will check the term details to see any nonpreferred, broader, narrower, and related terms, and they will also check for any scope notes or indexer notes.

Taxonomy Updates and Quality Control

A taxonomy used by human indexers presents particular concerns with respect to two interrelated issues: updating the taxonomy and maintaining indexing consistency and quality.

Communication and Updates

Maintaining and updating a taxonomy used by human indexers requires communication in both directions: from the taxonomist(s) to the indexers and from the indexers to the taxonomist(s). As the taxonomist who is continually updating the taxonomy, you need to inform the indexers of newly added terms, term changes, merging of terms, or splitting of terms. Meanwhile, the indexers need a method of informing you, the taxonomist, that there is a need for a new term, based on a new concept appearing in the content, or a need for additional nonpreferred terms or term relationships, because an existing term is difficult to find.

The taxonomist does not necessarily have to inform the indexer of every new term, especially not every new named entity term (person names, company names, etc.). New topical subjects, along with changes in such terms, however, are more significant, and the taxonomist should mention their availability. In addition to new and changed terms, other information regularly communicated to indexers might be suggested combinations or sets of terms for indexing certain new or recurring subjects or issues, whether current events or new topics from a newly acquired set of content. This communication can be in any form that is practical for the organization, such as an email distribution list, bulletins posted in an intranet, or collaboration workspace.

Communication in the other direction, from the indexers to the taxonomist(s), is also necessary. Indexers are often the first to notice new concepts appearing in the content, so they should have a method to suggest new terms. While this could be by email or through an intranet/collaboration bulletin, even more effective for gaining indexer input is to have a method for suggesting or nominating terms right within the indexing software interface. Sometimes, rather than suggesting a new concept/term, an indexer may want to suggest a new term name for an existing concept, to be considered either as a change or merely as a nonpreferred term. Although less likely, indexers might even suggest additional term relationships, based on their understanding of term usage from the texts being indexed. These more complex suggestions from indexers could be communicated either through a notes/messaging field in the indexing software or through email or collaboration bulletins.

Maintaining Indexing Quality

Human indexers need comprehensive indexing policy guidelines and training in order to perform consistent, accurate indexing.

Editorial Policy for Indexers

Usually the taxonomists who create the taxonomy are also those who write the policy on how to use it. At the very least, in writing indexing policy, taxonomists work closely with technical writers who document how to use the indexing software. Indexing policy would include the following:

- Criteria for determining whether a subject or name is sufficiently relevant for indexing

- The level of detail for indexing: how much information needs to be present on a given topic to make it worthy of being indexed

- The number of terms to assign to any given document and whether terms of certain types or facets must always be assigned

- The permissibility of combinations of certain terms

- The permissibility or requirement of using both a term and its broader term

- A threshold number of sibling narrower terms, at which point the broader term should be used instead (e.g., **apples, oranges, bananas, grapes**, or use instead the broader term **fruit**)

- Editorial style conventions (forms of entry) for taxonomy terms, to aid the indexer in looking up terms and in creating candidate terms

- If a weighting system is used for assigned index terms, the criteria for choosing primary versus secondary weights and whether the majority of assigned terms are expected to be at the primary or secondary level

The editorial policy for indexers should be comprehensive enough, so it is clear what constitutes correct versus incorrect indexing. Indexing is somewhat subjective, and two well-trained indexers will not index everything identically, but they should be close. A clear indexing policy is necessary, both to identify indexing errors and to prevent them from recurring.

Training for Indexers

An indexing supervisor or senior indexers typically train new indexers, but the trainer could be a taxonomist. If the indexing operation is completely new or there is just one indexer, then the responsibility for indexer training is most likely to fall on the taxonomist. An important part of training is instruction in the indexing policy, but if the new indexers are inexperienced, then training will also involve basic instruction in indexing principles, such as the goal to capture the "aboutness" of a document rather than matching words in the text to taxonomy terms. Another important part of training is reviewing sample indexing and providing feedback. Initial indexing can be on sample documents (which must be carefully chosen for their representative nature) and then, when performance is satisfactory, on live documents. Even live indexing requires monitoring and checking for a period of time, as the diversity of documents that require indexing might bring up questions not covered in the sample indexing.

Taxonomy Improvements

If policy and training are sufficient, continued inaccuracies in indexing can indicate a need for improvements in the taxonomy. The work of all indexers, even experienced indexers, should be periodically reviewed, not so much for the purpose of providing individual feedback but for overall quality control. Indexing results can be spot-checked, but statistics on term usage in indexing would also be useful. Incomplete or inconsistent indexing could point to the need for improvements in the taxonomy:

- If certain index terms are not used as much as they ought to be, this indicates the need for additional nonpreferred terms and perhaps also additional relationships to other terms.

- In a small taxonomy with no nonpreferred terms, the overlooking of a particular term might indicate that it needs rewording or even relocation to somewhere else in the taxonomy.

- If a term is overused, than perhaps the concept should be divided into two or more new terms.

- If two terms are frequently used in combination, this may indicate a concept in need of a single, precoordinated term.

- If a certain index term is misused, then perhaps you should reword the preferred term, create more nonpreferred terms, and/or add a scope note.

Levels of Vocabulary Management

Human indexers obviously can make good use of taxonomies, but they can also be permitted to use terms that are not in a taxonomy, that is, to create their own terms, either as candidate terms for the taxonomy or simply as keywords. Whether they do so, and to what extent, depends on an organization's editorial policy and the capabilities of the indexing software. Permitting indexers to propose new terms has its benefits, since they are the first to see new concepts and names in incoming documents. There are a number of possibilities for managing term suggestions from indexers, listed here from the most controlled to the least controlled:

1. The indexer uses terms only from the taxonomy. The indexer may suggest terms (candidate terms), but such terms must be reviewed and approved by the taxonomist first and thus cannot be used immediately for indexing the document at hand (unless the document is put on hold).

2. The indexer primarily uses terms from the taxonomy but is also permitted to suggest and immediately use additional candidate terms as "unapproved" terms, which the taxonomist will review later. (If the taxonomist subsequently changes an unapproved term name, the system still keeps track of the term the indexer entered so that the taxonomist can add it as a nonpreferred term to enable retrieval of the previously indexed document.)

   a) Unapproved terms are restricted to named entities, and the indexer cannot create subject terms.

   b) Unapproved terms may be created for any kind of term, whether named entities or subjects.

3. The indexer uses a combination of terms from the taxonomy and indexer-created terms (keywords) of all types. The indexer-created keywords, like author keywords, are *not* formally suggested to the taxonomy as candidate terms, and they may or may not be reviewed by a taxonomist.

   a) Taxonomy terms are in the majority, and keywords are supplemental.

   b) Taxonomy terms are used only for a few basic categories, and more of the indexing/tagging is done with keywords.

Each of these options involves some trade-offs affecting the simplicity of the indexing system, the ability to index new concepts not yet in the taxonomy, and the consistency of indexing. Option 1, requiring taxonomist approval of new terms, is relatively simple to implement with respect to technology, but since it cannot support new names and emerging concepts, it works well only for content that does not deal with current events or does not otherwise require a quick turnaround. Option 2, allowing unapproved or candidate terms in indexing but with the option for the taxonomist to "fix" them, is a good compromise that allows indexers to capture new concepts as needed while also ensuring vocabulary control. However, it is more complex to implement, so it is preferable for a relatively large indexing operation with multiple trained indexers. Option 3, permitting a dual system of a taxonomy and uncontrolled keywords, is relatively simple to implement but would present a more complicated set of three options to the end user: taxonomy terms, indexed keyword terms, and free text search strings.

Managing Folksonomies

Following the continuum of decreasing levels of control over a taxonomy described in the previous section, one might expect a fourth option whereby the indexer creates keywords, and these keywords immediately become available for repeated future use by this and other indexers, without a taxonomist's reviewing and approving them. This scenario actually takes place in what we call a *folksonomy*, except that the creation and use of a folksonomy typically does not involve people who work as indexers. It is the authors and/ or the users of the content—in other words, common "folk"—who create folksonomy terms or tags. The folksonomy approach has become easy to implement with the rise of commercial software for that purpose. Let us first consider the background of folksonomies.

While the uncontrolled terms in folksonomies might seem beyond the scope of a taxonomist's responsibilities, such uncontrolled terms can in fact reflect emerging concepts and are actually prime candidates for future taxonomy terms. Therefore, if relevant folksonomies are available, the taxonomist should pay close attention to them. At some point, a taxonomist may review and edit the folksonomy and convert some or all of it into a taxonomy.

Social Tagging and Folksonomy

New technologies that enable interactive use of the web, commonly referred to as the semantic web or Web 3.0, allow users to assign keyword tags of their choice to all kinds of web content. These tags can be used by the individual tagger for later retrieval, but other people may also view and use these tags. This type of uncontrolled indexing or tagging is called *social tagging* because anyone in an online community or society can tag any content, see the tags of others, and search on the accumulated tags. Furthermore, new social communities can be built around shared sets of popular content or popular tags. This phenomenon, which began around 2004, is also known as social bookmarking, collaborative tagging, social classification, social indexing, or ethnoclassification.

Social tagging can be done by the content creators (authors, photographers, etc.), the content viewers (readers or consumers), or both. The same content can be tagged repeatedly over time, rather than having a page or document indexed and then closed to future indexing, so social tagging is very dynamic. Even if the content remains static, the tagging can change over time, but usually the content is changing or growing as well.

The term *folksonomy* was coined by Thomas Vander Wal in July 2004 on the discussion group of the Information Architecture Institute (then called the Asilomar Institute for Information Architecture) in response to a question about what to call the new, informal social classification comprising user-defined tags on information-sharing websites. Following up on Eric Scheid's suggestion of a "folk classification," Vander Wal responded as follows: "So the user-created bottom-up categorical structure development with an emergent thesaurus would become a Folksonomy?"[5] A folksonomy should not be confused with a folk taxonomy. The latter is a concept that has been around much longer, a term in anthropology that refers to the unscientific naming and classifying of things by lay people within a given culture.

Websites or services that make use of social tagging include social-bookmarking management sites Delicious (delicious.com), Pinterest (www.pinterest.com), and Diigo (www.diigo.com), and the site for uploading and tagging images, Flickr (www.flickr.com).

Social tagging has its strengths and weaknesses. Its advantages over taxonomies include the following:

- It reflects trends, is up to date, and can monitor change and popularity.

- It is cheaper and quicker than building and maintaining a taxonomy.

- It is responsive to user needs.

- It facilitates democracy (as in votes for popular content and popular tags), the distribution of tasks, and the building of virtual communities of shared interest and knowledge.

There are also drawbacks to social tagging, which include the following:

- The tagging is inherently inconsistent, so there are serious deficiencies in precision and recall for content retrieval.

- The tagging is inevitably biased. Users may disagree with prior tagging.

- Social tagging does not scale well to a large volume of content when the number of users is held constant.

- For social tagging to be effective, it requires a critical mass of user involvement, which is not always possible.

A folksonomy differs from a taxonomy, not merely in terms of who creates it and the lack of authority control but also in the approach to its creation. A folksonomy represents a bottom-up creation of a vocabulary, as opposed to the top-down nature of a taxonomy. Actually, a folksonomy generally has no hierarchical structure, so it is probably incorrect to speak of bottom-up when there is no "up." Relationships between terms can be explicit, if the tagging software permits users to create such relationships, or implicit, by displaying tags that commonly co-occur. Users create relationships between terms based on their personal perceptions and biases, and they usually make no distinctions between hierarchical and associative relationships.

Folksonomies in the Enterprise

Within a few years, the phenomenon of social tagging spread from public websites to inside enterprises. The success of social tagging within an organization, however, depends on the number of people involved. An organization may not have a critical mass of employees, and even if there is a potentially large number, the level of participation may not be sufficient. People tend to engage in social tagging because they enjoy it, not because it is part of their job.

If a folksonomy is used within an organization, there is an opportunity to manage it or leverage it. Vocabulary for social tagging, although user created, can be semicontrolled. A taxonomist may periodically intervene to "clean up" tags by merging multiple synonymous terms, choosing a preferred term, and designating the others as nonpreferred terms. Taggers would then no longer use terms designated as nonpreferred, but they could still create new equivalent terms for the same concept. Even when a folksonomy comes under greater control, inconsistent and biased tagging will still occur as long as taggers can invent their own terms and need not follow an editorial policy. Commercial enterprise social-bookmarking software may not support folksonomy editing, so internal development may be necessary.

Social tagging is most suitable for collaboration and for following trends in a rapidly growing and changing content. Therefore, for organizations that want to support creativity and innovation, social tagging might be a good idea. It is not so appropriate for critical research, which requires retrieval of all the relevant documents on a topic. Marketing and customer relations departments may also implement social tagging, encouraging customers and potential customers to engage in tagging for the purposes of stimulating and gauging market interest. Thus, for differing purposes, an enterprise can have both a controlled vocabulary and a social tagging area. In addition to periodically cleaning up folksonomy terms, a taxonomist might evaluate, edit, and promote popular folksonomy terms into a taxonomy that is used for other search purposes. A folksonomy, thus, is not an alternative to a taxonomy but rather is supplemental. Each has its own place and purpose.

Endnotes

1. For an elaboration on the differences between tagging and indexing, see the author's blog post "Tagging vs. Indexing," *The Accidental Taxonomist* blog, February 28, 2014, accessed December 20, 2015, accidental-taxonomist.blogspot.com/2014/02/tagging-vs-indexing.html

2. Susan Klement, "Open-System versus Closed-System Indexing: A Vital Distinction," *The Indexer* 23, no.1 (April 2002): 23–31.

3. American Society for Indexing, *American Society for Indexing 2009 Professional Activities and Salary Survey* (Wheat Ridge, CO: American Society of Indexers, 2010), 12. The average range reported was $2 to $4/page, 70 cents/entry, or $31 to $35/hour.

4. From the subject authority file of Cengage Learning, Inc., accessed via its internal vocabulary management system, August 16, 2015.

5. Thomas Vander Wal, "Folksonomy Coinage and Definition" (February 2, 2007), accessed December 20, 2015, www.vanderwal.net/folksonomy.html

Chapter 7

Taxonomies for Automated Indexing

What's taxonomy got to do with IT!
—David Riecks

As we all know too well, the volume of electronic content is growing at an increasingly rapid rate, and at the same time, the need to find meaningful information is becoming more critical in our competitive, interconnected, global world. The task of indexing content to make it retrievable has become too great for human indexers in many contexts. Meanwhile, technologies for automated indexing have been improving. Although under certain conditions human indexing is still preferred, many organizations are turning to automated indexing to serve their needs.

Automated Indexing, Search, and Taxonomies

Automated indexing is a very broad notion that encompasses various technologies and techniques, some of which involve taxonomies and some of which do not. Automated tagging, auto-classification, and auto-categorization refer to automated indexing technologies that utilize taxonomies by automatically associating taxonomy terms with content items. The terms automated tagging, auto-classification, and auto-categorization (those methods that use taxonomies) are not formally defined and are used interchangeably. General search engines, on the other hand, perform different forms of automated indexing, without necessarily using taxonomies.

When to Use Automated Indexing

Automated indexing is, of course, more practical than human indexing when there is vast volume of content to index in a short period, although there is a trade-off in the form of lower levels of accuracy. Rapidly changing content (such as news), government intelligence, content of a very large enterprise, or other high-volume flows of data, such as emails and social media, and anything that may be called "big data," all benefit from automated indexing. Although accuracy is never as high as with skilled human indexing, if the volume of content is great, then near-perfect accuracy may not be needed to find desired information or discern trends. The following factors favor choosing automated over human indexing:

- A very large number of documents, which would require multiple human indexers and would be costly to index

- Content that changes quickly and perhaps unpredictably

- A need for speed in indexing, such as for time-critical information, current awareness, or news

- Relatively common document types or formats or pretagged (structured) content types

- Content related to a relatively uniform subject area or a single industry (so there is less ambiguity of terms)

- Text content only (although a few technologies can identify digital video and audio data)

- A corporate culture that is more comfortable with investing in externally purchased technology than in hiring, training, and managing human indexers

Consumer-oriented content (such as product/service directories), news and information publishers and aggregators, and large intranets are all areas in which indexing speed and volume are of greater concern than the improved accuracy yet higher cost of human indexers. This is not to say that automated indexing systems are cheap. They can be quite expensive, too, but over an extended period, they will most likely pay for themselves. Automated indexing systems also vary greatly in capability.

Structured content (such as database records) or unstructured content that already has structured metadata assigned to it is much easier to auto-index than is totally unstructured content. Thus, the original users of auto-categorization systems were large publishers or vendors of structured content. The trend toward creating more structured content within organizations, such as in technical documentation and reports, has resulted in more enterprise content that is suitable for automatic indexing. (That is not to say that the proportion of unstructured content has decreased.) At the same time, automated indexing technologies are improving with regard to unstructured content. So, for both these reasons, automated indexing is becoming more popular within organizations to make large volumes of internal content retrievable. The same automated indexing system may work on both structured and unstructured content.

Although automated indexing saves the expense of human indexers, it still requires human involvement to be effective. People need to create and maintain the taxonomies, of course, and human intellectual work is needed either to "train" the system on the taxonomy terms or to write rules for individual terms, as this chapter will explain in more detail.

Taxonomies and Search Software

Although search engines, whether for the entire web or for large websites or intranets, create what are called indexes, they do not usually make use of taxonomies. Search engines retrieve webpages by sorting words according to their location and retrieve the locations by matching search queries to the words or phrases listed in the search engine's inverted index of words. Algorithms and rules can increase the sophistication of matching search terms with words in webpages, but a taxonomy is not necessarily involved.

Building and updating a comprehensive taxonomy to support searching the entire World Wide Web would be nearly an impossible task. The closest that web search engines come to implementing any sort of controlled vocabulary is by including word lists of common misspellings or "fuzzy" matches, but such lists are certainly not taxonomies and not even complete synonym rings.

However, search software for a single site, such as an enterprise's intranet, a content management system, or software for searching across a corpus of online documents, may incorporate taxonomies. The scope of the subject matter, while still vast, is at least restricted to the interests of an organization, and the content may be more structured in its formatting and metadata. Site or enterprise search software, which is a growing niche industry, may or may not make use of taxonomies, however. Such software was originally based on web search-engine technology and thus did not incorporate taxonomies. But as enterprise search software has become more sophisticated and tailored to the enterprise's needs and as users come to appreciate the benefits of taxonomies, the incorporation of taxonomies in enterprise search is becoming more common.

A basic search engine matches user-entered query words with words or phrases found within the documents' metadata field (such as title) or anywhere in the text and returns those documents that are sufficiently relevant based on the position and frequency of those words, among other considerations. Relevance ranking takes into consideration many factors and may determine the display order of results. The deficiencies of free-text search are obvious. If the user enters a word in the search box but the text uses a synonym for that word and not the same word, the search engine misses the document. In other cases, the word entered by the user may occur in the text but not in the same context; it may have a different meaning or use, or it may occur in the text only because it is negated. In any of these cases, the search may retrieve an irrelevant document.

Search engines have become more sophisticated over the years. It is now common to match singular and plural forms of the same word. More specialized search engines also employ grammatical stemming so that words with the same root, such as **writers** and **writing**, will also match, perhaps with a lower relevance ranking than for an exact word match. More sophisticated search engines incorporate text analytics technologies to take grammar and inter-word relationships into consideration, relationships that can help determine whether a given word occurring in a text has the meaning intended by the words in the search query. Nevertheless, it remains difficult to discern concepts, and not merely words, without first establishing some kind of controlled vocabulary and a way to link text words to the taxonomy term.

Controlled vocabularies or taxonomies support search in two different ways: (1) through nonpreferred terms or synonym rings or (2) as browsable taxonomies. Synonym rings for each concept in a controlled vocabulary include terms likely to be searched and terms likely to appear in the content. This facilitates the matching of user-entered search strings with words or phrases in the content texts, as in the example illustrated in Figure 7.1. Despite the name, the terms in a synonym ring need not be exact synonyms but should in fact be nonpreferred terms in accordance with the guidelines described in Chapter 4. A synonym ring typically does not

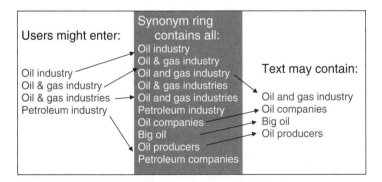

Figure 7.1 Example of how a synonym ring supports search for a concept

display terms in the user interface, whereas when the taxonomy makes a distinction between preferred and nonpreferred terms, the preferred terms are usually displayed.

In actual practice, the mere presence of a taxonomy with non-preferred terms does not guarantee that its nonpreferred terms will function as desired. Unless specifically set up to do so, in many cases search engines will ignore the relationships of nonpreferred terms to the preferred terms and will treat them as any other keywords.[1] As the taxonomist, you need to ensure that whoever configures the search engine takes into account the intended role of the nonpreferred terms.

The arrangement and display of terms for end-user browsing is another way in which taxonomies support search for automated indexing, just as they do for human-indexed concepts. In a hierarchical taxonomy, when the terms are visible and therefore browsable, users can browse and locate more specific subjects of interest, find out what is included in the taxonomy and what is not, and may find related subjects of interest. Users who are not entirely sure what they are looking for generally prefer a browsable hierarchical taxonomy to a blank search box. If a taxonomy or a set of categories is displayed to the user, then the software involved is more likely called auto-categorization or auto-classification software, rather than search software, because the interface includes categories. Faceted taxonomy displays, described in more detail in Chapter 8, also support search, but the indexing (or metadata tagging, as it may be called) requires a degree of human involvement, and so it is not a completely automatic method.

Automated Indexing Technologies

Just as there are different kinds of human indexing, there are also different forms of automated indexing and retrieval. The two different basic approaches to automated indexing and retrieval are information extraction and auto-categorization. They differ from each other both in technology and in purpose. Information extraction, which involves pulling information from text, focuses on identifying which key names, concepts, and data in a text are sufficiently significant in comparison with those with a mere passing mention. Auto-categorization, on the other hand, seeks to categorize each document based on what it is fundamentally "about." Information extraction is similar to back-of-the-book indexing in that it seeks to identify significant names and concepts within a chunk of text, whereas auto-categorization is more like article database indexing in that it assigns one or more taxonomy terms to describe the subject matter of the document as a whole. Consequently, results may differ between the two approaches. Information extraction is more suitable for disparate unstructured content, such as all the different documents a company might generate, including email, whereas auto-categorization is better for retrieval of traditional information, such as articles and related documents.

Finally, information extraction does not necessarily use a taxonomy, and when it does, it is usually a simple synonym ring. (Certain information extraction systems, though, can put named entities, such as geographic places and organizations, into a hierarchy.) Auto-categorization, on the other hand, usually involves a taxonomy, specifically a hierarchical taxonomy. As our interest is in taxonomies, this chapter will focus primarily on auto-categorization, after a brief look at information extraction and its most common form, entity extraction. Many automated indexing software products now combine information extraction and auto-categorization.

Information Extraction and Text Analytics

Information extraction, in some contexts called data extraction, and the overlapping fields of text analytics and text mining are technologies within the broader field of natural language processing that aim to extract useful information from varied unstructured content (that which lacks any metadata). These technologies, based on computational linguistics and pattern recognition, have been under development since the 1980s, building on natural language-processing research begun as early as the 1960s, and have produced commercial products since the 1990s. A newer, even broader field of content extraction has also emerged that encompasses technologies to extract information from any kind of content, including images, audio, and video, not just text. There are various technology approaches used in information extraction, including both statistics and rules-based techniques. A basic system might comprise components for the following tasks: dividing text into segments, sequencing text sentences, filtering out irrelevant sentences, detecting the basic parts of speech within sentences, parsing lexical fragments to produce a tree structure, semantically interpreting the parse tree, and so on. On top of these tasks, either rules or machine learning might be added.

Entity Extraction

Entity extraction, also called entity recognition or entity identification, is the most common form of information extraction and comprises technologies to identify named entities in text documents. Named entities include people names, company or organization names, locations, products, and sometimes named events or time designations. Proper nouns are, of course, easier to identify than other concepts, so entity extraction has a higher rate of reliability than concept-based information extraction. Therefore, some of the earliest automated indexing software was of this type. One of the first major commercial entity-extraction tools was NetOwl (www. netowl.com), which SRA International has been offering since 1996. Organizations utilizing NetOwl include several large publishers of online content, such as LexisNexis, Gale (a part of Cengage Learning), and IDT Payment Services.

There is a lot more involved, though, than just identifying words with capital letters that are not at the start of a sentence. Grammar-based linguistic rules and statistical models, as in topical auto-categorization, are required to develop an effective entity-extraction system.

Entity extraction thus does not necessarily involve a significantly different technology than the auto-categorization method previously described, but there are nuanced differences, requiring distinct software coding and rules. Thus, software products might be differentiated as either auto-categorizers or entity extractors. A single software product might also combine both, sometimes with the technology for one or the other feature developed by a third-party partner or vendor.

Entity extraction, along with its broader field of information extraction, does not presuppose an existing named term in a taxonomy, although in many cases it will make use of such terms. A controlled vocabulary will reconcile the variant forms of a name through its nonpreferred terms, but a new named term can also be extracted or indexed even if it is not included in a taxonomy. This may in fact be desirable to identify new names, especially of newly prominent people, companies, and products.

In addition to NetOwl (NameMatcher and EntityMatcher), other entity-extraction software products include Rosette Entity Extractor from Basis Technology (www.basistech.com/text-analytics/rosette/entity-extractor), Rosoka Extraction (www.rosoka.com/content/extraction), and OpenCalais from Thomson Reuters's subsidiary ClearForest (www.clearforest.com/solutions.html). There are also many others products that include entity extraction as a component of a larger auto-indexing solution, rather than as a stand-alone product, such as SAS Enterprise Content Categorization, Lexalytics Salience Engine, Open Text Content Analytics, Cogito Discover from Expert System, BA Insight's Classification software, and Data Harmony Metadata Extractor, to name a few.

Auto-Categorization

Auto-categorization or auto-classification refers to automatically associating appropriate taxonomy terms, often called categories, with a document, based on one or more different technologies that automatically analyze the text and compare it with data stored with the taxonomy terms and possibly other data as well. In addition to assigning documents to one or more categories, some auto-categorization systems, especially those that are called auto-classifiers, might also assign some other metadata values.[2]

Referring to "categories" rather than terms in such a taxonomy is not merely a matter of simplicity. The designation *category* implies something broader than the designation *term*. Auto-categorization does better at the broader category level than with subtly different specific terms, which call for the discernment of human indexers. The categories involved in auto-categorization might have some hierarchy to them, but in general they do not get as specific as the terms found in a thesaurus used for human indexing. Thus, auto-categorization may be best used with taxonomies that are not too large.

As with automated indexing software in general, there are different technologies and methods for auto-categorization. There are two fundamental approaches to auto-categorization involving predeveloped taxonomies and the possible role of a taxonomist: (1) machine-learning systems and (2) and rules-based systems. There are additional crosscutting technologies, and there are subtypes, so some literature on auto-categorization may list more methods. There is an additional auto-categorization technique of statistical clustering (also called semantic clustering), which does not necessarily require a pre-existing taxonomy, as it can automatically generate taxonomy terms. Therefore, as far as taxonomists are concerned, there are just the two methods of which to be aware.

Machine Learning-Based Auto-Categorization

Auto-categorization that is based on machine learning involves initially having the auto-categorization software "ingest" numerous sample documents that are already correctly indexed according to the taxonomy. This method is also called *catalog by example*. The system then uses algorithms and statistical analysis to "learn" patterns of text content to determine what kind of text is typically indexed with which taxonomy terms. Therefore, this method is also referred to as the "statistical method" for auto-categorization, although there are additional statistical methods that don't use machine learning. The statistical analysis is based on various techniques, including the following:

- Bayesian computations: Methods of probability and statistics named after the 18th-century mathematician Thomas Bayes

- Support vector machines: Classification performed initially by the construction of a hyperplane that separates the data into two categories

- Neural networks: Statistical analysis procedure based on models of the nervous system (less common than the other two techniques)

All these methods can "learn" from a collection of examples to discover patterns and trends and to determine what is useful and what is statistically rare.

In machine learning, feeding numerous sample pre-indexed documents is required for what is called *training the system*, and the documents are called *training documents*. The minimum number of training documents required and the degree of automated indexing accuracy achievable after training depends on various factors:

- The statistical method used

- The algorithms used

- The word count of the training documents

- The quality and content of the training documents

- The nature, meaning, and clarity (lack of ambiguity) of the individual taxonomy term

Depending on these circumstances, tens of documents or hundreds of documents could be required to train a particular term. Some documents provide very clear examples of a taxonomy concept, while others express it less concisely, directly, and clearly. It is possible that less than ten training documents might suffice under ideal circumstances, including a perfectly clear and unambiguous term and clear, simple training documents, but this is seldom the case.

If an existing indexing business or operation is migrating from human indexers to automated indexing, then there should be no difficulty in coming up with the desired number of pre-indexed training documents for a given term, except perhaps for some rarely used terms. This is because there already exists a large published collection of human-indexed content to tap for training documents.

If you are starting up an indexing operation from scratch, however, without an existing corpus of indexed documents, then coming up with training documents demands a lot more work.

Someone, often the taxonomist, must either test-index a large number of documents or identify training documents indexed by someone else for each term. Test indexing of documents is useful only to a limited degree. While it is a realistic method to determine what combinations of terms are often needed for typical documents, the documents used might not include some of the taxonomy terms. The other approach, taking each taxonomy term and finding suitable training documents, ensures that all terms are covered. However, finding ideal documents for training is not always easy and requires good online searching skills. It can also take a lot of time.

In some machine-learning systems, the training documents then yield additional automatically generated "keywords" from the multiple texts that are associated with the taxonomy term being trained. The statistical analysis assigns a percentage relevancy or weighting for each automatically generated keyword, but the taxonomist (or perhaps *machine-aided indexing analyst*) can manually change individual keyword relevancies if the automatically assigned relevancy seems too high or low (usually too high).

Whether starting with a corpus of pre-indexed content, test-indexing individual documents, or searching for new documents for each term, machine-learning automated indexing requires the additional step of quality testing. You will need to check samples of automatically indexed documents matched for each term to determine whether they are sufficiently acceptable (minimal inappropriate documents retrieved) and then make appropriate changes to the collection of training documents. This process involves removing training documents whose content is skewing the results and perhaps adding more appropriate documents or making refinements to the given term by adding or deleting nonpreferred terms. Depending on the nature and source of the training documents, you may even be able to edit the documents in order to provide more ideal content. All these adjustments are part of what is called *tuning* in the machine-learning process, and it can be a time-consuming task, even a full-time job. If the taxonomy is large, it may not be possible to check and tune every term, so only the high-usage terms get tuned.

Rules-Based Auto-Categorization

Rules-based auto-categorization puts more emphasis on matching text patterns than on statistical analysis. In rules-based auto-categorization, rules are created for each taxonomy term that instruct the system how to automatically index with that term. Humans, often taxonomists, write rules for taxonomy terms. Depending on the system, the rules may be simple or complex, and in cases of simple rules, the system may automatically create suggested rules, which the taxonomist can then edit.

In simple rules-based systems, the user (taxonomist) enters or edits automatically generated synonyms/nonpreferred terms for each term and additionally enters closely related keywords and phrases that are expected to be found in the same document. Unlike taxonomy nonpreferred terms, these keywords do not always have to be suitable for use as the preferred term. A distinction is made between truly equivalent nonpreferred terms and merely supporting keywords.

In systems supporting complex rules, also called semantic rules or Boolean rules, the rules are conditional statements that often involve Boolean logic and may use operators that look at word order, word proximity, and content structure to identify patterns in the text and apply taxonomy terms accordingly. The collection of rules is sometimes called a *rule set* or a *knowledge base*. Auto-categorization systems may automatically generate basic rules for every term, and the taxonomist then only needs to write additional conditional statements for the terms that are more ambiguous. Software that is entirely rules based is not quite as common as that which involves some additional statistical technology, such as machine learning-based auto-categorization, simply because greater human intervention is required, and the customers for auto-categorization tools tend to seek the most "automated" method. However, tools that combine rules-based and machine learning-based auto-categorization are becoming more common.

Sometimes a word found in the text matches a term in the taxonomy as a true synonym, in which case no conditional rules are required. However, when a term in the taxonomy has multiple meanings, rules are needed for clarification. Nonpreferred terms also require qualification through rules in order to serve as unambiguous matches. For example, the term **earthquakes** has a number of possible nonpreferred terms, but these all have other meanings: **quakes, tremors, tremblers,** and **aftershocks.** These all could be used as nonpreferred terms, provided there are rules restricting these terms to texts that also include certain other words or phrases, such as **Richter scale, disaster,** or **structural damage.**

Both topical concepts and named entities may utilize rules. Rules are especially useful for distinguishing individuals with common surnames (Smith, Brown, Johnson); names that could apply to individuals, organizations, or places (Washington, Columbus, Madison, Jackson); or names that are also common words (Bush, Rice, Gates).

Rules can refer to many different conditions regarding the word or phrase of text to match. These include:

- Truncation of the word

- The mention of other words in the text

- Proximity to other words in the text

- Relation to other words in the text, based on Boolean AND, OR, and NOT operators

- Initial capitalization or full-word capitalization

- Text placement within a sentence (a rule usually used in combination with capitalization)

Software tools vary in how they require the rules to be formatted, but a common construction involves IF, IF ELSE, or more complex variations. The following example, in which terms following the statement USE are in the taxonomy, comes from the Data Harmony Machine Aided Indexer User's Guide.[3]

Text to Match: norwegian

```
IF (MENTIONS "language")
   USE Norwegian language
ELSE IF (MENTIONS "country")
   USE Norway
ENDIF
ENDIF
```

Some complex rules-based systems also utilize regular expressions (*regex* for short), which are special text strings for describing complex search patterns. Writing regular expressions, usually done by someone called a knowledge engineer rather than a taxonomist, involves following numerous coding rules. It is like creating filter rules for incoming emails to automatically go into a spam folder or other folders, but without a dropdown list of options and with countless more possible rules.

Another feature of many auto-categorization systems, and especially rules-based systems, is the assignment of relative rankings or weightings for each supporting synonym, keyword, or phrase. Some words or phrases will be sufficient by themselves to get the document categorized to the corresponding taxonomy term; whereas other words or phrases, due to lower weightings, must be found in combinations with other listed words or phrases in order to meet the threshold for categorizing a document.

Since simple rules are not expected to achieve the same level of results as more complex Boolean rules and regular expressions, the auto-categorization software may additionally employ other classification technologies at the back end to generate terms and phrases to match against the taxonomy and associated weighted synonyms and keywords. There may also be language processing techniques that perform stemming on extracted terms and consider the lexical variants of terms. Instead of relying on exact matches to terms and their variants and keywords, some of these rules-based auto-categorizers involve "fuzzy matching," which can be based on either linguistic processing or statistical methods, including the additional use of training sets of documents.

Comparison of Auto-Categorization Methods

Regardless of the method, auto-categorization still requires human involvement, and that human is often the taxonomist who created the taxonomy and continues to maintain it. The tasks and skills required in ensuring that the auto-categorization system properly matches text with taxonomy terms are very different for each method, though.

Writing the rules for rules-based auto-categorization requires intimate familiarity with each taxonomy term and its appropriate usage, so usually the taxonomist who creates the taxonomy also writes the rules. In addition, high-level analytical and problem-solving abilities are needed. Skills in traditional command-line online searching are helpful, although not necessary, for constructing Boolean and nested search expressions, which may remind long-time librarians of command-line Dialog searching.

If regular expressions are also required, then the work is a little more like scripting or coding. You do not need to be a software programmer, but you do need to have a certain comfort level with coding, such as HTML or XML. Some information professionals get into this, and some do not.

The tuning of machine learning, on the other hand, requires the kinds of skills used by a periodical/database-type of indexer or an online searcher to come up with and/or evaluate sample training documents. Thus, former periodical indexers are well qualified for this task. In fact, taxonomist-level skills are not necessary, although one does need to be familiar with the taxonomy. A single taxonomist might have several other people, who are not taxonomists, aid in the task of identifying, assigning, and managing training documents to terms.

The degree of human involvement in auto-categorization systems has a direct impact on the indexing accuracy and retrieval success rate. This includes additional human effort to refine and improve a term's nonpreferred terms, training documents, or rules. In evaluating the success rates of different auto-categorization methods, vendors will claim that their system is better, but there are in fact too many variables for any accurate comparison of the methods. Machine-learning systems may have a 60–70 percent retrieval success rate without tuning,[4] but tuning can achieve a rate of more than 80 percent correct retrievals for certain unambiguous terms. With enough effort in the rules writing, rules-based auto-categorization may achieve a 90 percent success rate.[5] Unless technologies are combined, the core technologies have not been able to achieve higher success rates in more recent years. Rules-based auto-categorization tends to have a higher success rate than machine learning on average, simply because a high level of tuning is not a requirement to run a machine-learning system, and if sufficient training documents are lacking, there is not much that can be done. Writing rules for each term, however, is a necessity for rules-based auto-categorization to function at all, and whoever writes the rules has greater control over the end results than does the person who gathers training documents for a machine-learning system. In other words, because rules-based auto-categorization involves greater taxonomist involvement, it has the potential for higher success rates.

Automated Taxonomy Generation

Both rules-based and machine learning-based auto-categorization methods rely on prebuilt taxonomies (built by taxonomists) and match the terms in these taxonomies to the documents being indexed. Some auto-categorization vendors, however, have taken the notion of "automated" one step further by implementing technology to automatically generate what they call taxonomies along with the auto-categorization of content. The method usually used is statistical clustering, which involves the grouping together of documents that share words with the same meanings, as determined by a text analytics component that parses the text and then assigns these clustered documents to a category. Not only do these systems automatically create something like a taxonomy, but the categorization is also fully automated, requiring no humans to assign training documents or to write rules for each taxonomy term. Although more rudimentary than human-created taxonomies, these automatically generated "taxonomies" may even have a hierarchy. In such cases, though, a taxonomist usually creates the top-level categories. For example, many entity-extraction systems can populate predefined entity categories or facets with appropriate name terms upon search execution.

These automatically generated "taxonomies" are far from meeting the standards described in the ANSI/NISO Z39.19 guidelines. They also tend to include redundant concepts and mixed degrees of specificity (granularity).[6] However, such systems should not be dismissed merely as inadequate substitutes for human-crafted taxonomies but should instead be viewed as good sources for suggested terms that the taxonomist can edit into a proper taxonomy.

Automatic taxonomy generation software is typically offered as part of a text analytics package or suite, rather than as a stand-alone product.

Software for Auto-Categorization

Compared with the field of thesaurus management software, the field of auto-categorization and other automated indexing software, such as for entity extraction and text analytics, is a less mature industry segment, with companies appearing, disappearing, and being acquired at a relatively high rate. The software described in this section is not industry-specific, but there are also auto-categorization software products for specific industries, such as healthcare and law.

Auto-Categorization Software with Taxonomies

Commercial auto-categorization systems that utilize taxonomies handle these taxonomies in different ways. The software may

- come with preinstalled taxonomies that cannot be edited
- come with preinstalled taxonomies that the user may edit and extend through the user interface
- automatically generate a taxonomy that can be edited

- support the import of taxonomies but not the editing of those taxonomies

- support both the import of taxonomies and the editing of those taxonomies

There are also combinations of the aforementioned capabilities. For example, the systems that come with preinstalled taxonomies often also support the import of additional taxonomies. Finally, even auto-categorization software without a feature for taxonomies can often integrate with taxonomy management software through APIs (application programming interfaces), connectors, or custom programming. Vendor partnerships are widespread in this industry.

The auto-categorization software that comes with preinstalled taxonomies tends to cover specific vertical markets, such as pharmaceuticals, insurance, or law enforcement, and to include named entities, such as company names and geographic places. Product or industry types are also common as prebuilt taxonomies. From vendors in the United Kingdom, a typical preinstalled taxonomy is the Integrated Public Sector Vocabulary (IPSV), the standard vocabulary for use by local public sector agencies. Prebuilt taxonomies with auto-categorization systems are usually simple hierarchical taxonomies, not thesauri, and in addition to lacking associative term relationships, they may even lack nonpreferred terms. Chapter 1 mentions additional sources of prebuilt taxonomies.

Automated indexing/search software products that permit the importing of taxonomies vary with regard to the degree of complexity they can support in the imported taxonomies. For example, the auto-categorization software may not support associative relationships, only hierarchical, and it may be limited to a certain number of hierarchy levels. Even though it may be more efficient to build and edit a taxonomy in an external thesaurus management program and then import it into the auto-categorization system, such import limitations need to be kept in mind.

Auto-categorization software that utilizes taxonomies or simpler controlled vocabularies but lacks user interface features to edit those taxonomies was originally common, but as competing software products have added features, the inclusion of the ability to edit taxonomies to some degree is becoming more prevalent. The following are examples of auto-categorization products that include taxonomies but provide only limited ability to edit those taxonomies, at least according to the expectations of a skilled taxonomist: IBM Content Classification, Endeca Information Discovery from Oracle, IBM Watson Explorer (formerly Vivisimo), Attensity, Mindbreeze, Exalead, IDOL from HP (Hewlett-Packard), Salience from Lexalytics, and Aspire from Search Technologies.

These systems compete on the basis of their automatic indexing capabilities, and less attention is paid to taxonomy management features. In some cases, taxonomy management is an administrative feature and not a standard user feature. In some cases, the kinds of taxonomies supported are simple synonym rings. The software might not even call them "taxonomies" but rather something else, such as concept sets, concept matrix, category sets, concept libraries, or dictionaries. Additionally, since search/retrieval remains the primary goals of these tools, with taxonomy development only a supporting task, the vendors' literature on such software tends to focus on the needs of the content manager rather than the needs of the taxonomist. So it is difficult to discern the extent of the taxonomy management capabilities of these tools without trying them out. Evaluating auto-categorization software with taxonomy management is not a simple software evaluation, however, but ideally involves a proof-of-concept procedure.

There are several auto-categorization products that include a strong taxonomy management component with a well-developed user interface, likely to be used by a taxonomist, although they can create only simple hierarchical taxonomies, with no also associative (related term) relationships, like the taxonomies supported by the

SharePoint Term Store. Two examples are BA Insight and concept-Searching. Both of these are rules based, and it is more typical for rules-based auto-categorization software to have a good taxonomy management interface, since editing taxonomies, editing nonpreferred terms, and editing rules are tasks that go together.

BA Insight

BA Insight (www.BAInsight.com), founded in 2004 and based in Boston, Massachusetts, specializes in extending and enhancing enterprise search, and especially SharePoint search, through various applications, including auto-categorization software, along with implementation and consulting services. Its core auto-categorization product is called AutoClassifier, but there are also related tools utilizing text analytics for entity extraction, automated Content Type classification, and automatic "property mapping" for other metadata. The AutoClassifier product is fully rules based. Simple rule, that merge synonyms are initially automatically generated, and then the user can edit or enhance them. Rules can also be complex, making use of a scripting language, for example, VBscript. A Test Bench allows categorization results to be previewed in real time against the categorized documents, so that rules can be adjusted. The AutoClassifier includes taxonomy management as one of its main components, but the taxonomies are simple hierarchical taxonomies, since they are managed in the native SharePoint format. The taxonomy management user interface itself is easy and intuitive to use. The AutoClassifier fully integrates with SharePoint.

conceptSearching

The conceptSearching software is a web-based auto-classification and enterprise search product from Concept Searching Limited (www.conceptsearching.com), a company founded in 2002 in the United Kingdom. The conceptSearching product uses a proprietary statistical technology called Compound Term Processing, which Concept Searching introduced in 2003. Compound Term

Processing, based on Shannon Information Theory, automatically identifies multiword concepts and then computes the incremental value (i.e., additional meaning) of these compound terms over their component parts. The process uses algorithms, which adapt to each customer's content.[7] In addition to concept search technology, the integrated conceptSearching suite includes Taxonomy Manager and Workflow Manager. Through Taxonomy Manager the user can manage and adjust the weights of the keywords, or "clues," that the software automatically generates from the content and then quickly test the rules for accuracy. There are various taxonomy import formats, with SKOS and OWL being the easiest to import. The products integrate with all versions of SharePoint and many other platforms.

The conceptSearching product also offers various general industry taxonomies for sale from its taxonomy library. These are intended more as a means to accelerate a customer's taxonomy development process than to replace it. In fact,Concept Search's literature notes that the taxonomist or subject matter expert can edit that starter taxonomy in the tool to "further customize it to meet specific of unique organizational requirements."[8]

Taxonomy Management/Auto-Categorization Software Combinations

Software that fully supports taxonomy/thesaurus creation and management (as described in Chapter 5), instead of creating just simple hierarchical taxonomies, while also integrating with auto-categorization capabilities are the products supporting auto-categorization that are probably of the greatest interest to the taxonomist. These include offerings from Expert System, Access Innovations, OpenText, The Semantic Web Company (PoolParty), SAS, and Smartlogic. They offer product combinations for auto-categorization and for sophisticated taxonomy, thesaurus, or ontology management. In most cases (except for OpenText), taxonomy management is a stand-alone product, not merely a feature of auto-categorization software. The products described in the following paragraphs are not being endorsed and are thus presented in alphabetical order. Industry analysts would likely present potential customers with a different list of products, but the products are mentioned here because the taxonomist might encounter or use them.

Cogito Taxonomy Studio

Expert System (www.expertsystem.com), with global headquarters in Italy and with subsidiaries in the United States, the United Kingdom, France, Spain, and Germany, is the developer of an auto-categorization suite called Cogito Categorizer. In 2014 it introduced a taxonomy management tool, Cogito Taxonomy Studio, for the purpose of creating content-driven taxonomies and writing or editing rules for individual taxonomy terms for use in auto-categorization.

As Expert System was founded in 1989 and Cogito was developed in 1999, the company has had many years to build up a patented auto-categorization technology that uses a combination of statistics, term frequency, and linguistic clues combined with a "semantic network" to establish word meaning, which in turn supports the development of more complete categorization rules.[9] Cogito Categorizer, the core auto-categorization component, uses rules for each taxonomy term to categorize content, but training sets of documents may also be used to supplement the process and automatically generate rules that can be edited. In the other direction, the software can also be used to identify training sets of documents. Once created or edited, the auto-categorization rules are locked and can only be changed by administrator intervention, rather than allowing for changes based on the content of the documents being categorized, a feature aimed at preserving quality. Cogito Categorizer originally had a basic taxonomy creation feature, so it was only more recently that Expert System saw the need to offer a full-featured taxonomy management tool, Cogito Taxonomy Studio.

Cogito Taxonomy Studio can be used as a stand-alone product, as it incorporates its own rules-based auto-categorization capabilities, although it is generally used along with Cogito Categorizer for more sophisticated auto-categorization. Cogito Taxonomy Studio supports standard thesaurus relationships (hierarchical, associative, and equivalence), and taxonomies conform to SKOS guidelines. Taxonomies can be created manually from scratch, but the software also has a feature to extract concepts found in a set of documents as candidate taxonomy terms. Taxonomies can also be used outside the Cogito products, as Taxonomy Studio has a feature to export taxonomies, as OWL (based on RDF), SKOS, or text format. Taxonomy Studio can also import taxonomies in a SKOS format, and the company has a partnership with WAND to offer licensed, prebuilt taxonomies.

The Cogito product line was enhanced with complementary technologies through Expert System's acquisition of the France-based

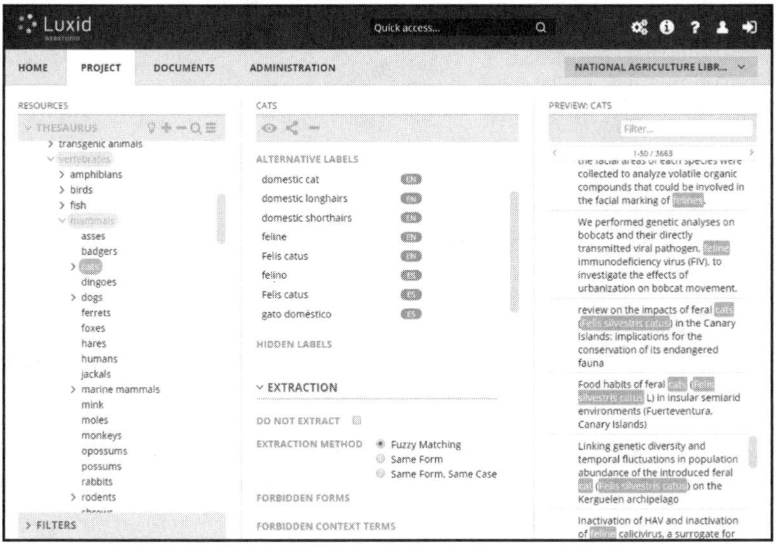

Figure 7.2 The user interface of WebStudio, for editing ontologies, managing the extraction of concepts from text, and reviewing autosuggested candidate terms. Display of nonpreferred (alternate labels) and hierarchical terms

competitor TEMIS and its Luxid Content Enrichment Platform in 2015. Like the Cogito line of products, the Luxid product family provides auto-categorization and related capabilities, involving text analytics and natural language processing in multiple languages; and as with Cogito, a taxonomy management tool called Luxid WebStudio was also added in 2014 (see Figure 7.2). Luxid WebStudio additionally supports ontologies (user-defined classes, relationships, and attributes), so we can probably expect additional ontology management capabilities coming to Cogito Taxonomy Studio in the future. Like Cogito Taxonomy Studio, Luxid WebStudio also has a synergy with content, since not only can taxonomy terms be automatically tagged to content, but candidate taxonomy terms can also be suggested from automated analysis of texts, and the user can review and add them to the taxonomy. One of the features of the Luxid product line is what it calls Skill Cartridges, which provide both generic and domain-/industry-specific statistical models, rules bases, and vocabularies to support information extraction and auto-categorization, and Luxid WebStudio also makes use of these Skill Cartridges.

Data Harmony MAIstro

As mentioned in Chapter 5, Access Innovations sells a large-scale taxonomy management system called Data Harmony Thesaurus Master (www.dataharmony.com). An additional product from Access Innovations is its Machine Aided Indexer (M.A.I.), which enables categorization through the rules-based method. M.A.I actually serves two functions: (1) machine-aided indexing, whereby the system suggests terms based on rules for individual documents, which the indexer can then accept or reject (the indexer can also add missing terms), and (2) fully automated indexing of documents in batch mode, typically used only after sufficient fine-tuning of the rules so that the top returns on the list are reliably accurate. According to Access Innovations's chief taxonomist Alice Redmond-Neal, most of the company's clients utilize M.A.I. for machine-aided indexing rather than for fully automated indexing and find it increases indexing speed up to 6.7 times that of completely manual indexing.[10]

While Thesaurus Master and M.A.I. are each available as separate products, an integrated system is also available, called Data Harmony MAIstro. In MAIstro, there are three tabs for the three window displays: Thesaurus Master, M.A.I. Rule Builder, and Test MAI. Thesaurus Master is the same as the stand-alone product for creating thesauri, the MAI Rule Builder is used to edit existing rules and also create new rules (basic rules are included programmatically), and Test MAI allows you to paste text from a document to test how well your rule works in assigning taxonomy terms to it. Although you can use the stand-alone M.A.I. by itself on any term list, in MAIstro the M.A.I. component automatically creates a basic rule for every term and nonpreferred term in the Thesaurus Master's thesaurus, and the terms and rules stay synchronized.

An additional feature is an internal statistics module that tracks the editor's term choices and compares them with M.A.I. term suggestions, sorting them as hits, misses, and noise to guide and prioritize the editor's fine-tuning of rules. Yet another feature is a drop-down menu for rule syntax autofill, which makes it easier to write a rule without memorizing all of the rule base syntax. Available extensions include Inline Tagging, MAIchem (a system for extracting chemical nomenclature within full text), Metadata Extractor, a search tool called Search Harmony, and Recommender (to retrieve more articles like a selected one). MAIstro has connectors to link to search engines and content management systems, including SharePoint.

Mondeca Content Annotation Manager

Mondeca S.A. (www.mondeca.com), whose Intelligent Topic Manager (ITM) was described in Chapter 5, also has an automated indexing (also referred to as "annotation") product called Content Annotation (CA) Manager, which works with the vocabularies managed in ITM. Not only does taxonomy/ontology software ITM serve as a source of vocabularies for auto-categorization, but CA Manager, through its processing of documents, also provides candidate terms for the vocabularies, which are exposed in the ITM Candidate Management user interface.[11]

The focus of CA Manager is not merely topical indexing, but rather involves adding metadata (structured annotations) to unstructured content, processing that content according to the Unstructured Information Management Architecture (UIMA) standard. CA Manager relies on the GATE (General Architecture for Text Engineering) open source text mining engine for information extraction, and other third-party text mining engines could be integrated. Auto-categorization is rules based and makes use of linguistic and semantic technologies in GATE. Thus CA Manager's features and strengths lie primarily in workflow management, connectivity (by providing content output in RDF format), and providing a flexible, scalable implementation.

OpenText Content Analytics

Following its acquisition in 2010 of Nstein, OpenText (opentext. com), a global information/content management software company based in Waterloo, Ontario, rebranded Nstein's automated indexing/search tool, Text Mining Engine (TME), as OpenText Content Analytics (OTCA).[12] The auto-categorization methods of OTCA combine the technologies of concept extraction, rules for terms, and the use of training documents. Users provide training documents for their own taxonomies, but all of the preinstalled taxonomies come already trained. OpenText also maintained the original software's Authority File and Taxonomy Manager components, combined and renamed as the OTCA Management Console.

The OTCA Management Console is a full-featured thesaurus management tool that supports hierarchical, associative, and equivalence relationships and term attributes in accordance with ANSI/NISO Z39.19 standards and other library group standards. Within the

Management Console, the taxonomist can build, maintain, and automate named entities in OTCA's Authority File Manager; and can build, maintain, and automate taxonomies along with machine-learning and indexing rules in OTCA's Knowledge Base Manager. Users can build taxonomies from scratch or import them in standard XML formats. Additionally, OTCA ships with sets of prebuilt taxonomies and authority files, such as the International Press Telecommunications Council taxonomy, the Industry Classification Benchmark database of companies and securities from Dow Jones, the Library of Congress Thesaurus for Graphic Materials, and others for geographic locations, organization names, people names, events, etc.

PoolParty Power Tagging

The Semantic Web Company, which provides the PoolParty Thesaurus Server software described in Chapter 5, also offers a set of auto-categorization modules called PoolParty Power Tagging (www. poolparty.biz/poolparty-powertagging). Rather than try to achieve general auto-categorization for any platform, PoolParty Power Tagging focuses on certain applications, with modules specifically for SharePoint, WordPress, Drupal, Atlassian's Confluence (a wiki platform), and a growing number of specific content management systems, including Jive, Alfresco, and Umbraco. With APIs, Power Tagging can work with other content management systems as well. The company introduced PoolParty Power Tagging in 2012, starting with PoolParty Power Tagging for Confluence. The technology used is based on machine learning from sample content in combination with linguistic processing and fuzzy matches. Taxonomists can also set rules to increase the precision of the built-in word sense disambiguation. PoolParty Power Tagging works in conjunction with an entity-extraction tool, PoolParty Extractor.

SAS Enterprise Content Categorization

SAS Institute, a company that has been providing business analytics software since the 1970s, within its category of "Advanced Analytics" (www.sas.com/en_us/software/analytics.html), offers a suite of automated indexing and taxonomy products called SAS Text Analytics. The SAS Text Analytics suite is based on the products of the company Teragram, which SAS acquired in 2008, and it includes the following: Enterprise Content Categorization, Ontology Management (described in Chapter 5), Sentiment Analysis, and Text Mining.

Enterprise Content Categorization (ECC) is an automated indexing product that has both auto-categorization and entity/concept extraction capabilities. For its rules-based auto-categorization, ECC supports the writing of rules with a graphical tree view of Boolean operators and commands for selection. It also supports use of regular expressions in rules. Additionally, the user can designate relative weightings of terms for a more statistical approach to auto-categorization.

ECC includes the capability for building, maintaining, and testing taxonomies. Taxonomies can be built from scratch, auto-generated and then edited, or preinstalled by SAS. Because ECC also comes with prebuilt taxonomies, nontaxonomists often use it, and thus less emphasis has been put on the manual taxonomy creation features. Although ECC does support creating the basic kinds of term relationships (equivalent, hierarchical, and associative), taxonomists may choose to use the other SAS product, Ontology Management, to build more complex thesauri and ontologies, which support custom relationships and term attributes. These ontologies can easily be exported into ECC for auto-categorization use.

Semaphore Classification Server

Smartlogic (www.smartlogic.com), whose Semaphore Ontology Editor is described in Chapter 5, also offers a rules-based classification engine called Semaphore Classification Server. The Classification Server has three components: Automatic Rules Creator, Rule Template Editor, and Semantic Processor. Utilizing taxonomies created in the Ontology Editor, the Classification Server has the capability to automatically generate rules based on the relationships of the terms in the taxonomy. The user can then edit those rules, create new manual rules that take precedence, and test those rules in the Rule Template Editor. The system supports over 30 different kinds of rules, with more rules added in more recent versions, and various kinds of wildcards. In addition, a text miner tool facilitates taxonomy and ontology development by suggesting additional terms. The Classification Server supports 31 different languages for classification. An additional Classification Review Tool is designed for testing sets of classification results for accuracy, and a Classification Analysis Tool allows the user to look at individual documents to see how they classify.

Synaptica Text Analytics & Auto-Classification System

The taxonomy management software vendor Synaptica (www.synaptica.com), described in Chapter 5, which has long offered a manual indexing component, in 2015 introduced an add-on module for auto-classification. Like Mondeca, Synaptica utilizes the GATE (General Architecture for Text Engineering) open source text mining engine for information extraction, which Synaptica has integrated with its taxonomy management tool. From the different components of GATE, Synaptica's Text Analytics & Auto-Classification System (TAACS) utilizes both rules-writing-based and training-set/machine-learning methods. Users of the software can then focus on the method that works best for their circumstances. Synaptica's auto-categorization tool is available in both internal client–server and cloud-hosted options.

Creating Taxonomies for Automated Indexing

Taxonomies for automated indexing, whether by information extraction or auto-categorization, are not fundamentally different from those for human indexing. After all, the end users and the search/retrieval interface may be the same, regardless of the indexing method. Taxonomists should try to follow the best practices suggested in the ANSI/NISO Z39.19 guidelines with respect to term format and relationships, no matter how the taxonomy is used. Nevertheless, automated indexing calls for certain considerations with respect to taxonomies.

Terms for Automated Indexing

Despite the increasing sophistication of automated indexing, no automated system can achieve the level of interpretation of subtle ideas that humans can. Therefore, a taxonomy used in automated indexing cannot support as great a number of concepts. This is particularly the case for statistical methods of auto-categorization. For example, in a taxonomy used by human indexers, you could maintain distinct concepts/terms for each of **insurance companies**, **insurance agents**, **insurance brokers**, and **insurance underwriters**, but automated indexing would not be able to distinguish the subtle differences among these terms. You should also avoid creating terms for both an action and a topic within the same taxonomy, especially if they share the same root, such as **investing** and **investments** or **contracting** and **contracts**, although in separate facets this might be acceptable. While the usage of one term or the other is clear to the trained indexer, it is difficult for an automated system to discern.

Precoordination works better for automated indexing, whether rules based or statistical, than leaving simple terms for postcoordination. Examples of precoordinated terms, explained in more detail in Chapter 3, include **software training**, **federal aid to education**, and **materials handling equipment industry**. Such phrase terms will more likely match phrases in the texts and what users may enter in the search box. As described earlier, leaving terms for postcoordination (such as **software** AND **training**) is more subject to ambiguity in search and retrieval. Meanwhile, subdivisions for structured indexing (also called second-level indexing), sometimes used for human indexing, especially of periodical literature, as mentioned in Chapter 6, are too complex for automated indexing.

Although with automated indexing there are no human indexers to read term notes, such notes are still helpful for the end user, so taxonomies for automated indexing often have scope notes or other forms of expanded explanations.

Nonpreferred Terms for Automated Indexing

Nonpreferred terms are especially important in taxonomies used for automatic indexing since a crucial part of the process is creating automatic matches between taxonomy terms and words in the content texts. In general, you will want more nonpreferred terms for automated indexing than for human indexing. While a human indexer will search and browse for different possible terms, the automated system must make exact matches, subject only to possible grammatical stemming and any filtering conditions in rules. On the other hand, for automated indexing you do not need phrase-inverted nonpreferred terms (such as **photography, digital**) that are useful to the human indexer who is searching for terms alphabetically. The following example compares possible nonpreferred terms for the term **presidential candidates** for human and automated indexing:

> Nonpreferred terms for human indexing of **presidential candidates**:
> **candidates, presidential**

> Nonpreferred terms for automated indexing of **presidential candidates**:
>
> **campaigning for president**
> **presidential candidate**
> **candidacy for president**
> **presidential hopeful**

> candidate for president
> presidential nominee
> presidential candidacy
> **running for president**

As shown in the preceding example, nonpreferred terms for automated indexing may include verbal phrases that do not conform to standard formats for terms. In fact, when it comes to proposing text string matches, there may be a blurred distinction between taxonomy nonpreferred terms and the suggested matches in a rules-based auto-categorization system. Where you put these suggested variant matches depends on the software system you are using.

For automated indexing, you might also want to distinguish between different types of nonpreferred terms, such as those that are auto-generated and those that are human-created. Acronyms can be ambiguous, especially in automated indexing. Thus, designating acronyms as acronyms and not just generic nonpreferred terms may help.

Term Relationships for Automated Indexing

Hierarchical relationships are the same whether a taxonomy is used for human or automated indexing, and polyhierarchies are useful in either application. Automated indexing tends to make use of hierarchical taxonomies, while thesauri are more common in human indexing.

Associative relationships may occur in taxonomies used in automated indexing, but they are not quite as common as in taxonomies used in human indexing. Associative relationships are highly useful for the human indexer, and they are also useful for the end-user searcher to suggest possible related concepts of interest. If there are no human indexers and no browsable display of a taxonomy to end users, then it is simpler to omit associative relationships, despite their potential usefulness. Furthermore, auto-categorization systems that make use of auto-generated keywords from content may automatically suggest related terms on the fly, based on shared keywords among the preferred terms.

Summary of Taxonomy Creation Differences

In creating taxonomies for human or automated indexing, there are different areas of emphasis. Taxonomies for human indexing should have

- extensive relationships, hierarchical and associative, between terms

- term notes for clarification

- additional common-use shortcuts and phrase inversions as nonpreferred terms

Taxonomies for automated indexing should have

- no subtle differences between terms

- precoordinated terms, but no structured subdivisions

- many varied nonpreferred terms, including non-noun phrases

In addition, automated indexing is more suitable for applying weighting or relevance ranking to assigned index terms, whether as primary or secondary, or by even further gradations measured in percentages. In human indexing, this process requires an additional step and decision for the indexer, but in automated indexing, especially that which is based on statistical methods, it is easy to implement.

The same taxonomy may be used for both human indexing and automated indexing. Within an organization, auto-categorization may be applied to some content while humans still index other content. There are also hybrid strategies of machine-aided indexing, which provide automated assistance to human indexers. The humans' skill and analysis are combined with software to raise productivity and speed, while still allowing indexer-editors to make final choices to ensure indexing accuracy. If a taxonomy is to be used for both human and automated indexing, whether separately or combined in machine-aided indexing, there are not necessarily any conflicts. You will need to put additional work into the taxonomy, though, so that it serves both methods of indexing well. Thus, it is important to know from the beginning how the taxonomy will be used.

Endnotes

1. Lynda Moulton, speaking at the Boston KM Forum, Waltham, Massachusetts, June 18, 2009.

2. Bernard Chester, "Auto-Categorization and Records Management," *AIIM E-Doc Magazine* 18, no. 2 (March 2004): 16.

3. *Data Harmony Version 3.3 User's Guide–M.A.I. (Machine Aided Indexer)* (Albuquerque, NM: Access Innovations, 2006), 53.

4. Bonnie Burwell, "Auto-Categorization Tools," *Intranet Professional* (Mar/Apr 2002), accessed December 20, 2015, www.intranetstoday .com/Articles/Editorial/Features/Auto-Categorization-Tools-56706 .aspx

5. Tom Reamy, email to author, June 23, 2009.

6. Louis Rosenfeld and Peter Morville, *Information architecture for the World Wide Web*, 2nd ed. (Sebastopol, CA: O'Reilly, 2002), 325. (The section on auto-categorization is not included in more recent editions of this book.)

7. John Challis (CEO/CTO of Concept Searching Ltd.), email to author, October 6, 2015.

8. "Jumpstart Taxonomy Development," Concept Searching Taxonomy Library, August 14, 2009, accessed December 20, 2015, www .conceptsearching.com/Web/Userfiles/File/ConceptSearchingTaxonomy Library.pdf

9. Product information within both paragraphs on Cogito Taxonomy Studio is partially from Bryan Bell (executive vice president, Expert System USA), email to author, October 26, 2015.

10. Alice Redmond-Neal (chief taxonomist, Access Innovations, Inc.), email to author, July 20, 2009, and Margie Hlava (president of Access Innovations, Inc.), email to author, July 21, 2009.

11. François Thibault (international sales director, Mondeca), email to author, October 21, 2015.

12. Open Text: Open Text Content Analytics Data Sheet, accessed December 20, 2015, www.opentext.com/file_source/OpenText/en_US/PDF/ open-text-content-analytics-product-sheet.pdf and Martin Brousseau (product manager at OpenText), email to author, October 2, 2015.

Chapter 8

Taxonomy Structures

Taxonomies: find, organise, discover.
—Patrick Lambe

We have discussed the importance of well-designed terms and relationships, as well as considerations in human and automated indexing, but a taxonomy usually involves structure as well. After all, the technical designation for a taxonomy or controlled vocabulary is *knowledge organization system*. If taxonomies are to organize knowledge, then they must be organized themselves. This chapter looks at structure via hierarchies, facets, and categories. These different methods of organizing and structuring a taxonomy are not mutually exclusive and may overlap. Chapter 9 addresses the impact of taxonomy structure, including both hierarchies and facets, on the display of the taxonomy.

Hierarchies

Hierarchies, also known as tree structures, are the extension of broader term/narrower term relationships to include every term within a controlled vocabulary. They are the defining feature of hierarchical taxonomies. The emphasis of a hierarchy is on categorization, classification, or sorting. They are created—and used—largely from the top down.

Hierarchies were originally developed to classify things—plants, animals, tools, products, books, or other creative works—but are increasingly used now to organize concepts or topics as well. Examples of hierarchies for classifying things include the following:

- Linnaean taxonomy for classification of living organisms
- Dewey Decimal Classification for books
- SIC or NAICS codes for businesses and industries
- Open Directory Project (www.dmoz.org) for websites

When classifying physical things, which can go into only one place, such as books on a shelf or an object in a museum, each taxonomy term can have only one broader term. However, most modern taxonomies exist in electronic form, and so do the items to which they refer, such as websites or digital media. Therefore, a concept can virtually exist in more than one place in the hierarchy. In other words, a term can have more than one broader term; this is called a polyhierarchy. However, even if a taxonomy supports polyhierarchies, they should be created with discretion. There still needs to be an overarching general structure that is logical and easy to use; too many polyhierarchies could become confusing. Designing a clear hierarchical structure takes more than just knowledge of the subject area, as there is often more than one way to create a hierarchy.

Certain subject areas lend themselves more easily to hierarchies than others. Those areas that already have a natural, intuitive, or standard classification scheme are good candidates for hierarchical arrangements of terms. Examples include geographic places, organizational or governmental department structures, industries/products, academic disciplines, scientific/natural objects, and chemicals. Subject areas that are more challenging to arrange into tree-type hierarchies include methods and activities, current events, and any broad area of knowledge.

Arrangements of Hierarchies

Even a "logical" hierarchy may not be as easy to create as first anticipated. When alternatives for classification exist, you first face the decision of how to design a categorization structure. Industries, for example, can be organized by a standard classification system, such as SIC or NAICS codes, or alternatively by vertical market sector, such as information technology (hardware, software, and services), healthcare, transportation, and media. A similar decision would be whether to organize products by material and manufacturing technology (metal products, glass products, plastic products, etc.) or by end use (office products, kitchen products, giftware, toys, etc.). In other areas, terms for organizations can be grouped differently, such as by their objectives (charitable work, political action, educational outreach) or by political or religious affiliation. Government agencies can be categorized by type or by state/country affiliation. Finally, places, which initially may seem perfectly simple to classify, can be organized either by geospatial location on the globe or by type of place (country, city, body of water, etc.). Figure 8.1 illustrates these two different ways to classify places.

Factors to Consider

In determining the arrangement of the hierarchy for your taxonomy, you need to consider user requirements and expectations.

Geo-spatial hierarchy				
Geographics				
- North America	- South	- Europe	- Asia	- Africa
-- United States	America	-- Eastern Europe	-- Middle East	-- East Africa
--- New England	-- Brazil	etc.	etc.	etc.
---- Massachusetts	etc.			
----- Boston				
Term-type hierarchy				
Geographics				
- Cities	- U.S. States	- Countries	- Continents	
-- Abijan	-- Alabama	-- Afghanistan	-- Africa	
-- Amsterdam	-- Alaska	-- Albania	-- Asia	
etc.	etc.	etc.	etc.	

Figure 8.1 Two different methods of displaying a geographic hierarchy

Ask yourself this: Based on their background and perspective, how would the majority of the users most likely classify the subject matter? For products, classification by end use makes most sense for users who are consumers, whereas classification by material type is more appropriate for wholesalers. For organizing national and international government agencies, a US-centric taxonomy structure would be appropriate for US federal employees but not for international users. For scientific or technical subject areas, while a "correct" hierarchy may exist, if users are not knowledgeable about the subject, then they will not know under which broader term to find desired narrower terms. For example, a classification of world languages based on language families (Indo-European languages, Ural-Altaic languages, etc.) makes sense if your users are scholars, but for the general public or younger students, classification by world region (European languages, Asian languages, etc.) might make more sense. User testing, if you have access to it, is ideal for supporting this kind of decision making. Having users participate in card-sorting exercises, described further in Chapter 10, can reveal valuable information about how your users prefer to categorize concepts.

In designing hierarchies, additional factors to consider include the following:

- Support of polyhierarchies: If the policy prohibits polyhierarchies, then input from stakeholders and user studies are even more critical in helping you decide how to arrange the hierarchies.

- Permissibility of node labels: If node labels (category designations, not linked to content, described later) are allowed, you will have greater flexibility to design truly accurate hierarchies.

- Retrieval inclusive of all narrower terms (also called recursive): If searching can automatically retrieve all content linked to a term's narrower terms, you should be extra careful that the hierarchies function as expected.

Named Entities in Hierarchies

A more specific issue in designing hierarchies is deciding at what level to relate corresponding named entity terms, if at all. A hierarchical taxonomy comprises primarily generic–specific hierarchical relationships, but instance relationships could be included within it. Sometimes named entities are in a completely separate list, an authority file (as discussed later in the section "Multiple Vocabularies and Categories"). Even if named entities are maintained separately, there still could be hierarchical relationships created between these entities and their corresponding generic terms. You then need to decide at what level within the generic hierarchy to create the relationships to the entity instances. Creating relationships from the most specific (lowest hierarchy level) generic term to named entity instances may seem to be the most logical policy, but it is not always best from the end-user perspective. Users might not know or expect to have to go so deep into the hierarchy to find named entities. Furthermore, entity relationships could change over time, requiring greater attention to maintenance.

In the following example, a generic-specific hierarchy of political occupations has instance relationship to named entities of individual people. As the taxonomist, you may choose to create the entity instance relationships to the most specific terms of **presidents** and **prime ministers,** or you may choose to relate all these named entities at one level higher to **heads of state & government**.

Heads of state & government	← names of all kinds of heads of state & government linked here, *or*
—Presidents	← names of presidents linked here
—Prime ministers	← names of prime ministers linked here

The reason to consider relating the names of individuals to the slightly broader **heads of state & government** instead of to one or the other of its narrower terms is that users might not know whether the head of state in a particular country is a president or a prime minister. It would be more convenient for these users to have a single alphabetical list for all. On the other hand, if the hierarchy belongs to the library of an educational institution, there may be an added objective to educate the student users as to the most complete and correct information. Another issue to consider is whether there are entities that do not neatly fall into a most specific generic term category (e.g., Vladimir Putin, whose title has switched between president and prime minister), in which case moving the entities up a level would be better.

Depth and Breadth of Hierarchies

Related to the issue of how to design the classification structure are decisions regarding the depth and breadth of each hierarchical level. For a taxonomy on a website, a popular rule of thumb is to go only three levels deep and have only six to eight concepts per level. These numbers are based on website user-experience design guidelines and practice,[1] which suggest that users have the patience to click down only to a third level and can scan only six to eight term entries at once. These conventions make sense for a small taxonomy displayed as a web navigation menu, where the space is confined to a strip along the top or a margin along the side. In reality, though, a taxonomy may have hundreds or thousands of preferred terms. Therefore, for a hierarchical taxonomy, you often need to consider how best to balance the number of levels (depth) and number of terms per level (breadth).

There are no hard rules on how to structure hierarchies. The following pair of examples shows how industry names could be placed in a deep hierarchy of many levels, which is what is done with NAICS industry codes, or in a flat alphabetical list, which in this case comes from the professional networking site LinkedIn.

NAICS (deep hierarchy)	**LinkedIn.com (flat list)**
Industries	Industry
- Transportation services	- Accounting
-- Air transportation	- Airlines/Aviation
--- Scheduled air transportation services	- Alternative Dispute Resolution
---- Scheduled air freight transportation services	- Alternative Medicine
etc.	etc.

Factors to Consider

Factors that may influence your decisions on the depth and breadth of a hierarchy include user expectations, the need to maintain consistency, and user interface design. The first consideration is the nature of the content and the users' needs and expectations. If the content for the taxonomy is scholarly or scientific or if the users are researchers or students, the users will expect many levels. A consumer- or news-oriented service, on the other hand, accessed by the public, would likely have fewer levels but a greater number of top-level terms and terms at each level. Areas that users understand as naturally hierarchical, such as industries/product types and geographic places, can support more levels of depth than subjects that are less intuitively hierarchical, such as business management topics.

Another issue to keep in mind is that, inevitably, the greater the number of levels, the less consistency there will be across levels.

This may or may not be important. If users are experts in the subject area or are using the taxonomy frequently, providing accurate terms is more important than providing a uniform-looking hierarchy. If, on the other hand, users are from the general public and are likely to be new to the taxonomy, then a logically organized taxonomy with a relatively consistent number of levels and consistent degree of specificity at each level would be desirable.

The user interface display, with its vertical or horizontal space limitations, also has an impact on hierarchy design decisions. Therefore, it is advantageous to know in advance what the interface will look like. If each level will display in a separate webpage, then as many terms as can fit onto one page in two or three columns without scrolling could work nicely. Such long lists of terms at the same level, however, may be difficult for the user to skim quickly and are more appropriate for alphabetized lists of proper nouns. If the taxonomy will display as an expandable tree in which sublevels appear, such as by clicking on a plus sign, then more than three levels is fine, but the number of terms per level ought not extend beyond a single-page length in a single column, because the position in the hierarchy cannot be seen. Finally, if the taxonomy will be implemented in facets (described later), then deep hierarchies are less likely to be needed or desirable. From the taxonomist's perspective, ideally the taxonomy design should dictate the user interface design, not vice versa. Often, however, a product development team designs the user interface without giving consideration to content and prior to creation of the taxonomy, and the taxonomist needs to adapt.

All, General, and Other

In certain areas, thesauri and full hierarchical taxonomies, by their nature, affect indexing and searching differently. One such area is the indexing and retrieval of *all*, *general*, and *other* topics pertaining to a taxonomy term that also has narrower terms.

"All" Uses of a Broader Term

Because a hierarchical taxonomy categorizes everything, users often expect to retrieve everything within a category at the broader level. This is sometimes called "rolled up" or "recursive retrieval." (The word *recursive* also has other usages in information science.) When the user selects a term, everything indexed to that term *and* everything that is indexed to all of its narrower terms are retrieved in a single, large result set. Whether the indexing is done by humans or is automatic, recursive retrieval can be implemented automatically. In taxonomies or thesauri that do not consist merely of one single hierarchy or a few large hierarchies, recursive searching is not so common or at least is not the default. Instead, a broader term is indexed to its broader/general treatment of the subject only. The following example, using the term **crafts**, compares recursive retrieval in a hierarchical taxonomy with nonrecursive retrieval in a less hierarchical taxonomy or thesaurus (remember, capitalization of terms is more common in hierarchical taxonomies):

Recursive retrieval:

Crafts ← retrieves content on all crafts, including beadwork, embroidery, etc.

> Beadwork ← retrieves content on beadwork

> Embroidery ← retrieves content on embroidery

Nonrecursive retrieval:

Crafts ← retrieves content only indexed with crafts, that is, crafts in general

> Beadwork ← retrieves content on beadwork

> Embroidery ← retrieves content on embroidery

"General" Usage of a Broader Term

If recursive indexing and retrieval is the default in a hierarchical taxonomy and if the user does not have the option to change it, then there needs to be an additional way to index and retrieve only the content that truly is of a general nature as it corresponds to a broader term's meaning. Typically, to achieve this, the taxonomist creates a category under the broader term that has the word *general* in it, as in the following example for **crafts**:

Crafts ← retrieves content on all crafts, including narrower terms and crafts in general

> **Crafts in general**   ← retrieves content on crafts in general
> **Beadwork**   ← retrieves content on beadwork
> **Embroidery**   ← retrieves content on embroidery

You could also name the term **General crafts** instead of **Crafts in general**. On the indexing side, there may or may not actually be a term labeled *general*, as such an additional indexing term is not needed. Indexing of general content could still be to the broader term name, in this case **Crafts**, but the display of such indexing would be associated with the *general* term, and the results attached to the broader term name, **Crafts**, are the sum total of recursive results. The need for a *general* term arises only in hierarchical taxonomies and specifically in those hierarchical taxonomies that default to recursive retrieval.

Sometimes the end user has the option to select either general or all/recursive retrieval, using a radio button or a check box. Indexing/retrieval systems in which terms correspond with numeric codes tend to allow this flexibility, whereby truncating the numeric code retrieves *all* narrower concepts and adding the trailing zeros matches the broader term only for *general*. In the following example, based on Predicasts2 industry codes (a historical periodical index), a search on **6300** is for insurance in general, whereas **63** would retrieve all insurance, including life and health insurance.

6300	Insurance
6310	Life Insurance
6320	Accident & Health Insurance
6322	Health Insurance

Allowing such end-user control is more likely to be an option in a system aimed at relatively expert users.

"Other" Usage of a Broader Term

Parallel with the idea of *general* terms is the idea of *other* or *miscellaneous*. If a specific topic arises in the content being indexed and there is no matching term in the taxonomy (yet), then the content item should be indexed with the next broader term. This is standard indexing practice, whether or not the concept is an explicit narrower term.

However, in the case of a hierarchical taxonomy in which broader terms are *not* used as index terms but only for recursive retrieval results and in which the broad concept itself is indexed with a *general*, a dilemma arises. The new narrow concept should *not* be indexed to a term used for *general*. The solution is to introduce yet another narrower concept called *other* or a variation thereof. Situations that call for such an *other* term are rare, and generally creating an *other* or *miscellaneous* term should be avoided, but sometimes it is a practical solution. Following is an example with **crafts**:

Crafts
> **Crafts in general**
> **Beadwork**
> **Embroidery**
etc.
> **Other crafts**

An example in practice is the SIC and NAICS industry codes/ terms, which have several industry classification types "for other establishments not elsewhere classified." The following are three separate examples of NAICS codes/terms:

1129	**Other Animal Production**
3329	**Other Fabricated Metal Product Manufacturing**
51119	**Other Publishers**

The distinction between *general* and *other/miscellaneous* may be too subtle for automated indexing to discern, so this structure works better with human indexing. If you are using automated indexing that is only questionably reliable in this area, it might be best to avoid creating *other* and *general* categories altogether. The broader term would simply be used for all of these (*all*, *general*, and *other*), and the distinctions would be sacrificed. Another possibility would be to combine *general* and *other*, since they are difficult to distinguish.

Node Labels

Another way to create a more detailed hierarchical structure in a taxonomy is by including what are called node labels. A node label can be considered a dummy term: a label to help organize the hierarchy, but not a real term used in indexing, hence the designation *label* rather than *term*. If implemented, node labels should be designated somehow (enclosed in brackets, or set in a different color, font, or style), so it is clear that they are labels and not index terms. Node labels can appear anywhere in a taxonomy, but the most common are of two kinds:

1. Broad categories: as top terms or at intermediate to high levels in the taxonomy

2. Facet indicators: for the most specific terms

You may find that the designations *facet indicator* and *node label* are used interchangeably, but technically a facet indicator is a kind of node label.

In a hierarchical taxonomy, it is typical to have named hierarchies, which are named for their top term, such as **Politics & Government**, **Business & Finance**, **Buildings & Facilities**, or **Occupations**, yet not have these top terms actually used in indexing, since they are too broad to be practical. These terms would then be designated as node labels that display to the users but cannot be linked to content. Even the human indexers see the node labels, which help structure the taxonomy, but the indexing software prohibits the use of the node labels in indexing. In some hierarchical taxonomies, not merely the top terms but even second-level concepts might be designated as node labels only, and only the lowest level(s) are actual indexing terms.

A particular kind of node label, called a facet indicator, is used to subcategorize a relatively large number of narrower terms, all at the same hierarchical level, by type or facet. This is the original application of the idea of "facets" in controlled vocabularies and is not exactly the same as top-level facets used to indicate complete separate taxonomies or vocabularies, which are discussed in more detail in the next section. When facet indicators are used, terms in a controlled vocabulary are first classified by subject area and then more narrowly by their facet aspect. Figure 8.2 is an example of the taxonomy term for **automobiles** and its narrower terms; the facet indicators appear in italics.

Use of brackets, angle or square, is another way to indicate facet indicators. Facet indicators tend to occur in thesauri used by human indexers, if they are implemented at all. They have become less common now that top-level facets have become more popular, but they remain useful for a thesaurus that is both broad in scope and detailed in coverage.

Automobiles
  by body type
    Coupes
    Sedans
    Station wagons
    Minivans
    Sport-utility vehicles
  by engine type
    Gasoline engine automobiles
    Diesel engine automobiles
    Electric automobiles
    Natural gas engine automobiles
    Alcohol engine automobiles
  by transmission type
    Automatic transmission automobiles
    Manual transmission automobiles

Figure 8.2 Facet indicators for types of automobiles

Facets

Facets are categorical groupings of terms within a taxonomy. They are used to support what is called faceted classification or faceted search. Facets serve to describe content from multiple angles, perspectives, or attributes. Top-level facets have some similarities with the previously described concept of facet indicators but are implemented somewhat differently. In the case of top-level facets, terms are generally classified first by facet, and then within each facet there might be a subject hierarchy. This is the opposite of how facet indicators work, whereby terms are classified first by subject and then by facet (such as by a subject **automobiles** and then by a facet indicator *by body type*). Facets in faceted classification each represent their own distinct hierarchy and are mutually exclusive. The facet values could be a flat list or, if numerous, organized into a hierarchy. The objective of facets is to allow for searching on multiple terms in combination (postcoordination), with one term from each facet. Whereas facet indicators in a hierarchical taxonomy are precoordinated, the facets in faceted search serve postcoordinated searching. In this sense, a facet is not merely a grouping of concepts but also a "dimension" of a query. In fact, the word *facet* comes from *face*, or side of something.

Types and Examples of Facets

The idea of faceted classification was first developed by the Indian mathematician and librarian S. R. Ranganathan in the late 1920s as an alternative to the Dewey Decimal Classification system for books, which he felt was inadequate because it permits only a single classification number for what are often multifaceted books. He called his system Colon Classification, as his call-number notation display made use of colons and other forms of punctuation to separate the various facet terms associated with the title being cataloged. Ranganathan developed a set of five broad facets:

- Personality: topic or orientation

- Matter: things or materials

- Energy: actions
- Space: places or locations
- Time: times or time periods

The colon classification did not catch on, largely because it was too complicated for the average user. Today, with the use of computers and database management software, colon-type coding schemes are not needed to implement faceted classification, and searching by facets has become easy to implement and use. Each content item is a database record, and each field of that record is described by a facet. Thus, faceted search is sometimes called *fielded* search.

Modern designations of generic facets include those suggested for enterprise taxonomies by Patrick Lambe in his book *Organising Knowledge* (2007):[3]

- People and organizations
- Things and parts of things
- Activity cycles
- Locations

Louis Rosenfeld and Peter Morville, in *Information Architecture* (2002, 2006, 2015) aka the "polar bear book," suggest the following as typical facets for the "business world":[4]

- Topic
- Product
- Document type
- Audience
- Geography
- Price

While it may be helpful to refer back to these generic facets, the nature of your content should be the primary determining factor in how you design your facets, if you choose to go this route. Faceted taxonomies and faceted search work best for content that is structured into records that all have at least some characteristics in common. Following are examples of more specific facets on various public websites:

For job postings at Simply Hired (www.simplyhired.com/a/jobs/advanced-search):

- Location
- Posted Within (date range)
- Job Type (Full time, Part time, etc.)
- Experience (years range)
- Education (degree)
- Special Features
- Job Boards (exclude, only)
- Recruiters (exclude, only)
- Company Size
- Company Revenue

For recipes at Food.com (Advanced search at www.food.com/recipe):

- Ingredient
- Meal
- Course
- Diet & Nutrition
- Occasion
- Cuisine
- Preparation

For cars at Kelley Blue Book (www.kbb.com/cars-for-sale):

- Make & Model
- Price Range
- Body Style
- Type (New/Used/Certified Pre-Owned)
- Fuel Type
- Engine
- Drive
- Transmission
- Doors (2 or 4)
- Exterior Color

For art collection objects at the Carnegie Museum of Art (www.cmoa.org/collection-search):

- Nationality
- Date Range
- Classification (type of art)
- Department
- Theme
- Location in the Museum

Implementing Facets

Facets work best with content that is of a somewhat consistent type. This way the same facets may be used across all the content. These could be collections comprising just news articles, technical reports, instructional materials, product data, or image files—but not a miscellaneous collection of all of these. Most of the content should be described by most of the facets, but it is not necessary that each facet apply to every content record. The more similar the content is, the greater the number of facets that can be supported. Thus, from the preceding examples, we see how job descriptions, which are quite uniform and structured, might be supported by up to eight facets, while other types of content would support fewer facets. For a diverse collection of articles, you might have as few as two facets—place and subject—and the subjects could comprise a large thesaurus or hierarchical taxonomy. This latter, more limited implementation of facets is actually quite common, though this type of taxonomy is not necessarily referred to as faceted.

The facets within a single taxonomy and content set can vary greatly. Some facets are relatively large, and some are very small. You could have a large hierarchical facet for over a hundred product types and another facet that contains only three or four values for types of users/customers. Facets also permit you to have taxonomy terms that are mere adjectives, since facets tend to describe the attributes of things. These could be qualities, colors, sizes, and so forth. In general, though, faceted taxonomies are not as large as purely hierarchical taxonomies or thesauri.

Developing facets also involves a slightly different analysis of the content than does developing regular term hierarchies. You look at the content to see the similar patterns and then determine all the different aspects and variables for searching. It is a top-down approach, coming up with facets first and populating them with terms afterward. Although usually it is clear which facet a given term belongs to, there are occasions when it is not so obvious. For example, it is common to have a location or place facet, which comprises geographic places. However, questions then arise regarding man-made structures and institutions. Institutions (schools, hospitals, museums, libraries, churches, etc.) are really organizations but sometimes are considered places as well. While in general they should not be included in a location facet, specific campuses and buildings could be. As another example, it is also common to have a facet for actions, activities, or events. This is often the case in a taxonomy for business information, which might include such concepts as **product introductions, orders/sales deals, partner contracts**, and **acquisitions and mergers**. Yet there may also be a general subject facet, which includes business-related topics, such as **management, finance**, and **human resources**. In this case, it might be difficult to decide whether certain topics, such as **sales, contracts**, or **joint ventures**, belong in the actions or in the subject facet. User search behavior, content, and indexing (manual or automatic) all need to be carefully considered in making such decisions.

Top-level facets are sometimes confused with hierarchies or categories. Categories, described in the next section, are not as strictly defined as facets and may refer to any grouping of terms. Hierarchies differ from facets in two ways. First, terms in hierarchies, unlike facets, are not limited to *aspects* of a search and thus are not necessarily set up for postcoordination, as in the case of one term from each of multiple facets. Terms may be selected from multiple hierarchies to simply describe several topics (not aspects) about a content resource. Second, while you cannot have polyhierarchies across different facets, because facets are distinct and mutually exclusive, hierarchies are not always strictly separated, and polyhierarchies may transcend them. To test whether your proposed groupings are indeed valid as facets, try putting the word *by* in front of each facet name, even if this will not be implemented in the display, and see if the facets make sense as a means of searching.

Facets can be combined with hierarchies in either of two ways: hierarchies within facets or facets within hierarchies. If the terms within a facet are topical in nature and too numerous to browse in a single, flat list, then it may be more user-friendly to organize them into a simple hierarchy. Typically the display of terms within a facet is not conducive to more than a two-level hierarchy. It's not unusual to have a hierarchy within only one or two facets, while the rest of the facets contain shorter lists of terms with no hierarchy. This is a method often employed in enterprise taxonomies. In taxonomies in which each facet contains a multilevel hierarchy, the designations *facet* and *hierarchy* may be used interchangeably.

The other combination, that of facets within hierarchies, is common within ecommerce product taxonomies. The end-user first browses a hierarchy of categories, and then once a specific (product) category is selected, then there is the option to filter the results by facets for each of various attributes, such as product-specific features. Figure 8.3 provides an example screenshot from the Sears

Figure 8.3 Facets for men's shirts on the Sears retail website, where facets can be expanded to reveal the terms/values within each (Source: www.sears.com)

retail website, where, after the user initially browses the hierarchical taxonomy of Clothing, Shoes & Jewelry > Clothing > Men's Clothing > Men's Shirts, then facets, some of which are specific to the selected topic of Men's Shirts, such as the type of collar, are available to refine the results further.

Facets can also cover metadata that is not limited to topical taxonomies. This information could include author, content type, file type, language, source, audience, etc., but each of these facets would still have its own controlled vocabulary. If managed separately by a metadata librarian and not a taxonomist, then these fields will more likely be called metadata rather than being called taxonomy facets. Different organizations manage such metadata differently.

Multiple Vocabularies and Categories

Hierarchies and facets are ways of organizing taxonomy terms that have a direct impact on how the end user browses and makes use of the taxonomy. There are additional ways to organize a taxonomy or set of taxonomies that are more administrative and may or may not impact the end-user display. These include having separate vocabulary files and having categories or classes in the taxonomy.

Separate Taxonomy/Vocabulary Files

A given body of content with its own indexing system and its own search/browse/retrieval interface, or what together might be called a single taxonomy "project," may have a single taxonomy or a set of multiple taxonomies, depending on how you define and organize your taxonomies. There is no standard to define what constitutes a single taxonomy as opposed to multiple taxonomies, since originally this word was not even used in the plural. Although all terms in a hierarchical taxonomy must belong to a single hierarchy, this does not necessarily mean that each hierarchy is its own taxonomy. Sometimes taxonomies are defined this way, but not always. Additionally, if the controlled vocabulary is not hierarchical, it may be even less obvious how to distinguish one vocabulary from another.

Factors that contribute to the designation of a single taxonomy/ thesaurus include relationship types, subject scope, and taxonomy usage. Generally, standard hierarchical and associative relationships do not transcend multiple taxonomies. An exception would be instance-type hierarchical relationships between topics in a taxonomy and named entities (proper nouns) maintained in a separate controlled vocabulary. Other types of relationships may link terms across multiple taxonomies, but they would likely be special-purpose relationships, such as equivalency mappings or translations. One taxonomy is for one subject area, although that subject area could be very broad, for example a taxonomy could be designed to support indexing of the topics in the daily news. Usually a taxonomy is more limited in scope, covering, for example just technology topics or just health topics. Generally, a single taxonomy is utilized in a single indexing/tagging method and with its own indexing policy. For the end user, a retrieval function is served by a single taxonomy, which might support a search function or provide a set of browse categories. In any case, sometimes the taxonomy owner or stakeholders, rather than the taxonomist, determines whether it is to be considered as one taxonomy or multiple taxonomies.

Whether hierarchical or not, it is often useful to break out a large controlled vocabulary into multiple vocabulary files, lists, or databases, both for administrative purposes and to support certain user interface features. Separate vocabularies can support the following:

- Continued distinctions between preinstalled, user-created, and user-imported taxonomies

- Different sets of descriptive attributes for terms (such as location for organization, NAICS codes for companies, birth/death dates for people, etc.)

- Different access privileges by different taxonomists and taxonomy-editing subject matter experts

- Different administrative policies, such as indexer rights to add and approve new terms

- Systematic enforcement of different editorial policies for term format, such as title capitalization for named entities but not for topical terms

- Special features for different types of terms, such as subfields for last name and first name and modifiers for products or works

- Indexing policies that require a minimum and/or maximum number of terms of certain types

- Use of auto-categorization or entity extraction with some vocabularies and not others

- Separate and more efficient searching and browsing by taxonomists, indexers, and end users, such as listing named entities alphabetically

- Implementation of features such as filtering in the end-user interface

One of the most common ways to break out controlled vocabularies is between named entities and topical subjects, due to a number of differences between these two types of controlled vocabularies. Separate vocabulary files may also be maintained for different kinds of named entities, such as for people, places, and organizations. You might choose to call your sets of topical subjects *thesauri* or *taxonomies*, while calling your named entities *authority files*, and manage them somewhat separately, perhaps by different taxonomists and perhaps even with different titles.

Distinct vocabulary files may still permit relationships between terms across these different vocabularies, but the databases need to be deliberately designed to do so. As long as the vocabularies are maintained in a kind of relational database management system, then it is possible to set up a kind of table for each vocabulary, with a standard set of fields, and have records within each table relate to records in other tables. Thus, for example, named entities in one vocabulary file can still be linked to their respective broader terms (instance-type) in another vocabulary file, such as linking **Mississippi River** to **rivers**. Leading taxonomy management systems support these cross-file relationships (such as Synaptica, which calls them objects), but simpler tools, such as MultiTes, do not necessarily include this feature.

Categories

Categories, also called classes, constitute an additional means of classifying and organizing terms in a taxonomy or set of taxonomies. Nearly all commercial taxonomy management software supports the use of such categories, often as defined within an administrative feature. Categories transcend hierarchies, facets, and vocabulary files and are applied to individual terms. Usually, though, terms within the same hierarchy belong to the same category, and we describe a narrower term as "inheriting" the category and other properties of its broader term. The taxonomist creates a set of category designations and applies them to taxonomy terms, in much the same way as an indexer applies terms to content. Categories are not types of terms, but rather part of the metadata of taxonomy terms. Categories can also be added to sets of terms in a batch method. The same taxonomy term may belong to more than one category. Depending on the purpose of the categories, the end-user searchers may not be aware of the presence of the categories, though.

Categories have unlimited uses, but a common purpose is to designate an intended end-use implementation of a set of taxonomy terms that are all in one master taxonomy. This could involve segmenting the taxonomies to serve any of the following:

- Different organizational uses, such as external website, extranet, intranet, product database, etc.

- Different group or department uses of internal enterprise taxonomies, such as human resources, finance, engineering, customer service, etc.

- Different industry markets or database products of published content taxonomies, such as healthcare, financial services, high tech, government, etc.

- Different classes that are defined for the purposes of customized, semantic relationships that are permitted only between terms belonging to certain pairs of classes, which is the case in ontology-like taxonomies

There are no rules or standards regarding how you define or word your categories. They simply reflect their purpose. Thus, the category names **human resources, finance, engineering**, and **customer service** could be used for designating department use, or the category names **healthcare, financial services, high tech**, and **government** could designate industry markets.

If your taxonomy management software does not support relationships between terms that are within separate vocabulary files, then you could also utilize categories as a means of breaking a single master taxonomy into differently administered subtaxonomies.

Thus, categories could be used for many of the same purposes as separate vocabulary files, such as designating taxonomy types, such as topics, named people, organizations, and places. As with separate vocabulary files, categories could also be implemented as a means for the end user to filter the taxonomy so as to contain only certain subsets of terms when performing a search in the user interface.

Categories can be used to provide a little more structure to an otherwise nonhierarchical thesaurus. If, for example, a hierarchical display is desired for a nonhierarchical thesaurus, then category names could be treated as top terms. Although this would not be an ideal hierarchy and the number of second-level terms might be very great, it could prove adequate as long as the thesaurus is not too large.

Finally, in software that combines thesaurus management and ontology management capabilities, categories may be used to designate "classes" as they are used in an ontology. When ontologists designate customized semantic relationships, they must specify between which classes a given relationship type will function. For example, a semantic relationship pair of "employs"/"is employed by" can only be used between terms within a Person class and an Organization class, and the relationships must point in the proper direction between the terms in those two classes. Ontology management software will enforce this requirement of classes and manages classes differently from generic categories, but sometimes thesaurus management software with customizable relationships and categories will be used instead to create an ontology-like controlled vocabulary, in which case the taxonomist should take care to set up the categories correctly. For example, the thesaurus management software MultiTes permits the creation of semantic relationships and customized categories, but the software does not enforce the use of categories as restrictive, ontology-like classes for the relationship types.

Endnotes

1. The "three-click rule" is popular in user-interface design but user testing has not proven its need, as indicated in the following article: Joshua Porter, "Testing the Three-Click Rule, *User Interface Engineering*, April 16, 2003, accessed September 19, 2015, www.uie.com/articles/three_click_rule

2. Gale Group, *The Gale Group Guide to Predicasts Codes* (Foster City, CA: Gale Group, 1999).

3. Patrick Lambe, *Organising Knowledge: Taxonomies, Knowledge and Organisational Effectiveness* (Oxford: Chandos Publishing, 2007), 34.

4. Louis Rosenfeld, Peter Morville, and Jorge Arango, *Information Architecture: For the Web and Beyond*, 4th ed. (Sebastopol, CA: O'Reilly, 2015), 304. These facets are also listed in the section on facets in previous editions of the book, 2002 and 2006, under the title *Information Architecture for the World Wide Web*.

Chapter 9

Taxonomy Displays

So many taxonomies, so little time.
—Seth Earley

A taxonomy has different kinds of users, and hence the same taxonomy may be implemented with different user interfaces or displays. Taxonomy users may include

1. taxonomists, searching and browsing the taxonomy in order to update and maintain it

2. human indexers or taggers, using the taxonomy to index or tag content

3. subject area researchers, using the taxonomy to better understand a subject area, without seeking linked content

4. end-user searchers, using the taxonomy to find specific content or discover information

All taxonomies are used at least by a taxonomist and by end users, but not all taxonomies display fully to the end users. Additionally, human indexers and possibly also subject area researchers use some taxonomies. These taxonomies are fully displayed, possibly with more than one format option. Taxonomies that are made available to third-party subject area researchers (which may include other taxonomists) are usually also used by human indexers, but not all taxonomies used by human indexers are provided in a displayable format to other parties.

The first section of this chapter discusses various standard displays of the type of taxonomy called a thesaurus, as used by taxonomists, human indexers, subject area researchers, and occasionally end-user searchers. The following sections look specifically at end-user displays of different kinds of taxonomies, not just thesauri. Options for taxonomy end-user displays are largely determined by the taxonomy organization and structure, which could be any of the following:

- A thesaurus of terms, with no dominating hierarchies
- A hierarchical taxonomy or taxonomies
- A set of facets or categories

Unlike the taxonomy itself, the design of the end-user display is often a decision involving more people than just the taxonomist. Nevertheless, the taxonomist usually contributes to the design of the end-user display at least to some degree.

Thesaurus Displays and Outputs

A thesaurus, in contrast to a simple hierarchical taxonomy, is often the most suitable kind of knowledge organization system when there is a relatively large controlled vocabulary and human indexers are involved. A thesaurus differs from a hierarchical taxonomy not only in its focus on the individual term and its relationships, both hierarchical and associative, but also in its flexibility with regard to different displays. Although you could sort a hierarchical taxonomy into a single alphabetical list of terms, if the taxonomy lacks non-preferred terms, then an alphabetical list is not very useful. It would be like a book index without *See* references or double posts. A single thesaurus, by contrast, can display its terms hierarchically or alphabetically, as we have already seen in the user interface display options of thesaurus management software described in Chapter 5.

Not only are there different display options in the interface used by the taxonomist, but the indexers, thesaurus researchers (not searching for content), and possibly even end-user searchers may also have the ability to choose different display or access options. Published thesauri typically have at least two formats, one for an alphabetical presentation of the thesaurus and one for the same thesaurus in a hierarchical presentation.

In addition to the different user interface display options, full-featured thesaurus management software offers various output or report options, which can be displayed to the screen or printed. These different output displays are useful for reviewing, sharing, or publishing the thesaurus. In addition to the general choice between hierarchical and alphabetical, there may be further variations on each of these formats. Types of thesaurus output displays include:

- Alphabetical simple list: Terms listed alphabetically without any details displayed

- Alphabetical flat format: Terms with all their immediate relationships (UF, BT, NT, RT) and notes if any (also known as a term record), and often the default alphabetical display for a thesaurus

- Full-term hierarchy: Terms with multiple relationship levels displayed (such as BT1, BT2, etc.; NT1, NT2, etc.)

- Top term hierarchy: A listing of only the broadest terms, each one including a display of its hierarchy of narrower terms underneath

- Permuted/rotated index: Terms listed by their component words (i.e., an alphabetic list of words within terms), and variations known as KWIC (keyword in context) and KWOC (keyword out of context)

Alphabetical Simple List

An alphabetical display of a thesaurus allows users to browse any section of the thesaurus for a term they have in mind. Users have an idea of what concept they want but are not sure of the exact phrasing of the term, so they look up the start of the first word. What

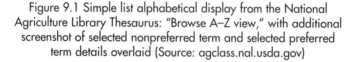

Search for Term   0-9 A B C D E F G H I J K L M N O P Q R S T U V W X Y Z

Search Results: Click on term to display record

Search

Next Page

Search options
Language
English

Search type
terms contain text

Terms per page
100

- *jaagsiekte*
- Jaagsiekte sheep retrovirus
- *jaboticaba*
- Jacaranda
- Jacaranda copaia
- Jacaranda mimosifolia
- *Jacaranda ovalifolia*
- Jacaratia
- *Jacaratia dodecaphylla*
- Jacaratia dolichaula
- Jacaratia mexicana
- Jacaratia spinosa
- *jacare*
- Jaceosidin
- *jack beans*
- Jack in the bush
- *jack in the pulpit*
- *jack pine*
- *jack pine budworm*
- *jack pine sawfly*
- *jack rabbits*
- Jackals
- *jackasses*
- *jackdaw*
- jackfruits

jack beans
Use
    Canavalia ensiformis

jackfruits
  RDF/XML Format:
    http://lod.nal.usda.gov/nalt/12648.rdf

  Persistent URI:
    http://lod.nal.usda.gov/nalt/12648

  Definition
    Resembling breadfruits, jackfruits are much larger
    and can weigh up to 100 pounds. It is usually boiled,
    tastes like potato, and is eaten as a vegetable in
    South Pacific and Malaysian cuisines.

  Definition Source
    NAL Thesaurus Staff

  Broader Term
    tree fruits

  Related Term
    Artocarpus heterophyllus

  Spanish
    fruta del pobre

  Subject Category
    E Economics, Business and Industry
    F Plant Science and Plant Products

Figure 9.1 Simple list alphabetical display from the National
Agriculture Library Thesaurus: "Browse A–Z view," with additional
screenshot of selected nonpreferred term and selected preferred
term details overlaid (Source: agclass.nal.usda.gov)

makes an alphabetical display especially useful is that often nonpreferred terms are interspersed, usually in a different typeface.
Users may have an option to show or hide nonpreferred terms in
any of the alphabetical display formats. An example of a simple list
alphabetical display is shown in Figure 9.1.

The simple list type of alphabetical display permits the quickest
browsing. This option is usually made available to taxonomists or
human indexers who are already somewhat familiar with the thesaurus and do not need to read all the details of a term to know
which term they want. Hiding nonpreferred terms supports even
more efficient browsing, but only if the user has a pretty good idea
of the wording of the desired term. Simple lists are less common
in end-user searcher displays. In any case, if an alphabetical list is

available, in an online environment it is typical to have terms in a simple list hyperlinked to their full-detail display, such as in the example shown in Figure 9.1.

Alphabetical Flat Format

The flat format is an alphabetical list of terms (usually both preferred and nonpreferred) with each preferred term having all of its nonpreferred terms, broader terms, narrower terms, related terms, and any scope note listed under it. This is often the default "alphabetical" output of thesaurus management software, and it is the commonly expected display of a thesaurus kind of controlled vocabulary. A subject area researcher interested in term details rather than linked content would also most likely seek out this display. An example excerpt of a flat-format alphabetical list of terms from the ASIS&T Thesaurus of Information Science, Technology, and Librarianship is shown in Figure 9.2.[1]

---

learned society publishers
BT publishers

learning
SN *Human learning; for artificial or machine learning, use "machine learning."*
BT educational activities
NT distance learning
     lifelong learning
     perceptual learning
RT knowledge acquisition
     machine learning

learning centers
USE media centers

learning disabled persons
BT disabled persons

Figure 9.2 Flat-format alphabetical arrangement of terms from
the ASIS&T Thesaurus of Information Science,
Technology, and Librarianship

The alphabetic flat format is common in printed thesauri, because all the term details are present, but there is no repetitive inclusion of terms, as is the case with full-term hierarchy display (which would take up more space). In the online medium, it has become less common to see a complete alphabetical listing with the flat-format display of terms. Instead, there might be a simple list, with the flat-format term details appearing in a separate window, as is the example in the second window in Figure 9.1.

The information provided for each term in flat-format display typically includes the following: nonpreferred terms (UF), broader term(s) (BT), narrower terms (NT), related terms (RT), and scope note. The broader terms and narrower terms displayed are those that are in immediate relationships, just one level up or one level down. In a bilingual thesaurus, a term's foreign language translation is also included. Less common but sometimes included is the term's ultimate broadest term, or top term, abbreviated as TT. For example, the multiterm hierarchy **products > software > business software > spreadsheet software** would be listed with the broader term and broadest term indicated as follows:

> **spreadsheet software**
> > BT **business software**
> > TT **products**

Online thesaurus term details now may also have a persistent URL and a link to the RDF/XML format of the term details (nonpreferred terms, broader term, narrower terms, related terms, scope note, etc.)

Hierarchical Term Outputs

Hierarchical reports or outputs from a thesaurus are also alphabetical. Each preferred term is listed in alphabetical order along with the term's hierarchical relationships. A hierarchical output of a thesaurus differs from the alphabetical output in three ways: (1)

typically only the hierarchical relationships are displayed (no scope notes, nonpreferred terms, or associative relationships), (2) the full hierarchy is displayed, instead of just the immediate broader and narrower terms, and (3) the alphabetical listing is of preferred terms only (nonpreferred terms are not listed). For a thesaurus that is not very hierarchical, that is, it is not organized under just a few broader terms, a "hierarchical" output may appear to be more alphabetical, and this can be confusing. A hierarchical report from a thesaurus does not necessarily look like a hierarchical taxonomy.

There are variations for hierarchical outputs, depending on whether only the narrower term hierarchy is displayed for a given term or both the narrower and broader hierarchy are displayed, and depending on whether the alphabetical listing is of all pre-ferred terms or just top terms. Finally, some published thesauri, such as the NASA thesaurus, include additional term information, such as related term and used-from relationships and definitions in its "hierarchical" display.

Full-Term Hierarchy

In a full-term hierarchy, not only are the immediate broader and narrower terms displayed at each term but also further broader and narrower terms of those terms, all the way out to the ends of the hierarchy. The number of hierarchical levels may vary among terms within the same taxonomy.

There are two kinds of full-term hierarchy displays: multilevel and two-way hierarchy. A multilevel display lists the relationships under the preferred term, with successive levels of hierarchy typically indicated by numerals following or by greater-than/less-than signs (angle brackets) preceding BT or NT, such as BT1, BT2 or >BT, >>BT. Additional relationships (UF, RT, Scope Note) may or may not be included. A two-way hierarchy is a more graphical representation of a term's placement in a hierarchy, displaying its broader terms above it and its narrower terms below it and making use of indentations,

Multi-Level Hierarchy	Two-Way Hierarchy
Recreation facilities	: : Facilities & Infrastructure
UF: Recreation centers	: Public buildings & facilities
UF: Recreational facilities	**Recreation facilities**
NT1: Amusement parks	. Amusement parks
NT1: Athletic facilities	. Athletic facilities
NT2: Fitness centers & gyms	. . Fitness centers & gyms
NT2: Skating rinks	. . Skating rinks
NT2: Swimming pools	. . Swimming pools
NT2: Tennis courts	. . Tennis courts
NT1: Bowling alleys	. Bowling alleys
NT1: Golf courses	. Golf courses
NT1: Skiing facilities	. Skiing facilities
NT1: Stadiums & arenas	. Stadiums & arenas
BT1: Public buildings & facilities	
BT2: Facilities & Infrastructure	

Figure 9.3 Full-term hierarchy displays, both multilevel and two-way

carats, periods, colons, or other punctuation. A typical display might use successive periods (ellipses) preceding each narrower term and colons preceding each broader term. Figure 9.3 contrasts a multilevel hierarchy and a two-way hierarchy for the same term.

If using greater-than/less-than signs, then the full-term hierarchy for *recreation facilities* would include the following terms and notation:

<< Facilities & infrastructure
< Public buildings & facilities
Recreation facilities
> Amusement parks
>> Athletic facilities

Top Term Hierarchy
A top term output from a thesaurus is the same as the hierarchical display of a thesaurus in the user interface and is the same as the full

hierarchical display of a hierarchical taxonomy. It is an alphabetical list of preferred terms that have no broader terms, and under each is the full hierarchy of narrower terms for each, usually arranged with indents or series of periods. Unlike the full-term hierarchy display, the top term display does not involve any repeated inclusion of terms, except in the case of polyhierarchies. Nonpreferred terms, related terms, and notes are not included in this display. Relatively flat taxonomies will have a high number of top terms, whereas more structured hierarchical taxonomies will have a limited number of top terms. Figure 9.4 presents two different thesaurus top term display excerpts, one more hierarchical than the other.

A top term report is a useful way for a taxonomist to check the hierarchical balance of a thesaurus. For end users, a top term display is desirable for a more hierarchically structured taxonomy or

Top term display excerpt showing a single top term in a hierarchical thesaurus	Top term display excerpt showing three top terms in a relatively flat thesaurus
Politics & Government	**Political actions**
. Domestic policy & programs	. Campaigning
.. Agricultural policy	. Lobbying
.. Economic policy	. Political protests
... Monetary policy	
... Fiscal policy	**Political ideologies**
.. Energy policy	. Conservatism
.. Health policy & programs	. Environmentalism
.. Social policy	. Liberalism
. Foreign policy	.. Socialism
.. Appeasement	
.. Bilateralism	**Politicians**
.. Foreign assistance	. Political office holders
... Foreign military assistance	. Political candidates
.. Foreign intervention	
.. Unilateralism	

Figure 9.4 Top term hierarchy display excerpts: one more hierarchical and one less hierarchical

thesaurus. For a taxonomy that has little hierarchy (is relatively "flat"), though, this display has less value for end users.

Permuted Index

A permuted index, also called a rotated index, takes each word within a term (most of which are multiword phrases anyway), sorts these words alphabetically, and displays all the terms with the given word (keyword) in it, grouped together by the keyword. Each taxonomy phrase-term thus appears more than once in the display, under each of its constituent keywords. This display is called an index because it is indeed an alphabetical index of words within terms. There are two variations on the display, KWIC and KWOC.

An alphabetical display of a KWIC or KWOC index can provide a useful way to search for terms in a printed list. In the online environment, however, such an alphabetical display is unnecessary, so the permuted index, especially the KWIC format, is rarely seen anymore. Instead, a user interface, whether for indexers or end-user searchers, may offer the option of searching for words *within* terms and then return a list of matching taxonomy terms. This type of search essentially achieves the same objective as a permuted display.

Thesaurus Displays for End-User Searchers

The various thesaurus displays described in the preceding section are typically an option reserved for the taxonomist and human indexers and sometimes for subject area researchers if the thesaurus is publicly available. However, end-user searchers do not usually have the option to select from such varied thesaurus displays for several reasons:

- Search product designers have enough other features to worry about, as they need to support search, discovery, alerts, reports, saving and sharing search results, and the like.

- Having different ways to view a thesaurus may provide more information than is needed by the untrained searcher.

- End-user searchers generally do not have as great an understanding of thesaurus principles, so they would not readily know what is meant by the relationship codes (BT, NT, RT, UF, TT) or the display type designations (flat, multilevel, two-way hierarchy, or permuted).

- The thesaurus in electronic format can be searched anyway, so numerous types of browsable displays may not be needed. A single hierarchical browse display may be offered as an option in addition to the search box, but additional, alphabetical displays may be deemed unnecessary if there is also a search option. While a subject researcher may on occasion still browse a printed or PDF thesaurus or taxonomy, end-user searchers today view and use taxonomies in electronic format only, usually via the web.

If an alphabetical browse interface is available, then it may be divided into sections for each letter of the alphabet, as shown in Figure 9.5 for ERIC Thesaurus.

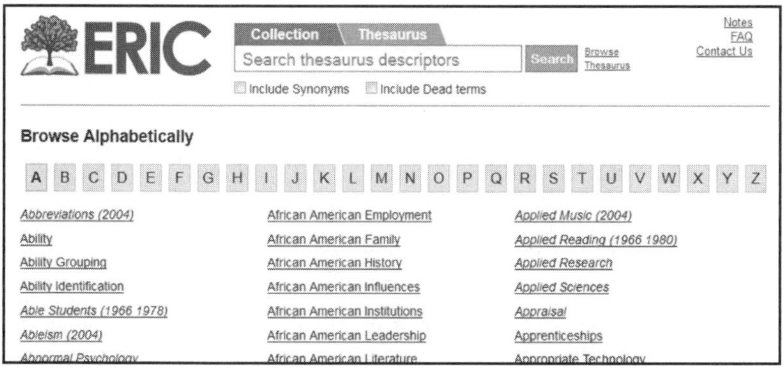

Figure 9.5 ERIC Thesaurus's A–Z browse display (Source: eric.ed.gov)

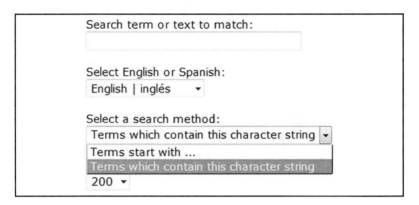

Figure 9.6 USDA Thesaurus's search options for terms beginning with or containing text (Source: agclass.nal.usda.gov)

If the thesaurus is extremely large, then such alphabetical browsing may not be practical. In this case, users might have just two ways to access terms in the thesaurus, via a hierarchical view or a search box. The search feature, though, should ideally permit the option of searching for both the following:

- Terms beginning with a word or string

- Terms containing a word or string

The user then retrieves a limited alphabetical list of thesaurus terms. Figure 9.6 shows an example of a search box that presents both search options.

Hierarchical Taxonomy Displays

A typical hierarchical display has narrower terms indented under their broader terms, but large hierarchies can go on for dozens of pages. While a lengthy hierarchy could be browsed across many printed pages, this would be quite impractical on screen. The online medium, however, presents alternatives. While there are various kinds of end-user displays of online hierarchical taxonomies, they all have in common some sort of interactive display that permits the user to navigate down from the top terms to terms that are more specific.

Although the presentation of a hierarchical taxonomy is similar to a top term hierarchical display of a thesaurus, there are stylistic differences. A hierarchical taxonomy does not necessarily use the designation NT or series of periods preceding narrower terms but usually relies simply on indentation and perhaps a different type-face. Sometimes there are also graphical representations for the hierarchy. Additionally, to reflect their heading/category nature, terms usually have initial capitalization, unlike terms in a thesaurus. Finally, terms in a hierarchical taxonomy are often called *categories* or *subjects*, rather than *terms*, to reflect the categorical nature of the hierarchy.

Hierarchical Display Types

There are several common online formats for displaying hierarchical taxonomies to the end user:

- One level per page or screen view, with terms hyperlinked to the next level of their narrower terms

- Expandable trees of terms, in which clicking on a term reveals its narrower terms beneath

- Fly-out subcategory lists, displaying like submenus

One Level per Page

Using a separate webpage to display each level of a taxonomy has been the traditional method for displaying web-based hierarchical taxonomies, as it requires less time and bandwidth to load subsequent level pages. Each term is hyperlinked to a new page that displays all its narrower terms. This was the format of the Yahoo Directory of the web, which existed from 1994 to 2014, and the same format and style is followed by the Open Directory Project (www.dmoz.org). It is more common to have a variation of this format, whereby two levels are presented on the first page and then one level per page follows at deeper levels. An example, Figure 9.7, shows the Superpages site, where the first level and selected terms of the second levels are displayed on the first page, but then new pages are displayed for deeper levels (in this case, geographic rather than topical).

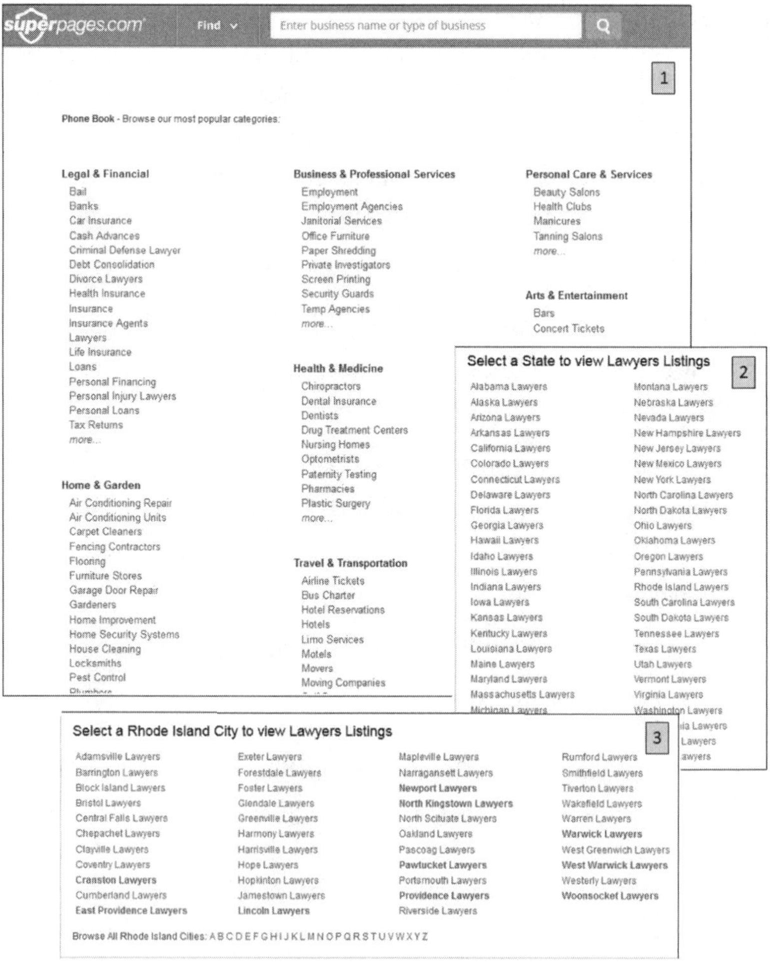

Figure 9.7 Three successive screenshots from the Dex Media Superpages yellow pages directory hierarchy, in which each lower level of narrower terms is on its own new webpage (Source: www.superpages.com/yellowpages)

This method of separate levels on each page has several advantages:

- There can be a large number of terms at any given level, so it works with a relatively large taxonomy.

- It works well with polyhierarchies.

- It is technically easy to implement.

Disadvantages to this method are as follows:

- The display often takes up the entire screen and does not permit space for search results or other content.

- Users can only see one level in one hierarchy at a time.

- It is less suitable when the taxonomy has varied levels or a narrower level consisting of just one or a few terms.

- There is often no prior indication whether the next level will have additional narrower terms or will finally link to the content.

In this type of user interface, the navigation path hierarchy typically displays near the top of the window, so even when at a deeper level, the user still can keep track of the higher levels/broader terms, such as the following example from eBay (www.ebay.com/chp/Alarm-/13856):

Home > All Categories > Collectibles & Art > Collectibles > Clocks > Vintage (1930-69) > Alarm

The terms in the path are hyperlinked to the page where they are the broader term so that the user can easily go back to any previous broader level. This is sometimes referred to as a *breadcrumb trail* because it shows where you have come from and how to get back, a metaphor based on the story of Hansel and Gretel, who dropped breadcrumbs as they walked through the woods in order to find their way back home.

Expandable Tree Hierarchy

Another method for displaying a hierarchical taxonomy, an expandable tree hierarchy, is more graphical and interactive. It permits the user to click on a term or a plus sign next to it to display its narrower terms, usually indented underneath it or possibly in a new column to its right. Unlike the display with one level per screen, in an expandable tree, all of the higher levels of terms continue to display, even as each narrower level is displayed. Figure 9.8 presents an example from the *USA Today* newspaper's categories of new stories.

The expandable tree method has the following advantages:

- The hierarchical nature is made obvious to the user, and the format is familiar to users of Windows Explorer (analogous to folders on the desktop).

- It allows the user to visualize the taxonomy and supports a more interactive exploration of the hierarchy.

- The presence or absence of a plus sign next to a term makes it clear whether there is a lower level under the term.

- Inconsistent numbers of levels and terms per level are easily accommodated.

- The display takes up only part of the screen width, allowing for the display of other content in the remainder of the window, such as content tagged with the term.

Disadvantages to this method include the following:

- It is not suitable for displaying a large taxonomy or a large number of narrower terms at a given level, because when terms are expanded, the higher levels get pushed out of view. (Scrolling to see all the terms causes their broader term to scroll out of view.)

- It cannot accommodate polyhierarchies very well, due to the limited space of the display window, and they may even be confusing to the user if polyhierarchies are included.

- It may tend to take longer to load and display, due to the graphic features.

- Implementing the display requires greater expertise and resources in web-page development.

Figure 9.8 Expandable tree hierarchy of the *USA Today* Content Tree
(Source: content.usatoday.com/community/tags/topic-index.aspx)

Because of the resources required, both human and bandwidth, expandable tree hierarchies are generally not deployed on public websites, but rather are used within software applications or on intranets within an organization.

Fly-Out Subcategory Lists

The fly-out subcategory design is a more recent display type, and it seems to be growing in popularity for public website-displayed hierarchical taxonomies. When a user selects a category, a list of subcategories then appears (flies out") typically to the right of the list of top categories. This design style is similar to fly-out sub-menus found in website navigation. The only difference is that this is not website navigation but rather a hierarchy of taxonomy terms, which are each linked to multiple items, not single webpages.

This method is used as the transition from the top level to the second level in the major retail websites of Best Buy, Target, Walmart, and in a modified form (displaying below rather than out to the right) on the Sears website. It is also used at the lower level of the hierarchical taxonomy on eBay. An example of fly-out categories is in Figure 9.9, from the video course vendor Lynda.com, in which the top-level term Video is selected.

Choice of Display Type

A large taxonomy is best suited for display on one level per screen, whereas small taxonomies can be accommodated with the expandable graphical tree display. Broad hierarchies, with many terms per level, are better displayed with one level per screen, whereas deep hierarchies work better in expandable trees. The expandable tree has become more popular with web designers regardless of taxonomy size and structure, however, because it is more attractive and interactive. Meanwhile, the demands in technology and bandwidth necessary for the interactive graphical displays have become less of an issue. In practice, the design of an attractive display often

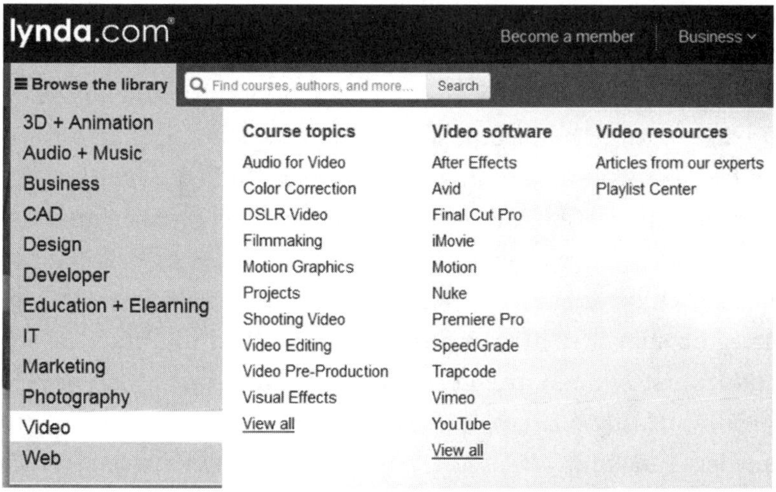

Figure 9.9 Fly-out subcategories on the site Lynda.com (www.Lynda.com)

takes precedence over suitability for a given taxonomy. Thus you, as the taxonomist, might simply be instructed to create a taxonomy for an expandable tree rather than being asked for your input on interface design.

With either kind of display, it can be difficult to navigate too many levels, just as with term hierarchies in a thesaurus. If the interface displays one level per screen, then a maximum of three levels is generally considered user-friendly. With an expandable tree, perhaps up to four levels is acceptable. Studies show that users of a public website typically do not have patience for more, especially if they are visiting the site for the first time. They are eager to find information quickly, and they will move on to a different website if they do not find it soon enough. Taxonomies for content for a more restricted audience (such as on an intranet for employees, a specialized subject area, or some kind of reference information source) may have more levels, and indeed their users will expect more levels. Each taxonomy is unique, though, so you should not try to adhere to any strict rules on numbers of levels.

Sort Order Options

With hierarchical displays, the user may have various options for sorting terms within the same hierarchical level (sharing the same broader term). The default sorting in any system is alphabetical, and while this is usually fine, sometimes a different order is more suitable. Any set of terms having to do with time, events, sequence, or procedures could be arranged chronologically or sequentially instead. Other orderings of concepts might be based on well-known categorizations, such as industries arranged in the order of SIC codes (first agriculture, then mining, manufacturing, wholesale, retail, and lastly services). Variations in sort order can be applied to any level, including the top-level terms. If you have usage studies on what the most popular terms are, then popularity could even be used as a basis for sort order. An example of somewhat sequential ordering of six narrower terms is the following:

Personnel management
> **Recruiting**
> **Hiring**
> **Training**
> **Promotions**
> **Letting go of employees**

In general, the shorter the list, the less important alphabetical sorting is. If you have 20 to 30 terms or more at the same level displayed together, alphabetical is probably best, but with fewer than 10 terms, you should consider other, more "logical" sort orders. In addition, for predictability the sort order method should be consistent throughout the taxonomy. If you choose alphabetic, then use it throughout. If you choose nonalphabetical "logical," then use that throughout, although you can vary the actual logical basis by grouping.

Another issue in sort order, regardless of number of terms at a level, is that whenever there is any *general* or *other/miscellaneous* category, it should *not* sort alphabetically. *General* should appear first in the list, not under *G*, and *other/miscellaneous* should be at the end, not under *O* or *M*.

Term Display Names in Context

For hierarchically displayed taxonomies, the taxonomist has the option of creating short, simple term names whose meanings will be understood within the context of the broader term. *General* and *other* are examples, but you could use simple contextual term names for any concept. The following pairs of examples illustrate the difference between short, simple term names, whose meaning is known in context, and their corresponding, unambiguous, longer term names:

Simple terms, (understood in context):	Full, unambiguous terms:
Human resource management	**Human resource management**
-- Recruiting	**-- Recruiting employees**
-- Training	**-- Training employees**

The display with term names that are understood in context is thus similar in a way to subdivisions of main entries in a back-of-the-book index, in which the subdivision names might be of a rather general nature. The function in hierarchies is to label narrower terms, however, not precoordinated main entry/subentry combinations. Thus, if the same narrower term names are applicable with different broader terms in different hierarchies, then they should be treated as different terms, with different administrative identifiers and different names displayed to a human indexer. **Display name** can then be one of the equivalent variants of a term.

Node Label Usage

In a hierarchical presentation, sometimes all broader terms function as node labels, with only the narrowest terms ("leaf" nodes) linked to content. This structure contrasts with a thesaurus, in which all terms at all levels are expected to be linked to content, unless they are specifically designated as a node label, which is relatively rare. The use of node label broader terms is especially common in hierarchical taxonomies displaying one level of terms per page. After selecting a term, the next page would display either a list of content results for that term or a list of narrower terms for that term, but not a combination of both narrower terms and content results. This is the case with the Superpages taxonomy in Figure 9.7.

In other hierarchical taxonomies with one level of hierarchy per page, the terms at only the top/first levels are node labels, whereas terms at lower levels are linked to content while still having narrower terms beneath them. This structure requires a little more creativity in the display in order to show both content results and narrower terms. As an example, in the Amazon.com website, shown in Figure 9.10, the top two levels, **Books & Audible** and then **Books**,

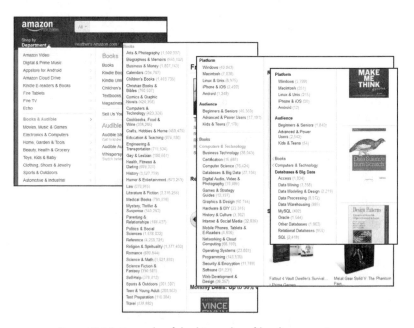

Figure 9.10 Example of the hierarchy of book categories on Amazon.com, which shows node labels for the first two levels on the first screenshot and then recursive retrieval categories on successive levels (www.amazon.com/gp/site-directory)

are node labels. After that, all subcategories link to content, while also having subcategories.

In an expandable tree display, broader terms also may or may not be node labels, although they are less frequently node labels than in the one-level-per-page display, because there is usually space on the screen adjacent to the tree to display retrieval results.

Recursive Retrieval

In a hierarchical taxonomy, even if linked content is available for a selected broader term, that content might not actually be indexed to that term for its "general" usage. Instead, that linked content could be exclusively the result of recursive retrieval. Recursive or "rolled up" retrieval returns inclusive results for all of a broader term's narrower terms. Typically, when there is space in the window to the right of the hierarchy (as in an expandable tree display), search results are displayed for terms at any level in the hierarchy, except perhaps for the top terms. The default *all* is more common, however, than *general* in a hierarchical taxonomy display result, especially if less sophisticated automatic indexing is involved. Thus, the broader term that provides only recursive retrieval serves as a node label on the indexing side but operates as an *all* index term on the retrieval/end-user display side.

Some end-user displays provide the total count of matched records per term, as is the case with the Amazon.com results in Figure 9.10, which are the numbers in parentheses following the term. If the number next to a broader term is very high, equal to or greater than the sum of the numbers next to all of its narrower terms, that indicates that the broader term is providing recursive results.

Fielded Search and Faceted Displays

The third main kind of access to a taxonomy and end-user display is fielded search. A fielded search display presents a means for the user to select or enter a vocabulary term for each of several search values or fields. These fields can be facets or merely vocabulary files or categories, as described in Chapter 8. The user may enter terms in search boxes that clearly depict fields, or each "field" may merely be a display of a short hierarchical list, from which the user selects a term. The end users may or may not be able to actually see and browse the taxonomy in a fielded search interface, but preferably they can, if it is not too large.

Faceted Search Displays

A powerful application of fielded search is its use with facets, even if blank "fields" are not always used in faceted search, also called faceted navigation. A fielded search display of a faceted taxonomy presents the user with all the facets and the option to choose a term (often just one) from each facet and execute a search on them in combination, either after making all selections or in a step-by-step fashion. If it is a step-by-step method, then search results are displayed on a selection from the first facet and then are narrowed on selections of terms from subsequent facets, with the search set becoming smaller at each step. The order in which the user makes selections from the facets ought not to matter. Allowing the user to refine the search step by step has the advantage that if a step returns zero results, it is clear which condition (which facet) could not be met. A breadcrumb trail may also be used in faceted search results, even though the path is not always in the same sequence, as the user may select from facets in any order.

Figure 9.11, from the product review site Buzzillions (www .buzzillions.com), presents an example of a faceted display that involves step-by-step narrowing in a series of three screenshots. Although "fields" are not apparent, each column/category represents a facet for selection. After using a traditional hierarchical taxonomy to arrive at the category for **LCD Monitors**, the user sees the facet options at the top of the screen. The user may select from any facet in any order. In this example, the user first chose a brand, which limited the result from 1543 to 80 items, then made a selection from "by Greenness," which limited the results further to

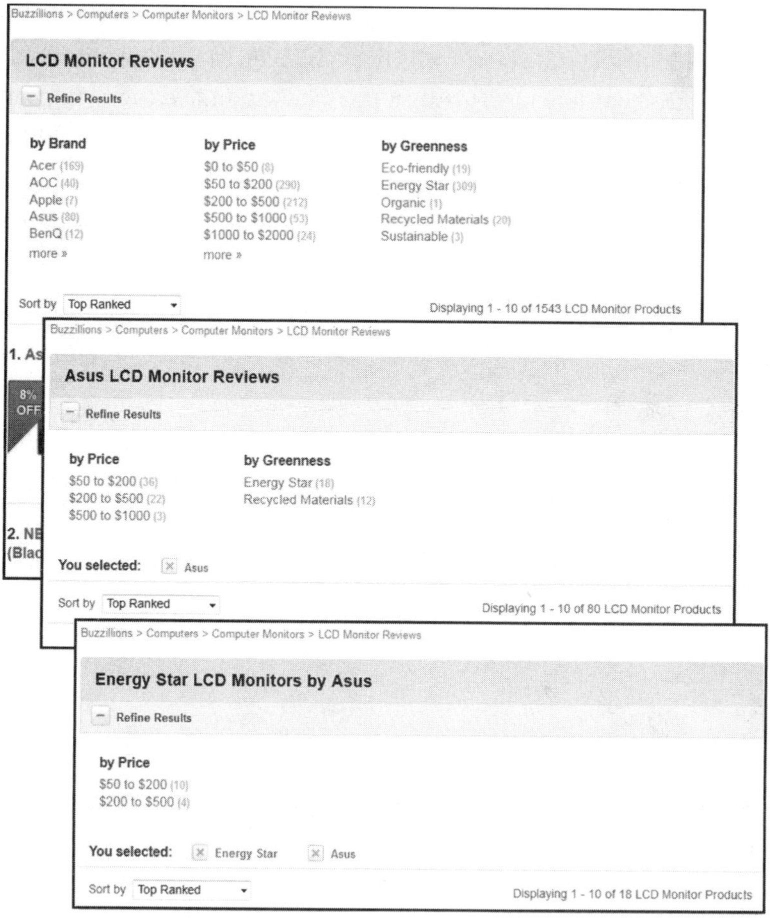

Figure 9.11 Facets for limiting search results for LCD Monitor reviews on the
Buzzillions website (Source: www.buzzillions.com)

18 items. The selected values are listed as "You selected," with an
X-box option to deselect and back out, perhaps in a different order
than the facet options were first selected.

There are various options for displaying the terms within a facet.
Unlike thesauri or hierarchical taxonomies, faceted taxonomies
tend to be relatively small, so it may be possible to display all the
terms within a facet in a single view. If there are numerous facets,
then it might not be practical initially to display all terms under all

facets. A scrollbox, pull-down menu, or pop-up list may be implemented to display the terms within each facet. Another option is to display the first few terms within the facet and have the hypertext "Show more..." linking to the full list. Finally, the facets could be expanded and collapsed to show the terms within some of them at a time. Figure 9.12 from the North Carolina State University

Figure 9.12 Facets for narrowing search results for library materials at the North Carolina State University Libraries (www.lib.ncsu.edu/catalog, Under Browse New Titles)

Libraries is an example of expanded and collapsed facets and the use of the "Show more" link to display only the start of the list of terms within each facet.

A small taxonomy also allows for more flexibility with the sort order of terms. The nature of facets, which tend to describe attributes, also makes them suitable for logical orderings rather than alphabetic. For example, facets for date, price, size, age, or other numeric ranges are common, and you should order these numerically from lowest to highest. Sometimes terms within facets are by default listed in the order of the number of records to which they link. Figure 9.12 from the North Carolina State University Libraries lists the facets by order of importance, rather than alphabetical, starting with Subject, and terms within the facets are ordered by the number of records.

While traditionally the user may select only one facet at a time, the user interface could be designed to support multiple selections. This is done by providing check (tick) boxes next to each term. The user can select any number at once. In the example (Figure 9.12), from the North Carolina State University Libraries, the first limiting option has check boxes for Currently available, Available online, and/or New titles.

Just because a taxonomy is organized into facets, there is no guarantee that the user interface will implement them for actual faceted searching. A simple user interface might offer the user the choice of browsing or searching by one type of metadata value or another, but not support a search on multiple facets in combination. In Boolean search terms, faceted search is based on the AND combination, rather than OR. Thus, if you develop a faceted taxonomy, you will want to make sure that it is properly supported in the search user interface.

Fielded Search Without Facets

Not all cases of fielded search involve facets. As discussed in Chapter 8, a taxonomy project may comprise multiple controlled vocabularies or taxonomies, and users could search each of these vocabularies individually through its own field in a fielded search interface. For example, in a set of controlled vocabularies for indexing a database of articles, personal names and company names (as appearing in article text content) are often maintained in separate vocabularies, and they may appear to the user as separate fields to search as well. This helps avoid ambiguity among term names. These fields are not really facets, though, because they are not attributes or dimensions of a periodical article; they are just a different kind of vocabulary.

A user interface that presents fielded search is often called advanced search. In a graphical display, this is somewhat of a misnomer, since it is very simple to use, and one does not need to be an "advanced" searcher. Often each field type has its own search box. In many cases the listed fields are all predefined.

In addition to controlled vocabulary fields, fielded search may include fields for nonvocabulary data, such as accession number, free-text fields for title or abstract, and date. While such fields represent useful metadata, they, likewise, are not taxonomy facets. Figure 9.13 shows an example of a fielded search user interface (from advanced search) for clinical trials at ClinicalTrials.gov, a service of the US National Institutes of Health. Fields with controlled vocabularies are those with a filled-in value and a down arrow, to select from a drop-down list of options. Other fields support keyword searching, and other fields are for other metadata, such as gender, age, phase, date, etc., which are grouped under Additional Criteria.

In other cases of advanced/fielded search, there is more flexibility, the user chooses the designation of the field from a drop-down list, and multiple, definable search boxes are provided to combine in Boolean searching. A choice of different Boolean operators (AND, OR, and NOT) may also be available in drop-down lists. This is the case in Figure 9.14, the advanced search for the Gale Business

---

Advanced Search

Fill in any or all of the fields below. Click on the label to the left of each search field for more information or read the Help

Search Terms:		Search Help
Recruitment:	All Studies	☐ Exclude Unknown status
Study Results:	All Studies	
Study Type:	All Studies	
	All Studies	
	Interventional Studies	
Targeted Search	Observational Studies	
Conditions:	-- Patient Registries	
	Expanded Access Studies	
Interventions:		
Title Acronym/Titles:		
Outcome Measures:		
Sponsor/Collaborators:		☐ Exact match
Sponsor (Lead):		☐ Exact match
Study IDs:		

Locations

State 1:	--- Optional ---
Country 1:	--- Optional ---
State 2:	--- Optional ---
Country 2:	--- Optional ---
State 3:	--- Optional ---
Country 3:	--- Optional ---
Location Terms:	

Additional Criteria

Gender:	All Studies
Age Group:	☐ Child (birth–17) ☐ Adult (18–65) ☐ Senior (66+)
Phase:	☐ Phase 0 ☐ Phase 1 ☐ Phase 2 ☐ Phase 3 ☐ Phase 4
Funder Type:	☐ NIH ☐ Other U.S. Federal agency ☐ Industry ☐ All others (individuals, universities, organizations)
Safety Issue:	☐ Has an Outcome Measure designated as a safety issue
First Received:	From _____ To _____ (MM/DD/YYYY)
Last Updated:	From _____ To _____ (MM/DD/YYYY)

Figure 9.13 Fielded search options for searching clinical trials at ClinicalTrials.gov (www.clinicaltrials.gov/ct2/search/advanced). The drop-down list of options in the screenshot is selected for the field of Study Type

Collection online subscription database. For the search field, the user selects from a drop-down the fields to be searched. Although three blank search fields are provided, the user may use any number in combination. An advantage of this method is that the user can repeat the same field designation for more than one search box and thus search on multiple terms from within the same field. The disadvantage with this method of using generic fields is that the user does not have the option of looking up controlled vocabulary terms from a drop-down list, which would only be possible for a predetermined field.

The subject descriptors used for fielded search in a set of taxonomies may be developed and maintained according to thesaurus standards or just as a simple hierarchy. You should not consider the user interface implementation of fielded search to be in any way a restriction on how you choose to develop the taxonomy.

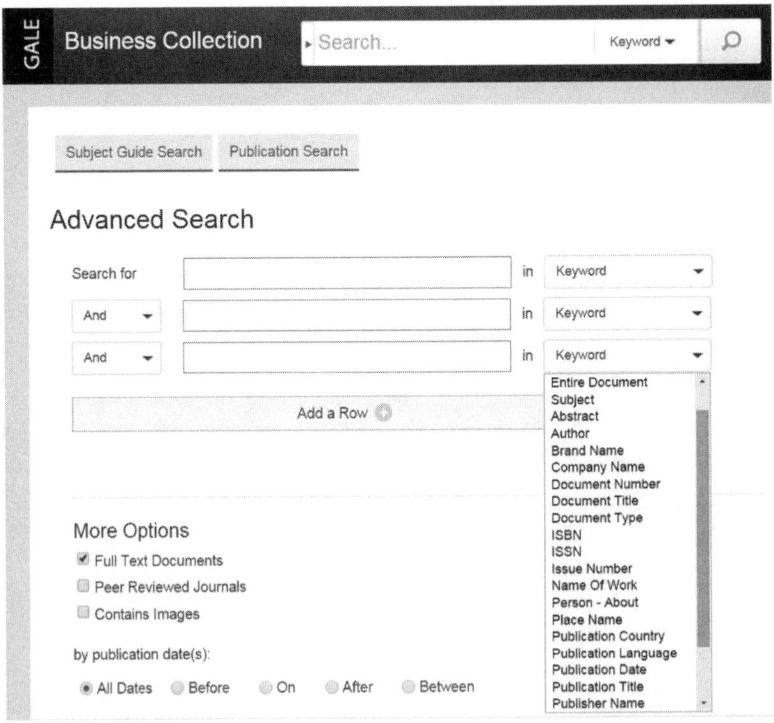

Figure 9.14 Advanced Search of Gale Business Collection subscription database, with the drop-down list of field options opened[2]

Endnotes

1. Alice Redmond-Neal and Marjorie M.K. Hlava eds. *ASIS&T Thesaurus of Information Science, Technology, and Librianship*, 3rd ed. (Medford, NJ: Information Today, Inc., and the American Society for Information Science and Technology, 2005), 77.

2. Access to the Gale databases (*www.gale.com*) in not through a public website, but by subscription, and available to patrons of subscribing public or academic libraries.

Chapter 10

Taxonomy Planning, Design, and Creation

Taxonomies: turning data into knowledge.
—Nick Berry

Creating, or even revising, a taxonomy is a significant project that eventually becomes a knowledge base that requires continual maintenance. Other books and articles go into the subject of taxonomy planning and project management at greater length than there is space for in this chapter. In one such book, *Organising Knowledge*, the author Patrick Lambe suggests the following six steps for preparing a taxonomy project and discusses each in detail:[1]

1. Meet with the project sponsor (to map key stakeholders and activities, learn the purpose and intent of the project, determine the technology available, and assess the knowledge and information management context).

2. Engage the stakeholders.

3. Refine the project purpose, and get the sponsor's agreement.

4. Design the approach.

5. Build a communication plan.

6. Start the process for taxonomy governance.

Another suggested approach to taxonomy projects comes from Darin Stewart in his book *Building Enterprise Taxonomies*.

He describes the taxonomy development cycle as comprising five phases:[2]

1. Research (including stakeholder interviews and a content audit)

2. Strategy (developing the taxonomy plan and governance document)

3. Design

4. Implementation (actually building the taxonomy)

5. Administration (maintenance of the taxonomy)

Since accidental taxonomists are not always taxonomy project managers, we will not present detailed project management instructions here. Rather, this chapter looks at key issues pertaining to taxonomies as projects, including their planning, unique issues of enterprise taxonomies, taxonomy creation processes, taxonomy implementation and interoperability, and taxonomy governance.

Planning for a Taxonomy

Because a taxonomy is something created for future, long-term use, planning is very important. Planning involves asking questions, conducting research, and preparing a written taxonomy plan, which can also serve as a governance document throughout the taxonomy creation process and for ongoing maintenance of the taxonomy. By now, you should know the details of how to create or edit a taxonomy, but if someone says to you, "We need a taxonomy, and we hear you know how to create taxonomies. What do you need to know to get started?" would you know how to answer and how to proceed? Even people with some taxonomy experience may be unsure how to respond initially to a new and different project. Planning involves asking the right people the right questions, conducting additional research, and developing a taxonomy design and strategy.

Project Questions

The first step in a taxonomy project is to meet with the key person or people connected to the project to get answers to fundamental questions about the intended taxonomy. If a single knowledgeable taxonomy manager is already in place and you come into the project simply to build the taxonomy, then you need only ask the taxonomy project manager the questions listed in this section. If, however, the taxonomy project manager does not yet have all the answers and is hoping that you will help come up with them or if you *are* the taxonomy project manager, then you need to speak with all of the stakeholders in the project.

A definition of a stakeholder is "anyone who has a vested interest in the project, can be affected by the change initiative that the project represents or has the power to influence the project" (Declan Chellar).[3] Who exactly the stakeholders are will vary depending on the type of organization and purpose of the taxonomy. If, for example, the taxonomy is for a web-based subscription information service, then the stakeholders include the project manager, someone responsible for overseeing content creation or aggregation, any key content vendor(s), someone responsible for indexing, someone responsible for web user interface design (such as an information architect), and someone responsible for marketing and getting user feedback.

Whether you are meeting with the taxonomy owner/manager or you as a taxonomy manager are meeting with a number of stakeholders, you should be asking the same fundamental questions before beginning work on the taxonomy:

1. Purpose: What will the taxonomy be used for?

2. Users: Who are all the users of the taxonomy, and who are the end users in particular?

3. Content: What content will be covered by the taxonomy?

4. Scope: What are the topic area, scope, and limits?

5. Resources: What are the project's resources and constraints?

If the project owner cannot sufficiently answer all these questions, find out whom else you should ask. Answers may come from more than one person.

Purpose

Although a single taxonomy often serves multiple purposes, typically there is a primary purpose in mind. Recall from Chapter 1 that there are three main applications of taxonomies:

- Indexing support (manual or automated)

- Retrieval support (including both search and discovery)

- Organization and navigation support

If a taxonomy's primary purpose is to ensure comprehensive, accurate, and consistent manual indexing/tagging, then you will probably want more of a thesaurus-type of taxonomy. Nonpreferred terms and relationships should facilitate indexers in finding the preferred terms, and indexing policies must be established. If a taxonomy's purpose is to support automated indexing, then a synonym ring-type taxonomy may be all that is needed. If a taxonomy's primary purpose is to serve retrieval, then a taxonomy structure that best serves end-user needs, such as a balanced hierarchical or faceted structure, is best. Finally, if a taxonomy's objective is to serve website organization and navigation, then it should be hierarchical and relatively small, should have term names that fit well as menu labels, and may not need additional term relationships.

Users

The purpose of a taxonomy will determine to a certain degree who the taxonomy users are (e.g., whether the users include indexers), but there are other variables to consider among users as well. If indexers are involved, it makes a difference whether they are dedicated indexers, content creators/authors, or editors and whether they are experts in the subject matter. Dedicated, trained indexers can deal with a large, generalized taxonomy, but expect consistency in depth, breadth, and term style. Authors, on the other hand, seek terms that match the language of their writing and need a simple taxonomy without extensive indexing policies.

End users could be internal organization members, students, subject area specialists, the public, or various subsections of the public. Not only would different audiences look for different preferred terms, but different kinds of users may also have different expectations regarding the display of the term details, including/excluding nonpreferred terms and other relationships. Internal users may expect internal jargon and a structure that reflects the organization. A taxonomy used by students will likely need additional educational features, such as scientifically correct hierarchies and generous use of scope notes. Subject matter experts tend to expect deep taxonomies. A taxonomy for the public ideally is no more than three levels deep if hierarchical, or it could be faceted if the content is appropriate for a faceted taxonomy. In either case, the display should be very intuitive to use.

It can be tricky if the same taxonomy will be used by multiple types of users, which is most often the case with the taxonomies of large information vendors. Margot Diltz, retired senior manager of editor policy at Cengage Learning, explained as follows:

> It is a challenge to create a single taxonomic system that satisfies the needs of a range of audiences, that is, the expert and the generalist or the child and the adult. When the taxonomy is meant to meet the needs of all possible users, the results are likely to mean compromises that leave the taxonomist less than satisfied.[4]

Content

The range of content covered by a taxonomy can be a moving target. Once a taxonomy project is proposed, stakeholders may suggest additional content types not originally envisioned in the inclusion. This problem applies to both taxonomies used by information vendors and those used just internally. Thus, when planning a taxonomy, it is important to take a broad view and consider all the types of content likely to be included, even if some will not be incorporated until later.

In addition to the subject area of the content, the type of content affects the taxonomy design. The content could be text only or could consist of other media, such as image files, audio files, or video files, or it could be a combination. Image-only content tends not to make use of broad or abstract taxonomy concepts (such as **diseases**, **mergers & acquisitions**, and **human resources**), as text content might. Furthermore, if the type of content is relatively uniform, then a faceted taxonomy might be most suitable. The nature of the content, volume, and rate at which it changes or grows all factor into deciding whether indexing will be manual or automatic, and the type of indexing also affects the taxonomy design.

Scope

While the content to be indexed is the determining factor in the subject scope of the taxonomy, any body of content will include off-topic documents. Thus, a policy is needed from the beginning to determine what types of subjects can be included in the taxonomy. There is also the question of what kinds of named entities should be included for people, organizations, products, places, document titles or names of works, laws, events, and so on. If the taxonomy is faceted, you only need to include facets that are relevant to the search process. If not everything is covered, that's still OK. It can be easy to lose sight of a taxonomy's scope, especially if term relationships lead to creating more terms of only marginal relevance to the project.

Resources

Project resources or constraints include the following:

- Skills and expertise: Of project managers, indexers, and other taxonomy editors

- Funding: For staff and for software, hardware, and networking services

- Timing: When a completed taxonomy needs to be implemented

- Stakeholder role: Of the project owner, managers, partners, content vendors, and/or key clients, and so on, who may have certain expectations for the taxonomy and who may or may not be actively involved

- Technology: Capabilities of the software used for indexing (human or automated), the software used for search/retrieval, the information architecture and user interface design, and how the data is stored—for example, the taxonomy may be implemented in a document management system that does not support polyhierarchies

- Technical support: For software, hardware, and networking/telecommunications requirements and the hosting of the data

Limited resources can obviously affect the size and complexity of the taxonomy.

Additional Considerations

Sometimes the taxonomist reports to a project manager, and sometimes the taxonomist *is* the project manager. In the latter case, such as in the role of a taxonomy manager or taxonomy consultant, there are many other issues to consider. These include typical project management concerns that are covered in other books. Some questions pertaining specifically to taxonomy project management include the following:

- Which people will be involved in the taxonomy creation, management, support, and approval? This typically involves people from different departments.

- Who is required to give approval, and at what level of decision making in creating the taxonomy is approval needed? Someone other than the taxonomist might decide the taxonomy format, specific top terms, and an approximate number of hierarchical levels.

- Who will be responsible for setting taxonomy usage policy? Most likely, it will be you, the taxonomist, but the policy will still need approval.

- Who will document taxonomy usage and policies? It might be a taxonomist-consultant, or it might be the taxonomy owner.

- How will the taxonomy fit in with other document-level metadata, and who is responsible for this? It's a gray line between taxonomy and other metadata, such as document type, content type, discipline, or audience, and if a metadata librarian is involved in that area, you need to work together.

- How will ongoing support and maintenance be handled? Who will be responsible, and how much time will be devoted to such tasks?

If you are *not* in a project manager role and someone else is taking care of all of the preceding issues, you as the taxonomist or taxonomy editor still need to address some key questions before you plunge in and start creating terms and relationships:

- Will the structure of the taxonomy be a relatively flat controlled vocabulary, a hierarchical taxonomy, or a taxonomy organized into facets?

- Will the technology fully support faceted search?

- If hierarchical, will polyhierarchies be permitted?

- If hierarchical, approximately how many top terms should there be, and how many levels deep should the taxonomy go?

- Will associative relationships be included and supported?

- Will the nonpreferred terms be displayed to the end users?

- What kinds of additional information should each term have (such as scope notes or other attributes)?

- Will the taxonomy (or taxonomies) be segmented or classified in such a way that separate files or category designations would be applicable?

In some cases, answers will not be immediately available to these questions. You may need to conduct further research and perhaps even perform some test development of the taxonomy before the answers become apparent. This is one of the differences between serving as a taxonomy editor versus serving as a taxonomy manager or consultant. If you are a taxonomy editor, someone else should answer these questions for you. As a taxonomy manager or consultant, though, you will need to do research to determine the answers yourself.

Research for a Taxonomy

To a large extent, conducting research for a taxonomy project involves gathering sources for terms (discussed in Chapter 3), but research is also needed to support decisions regarding the taxonomy's size, scope, structure, display, and other features. In some cases, the same research can yield both terms and answers to these other taxonomy design questions.

Possible research tasks include the following:

- In-depth interviews of primary stakeholders, interviews of additional stakeholders, and perhaps interviews with some of the potential taxonomy users

- A content audit or content inventory (see Chapter 3 for details and an example)

- Analysis of word or phrase lists generated by simple text analytics tools from sample content

- Analysis of search logs (when a search engine is already in use) and click-trail reports of such reporting tools, if available

- Research into the functions of any existing search/ retrieval systems the organization may have and/or methods used for search/retrieval for similar content in similar organizations

Stakeholder Interviews

Interviewing stakeholders means scheduling individual meetings, either face-to-face or by phone, with the taxonomy project sponsors, leaders, managers, and team members and with key people in other departments who will be involved in or have some stake in the taxonomy. In preparation, you need to identify the stakeholders for interviews and draw up interview questions. Plan for each interview to last perhaps 30 to 60 minutes. The interview questions should seek to understand

- the goals and objectives of the taxonomy, especially from a business sense

- weaknesses or failings of the current search/findability

- needs or desires for the functionality of a new or improved search/browse system

- the basic kinds of content

- the information systems currently used and those that are expected to be added or retired

- the challenges foreseen

- the nature of content creation, by whom, according to what policies, and the like

Questions can deal with both the big picture and with details. It may be necessary to have two slightly different sets of questions depending on the type of stakeholder, such as one set for those who would be indexing or tagging documents and one set for those who would be primarily looking for documents. Some questions would be the same for everyone, but some would be different. Examples of questions for stakeholders who add content and would tag or index with a future taxonomy could include:

1. What kind of documents do you and/or your group members upload/add to the system?
2. What is the process of uploading/adding content and categorizing content?
3. Is content tagged or supposed to be tagged when uploaded?
4. If so, are there other issues with the tags?

Examples of questions for stakeholders who need to find content and who would browse a future taxonomy could include:

1. Are you looking just for specific documents, or do you also look for information/answers to questions from any content sources?
2. How do you look for documents?
3. What are the keywords you use or would like to use?
4. What difficulties do you encounter (specific examples) in finding documents?

You may wish to use a table or spreadsheet to record the results of the interview questions, with a row for each stakeholder and a column for each question. You can then glance at all the results to discern any patterns.

Search Logs and Click-Trail Reports
Search query logs record search behavior, and click-trail reports record browse/navigation behavior. Both are useful for developing taxonomy terms in different ways.

Search query logs provide ideas for preferred and nonpreferred terms. They are simple to interpret because they list keywords/ search strings that users have entered, presenting them in usage order. Query logs are often a standard administrative feature of search software.

Click-trail reports, on the other hand, can provide ideas for structuring a hierarchy of terms. These reports usually show the series of web-page titles that a user clicked through to navigate to the desired information, with a list of trails for each final destination page. Thus, you can discover the most prevalent paths users take to a destination page. These paths provide insight into what most users consider the logical hierarchy or category for the information on the destination page. Web analytics software packages that offer click-trail reports include ClickTale (www.clicktale.com), Clicky (www.getclicky.com), and iWebTrack (www.iwebtrack.com).

Taxonomy Design Plan

The answers to all the aforementioned questions form the basis for a taxonomy design plan. The extent and details of such a plan will depend to a certain degree on the organization's documentation requirements. Formal approval of a plan may or may not be required prior to starting work on building the taxonomy. The plan should address at least the following issues:

- Purpose and users of the taxonomy

- Scope of the taxonomy and of the indexed content

- Tools used for creating and managing the taxonomy

- Sources for the taxonomy terms

- Systems used for implementation and end use of the taxonomy

- Expected user interface features

- Indexing method(s)

- Structure/type of taxonomy, relationship types

- Project timetable with milestones and prerequisites

This taxonomy design document—which you may call a project plan, requirements document, or another name that fits into your organization's documentation policy—can be considered the first major "deliverable" of a taxonomy project. The taxonomy design plan can then be the basis for future documentation of the taxonomy, which you will develop as you create the taxonomy. While the general taxonomy design issues should be decided in advance, certain details tend to get resolved later, once you actually begin creating the taxonomy. Such details could include term format (such as whether to use parenthetical qualifiers), the use of certain term note/description fields, and procedures for updating the taxonomy. Furthermore, technical requirements can change, especially if the user interface is still under development or the content management system/search software is subject to change. (Taxonomy projects are often launched at the same time that new software systems are introduced.) You will update the documentation throughout the taxonomy creation process, and it will be complete only when the taxonomy is complete. Then it is no longer a "plan" but becomes the "governance" document, a policy document to "govern" the taxonomy.

Taxonomy Structural Design

It is at this stage that you will make all structural decisions about the taxonomy, if they have not already been made for you. Structural issues include deciding whether the taxonomy will

- have any portions licensed from external sources (see Chapter 1)

- be predominantly hierarchical, faceted, or organized as a thesaurus

- have associative relationships

- be maintained as a single file/thesaurus or as multiple taxonomies/vocabularies/files

- include additional term types or categories that might be applied to organize the taxonomy

As mentioned in Chapter 5 with respect to taxonomy management software features, assigning categories to terms enables support for certain end-use search interface characteristics and other administrative capabilities. You could also use categories to distinguish

- generic terms from named entities

- terms that the you decide may be permitted to have certain semantic relationships

- terms that belong within a facet for a faceted taxonomy

There could be a master taxonomy, for example, and subsections categorized for certain audiences or services.

Number of Taxonomists

In planning the timetable for completing the taxonomy, you need to consider how many people will be directly working on it. Whether a single taxonomist will suffice or whether there should be a team of people working on the taxonomy depends, obviously, on the taxonomy size, the project deadline, and the budget. One taxonomist can create an entire taxonomy for a project if there is sufficient time, perhaps a period of several months. Even if one taxonomist working full time could undertake the entire project, it may be desirable to have multiple taxonomy editors, who would be working only part-time on the project (whether they are on staff or contracted freelancers). As we have seen, there are many subjective decisions that the taxonomist must make, so it is good to have other taxonomists to consult for opinions. If there are multiple taxonomists, the work could be divided among them in different ways:

- By taxonomy hierarchy, facet, authority file, or subject area

- By task/function: interviewing stakeholders, performing a content audit, constructing the initial taxonomy structure, researching terms and relationships, conducting card sorting or other user testing, editing, and so on. (Some of these tasks must be performed sequentially.)

In contrast with the work of indexers, there are no reliable average rates for estimating how many terms a taxonomist can create per hour. There are too many variables, and individual terms may or may not require research. Fortunately, a considerable amount of taxonomy work can be done off-site. Therefore, employing remote freelance taxonomists, which is more appropriate for part-time, short-term work anyway, may work quite well for a taxonomy project.

Enterprise Taxonomies

Enterprise taxonomies have recently been receiving a great deal of attention. *Enterprise* is not limited to a company or business but could refer to any large organization, including nonprofits and government agencies. It sometimes seems as if all taxonomies these days are enterprise taxonomies, because (1) it is true that most *new* taxonomies are indeed enterprise taxonomies, and (2) taxonomies that are not created for an enterprise are less likely to be called taxonomies but rather *thesauri* or *controlled vocabularies*. A greater number of new and planned taxonomy projects are for enterprises, simply because that is where the greatest market is. Most information vendors who use taxonomies to provide content for customers or the public, rather than for an internal enterprise, already have taxonomies in place. The number of new information vendors is relatively small, whereas the number of enterprises of various kinds that can benefit from a taxonomy to make their documents and other content easier to manage and find is vast.

Enterprise Taxonomy Characteristics

The significant features of an enterprise taxonomy are the following:

1. Its primary users are members of the enterprise (employees and perhaps also contractors).

2. The content to be indexed with the taxonomy is largely created/authored by members of the enterprise.

3. The taxonomy unifies concepts/vocabularies from various departments to universally serve the entire enterprise (but does not necessarily include all content in an enterprise).

There may be some differences of opinion as to whether an enterprise taxonomy ought to cover *all* shared content of an enterprise. In practice, this is rarely achieved. What makes a taxonomy an enterprise taxonomy, though, is that it covers content in multiple departments for multiple purposes and has users from multiple departments of the organization.

An enterprise taxonomy is often implemented within an enterprise content management system, a document management system, SharePoint, or an intranet or extranet (like an intranet, but with additional access to partners, vendors, clients, and so on, but not the general public). Access through a public website is also possible but would likely be of secondary importance and may include only parts of the taxonomy.

An enterprise taxonomy is often a faceted taxonomy with a hierarchy of terms within the larger facets. Typical facets would be document type or content type, line of business and then product or service type, functional area or department, location or region, and possibly the catch-all facet of topic. There may be a facet for phase, stage, or lifecycle of a product or service. Market segment, customer type, or audience could also be a facet. For companies in highly regulated industries, there may even be a facet for laws and regulations. The types of documents within an organization can be quite numerous and of highly specific types, such as "Securities loan agreement registration." This may result in a relatively large, hierarchical taxonomy within a facet for document type. At some point, the distinction between document type and topic can get blurred, so taxonomy policies need to be developed and followed.

Developing an enterprise taxonomy has its own particular requirements. Because it involves various departments and people within an organization, a significant number of people have to be consulted in the taxonomy development process, including stakeholders and representative users. Enterprise taxonomy stakeholders include

- the project sponsor/owner

- the manager (upper management)

- members of a taxonomy project team

- managers of departments whose existing vocabularies (which may or may not currently be controlled) will be utilized

- content creators, who want the documents they write to be found through the taxonomy

- information technology engineers who will be responsible for implementation and technical support

- the intranet/extranet webmaster(s)

- key "power" users

Users of an enterprise taxonomy include potentially all employees of an organization. Thus, unlike externally facing taxonomies, test users are easily accessible, although they may be at various remote locations.

The subject matter scope of an enterprise taxonomy can be quite varied and needs to be carefully considered, as there are different options for how inclusive it may be. The scope could include any or all of the following:

- Products and services (names, descriptions, features, user issues)

- Technology and technical terminology (science, research and development oriented)

- People and their areas of expertise

- Human resources and management subjects (policies, procedures, programs)

In addition, you need to recognize the existence of proprietary/nonpublic terminology that would never be known to anyone outside of the enterprise. All enterprises have, to some degree, their own jargon, acronyms, project code names, and so on, which are totally unique and not defined anywhere outside that domain. You need to look for that language and be sure to include it.

Enterprise Taxonomy Project Tasks

The steps for creating an enterprise taxonomy are not too different from those involved in creating any taxonomy, but greater attention is required in certain areas, especially with respect to the research and information-gathering phase. A workshop with stakeholders is one possible method to brainstorm facets and terms for an enterprise taxonomy. In addition to interviewing stakeholders, it is both possible and beneficial to interview select users, since the users are people within the enterprise rather than external customers, so the users are more accessible. Web search logs are typically available to analyze for search terms that have been entered, and these should not be overlooked. A content audit is usually relatively involved and complicated in an enterprise, due to the diversity of content.

For top terms of an enterprise taxonomy, you need to look harder to identify organizing principles, problems, and tasks. This is not as simple as for a retail product taxonomy.

The documented design plan of an enterprise taxonomy also carries more weight, because actually developing the taxonomy may be contingent on acceptance of the plan, which is not necessarily assured. Some managers may be skeptical of the cost-benefits of a taxonomy.

Stakeholder Workshop

Conducting a full-day or two-day taxonomy workshop with most of the key stakeholders (10–15 perhaps) participating in the same room is a common technique among taxonomy consultants. The taxonomy consultant may start out by explaining what an enterprise taxonomy is and how it can help the organization, and what facets are and how they work. Then the consultant asks individuals around the table in turn to suggest types of content and topics of search. These are written down on a board and then reviewed, eliminating some and combining near duplicates, and grouped into categories or facets. This method not only quickly generates a set of candidate taxonomy terms and facets upon which most key stakeholders already agree but also engages the stakeholders more and gets their buy-on on the whole idea of the taxonomy and the process to create it.

Stakeholder and User Interviews

The stakeholders in an enterprise taxonomy project tend to be a larger and more diverse group than stakeholders in a taxonomy for customer-only information services. In addition to the taxonomy project leader, manager, and/or sponsor, you should include a manager from each department whose content will be included and from each department that will use the taxonomy, which essentially includes all departments of an enterprise. If a taxonomy workshop was held, the stakeholders who are interviewed may include most of the workshop participants plus some additional people.

User interviews, which should come after the stakeholder interviews, ought to include at least two representatives from different functional areas, such as human resources, marketing, sales, customer service, finance, research, and product development. User interviews are typically not as long as the stakeholder interviews. Interview questions should center on what kinds of information are needed within a given function area, how the current system falls short, how a desired search system should work, and any other "wish list" items. At this stage, these are still planning questions. Later, when there is a draft or test taxonomy to review, you will consult with the users and stakeholders again.

Enterprise Content Audits

As discussed in Chapter 3, a content audit or content inventory is an important step in gathering sources for terms for any taxonomy. In an enterprise, there is an even greater variety of content that the taxonomy may cover, all of which should be included in a content audit. The taxonomy may cover the following types of content:

- Employee handbooks
- Manuals and guidelines
- Transaction records
- Policies and procedures
- Reports and white papers
- Standards
- Marketing literature
- Product data
- Internal employee newsletters
- R&D development documents
- Training materials
- External publications
- Schematics and drawings
- Customer support documents
- Project documents

Furthermore, there may be a variety of different document types or file formats to consider, including the following:

- Web-page files (HTML)

- PDF documents

- Word-processed documents

- Documents in other publishing formats

- Presentations

- Spreadsheets

- Online help files

- Image files

- Videos

- Database records

- XML files

- Paper (such as from archives or external sources)

Electronic documents could be web/intranet pages or shared files on servers or could be located in document management systems or on individual hard drives.

Although an enterprise taxonomy will be used across the entire enterprise and should include vocabulary for the entire enterprise, this does not necessarily mean that every single piece of content must be included. You would exclude emails, confidential employee records, receipts attached to expense reports, forms, vendor- or partner-produced literature, and so on. You might also determine that some content will stay in separate repositories; for example, logs of customer calls will stay in the customer contact system, and forms filled out by individual employees will be kept only in the human resources files.

The content audit needs to be more detailed for an enterprise taxonomy than for other kinds of taxonomies. In addition to writing down the term/concept and its source, other information to record for each concept includes audience, document type, and possibly the content management system in which the document is stored. In *Building Enterprise Taxonomies*, Darin Stewart suggests that data from an audit include the following:[5]

- Content (or document)
- Category (or document type)
- Source (application, database, or external provider)
- Location (URL, file system path, or hard copy location)
- Stakeholder (author, producer, consumer, or executive)
- Organization (stakeholder affiliation)
- Term

Content determined to be redundant, obsolete, or trivial (ROT) may also be marked as such.

A complete content inventory is usually not possible nor necessary for an enterprise taxonomy. Locating and recording all content in an enterprise would be nearly impossible due to its sheer volume, and much of it may be of little relevance anyway. Rather, you need to identify the most critical content for the audit. Stewart refers to "critical core content" in identifying what should be surveyed during an enterprise taxonomy content audit.[6]

Taxonomy Creation Process

Actually creating a taxonomy involves entering the concepts and terms identified in the planning and research stage into some taxonomy management tool, adding the appropriate term relationships and possible additional information, getting intermittent feedback from stakeholders and test users, and making further revisions as needed. This is the core of the work of taxonomists and what defines their work. And for most taxonomists, especially those who are not also involved in project management, this is the bulk of their job.

Steps for Building a Taxonomy

Planning for a taxonomy, as described in the first section of this chapter, involves answering basic questions regardless of the kind of taxonomy. But when it comes to actually building the taxonomy, there are different methods. Broadly speaking, the approach to building the taxonomy can be either top-down, bottom-up, or some of each, depending on the type of taxonomy. Hierarchical and faceted taxonomies tend to involve more of a top-down approach. The approach will also depend on the primary source for terms. If a significant number of terms are suggested by the taxonomists, subject matter experts, information architects, or a product manager, then more of a top-down design would result. If most of the terms originate in sample content, a bottom-up approach makes more sense.

Steps for Building a Hierarchical or Faceted Taxonomy

The basic steps for creating hierarchical taxonomies are the following:

1. Gather term concepts from a content audit, stakeholder interviews, and other sources.

2. Identify the top categories or facets based on analysis of patterns and scope of concepts, and list these (ideally in a spreadsheet).

3. Come up with example second-level terms for each category (but not necessarily all second-level terms) and possibly even a few third-level terms.

4. Present this top-level "straw-man" taxonomy to the taxonomy owner(s) or stakeholders for initial review and feedback and make revisions as requested. ("Straw-man" in this context means that, like straw, it can easily be torn down and rebuilt.)

5. Making full use of all the concepts gathered, fully build the taxonomy out to lower levels, possibly still in spreadsheet software if it is a small taxonomy or else in a taxonomy/thesaurus management tool.

6. Implement, conduct user testing, and revise as needed.

Since a hierarchical taxonomy is simpler than a thesaurus, at least once the basic hierarchies have been defined, the taxonomist's role could diminish after Step 4. At that point, internal subject matter experts, more intimately familiar with the content, could build out the taxonomy to further depths, as long as the taxonomist provides the guidelines and some review.

Although the top terms are defined first, with sample second-level terms next, often the procedure involves identifying the narrowest terms next, after the top terms, and then grouping the narrowest terms to come up with possible intermediate-level terms. Thus, even for a supposedly top-down hierarchy, you may actually perform some bottom-up taxonomy building, while still presenting a straw-man taxonomy consisting of only the top two levels. It is not unusual to start out creating the taxonomy from both the top and the bottom and to leave the middle for last.

Steps in Building a Thesaurus

The steps for creating literature/digital asset retrieval thesauri are similar to those for creating hierarchical taxonomies but not identical. Top categories may or may not need identifying, and unlike a hierarchical taxonomy, there is no point at which the taxonomist can "pass off" the taxonomy building to subject matter experts.

The taxonomist must do all the development of a thesaurus, except perhaps for named entities:

1. Gather term concepts from samples of the content being indexed.

2. Analyze the collected terms and organize them into lists within the same subject area at the same level "offline," whether in a spreadsheet (preferable) or in a text document.

3. Obtain feedback on some of the more significant term lists as deemed necessary, and then import them into thesaurus management software.

4. Making full use of all the gathered concepts, fully build out the thesaurus of terms and relationships in a thesaurus management tool, consulting reference sources (dictionaries, glossaries, other thesauri) and subject matter experts as needed.

5. Implement the thesaurus, test it with sample indexing, and revise it, filling in apparently "missing" terms and relationships.

When it comes to the most involved phase, actually building out the thesaurus of terms and relationships (Step 4 in the preceding list), there are basically three different possible approaches:

1. Complete each term's set of nonpreferred terms, full relationships, notes, and all attributes, then slowly add more terms. This approach works best for named entities, where interterm relationships are minimal or at least rather simple, but term details might be quite extensive.

2. Add a number of terms quickly, and then go back later to add the terms' details and relationships. Adding multiple terms could be done offline and then imported, but if the thesaurus software does not have an easy importing feature, it may be quicker to add terms of less than a dozen or so manually. This approach is more appropriate when there are a significant number of terms at the same level or when you have a list of technical terms that require research and you want to do all of the research later.

3. Adopt a hybrid approach, in which you add terms, create their nonpreferred terms and any scope notes or other term details, then go back and create relationships later; or create hierarchical relationships at the time of term creation, and add only the associative relationships later. This approach can work for various kinds of terms, and the specific procedure is more a matter of how the taxonomist may think: fully defined terms first, relationships second.

If you do postpone any relationship creation after creating a number of terms, obviously you should keep good records of which terms still require relationships.

In either case, whether you are building a hierarchical taxonomy or a thesaurus, you will likely develop a considerable number of terms offline, such as in a spreadsheet. You can then import or load the terms in batches into a thesaurus management tool, where you can create relationships and add other data. When you add terms later, though, during the taxonomy maintenance phase, you will need to create each one individually. Therefore, you will likely do all maintenance taxonomy work in the thesaurus management software.

Card-Sorting Exercises

The taxonomy-creation process involves periodic input from stakeholders and/or test-users. This input is not limited to approving lists of terms but could also involve input into the structure in the case of a hierarchical taxonomy. You can gather this input through a procedure called card sorting. As the name implies, card sorting involves having test-users sort into categories small cards or pieces of paper on which you have written the names of candidate taxonomy terms. From the sorting results, you can get an idea of how users believe hierarchies should be arranged. Card sorting is usually used for only two levels of a hierarchy at a time, typically the top level and a second level. Card sorting reveals the way searchers think about the concepts and has been a technique utilized by information architects for web navigational taxonomies for some time. While often associated with navigational taxonomies, this method can be used for the top two levels of any hierarchical taxonomy.

The number of cards/terms should be limited so that the card-sorting participants can easily scan the groups and work with them. Ideally, there should be about four to eight top-level categories, and within each of these categories a similar or slightly higher number of terms. Thus, the total number of second-level terms involved might range from 20 to 60. With more than that, the technique becomes unwieldy.

There are two kinds of card-sorting exercises: open card sort and closed card sort. An open card sort does not predefine the broader categories. The participants themselves must categorize the cards as they deem appropriate, determining both the names of the categories and how many categories there should be. A closed card sort is simpler for the participants. You provide them with the top-level categories, and they merely sort the second-level concepts into those predefined categories. You can choose either method or use both in sequence. An open card sort would be useful earlier on in the taxonomy development process, when you have not yet determined the top-level terms, and a closed card sort would come later.

Card sorting no longer requires having participants sort index cards on a conference room table in your presence, although there are benefits to doing it live if you can. Card-sorting software allows you to conduct card-sorting exercises with remote participants.

Web-based, SaaS card-sorting tools that offer subscription uses include OptimalSort (www.optimalworkshop.com/optimalsort) and User Zoom Card Sorting (www.userzoom.com/card-sorting). A list of web-based and stand-alone card-sorting software is available at the website of the book *Measuring the User Experience* (www.measuringux.com/CardSorting). These tools, which allow the users to move "cards" by a drag-and-drop feature, offer both open and

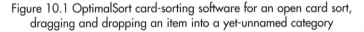

Figure 10.1 OptimalSort card-sorting software for an open card sort, dragging and dropping an item into a yet-unnamed category

closed card-sorting exercises. Figure 10.1 is a screenshot of an open card sort via OptimalSort.

Although conducting a card-sorting exercise is relatively simple, you should design it carefully to get the most out of it. If you have no prior experience with running a card-sorting exercise or merely want to learn more, Donna Spencer's book *Card Sorting: Designing Usable Categories* (Rosenfeld Media, 2009) covers the field in great detail.

As mentioned previously, card sorting may be used when trying to determine the top two levels of a hierarchical taxonomy. It is not practical for more than two levels at once, and it does not work for faceted taxonomies (unless testing only a single facet), since the nature of facets is to allow multiple methods of classification. For these reasons, many taxonomy projects are not suitable for card sorting.

Taxonomy Testing

After a taxonomy is created but before it is available for use, it is good practice to test the taxonomy. This procedure is also called taxonomy validation, implying that the taxonomy is indeed well designed and some testing is needed merely to validate it. Since a taxonomy is used both for indexing and retrieval, ideally two sets of tests take place. Testing for indexing can be done before the taxonomy is implemented, utilizing an offline version of the taxonomy. Testing for retrieval, however, requires some degree of system implementation, such as in a test environment of the system.

Testing a Taxonomy for Indexing Content

Several users who would likely index the content (or manage the automated indexing of content) should each be asked to provide several sample content items that they would add to the system and index. Both the taxonomist and the users then go through a simulated process of indexing, looking at the content item and at the taxonomy, and noting which terms from the taxonomy they would choose and whether they have difficulty finding terms, or perhaps do not find an expected term. The taxonomist may follow up with conversations with the test-indexing users or may simply utilize the test participants' notes. The taxonomist then identifies the terms that need to be added to the taxonomy, the terms that need clarification, and the terms that would be added merely as nonpreferred terms to existing terms.

Texting a Taxonomy for Finding Content

Testing the taxonomy for its effectiveness in content retrieval involves working with varied stakeholders in developing sample queries to see if the appropriate content is retrieved. Queries should be created only for content that is known to exist in the repository. The taxonomist may execute sample searches, but it is also a good idea to have representative users, if available, do the testing. They can search or browse the taxonomy for terms they expect to be linked to the desired content.

Testing should evaluate both recall and precision. Poor recall means that users could not find the content or could not find it easily enough. This would suggest that the taxonomy is not specific enough in some places, that terms were hard to find due to a lack of nonpreferred terms, or that indexing was insufficient. Poor precision means that users retrieve the wrong content in addition to the correct content. This suggests that certain terms are ambiguous (not precise enough) or that the content is over-indexed, with terms tagged to content that is not sufficiently relevant.

Taxonomy Governance

Even after a taxonomy is created and implemented, it is never entirely finished. All taxonomies require some updating over time, some more often than others. Keeping a taxonomy up to date requires having policies, methods, and procedures for maintenance and requires a documented understanding of who is responsible for the taxonomy over time. These documented policies constitute what is called taxonomy governance.

Governance, a term that in the past decade has been used in project management and especially in the information technology sector, refers to all the processes for managing a project, with particular emphasis on accountability. Governance deals with policies and procedures, including roles and accountabilities, standards, process methodologies, and communication methods. For taxonomies, governance is important not only for the design and building phases but also for the continued maintenance of the taxonomy. As mentioned previously, the initial taxonomy design plan document should become the basis of the governance document. This document is both followed and enhanced as the taxonomy is built, implemented, and maintained.

In considering the scope of taxonomy governance, you need to determine the following:

- The kinds of rules that should be followed for adding, changing, moving, or deleting terms or relationships

- The group that should maintain the taxonomy

- The various kinds of changes that may be expected to occur and possibly even their costs

- The kinds of information needed to determine appropriate changes (such as statistics for terms' indexing usage)

- The processes for changes

- Specific methods for handling comments, appeals, issue logs, announcements, update schedules, and so on

Possible methods for communicating with indexers have already been discussed in Chapter 6, but other individuals and groups will also want to propose changes to the taxonomy, so they, too, need to be covered in the governance document. Governance methods vary significantly among organizations and can involve primarily a single person, a couple of people, or a large cross-functional team.

The taxonomist or taxonomists who initially created the taxonomy are not necessarily the persons responsible for carrying out needed updates over time. Creating the taxonomy may involve an outside consultant or contractor or someone temporarily assigned to the project for the time-consuming design and building phase, while the less intensive work of maintenance later becomes someone else's task. The taxonomy could live on for decades after the employee(s) who created it left the organization. Alternatively, the taxonomy may have been inherited through an acquisition or partnership or adopted from another department. No matter what the circumstances, whether you are an employee or contractor, whenever you create a taxonomy, you should expect that the taxonomy will need to be maintained at some time or in some place without your own continued direct involvement. Therefore, documented policies are very important. On the other hand, if you come in to manage or update an existing taxonomy, be sure to ask for all documentation pertaining to the taxonomy.

There might not be a single taxonomy governance document but rather several relevant documents. Taxonomy governance deals with the taxonomy and all associated materials/documents, including

- an editorial style guide (which may be written for the taxonomy specifically or included within a larger guide for content creation in general)

- an end-user (searcher) guide

- indexing guidelines for indexers or for people using automated indexing systems

- any metadata standard of which controlled vocabularies are a part

- a broader product requirements document of which the taxonomy is a part

- team rules and procedures

An editorial style guide addresses issues involved in creating taxonomy terms and relationships, including capitalization, abbreviations, use of special characters, plurals, length limits, foreign words, inverted forms, punctuation within terms, and formats for certain kinds of named entities. Issues concerning term relationships include the number of relationships per term, polyhierarchies, use of associative relationships or additional customized relationships, and so on. There may be some overlap between the taxonomy editorial style guide and an indexing guide, especially regarding permission for indexers to create unapproved terms.

Because governance is so closely tied to maintenance, one might assume that taxonomy governance is the same as maintenance, but it is not. As we have seen, governance issues start with the taxonomy design plan. It is important to keep governance issues in mind from the start of a taxonomy project. Chapter 11 discusses taxonomy maintenance.

Endnotes

1. Patrick Lambe, "Preparing for a Taxonomy Project," Chapter 7 in *Organising Knowledge: Taxonomies, Knowledge, and Organisational Effectiveness*, 153–83 (Oxford: Chandos Publishing, 2007).

2. Darin L. Stewart, *Building Enterprise Taxonomies* (Portland, OR: Mokita Press, 2008), 70.

3. Declan Chellar, "Who Are Your Stakeholders?," *The Project Management Hut* (June 25, 2009), accessed December 20, 2015, www.pmhut.com/who-are-your -stakeholders

4. Margot Diltz, "Taxonomy Work Impressions Survey" survey response, September 22, 2009.

5. Stewart, *Building Enterprise Taxonomies*, 78.

6. Ibid., 77.

Chapter 11

Taxonomy Implementation and Evolution

Taxonomies: adding a little to your data so that
you can get a lot more out of it.
—Bob DuCharme

Taxonomy work involves more than just building new taxonomies. After all, full-time employed taxonomists tend to keep their jobs after they finish building a taxonomy. Chapter 2 lists a number of related duties that taxonomists perform, including documentation, test-searching, and indexing support. In addition, and more significantly, a taxonomy needs to be implemented in different systems, maintained, revised, adapted to new indexing or search implementations, merged or mapped with another taxonomy, and possibly translated into another language. You might maintain, revise, or adapt the taxonomy that you created, but you could also be required to manage and adapt a taxonomy created by someone else. As noted earlier, a taxonomy is never done. Because taxonomies are used to support the indexing of ever-growing and ever-changing content repositories, their terms must be updated and modified in keeping with evolving topics. Over time, you may also be able to collect data on what keywords end users are using, and thus you can modify terms to more closely match.

Taxonomy Exchange and Interoperability

A taxonomy is not fully functional if left in a taxonomy management system. Although some taxonomy management systems include modules for indexing (manual or automated) and/or search, most likely your content resides somewhere else, and at least some of your end users also use different systems for searching or browsing. Therefore, the completed taxonomy needs to be implemented or deployed into other systems to be used. This process typically involves exporting the taxonomy from your taxonomy management system and then having it imported into other systems. An existing taxonomy already in use may also need to be implemented into other systems, such as those of third-party partners or vendors. The ability to use data, in this case a taxonomy, in different applications, implementations, or software systems, whether proprietary, commercial, or open source, such as on the web, is known either as "exchange" or "interoperability." The term "interoperability" covers both the exchange of data to allow the same taxonomy to be used between different systems and also the linkages between different controlled vocabularies, which is discussed later in this chapter in the section of Mapping Taxonomies.

A taxonomy contains complex information, so a standard interoperable format is needed for exporting and re-importing or for importing an external licensed taxonomy. A CSV (comma-separated values) file format, typically derived from an Excel file, can serve this purpose, but it lacks any standard definitions. Therefore, the CSV format typically requires manipulation to set up the columns as required by a specific application, which is easier to do in relatively simple taxonomies than in complex thesauri. A more robust interoperable format, suitable for even complex thesauri, is XML, but it too requires further standardization.

XML

XML (www.w3.org/XML), which stands for eXtensible Markup Language, uses nested tags, like HTML, but the creator can define the tags. Definitions for the tags are stored in a related document called a schema. All commercial taxonomy management software supports some form of XML exporting of the taxonomies, so you

```
<CONCEPT>
  <DESCRIPTOR>Bookplates</DESCRIPTOR>
  <SN>Book owners&apos; identification labels; usually intended for
pasting inside a book.</SN>
  <UF>Book plates</UF>
  <UF>Ex libris</UF>
  <BT>Labels</BT>
  <NT>Armorial bookplates</NT>
  <RT>Ownership marks</RT>
</CONCEPT>
```

Figure 11.1 An example of XML output for a single preferred term,
"Bookplates," from the thesaurus software MultiTes
(same selected record as in Figure 5.4)

do not need to create your own XML tags. Figure 11.1 is an example of XML output generated by the thesaurus software MultiTes for a single preferred term, "Bookplates," from the Getty Art & Architecture Thesaurus.

XML tags are user defined and not standard, in contrast to HTML or various metadata standards (e.g., MARC or Dublin Core). Therefore, the tags used with an XML taxonomy export file have varied in different thesaurus software products. Others have followed a quite different tagged format, with more specifics, such as the following:

<relationship type="associative" name="Related To" termId="51">Child care**</relationship>**

Thesaurus software usually does not include a schema document, and even if it did, it would not cover any user-defined relationships, categories, or notes. Therefore, if you want to import a nonstandard XML file from thesaurus management software into an indexing system, content management system, or another taxonomy management software application, you need to write the schema yourself, find someone in your organization who can, contract the thesaurus software vendor for the additional service, or, if licensing an externally published taxonomy, contract the thesaurus vendor to do it.

Zthes

In an attempt to provide a standard for the various possible XML tag specifications for thesauri, beginning in 1999 the British software engineer Mike Taylor developed an XML schema specific for the "semantic hierarchies" of terms as described in ISO 2788 (the predecessor at the time to ISO 2596) and ANSI/NISO Z39.19, which is called Zthes (zthes.z3950.org), the "Z" coming from Z39.19.

The Zthes schema specifies the following elements: termId, termUpdate, termName, termQualifier, termType, termLanguage, termVocabulary, termCategory, termStatus, termApproval, term Sortkey, termNote, termCreatedDate, termCreatedBy, termModified Date, termModifiedBy, postings, and relation. Subrecords specify the relation (relationship) type. Figure 11.2 is an example of Zthes XML of the NASA Thesaurus (www.sti.nasa.gov/sti-tools/#thesaurus).

Zthes gained a sufficient reputation as a thesaurus standard that several thesaurus software vendors have supported it as an export format, including Data Harmony, Synaptica, and (previously) Smartlogic Semaphore. Zthes, however, has not stayed up to date, and is limited to thesauri only and designed for other kinds of

```xml
- <term>
    <termId>43731</termId>
    <termUpdate>add</termUpdate>
    <termName>galactic clusters</termName>
    <termVocabulary>NASA Thesaurus</termVocabulary>
    <termNote label="Scope Note">RESTRICTED TO CLUSTERS OF GALAXIES; EXCLUDES OPEN CLUSTERS</termNote>
-   <relation weight="100">
        <relationType>UF</relationType>
        <termId>183534</termId>
        <termName>galaxy groups</termName>
        <termVocabulary>NASA Thesaurus</termVocabulary>
    </relation>
-   <relation weight="100">
        <relationType>BT</relationType>
        <termId>61022</termId>
        <termName>celestial bodies</termName>
        <termVocabulary>NASA Thesaurus</termVocabulary>
    </relation>
-   <relation weight="100">
        <relationType>NT</relationType>
        <termId>62525</termId>
        <termName>local group (astronomy)</termName>
        <termVocabulary>NASA Thesaurus</termVocabulary>
    </relation>
```

Figure 11.2 An extract example of ZThes1.0 representation for a single preferred term, "galactic clusters," from the NASA thesaurus. (The NT and RT relations are too numerous, so to save space only the first three are shown.)

controlled vocabularies. So, without a revision since 2006 and with the growing demand for Semantic Web interoperability standards instead, its support by thesaurus software vendors has dropped.[1]

RDF, OWL, and SKOS

The RDF (Resource Description Framework) language, or variations of it, is also used as an interoperable format for taxonomies. RDF (www.w3.org/RDF), supported by the World Wide Web Consortium (W3C), is a framework rather than a strict standard. RDF, which is expressable in XML syntax, was designed for describing web resources and giving each resource and the resource's attributes persistent identifiers, such as URIs or URLs. An extension of RDF deals specifically with a vocabulary description language but does not get into such specifics as term relationship types. Rather, it provides a mechanism for the user to define them. Although RDF uses XML syntax, it is more complex than a tagging language, since it uses what are called *classes, properties, resources,* and *collections.* A better analogy for RDF syntax would be the coding used in object-oriented programming languages.

What is more relevant for taxonomies are two other W3C standards or specifications built on RDF: the Web Ontology Language (called by a slightly indirect acronym, OWL) and the SKOS. Since there are no W3C standards specifically for thesauri, these are the most appropriate.

OWL (www.w3.org/2001/sw/wiki/OWL), a formal W3C recommendation of 2004, is a semantic markup language for publishing and sharing ontologies on the web and supports Semantic Web applications. OWL features a larger vocabulary, a stronger syntax, and greater machine interpretability than does RDF. As OWL is intended specifically for ontologies, rather than simpler thesauri or taxonomies, it may actually be more than you need. A revised version of OWL, OWL 2, was published in 2012, which includes some new features, functionality, and expressivity. Taxonomy/ontology management software that supports RDF/OWL exporting includes

Data Harmony, Mondeca, PoolParty, Protégé, SAS, Semaphore, Synaptica, and TopBraid EVN.

SKOS (www.w3.org/2004/02/skos) is a proposed standard that is an application of RDF specifically for knowledge organization systems, such as thesauri and taxonomies. SKOS was published as a W3C "recommendation" in 2009, and while it is often considered a "standard," it remains a work in progress. The word "simple" in the name implies that it is simpler than OWL. In SKOS, the fundamental element is a concept, rather than a "term," and SKOS also defines preferred and alternate (nonpreferred) labels for concepts, along with (scope) notes and definitions. SKOS also supports foreign language equivalents of a concept and additional alternate (nonpreferred) labels within those other languages. Standard relationships between concepts are broader, narrower, and related relationships, but customized relationships can also be supported.

```
- <PreferredTerm rdf:ID="PT43731">
    <termId>43731</termId>
    <termUpdate>add</termUpdate>
    <termName>galactic clusters</termName>
    <termVocabulary rdf:resource="#NASA_Thesaurus"/>
    <termNote rdf:resource="#PT43731-ScopeNote"/>
    <firstTermInRelation rdf:resource="#PT43731-UF-NPT183534"/>
    <secondTermInRelation rdf:resource="#NPT183534-USE-PT43731"/>
    <firstTermInRelation rdf:resource="#PT43731-BT-PT61022"/>
    <secondTermInRelation rdf:resource="#PT61022-NT-PT43731"/>
    <firstTermInRelation rdf:resource="#PT43731-NT-PT62525"/>
        .
        .
    <firstTermInRelation rdf:resource="#PT43731-RT-PT64494"/>
    <secondTermInRelation rdf:resource="#PT64494-RT-PT43731"/>
  </PreferredTerm>
- <ThesaurusNote rdf:ID="PT43731-ScopeNote">
    <noteLabel>Scope Note</noteLabel>
    <noteValue>RESTRICTED TO CLUSTERS OF GALAXIES; EXCLUDES OPEN CLUSTERS</noteValue>
  </ThesaurusNote>
- <UF-Rel rdf:ID="PT43731-UF-NPT183534">
    <firstTerm rdf:resource="#PT43731"/>
    <secondTerm rdf:resource="#NPT183534"/>
    <relationWeight>100</relationWeight>
  </UF-Rel>
- <BT-Rel rdf:ID="PT43731-BT-PT61022">
    <firstTerm rdf:resource="#PT43731"/>
    <secondTerm rdf:resource="#PT61022"/>
    <relationWeight>100</relationWeight>
  </BT-Rel>
- <NT-Rel rdf:ID="PT43731-NT-PT62525">
    <firstTerm rdf:resource="#PT43731"/>
    <secondTerm rdf:resource="#PT62525"/>
    <relationWeight>100</relationWeight>
  </NT-Rel>
```

Figure 11.3 An extract example of OWL (XML) representation for the concept "galactic clusters," from the NASA thesaurus. (Vertical periods denote text cut out to save in the figure.)

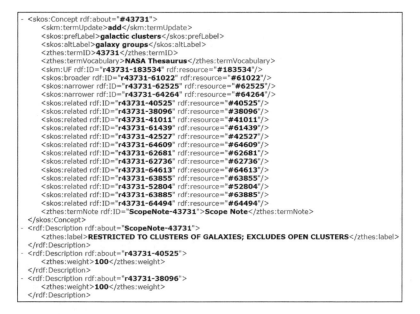

```
- <skos:Concept rdf:about="#43731">
    <skm:termUpdate>add</skm:termUpdate>
    <skos:prefLabel>galactic clusters</skos:prefLabel>
    <skos:altLabel>galaxy groups</skos:altLabel>
    <zthes:termID>43731</zthes:termID>
    <zthes:termVocabulary>NASA Thesaurus</zthes:termVocabulary>
    <skm:UF rdf:ID="r43731-183534" rdf:resource="#183534"/>
    <skos:broader rdf:ID="r43731-61022" rdf:resource="#61022"/>
    <skos:narrower rdf:ID="r43731-62525" rdf:resource="#62525"/>
    <skos:narrower rdf:ID="r43731-64264" rdf:resource="#64264"/>
    <skos:related rdf:ID="r43731-40525" rdf:resource="#40525"/>
    <skos:related rdf:ID="r43731-38096" rdf:resource="#38096"/>
    <skos:related rdf:ID="r43731-41011" rdf:resource="#41011"/>
    <skos:related rdf:ID="r43731-61439" rdf:resource="#61439"/>
    <skos:related rdf:ID="r43731-42527" rdf:resource="#42527"/>
    <skos:related rdf:ID="r43731-64609" rdf:resource="#64609"/>
    <skos:related rdf:ID="r43731-62681" rdf:resource="#62681"/>
    <skos:related rdf:ID="r43731-62736" rdf:resource="#62736"/>
    <skos:related rdf:ID="r43731-64613" rdf:resource="#64613"/>
    <skos:related rdf:ID="r43731-63855" rdf:resource="#63855"/>
    <skos:related rdf:ID="r43731-52804" rdf:resource="#52804"/>
    <skos:related rdf:ID="r43731-63885" rdf:resource="#63885"/>
    <skos:related rdf:ID="r43731-64494" rdf:resource="#64494"/>
    <zthes:termNote rdf:ID="ScopeNote-43731">Scope Note</zthes:termNote>
  </skos:Concept>
- <rdf:Description rdf:about="ScopeNote-43731">
    <zthes:label>RESTRICTED TO CLUSTERS OF GALAXIES; EXCLUDES OPEN CLUSTERS</zthes:label>
  </rdf:Description>
- <rdf:Description rdf:about="r43731-40525">
    <zthes:weight>100</zthes:weight>
  </rdf:Description>
- <rdf:Description rdf:about="r43731-38096">
    <zthes:weight>100</zthes:weight>
  </rdf:Description>
```

Figure 11.4 An extract example of SKOS (XML) representation
for the concept "galactic clusters," from the NASA thesaurus

Most dedicated taxonomy management software, as listed in Chapter 5, supports exporting to SKOS now. Figures 11.3 and 11.4 present examples of OWL and SKOS representations of XML of a preferred term/concept in the NASA Thesaurus (the same as was presented in Figure 11.2 in ZThes, for comparison). The narrower and related concept relations are too numerous, so to save space only the first are shown (www.sti.nasa.gov/sti-tools/#thesaurus).

Additionally there is SKOS-XL, which defines an extension describing "lexical entities," or terms, which are part of a concept. SKOS-XL thus helps support added metadata for specific terms (labels) that are part of a concept. Some, but not all, taxonomy management software that supports SKOS also supports SKOS-XL.

Thesaurus Standards and Exchange Formats

The World Wide Web Consortium is not the only organization interested in knowledge organization system exchange and interoperability. Coming from the other direction, the organizations that have developed thesaurus standards, the International Organization for Standards (ISO) and the National Information Standards Organization (NISO), have also more recently been working on exchange format recommendations for thesauri and other controlled vocabularies, which were out of the scope of the original standards documents.

When ISO updated its thesaurus standards, replacing 2788:1986 *Guidelines for the establishment and development of monolingual thesauri* and ISO 5964:1985 *Guidelines for the establishment and development of multilingual thesauri* with a set of new standards, ISO 25964 parts 1 and 2 (in 2011 and 2013), *Thesauri and interoperability with other vocabularies*, in addition to the original standards' content, there are new sections added to ISO 25964 - Part 1 that deal with thesaurus data management, sharing and exchange. These are the sections: 14. Guidelines for thesaurus management software, 15. Data model, 16. Integration of thesauri with applications, 17. Exchange formats (listing options of MARC, SKOS, and Zthes), and 18. Protocols. In the Data model section, the recommendation is to use XML, and a specific UML (Unified Modeling Language) data model is proposed.[2] ISO 25964 - Part 2, in the section on technical aspects of managing data (section 15.2.2), states: "A SKOS-compliant format is recommended if use in the Semantic Web is desired." During 2012–2013 members of an ISO 25964 working group developed a set of linkages between the elements of the ISO 25964 standard and the SKOS data model, called "Correspondence between ISO 25964 and SKOS/SKOS-XL models" (www.niso.org/schemas/iso25964/#skos).

Although ANSI/NISO Z.39.19 (2005) does not discuss exchange formats, such as XML or SKOS, the National Information Standards Organization (NISO) launched in 2015 a working group project, "Development of Standards to Support Bibliographic Data Exchange." Despite "bibliographic" in the name, the focus of the group is largely around vocabularies. One of the subgroup working areas for new guidelines or standards is focused on policies supporting vocabulary use and reuse.[3]

Taxonomy Updating

A taxonomy is never finished. As soon as it is implemented, it undergoes testing and revision, and continued use will dictate further enhancements. All taxonomies require ongoing maintenance, and many taxonomies also undergo more significant revisions or restructuring over time.

Taxonomy Maintenance

A taxonomy requires continual maintenance. Various kinds of changes can necessitate updates to a taxonomy:

- Ongoing user feedback suggests improvements.
- Quality control indicates preventable indexing inaccuracies.
- Additional content brings up new concepts.
- Certain previously included content is excluded or discontinued.
- New trends, buzzwords, and terminology arise in existing content.
- New audiences, users, markets, or implementations are added.

Taxonomy updating can be done continually or as periodic revision projects. If you have continued responsibility for the taxonomy, then you need to keep abreast of all the possible areas that may affect the taxonomy. This involves reviewing the following:

- Newly added content sources
- Parts of the taxonomy or vocabularies covering rapidly changing topics (e.g., events, news, and technology)

- Direct feedback from users (both indexers and end users)

- End-user search logs for additional search strings entered

- Term usage data in indexing/tagging (human or automated) to determine:

  - High-use terms needing further differentiation through the addition of more specific terms

  - Low/no-use terms that should be removed or merged

  - Identifiable indexing errors that point to the need for clarifying terms

When merging one term with another, not only do you convert a preferred term (the obsolete term) into a nonpreferred term for another preferred term, but ideally you want all of the obsolete term's nonpreferred terms to become nonpreferred terms for the newly merged preferred term. If there is a scope note for the obsolete term, that too should be moved over to the designated preferred term, but the taxonomist should review and edit the transferred or combined note. Some, but not all, taxonomy management software has a merge feature that, in a single step, allows a designated preferred term automatically to inherit the nonpreferred terms, notes, and other attributes of an obsolete term that is merged into it.

If the taxonomy set is segmented into subtaxonomies, vocabularies, facets, or authority files, some of these vocabularies will require more frequent updating than others, depending on their coverage. As a rule, named entities require more frequent updates than topical terms. Concepts should have some staying power, whereas relevant people, products, organizations, and so on may come and go. For example, new terms for types of products occur less frequently than new named product models. Simply keeping abreast of the latest news within a field is also a good idea for the taxonomist in charge of taxonomy maintenance.

When it comes to reviewing the indexing, you need to define what the thresholds are for "high-use" terms and "low-use" terms and determine what counts as an error. High use may be defined relative to other terms, but you should also consider how search results display. Depending on the user's ability to narrow results, one, two, or three screenfuls of search results per term (10, 20, or 30 records) could be considered enough. Low-use terms could be anything with fewer than three matches, but you also have to consider the time span. In the case of errors, it is necessary to have a clearly defined policy as to what constitutes an error, as well as a procedure to identify and track errors. Indexing is sometimes subjective, so you need to draw the line between "good enough" and "not good enough."

Ideally, you should use the same thesaurus software used in creating the taxonomy (as described in Chapter 5) to make updates to the taxonomy. Updating a taxonomy may include any of the following:

- Creating new terms
- Splitting existing terms (creating two new terms and removing an old one)
- Deleting terms
- Merging terms (including deleting a term and making it nonpreferred for an existing term)
- Changing the wording of a term (including keeping an old name as a nonpreferred term)
- Adding relationships (hierarchical or associative) between existing terms
- Deleting relationships between existing terms
- Changing relationships between existing terms (deleting and replacing with a different relationship)
- Adding nonpreferred terms to an existing term
- Adding scope notes to existing terms
- Adding other new information, attributes, categories, and so on to existing terms

- Moving a branch/subhierarchy within a hierarchical taxonomy to a new location

If the taxonomy/thesaurus software and the indexing system are integrated, there should be no complications when it comes to updating the taxonomy. But if, as is often the case, the taxonomy is maintained in one software system and indexing and/or search is conducted in a different system, the taxonomy updates need to be ported to it. If possible, set up some kind of schedule for regular updates, whether daily, weekly, or monthly. Taxonomy updates might need to be scheduled during a time when indexing is not taking place, perhaps outside regular working hours.

Then there is the matter of applying new or changed taxonomy terms to previously indexed content. Nonpreferred terms should take care of this automatically in the case of simple term changes. But if you create new terms or split an existing term into two terms, then retroactive indexing can be an issue, and this task may fall to the taxonomist and not the indexers. There may be the resources to retroactively index only selected documents that are considered important rather than all possible documents pertaining to the new term. One option is to have scripts written to make global changes to indexing when terms change in the taxonomy, or you can make use of interfaces that display term splits along with associated records so that you can assign more precise terminology to older documents.

Taxonomy Revisions

A taxonomy could require significant revisions for various reasons. Its maintenance may have been neglected over several years due to lack of a taxonomist, and evolutionary changes in content and audience/market over time eventually necessitate a more thorough review and overhaul. A conversion from human indexing to automated indexing would require a reexamination of the taxonomy to eliminate ambiguous terms and to increase the number of nonpreferred terms. If accumulated content has increased beyond initial expectations, it might be deemed necessary to expand a relatively small taxonomy in order to support indexing in detail (granularity), for more refined search results. A hierarchical taxonomy that previously excluded polyhierarchies may now permit them. More complex taxonomy revisions involve implementing a decision to convert a controlled vocabulary into a thesaurus or a hierarchical taxonomy or to convert a thesaurus or hierarchical taxonomy into a faceted taxonomy.

For example, a number of literature retrieval vendors in the United States chose initially to base their controlled vocabularies on Library of Congress Subject Headings (LCSH), because it was the largest general-purpose controlled vocabulary available. However, for many decades it lacked hierarchical relationships between terms (with no distinction between hierarchical and associative relationships). Organizations that used controlled vocabularies based on LCSH and later decided it would be better to have a true thesaurus then had to undertake a major taxonomy revision project to convert generic *See also* relationships into proper broader term (BT), narrower term (NT), or related term (RT) relationships. For a controlled vocabulary of tens of thousands of terms, this kind of project can take years.

Taxonomy revision projects follow some of the same steps as new taxonomy projects, depending on the type of revision. If there has been a significant change in content, then a content review or audit is required. If a taxonomy is to be totally restructured, then stakeholder interviews would be a good idea. More specifically, if a controlled vocabulary will be converted to a hierarchical taxonomy, then a card-sorting exercise would also be a good idea.

Combining Taxonomies

In addition to revising a single taxonomy, a common taxonomy management project involves combining two or more taxonomies. Different ways to combine taxonomies include the following:

- Integrating: Combining separate taxonomies on different subjects into a single master taxonomy for combined use

- Merging: Combining two redundant taxonomies in the same subject area into one (not retaining them as distinct)

- Mapping: Enabling one taxonomy to be used for another in the same subject area, while retaining them both as continued distinct taxonomies

Integrating focuses more on structure, whereas merging and mapping tend to ignore the structure and the relationships between concepts and focus on the terms. In all cases, the combined taxonomies may have previously been used separately. Integrating or mapping can also be used to combine an existing taxonomy with a newly created one.

Integrating Taxonomies

Integrating taxonomies involves combining previously separate vocabularies, hierarchies, authority files, or subtaxonomies that have different concepts into a single master taxonomy. Integrating allows for combined use in the same search/browse user interface and for a shared content repository. ("Combined use" does not, however, mean that terms from the different taxonomies must be combined in search execution, as in a faceted search.) The subject area scope of the different taxonomies may be related, but for the most part, they should not be overlapping or redundant, as the objective is to have them supplement each other. If the taxonomies were redundant, then the strategy would be to merge, rather than integrate, them. Reasons to integrate taxonomies include, but are not limited to, the following:

- A larger organizational taxonomy is built by combining existing departmental taxonomies.

- An additional facet is added to an existing faceted taxonomy, based on user feedback.

- A manufacturer or distributor adds a new product line, requiring that a new product/topic hierarchy be added to its website.

- An online database provider adds a new database product that requires a new authority file.

- An internally created taxonomy is supplemented by a purchased/licensed taxonomy in a complementary subject area in order to expand its scope.

- A company expands into a new geographic market and needs to add geographic and named organizational terms to cover that area.

- An organization acquires or merges with another organization, and their taxonomies in various operational areas need to be integrated.

Integrating taxonomies works well for hierarchical or faceted taxonomies, in which it is not difficult to add a hierarchy or facet. It is also quite simple to add a new named entity authority file to a collection of controlled vocabularies. Supplementing an existing topical thesaurus with an additional subject area, however, is more complicated. This is because at some point you will need to create relationships between the existing terms and the newly added terms, even if only associative relationships, and you will need to individually identify the relevant terms.

The previously separate taxonomies may have been created within the same organization, but most likely they originate from different sources. In some cases, the taxonomy to be integrated is sufficiently complete and fully structured, while in other cases, it requires significant editing and restructuring to conform to the format and standards of the rest of your taxonomy. While it may even be necessary to build a new subtaxonomy from scratch, this is not likely to occur at this stage, when resources are focused on taxonomy enhancement rather than construction. In other words, the person responsible for managing a taxonomy may not have the additional time needed to build a new subtaxonomy.

The main work for a taxonomist in an integration project is to study the potential issues and make recommendations for the integration, especially with respect to the overall taxonomy structure and any relationships between new terms and those already in the taxonomy. You will also need to come up with indexing and editorial policies for the new taxonomy and incorporate them into the existing governance procedure and documentation.

Assuming that the taxonomy to be integrated comes from an external source, the most crucial issue to deal with is data exchange (interoperability). As previously mentioned, any taxonomy that is imported in a nonstandard XML format will need a schema. Even if the format is not an issue, a taxonomy from another source will incvitably lack some of the values associated with terms in your existing taxonomy. These could include sequential numbers, categories or classes, additional attributes, additional relationship types, and history notes. (The imported taxonomy could have additional attributes, but those could be simply ignored.) Some of this information can perhaps be added in batches to the terms in the new taxonomy, while other information may have to be added to terms individually, and some information may simply be omitted because there is no support for it.

Merging Taxonomies

Another type of project involving pre-existing taxonomies is the complete merging of two or more taxonomies. Pre-existing taxonomies in the same or similar subject areas may need to be combined under various circumstances, including but not limited to the following:

- A new enterprise taxonomy replaces the separate taxonomies of multiple administrative departments.

- An information vendor merges different search taxonomies that had previously been used for different search products (used for different markets, media, content, etc.).

- A folksonomy is incorporated into the taxonomy.

- An organization acquires or merges with another organization, and their redundant vocabularies (whether they are enterprise taxonomies or consumer search taxonomies) are merged.

- An internally created taxonomy is combined with a purchased/licensed taxonomy in the same subject area to enhance it.

In merging two or more taxonomies, the process will be simpler if you can designate one taxonomy as the primary or dominant taxonomy into which you will merge the other(s). The decision as to which taxonomy is primary might be made for you, such as when one organization acquires another (typically the acquirer's taxonomy is primary). In other cases, it may not be obvious or even matter which taxonomy should be dominant. You will need to scan both or all taxonomies involved to compare and choose the dominant taxonomy. The dominant taxonomy may be the one that is significantly larger, has greater breadth, has greater depth, has the best skeleton or top structure, is more highly structured if that is important, or is generally a "better" taxonomy in accordance with standards and best practices.

The first step in merging involves automated matching to compare the two taxonomies to identify and classify matches, whether exact or close. Some commercial taxonomy applications, such as Synaptica and Wordmap, include an automatic vocabulary-matching feature, which is especially useful if both taxonomies are already managed in that software. Often one taxonomy is from an external source, so having someone write a custom program or script (e.g, Perl scripting language) to compare the vocabularies might be easier if resources permit. You should compare only two taxonomies at a time. If there are more than two taxonomies to be merged, compare each merging taxonomy with the primary taxonomy separately. Merging focuses on terms only; hierarchical and associative relationships are ignored during merging. Equivalence relationships, on the other hand, are important in merging.

In any case, an output for human review would typically be in a table or a spreadsheet with one column for one taxonomy, a second column for the other taxonomy, and corresponding matched terms in the same row. In a third column to the side or in between, you as the reviewer may enter *y* or *n* for *yes* or *no* to accept or reject the match or perhaps enter some other notation to provide a more specific judgment about the relationship between the pairs of terms.

Automated matching should identify and list the following types of matches, along with the match type (the basis of the match). If you are using your own scripting language, then the following should be sequential comparison passes:

1. Exact matches of a preferred term in the merging taxonomy with a preferred term in the primary taxonomy.

2. Exact matches of a preferred term in the merging taxonomy with a nonpreferred term in the primary taxonomy. For example, the primary taxonomy has the term **cars**, and the merging taxonomy has **automobiles USE cars**.

3. Exact matches of a preferred term in the primary taxonomy with a nonpreferred term in the merging taxonomy (whereby the corresponding preferred term in the merging taxonomy does not match any term in the primary taxonomy). For example, the primary taxonomy has the term **cars**, and the merging taxonomy has **cars USE automobiles**, but the primary taxonomy does not have automobiles, even as a nonpreferred term. (In these circumstances, automobiles will become a new nonpreferred term in the final merged taxonomy.)

4. Matches of a nonpreferred term in the merging taxonomy with a nonpreferred term in the primary taxonomy (for which the corresponding preferred terms do not exist in either taxonomy), although this would be rare. For example, the primary taxonomy has **cars USE autos**,

and the merging taxonomy has **cars USE automobiles**, but the primary taxonomy does not have **automobiles**, and the merging taxonomy does not have **autos**. The corresponding preferred term (**automobiles**) of the nonpreferred term (**cars**) within the merging taxonomy should be considered as an additional nonpreferred term for the corresponding preferred term (**autos**) in the primary taxonomy.

5. Close, but not exact, matches between a preferred term in the merging taxonomy and a preferred term or nonpreferred term in the primary taxonomy (also called *fuzzy matches*), based on ignoring the following differences between pairs of terms:

   a. Hyphens, parentheses, punctuation, and spaces (such as **healthcare/health care**)

   b. Plural/singular (such as **teaching method/teaching methods**)

   c. Common abbreviations and acronyms (such as **and/&**, **dept./department**), based on a provided list

   d. Words of a term appearing in a different order (such as **photography, digital** and **digital photography**)

   e. The addition of certain listed words, such as *industry* or *services* (as in **healthcare** and **healthcare services**)

   f. Different grammatical endings on the same root word (such as **production/producing**)

For matches to preferred terms in the primary taxonomy (the first and second types of matches in the preceding list), nothing needs to be done, and no human (taxonomist) review is necessary. For all subsequent types, a taxonomist should review the automatically generated matches. Table 11.1 summarizes the kinds of automated term matches between a "merging taxonomy" and the "primary taxonomy" and indicates which types require review by a taxonomist.

Table 11.1 Automated term matches that require review by a taxonomist

Merging Taxonomy	Primary Taxonomy	Review?
Exact matches of:		
Preferred term	*Preferred term*	
Preferred term	*Nonpreferred term*	
Nonpreferred term	*Preferred term*	yes
Nonpreferred term	*Nonpreferred term*	yes
Inexact matches of:		
Preferred term	*Preferred term*	yes

Additional types of matches will generate candidates for non-preferred terms from the merging taxonomy, and the taxonomist should approve them for addition to the primary taxonomy. Depending on the reason for designating one taxonomy as primary, you might also make use of the match results to consider whether to change the name of a preferred term of the primary taxonomy to that of an equivalent term used in the merging taxonomy, if it seems like a better wording for the concept.

After the automated matches have been generated, you need to analyze the remaining unmatched terms from each taxonomy more closely. You can temporarily sort and interfile them alphabetically, with terms from each taxonomy distinguished from each other in some way, such as font style. Then you can scan the list for additional potential matches based on the start of the terms. It is here that your skills in identifying valid equivalence relationships come into play.

Finally, in cases where there are completely different terms in the two taxonomies, there is no need to change terms in the primary taxonomy, and you should evaluate unmatched terms from the merging taxonomy individually for possible inclusion in the taxonomy. You need to pay special attention to where these terms might belong hierarchically when added to the primary taxonomy. If the new terms from the merging taxonomy comprise entirely new hierarchies or subhierarchies, it might make more sense to import the terms along with their relationships, rather than having to recreate the hierarchical relationships between them.

Mapping Taxonomies

In certain circumstances, two pre-existing taxonomies covering the same subject area may be integrated to serve unified retrieval yet remain intact for continued separate use as well. This combination enables one taxonomy to be used at the front end (in the searcher's user interface) while the other taxonomy is used at the back end (indexed to the content) for a specific content set. Thus, the taxonomy that the user sees at the front end continues to retrieve its content as before, along with additional content indexed with the other taxonomy. The taxonomies are matched, or more specifically "mapped," term-by-term where matches are sufficiently equivalent. Hierarchical and associative relationships are largely ignored for mapping.

The notion of mapping is probably most familiar to information professionals who work with metadata, since mapping projects are frequently used to support interoperability among metadata stored in different standards, such as MARC and variations of Dublin Core. As there are standards of metadata, so are there somewhat standardized mapping tables, known as *crosswalks*. In fact, "crosswalks" is sometimes used to mean mappings. Vocabulary or taxonomy mapping is quite different, however. Instead of mapping metadata (instructions for data), you are mapping the actual data, which is every term in a taxonomy.

Situations in which one taxonomy is mapped to another include, but are not limited, to the following:

- Selected internal content from an enterprise taxonomy is made available on a public website that has a different, public-facing taxonomy.

- A content provider with a taxonomy partners with a third-party information vendor with its own taxonomy to expand the market of its content.

- A provider of scientific/technical/medical content, which already has a detailed taxonomy, develops a new information service aimed at laypeople or students and creates a simpler taxonomy for it.

- A large collection of search log query terms needs to be integrated into the taxonomy as additional nonpreferred terms.

- Federated search, involving multiple data repositories, each with its own search engine and taxonomy, is implemented.

- Content will be made available in a different language region, and a comparable taxonomy already exists in the other language.

In a mapping project, it is important to know which taxonomy will appear in the user interface and which taxonomy will be linked to content. You need to be aware of the direction of information flow, which is from content to user, and thus map in this same direction, from the terms in what we will call the *indexing taxonomy* to terms in the *retrieval taxonomy*. Since mapping involves making equivalence relationships between the terms in one taxonomy and the terms in the other taxonomy, one taxonomy is being collectively "used for" the other taxonomy. Therefore one taxonomy needs to be preferred, like a preferred term, and the other taxonomy is nonpreferred. The preferred taxonomy is the retrieval taxonomy, and the nonpreferred taxonomy is the indexing taxonomy.

As with merging projects, mapping involves automatic matching first, followed by a human review. You can use the same series of matching types listed for merging taxonomies for mapping taxonomies, and you can use the same tools to do it. There are two main differences, however, between merging and mapping. First, in projects involving merging, any remaining unmatched terms are simply added to enhance the merged taxonomy, but in mapping, you are not creating a new taxonomy or adding new terms, so any unmatched terms unfortunately cannot be utilized. Second, creating matches for mapping is not limited to equivalence relationships. A narrower term can be mapped to a broader term, as long as it is going from the indexing taxonomy (NT) to the retrieval taxonomy (BT). This is an application of *upward posting*, whereby a broader term can be used for a narrower term. Consequently, it may happen that more than one narrower term in the indexing taxonomy is mapped to a single term that is broader in the retrieval taxonomy. Many-to-one mapping is acceptable but should not be too extensive.

With narrower-to-broader mapping permitted, automated matching could also include phrase matches of terms in the retrieval taxonomy that are phrases within terms in the indexing taxonomy. This is because a noun phrase found within a longer noun phrase has a good chance of being more generic (broader) than the longer and thus more specific noun phrase. For example, see the following:

Indexing taxonomy:	*Retrieval taxonomy:*
HDTV television sets	**television sets**

Television sets is a noun phrase within **HDTV television sets**, whereby the shorter phrase of **television sets** is indeed the broader concept. So the narrower term **HDTV television sets** would be automatically mapped "upward" to **television sets**. Not all term-within-a-term phrases are hierarchically related, however, so you should review such automated matches carefully.

As with merging taxonomies, it is easiest for you to quickly review numerous automated matches if they are in a spreadsheet format, where one column is used for the indexing taxonomy and another column for the retrieval taxonomy with matched terms in the same

	A	B	C
1	Private universities and colleges	n	Private colleges
2	Procarbazine hydrochloride	b	Procarbazine
3	Progressivism (United States politics)	b	Progressive movement
4	Projection	n	Projection (Drawing)
5	Prolactin	n	Prolactin test
6	Promethazine hydrochloride	b	Promethazine
7	Promoters (Entertainment)	b	Promoters
8	Propaganda, American	ok	American propaganda
9	Propellant actuated devices	b	Propellants
10	Propellers, Aerial	ok	Aircraft propellers
11	Propellers, Variable pitch	ok	Variable pitch propellers
12	Property tax	ok	Property taxes
13	Propfan engines	b	Engines
14	Propiomazine	b	Antipsychotic agents
15	Prose poems	ok	Prose poetry
16	Prosthesis	b	Prostheses and implants
17	Prosthodontics	ok	Dental prostheses

Figure 11.5 A mapping table representing an indexing taxonomy in column A, a retrieval taxonomy in column C, and taxonomist notes in column B: *ok* is equivalent, *b* is broader (so also *ok* for upward posting), and *n* is not acceptable

row. Figure 11.5 is an excerpt of a mapping table in which column A contains the indexing taxonomy, column C is for the retrieval taxonomy, and column B is where the taxonomist has marked the acceptability of the mapping as OK, not OK (n), and broader (b, which is acceptable for upward posting). For example, **promoters (entertainment)** has **promoters** as a broader term, but **prolactin** is neither equivalent to nor narrower than **prolactin test**, so this is not a match.

In mapping projects, it is all right if you cannot map a term in the retrieval taxonomy to a term in the indexing taxonomy because the retrieval taxonomy terms still have other uses. If, however, you cannot map a term in the indexing taxonomy to a term in the retrieval taxonomy, then any content indexed with that term will not be retrievable with the mapped taxonomy. Whether you should add any preferred terms to the retrieval taxonomy is another question, which is beyond the scope of the mapping project. This should be decided early on, though, so that you can identify these terms while reviewing the matches.

Guidelines for mapping thesauri are presented in ISO 25964-2 *Thesauri and interoperability with other vocabularies* -- Part 2: *Interoperability with other vocabularies*, and their inclusion was new to this 2013 version of standards. In fact, the kind of "interoperability" that this document discusses is mostly mapping, and roughly half of the standard (34 pages) deals with mapping between thesauri. (In other parts of the standard, there are guidelines for mapping between different types of vocabularies, such as between a taxonomy and a thesaurus, or between a name authorities and a thesaurus.) The different kinds of mapping ISO 25964 describes are hierarchical, associative, exact, inexact, and partial mappings. While ANSI/NISO Z39.19 is generally considered equivalent to ISO 25964, the sections on mapping thesauri are currently found only in ISO 25964 and not in ANSI/NISO Z39.19-2015.

Since mappings between active taxonomies is something that must be maintained, in contrast to integration and merging projects, taxonomy management software can support mappings between vocabularies as yet another kind of relationship. Most major taxonomy management software now has this mapping support feature. An additional automatic vocabulary-matching feature included in some taxonomy management software, as mentioned in the previous section on merging taxonomies, may also be used for the initial task of mapping.

Furthermore, SKOS includes specifications of standard mapping relationships. Since use of SKOS assumes that some automated process of mapping might be involved, the SKOS recommendation includes several different kinds or levels of mapping, which are described in the ISO 25964-2 standard: closeMatch, exactMatch, broadMatch, narrowerMatch, and relatedMatch.

Linked Data Taxonomies

Another, newer way to connect taxonomies is through Linked Data methods. Linked Data is a set of W3C specifications for web publishing that makes the data or content part of the Semantic Web. This means that instead of manually following individually created hyperlinks, semantic links and computer readable formats support automated relevant linkages among web content. Linked Data, coined by Tim Berners-Lee of the World Wide Web Consortium in 2009, comprises (1) URIs as names of things, (2) HTTP URIs for looking up, (3) using W3C standards (RDF and SPARQL) to describe the content, and (4) links out to other URIs (www.w3.org/DesignIssues/LinkedData.html). Additionally if the information is available on the web with an open license, then it is considered to be Linked Open Data (LOD). An example of a Linked Data dataset is DBPedia (an extraction of Wikipedia).

Taxonomies can make use of Linked Data or Linked Open Data in various ways. Although serving as labels to linked content is the most common method, taxonomy terms (actually concepts) themselves can be the content that is linked to. If taxonomy concepts are individually assigned URIs and HTTP addresses, are in an RDF

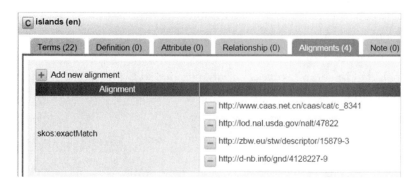

Figure 11.6 Screenshot from the VocBench open source taxonomy management software, which makes use of Linked Data to link a concept, "islands," in its taxonomy to the same in other taxonomies on the web

format (such as SKOS), and links are actually made, then concepts in one taxonomy can link to those in another taxonomy somewhere else on the web. An example can be seen in the preloaded AGROVOC Thesaurus within the open source, web-based VocBench taxonomy management software. Figure 11.6 shows a screenshot from within the VocBench application, where the taxonomy concept "islands" is selected. Under the tab for the concept's Alignments are four URLs/URIs linking directly the same concept/term in four other controlled vocabularies on the web.

Multilingual Taxonomies

With the global expansion of business and information, adding a second-language version to a taxonomy is not uncommon. A taxonomy in more than one language enables:

1. Users to search content that includes text and/or metadata in multiple languages, by using a single taxonomy in their own language, which is mapped to the foreign language taxonomies

2. Different users who speak different languages to search the same body of content (which may be in one language or more), using a taxonomy in the user interface in their native language

(In either case, after retrieving a document in a foreign language, the user could have it translated.)

An example of a publicly accessible, multilingual online thesaurus is the AGROVOC Thesaurus of the Food and Agricultural Organization (FAO) (aims.fao.org/vest-registry/vocabularies/agrovoc -multilingual-agricultural-thesaurus) in which selected concepts display all other language equivalents plus any alternate labels (nonpreferred terms) within those languages. (See Figure 11.7.) The user can also designate the language in which to search the thesaurus, and a search term in any language will retrieve the same

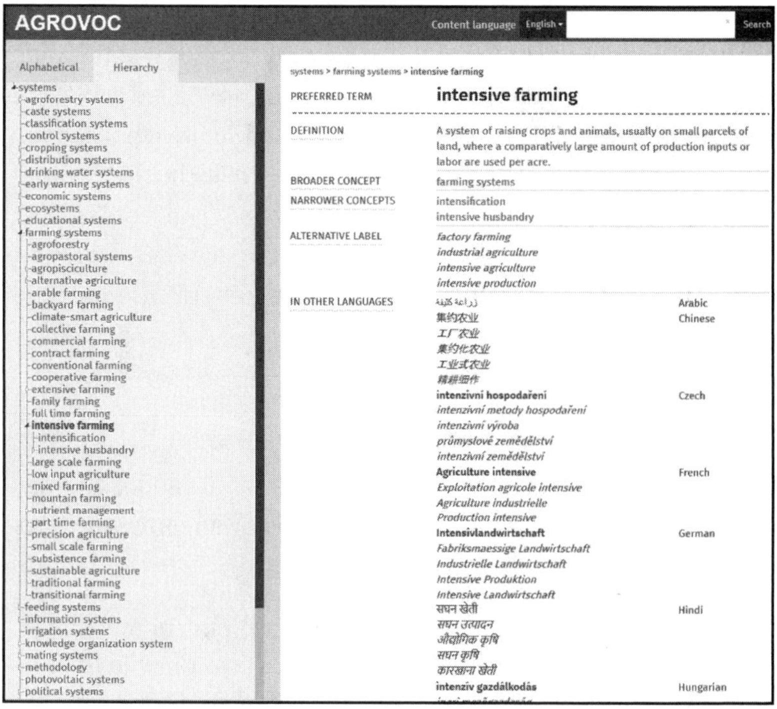

Figure 11.7 Display of a selected English-language term in the AGROVOC Thesaurus showing its multiple language equivalents with alternate labels in italics (aims.fao.org/vest-registry/vocabularies/agrovoc-multilingual-agricultural-thesaurus)

concept record, but the broader, narrower, and semantic/related relationships will display for the selected language.

Multilingual Taxonomy Development

A second-language version of a taxonomy should be treated as another way of combining two taxonomies, essentially by mapping, rather than as a simple translation of a taxonomy into another language. Merely adding translations to terms would not support navigation between terms with hierarchical or associative relationships within a second language, and the translation is then no more helpful than a scope note. Furthermore, not every term in one language has an exact translation in another language, especially in the case of nonpreferred terms. In the mapping analogy, the retrieval taxonomy is in the language of the searcher, and the indexing taxonomy is in the language of the content. However, the role of the different language taxonomies is typically dynamic, depending on the language of the user and the accessed content at any given time. The taxonomy in either language could be the retrieval taxonomy or the indexing taxonomy. Therefore, mapping has to go in both directions, which means that matches between terms in both language taxonomies need to be more exact. Narrower-to-broader mappings will not work in both directions. ISO 25964-1, Section 9, "Equivalence across languages," discusses these issues in greater detail.

While some taxonomies are designed to be bilingual or multilingual from the start, it is a more typical scenario that an organization adds a second language after a taxonomy has been in use. Either a taxonomy is translated term-by-term, or if an equivalent taxonomy already exists in the desired second language in the same subject area(s), it may be preferable to map the second-language taxonomy to the original (English-language) taxonomy.

This is not a typical mapping, because, as mentioned previously, equivalence must operate in both directions rather than one-way. A translator, rather than a taxonomist, should handle this mapping, since awareness of broader/narrower distinctions is not even needed, but translation experience is important. It will also likely be necessary to add terms to the second-language taxonomy when it lacks equivalent terms.

Whether translating a taxonomy or mapping to a second-language equivalent taxonomy already in existence, it is important to remember that the matches need to be for concepts, not term names. In addition, even if you are focusing on concepts, not terms, not all relationships between terms will match exactly in another language. When concepts in two languages are not perfect matches, the relationships between them most likely vary slightly as well. There are also cultural influences on what constitutes a relationship.

If a taxonomy is to be translated, it is more complicated than a typical translation project. Professional translators translate text in sentences, and they discern the meaning of potentially ambiguous words from the context. A taxonomy is a list of terms out of context. Instead of reading sentences, the translator of a taxonomy needs to look up a term's nonpreferred terms, scope notes, and hierarchical and associative relationships to be certain of the meaning of the term. Typical translation fees based on per-word rates cannot be applied in such situations, since it takes time to translate each term. Furthermore, while translators typically translate only into their native languages, a sufficiently bilingual translator who has experience translating in both directions is preferable for translating a taxonomy because all translations of taxonomy terms will need to function in both directions to support both the retrieval of multilingual content and the browsing by different language users. In addition, since you are unlikely to find a translator who is also a taxonomist, you should arrange for a native speaker of the second language who is an information specialist/librarian to review the translated taxonomy.

Other matters to take into consideration when developing multilingual taxonomies are support for characters in the writing systems of other languages, translation of the user interface, and adaptations for cultural differences. Remember to have everything in the user interface translated, including menus, instructions, pop-ups, help files, and so on. Other language-specific issues to consider include the editorial style for displayed terms (such as the use of plural forms and capitalization) and the "logical" sort orders of terms. Taken collectively, translation plus other language and region-specific adaptations (currencies, measurements, date/time formats, etc.), particularly for software and online user interfaces, is referred to as *localization*. There are companies and consultants that specialize in providing software and interface localization services. Finally, there are cultural differences in user search behavior that you may need to take into consideration. For example, it is possible that in another country, a different facet might be used for the same content because in that culture different criteria are important.

Finally, attention must be paid to governance and maintenance of taxonomies in multiple languages. Often a contract translator translates a taxonomy but is no longer available to help maintain it. When new terms are added or existing terms are changed in the English-language taxonomy, someone needs to take care of adding or changing the second-language equivalents. Too often organizations fail to keep taxonomies in second languages as up to date as the taxonomy in the original language. It is also important to have a native speaker of the second language periodically check the function of the taxonomy for quality control purposes.

Software Management of Multilingual Taxonomies

Almost all taxonomy management software now supports multilingual taxonomies in some form or another. Such software supports special characters and often different language scripts, and also has features for designating a language, as vocabulary metadata. The actual management of multilingual vocabularies, however, with equivalent translations linked to each other and relationships between terms within additional languages, can vary.

Traditional thesaurus management software (not SKOS based) that has a designated multilingual feature would typically treat links to language translation terms as a completely different relationship type. Although language translations are "equivalent" terms, the relationship type is not a form of thesaurus equivalence, because traditional equivalence is to designate nonpreferred terms, and terms in another language are not nonpreferred. All languages have their own preferred terms and nonpreferred terms. Rather, the link between translations of the same term in different languages is a kind of equivalent vocabulary relationship, similar to a relationship to maintain the mapping of vocabularies.

In thesaurus management software that does not have dedicated multilingual taxonomy support but does support customized relationships, you could create customized relationship types for translations, such as one called EN>FR and its reciprocal called FR>EN, to support links between English- and French-language preferred terms. The hierarchical and associative relationships between terms in one language, however, would have to be manually recreated between terms in the second language. While this is added work, it does allow more flexibility, especially in the more subjective area of when to create associative relationships.

In truly multilingual thesaurus software, use of a language equivalency relationship will additionally cause the automatic inheritance of hierarchical and associative relationships among terms in the first language to occur between terms within the second language. Nonpreferred terms are always created individually and are not linked between languages. MultiTes and Synaptica are examples of thesaurus software that have this feature. MultiTes has supported multilingual thesauri since its inception, which is what the prefix "multi" in the product name stands for. In MultiTes, you can also toggle between which language is set as the "active language," that is, the language whose alphabetical display and hierarchical reports are the default.

The SKOS framework supports multilingual vocabularies by having concepts instead of terms, so a concept may have multiple preferred labels, each in a different language, and multiple nonpreferred labels for each language. Thus, SKOS-based vocabulary management software is natively fully multilingual. The only possible limitations are the number of foreign language special characters and scripts the software may support. As newer vocabulary management software tends to be SKOS based, full multilingual vocabulary support is becoming more common. Figure 11.8 shows an XML presentation in SKOS of a vocabulary concept in three languages, English, French, and Spanish, with an additional alternate label in each of the three languages.

```
- <rdf:Description rdf:about="http://www.fao.org/aos/concept#35279">
    <skos:altLabel xml:lang="es">Dietas bajas en proteína</skos:altLabel>
    <skos:altLabel xml:lang="en">Low protein diets</skos:altLabel>
    <skos:related rdf:resource="http://www.fao.org/aos/concept#6251"/>
    <rdf:type rdf:resource="http://www.w3.org/2004/02/skos/core#Concept"/>
    <skos:altLabel xml:lang="fr">Régime pauvre en protéine</skos:altLabel>
    <skos:prefLabel xml:lang="es">Dietas restrictas en proteínas</skos:prefLabel>
    <skos:prefLabel xml:lang="en">Protein restricted diets</skos:prefLabel>
    <skos:inScheme rdf:resource="http://iaaa.unizar.es/thesaurus/AGROVOC"/>
    <skos:prefLabel xml:lang="fr">Régime allégé en protéine</skos:prefLabel>
    <skos:broader rdf:resource="http://www.fao.org/aos/concept#7714"/>
  </rdf:Description>
```

Figure 11.8 SKOS XML of a vocabulary concept, "Low-protein diets," in English, French, and Spanish from the AGROVOC Thesaurus

Endnotes

1. Stuart Laurie (director of sales engineering, Smartlogic), phone call with author, October 15, 2015, explaining why Semaphore discontinued its ZThes export option, as fewer users are interested in it.

2. Details of the ISO XML schema "Format for Exchange of Thesaurus Data Conforming to ISO 25964-1" on the NISO website, accessed December 20, 2015, www.niso.org/schemas/iso25964/schema-intro and the graphic of the UML model is available at www.niso.org/schemas/iso25964/Model_2011-06-02.jpg

3. National Information Standards Organization, "A Proposed NISO Work Item: Development of Standards to Support Bibliographic Data Exchange," December 18, 2014, accessed October 28, 2015, www.niso.org/apps/group_public/download.php/14152/Bibliographic%20Road map%20Work%20Item%20Final%20for%20Voting%20Members.pdf

Chapter 12

Taxonomy Work and the Profession

If you find what you're looking for, thank a taxonomist.
—J. D. Henry

An accidental taxonomist could be asked to create, revise, or map a taxonomy, and after the project is finished, resume his or her previous job responsibilities. Often, however, an accidental taxonomist remains a taxonomist, in both job responsibilities and professional life. This chapter describes the characteristics of taxonomy jobs, whether full time or freelance, and also suggests sources where taxonomists might look for continuing education and professional networking opportunities.

The Nature of Taxonomy Work

The heart of being a taxonomist is dealing with concepts, figuring out what words are best to describe them, and determining how best to relate and arrange the concepts so that people can find the information they are seeking. The task requires a degree of logic as one must scrupulously analyze relationships between terms. It is neither entirely technical/mathematical nor entirely linguistic but a little of each. You always need to keep in mind how others might look for information when considering how to word a term, create nonpreferred terms, structure relationships, and contribute to the design of the user interface display. Helping people find information is indeed rewarding, but unlike a traditional librarian, you may never meet the people whom you are helping. If you work within a large organization to develop and maintain its internal taxonomies, however, then you do have the added benefit of constantly being able to check with users to find out how the taxonomy is serving them and how it can be improved. However, you would not deal with the diversity of subject areas that a taxonomist working for an information provider or a contract taxonomist encounters.

While the skills and qualifications taxonomists need (listed in Chapter 2) are similar for any kind of taxonomy work, the actual working environment, conditions, responsibilities, and related duties can vary greatly. These depend on whether the taxonomist is a full-time employee, a temporary contract employee, a consultant, or a freelancer and, in the case of a full-time employee, whether taxonomy work is the primary job responsibility.

What Taxonomists Enjoy About Their Work

Our survey in May 2015 of those engaged in taxonomy work asked the open response question: "What do you enjoy about taxonomy work?" The 90 responses revealed that the vast majority enjoy taxonomy work for reasons that fall under one or more of the following general categories, listed in order of the number of responses, and many actually did list a combination of such reasons:

- Organizing information, and for some a more intellectual extension of modeling knowledge

- Solving problems and "puzzles"

- Helping people find the content they need or want

- Dealing with language, words, and meaning

- Learning new subjects

In the area of organizing information, some of the responses were:

- I LOVE sifting out similarities and differences, cross-referencing and adding synonyms, and sorting and standardizing terms. —Margaret Nunez

- I enjoy the structural interconnections and bringing alignment between metadata, taxonomies, and ontologies, and the content delivered in the customer/ user experience on websites and in web applications. —Allan Grohe

- I love how a well-planned taxonomy gives us the flexibility to develop intelligent content models. —Vinish Garg

- The division of a body of knowledge into discrete yet related concepts, while envisioning how a searcher would think of the information.

In the area of being challenged and solving problems and puzzles, responses included:

- I really love the puzzle involved in parsing out the right way to categorize content. Especially when these categories might overlap and need to intersect each other in ways that specifically benefit the user.

- It combines language and technology in interesting ways. There are complicated puzzles to solve and rarely a "right" answer. Taxonomy work utilizes my attention to detail.

- I love the daily challenge of the work. No two days are ever the same.

Examples of responses on the subject of helping other find what they are looking for included:

- It's just something I feel passionate about. I love knowing that the work I do will help users find or discover the right people or content.

- I like lining up points of view to provide better understanding and usability.

- I also love to teach others how they can improve findability through tagging. Seeing those a-ha moments in their eyes is almost better than a paycheck.

- The work itself is systematic and methodical, and if the taxonomies are deployed well, can result in major improvements in the client's information and knowledge environment. —Patrick Lambe

Regarding working with languages, some responses were:

- First off I love how creative you can be when finding the perfect words to describe whatever the user wants.

- I like the tricky intersection between the informality of language/meaning and the formality of structured relationships.

- I love vocabulary and its relationship to other words, the structure of the taxonomy.

Comments about getting to learn new things through taxonomy work included:

- I'm always learning! It requires a breadth of knowledge and a willingness to learn and research.

- Talking to subject matter experts and understanding how they classify concepts in their minds.

- Working with taxonomy is about gaining a deeper understanding about what the taxonomy is about. If it's the enterprise taxonomy for a business, it's truly understanding what makes that company tick. If it's a taxonomy about an idea or an industry or a process, it's about becoming thoroughly educated in those items as well. —Seth Maislin

Some further comments of what is enjoyable about taxonomy work included:

- The analysis, creativity and stakeholder engagement.

- I enjoy the far-reaching impact that is possible for such little effort.

- I enjoy the product development aspect, integrating taxonomies into the user experience. How to do this well is a challenge without it feeling clunky and forced.

- What I like most about working on taxonomies is that they're at the heart of the problem. Good information retrieval relies on good indexing, and good indexing simply isn't possible without a good taxonomy to work with. Like any craftsman's product, a well-crafted taxonomy is a combination of artistry and technical skill that is well structured for its purpose.
  —John Magee[1]

What Challenges Taxonomists Face

Our survey also asked the question, "What are pain points or challenges in your taxonomy work?" What is particular to the field of taxonomy is getting others to understand a taxonomy's role and value and how those who are stakeholders should and should not be contributing.

Responses around achieving stakeholder understanding and buy-in included:

- Frequently my biggest challenge is justifying the work to begin with. A lot of companies want fast solutions of which taxonomy is not. Nor should it be. So getting buy-in and once you have that tagging is very challenging.

- Articulating the ROI of taxonomy work.

- Stakeholder buy-in is challenging. Explaining how much time, effort and money an enterprise taxonomy requires is a tough sell … especially since the benefits are not immediately evident.

- People not understanding what I am talking about, understanding the value, or wondering why development will take "so long."

Sometimes interest in the taxonomy is too great, where there are competing interests, expectations, and requests, as suggested by the following comments:

- Too many opposing or conflicting opinions of how the taxonomy should be structured.

- Employees want to reflect organisational structure into the taxonomy.

- Company politics and self-styled "experts" who are product managers, librarians with no taxonomy experience, or marketing people.

- Contributors who insist that more keywords are better.

- Outside influences/marketing and sales reps requesting to alter taxonomy to better fit key words and buzz terms as opposed to technical terms.

- Different people in our organization expect different things out of our taxonomy.

The lack of ideal tools or technology is also an issue for some with such responses as:

- Setting up a system and processes to get the metadata aligned is frustrating and slow going.

- Finding good software that isn't enterprise-level.

- SharePoint—people are often forced to use it, and it is really not that great at anything, especially taxonomy management.

- Software not intended for taxonomies

- Keeping up with shifting technologies.

Limited resources, such as in time or money, are typical concerns:

- The most difficult challenge for me is advocacy for appropriate resources (e.g., tools, personnel)

- Having to move quickly without the proper time to consider the implications of additions or changes

- Finding the time to do it well

- The expense and effort involved in classification can limit project scope

Some other comments of note regarding difficulties faced in taxonomy work included:

- The two biggest challenges I have had are (1) getting assurance that the taxonomy will be maintained after completion and (2) explaining how a taxonomy is useful to teammates with different professional backgrounds.

- Getting follow-through from business teams, walking the line between business and technical communication, poor data quality, explaining how the taxonomy works, finding all stakeholders in a project.

- Balancing standards/best practices with actual needs of customers, systems.

- (1) Acquiring quality taxonomy tags when the taxonomy is deployed. (2) Ensuring continued maintenance and governance of the taxonomy once deployed. —Patrick Lambe

Employment Opportunities

Taxonomists work for varied employers: governments, international agencies, publishers, information providers, online retailers, consultancies, software vendors, and large corporations in any industry, with examples named in Chapter 2. The fact of the matter is that taxonomists often move around from one industry to another, between products and services, between profit-making and non-profit enterprises, which certainly contributes to interesting careers. Only some fields, such as medical, pharmaceutical, and scientific/technical publishers, tend to require subject matter expertise.

Dedicated, full-time, permanent taxonomist positions exist, but they are still not very common compared with other types of positions. Any large corporation or government agency that cares to structure and organize its terminology has enough ongoing information management needs to keep at least one full-time taxonomist busy all the time and at times needs even more assistance. However, one or two taxonomists out of a staff of thousands do not amount to much of the labor force. Businesses involved in the sale of indexed content also employ taxonomists and may even support a small team of taxonomists, but such businesses are few. The job-seeking taxonomist who does not wish to relocate may have to wait a while before a position opens up.

If you are searching for a *taxonomist* job, you will find relatively few openings in any given geographic area. It's not merely a matter of the diversity of job titles used (see Chapter 2), though that does complicate the search. The fact is that the number of positions in which taxonomy is the primary role is rather limited, and the number of open positions is much smaller still. What is more common, however, are positions in which taxonomy is one of several responsibilities. A search on *taxonomy* or *taxonomies* within the job descriptions of open positions yields many more results than a search for *taxonomy* or *taxonomist* limited to the job title. For example, on October 30, 2015, the aggregate job search board Indeed.com listed only 15 jobs with *taxonomist* and 28 *taxonomy* in the title for all of the United States, but 1,776 with *taxonomy* in the job description (after excluding jobs with the words *biology*, *biologist*, *plant*, and *zoology*), with such titles as business analyst, technical writer, data modeler, digital content specialist, and so on. What this means is that you need not be a *taxonomist* to find yourself using taxonomy skills in your job.

Although the number of jobs may be relatively small, they are growing. The exact same search conducted on Indeed.com six years prior (September 30, 2009) yielded only six jobs total with *taxonomist* or *taxonomy* in the title and less than 1,000 with the words in the job description.

A resource for locating jobs that comprise primarily taxonomy work is the Yahoo! mailing list group called Taxonomy Jobs (*groups.yahoo.com/neo/groups/taxonomy-jobs*). Job postings are from employers and recruiters, who proactively submit such job announcements, but many other taxonomy job openings are not included on this list.

Taxonomists as Contractors

A taxonomy project can take a considerable amount of work for only a temporary period of time. This usually applies to the design and creation stage, but revision and integration projects can also demand periods of intensive work. Thus, to supplement internal resources, a great deal of taxonomy work is done by contractors, whether consultants, or temporary employees. For small operations, these outsiders can take the place of a full-time taxonomist employee, but for larger taxonomy needs, they merely supplement the work of in-house experts.

Some differences in working conditions between employees and contractors are common across industries, but there are also certain specific differences with regard to taxonomy work. For contractors, the biggest benefit is that a lot of taxonomy work can be done at home, and thus they can work for clients in other parts of the country or even in other countries. Most taxonomy management software permits remote access, but many contract projects require only Excel. Contractors also encounter a variety of subject areas to work on, and when working on terms, this diversity is important to many. (As a contractor, I have worked on taxonomies for consumer products, industry categories, insurance, news, business management, travel, food, mining, banking, academic fields of study, transportation, travel, and names of writers, among other areas.)

On the negative side, contractors usually lack access to the latest software and other technical support services. Tasks such as comparing or merging lists of terms could often benefit from scripts that perhaps only more technical colleagues at an office can provide. It is difficult for a contractor to design a taxonomy for a content management system without the benefit of ever having been the user of any content management system or for SharePoint if they are not a user of SharePoint. Finally, the self-employed taxonomist does not have the support of workplace colleagues who can provide input and answers to questions for subjective taxonomy-building tasks. (Of course, not all taxonomist employees have as much co-worker support as they would like either, particularly if they are the only person in an organization who is knowledgeable about taxonomies.)

For a self-employed person seeking taxonomy work, there are plenty of opportunities, but there is a distinct difference between working as a *consultant*, directly for a client, and working as a *freelancer*, a step removed from the taxonomy's users. The nature of the work and the working conditions for each role are quite different.

Working as a Consultant

One of the main distinctions between consultants and freelancers, in general, is that consultants tell their clients what to do, whereas clients tell their freelancers what to do. To be fair, consultants usually (but not always) undertake work on actually constructing the taxonomy as well, but consultants are expected to do at least some consulting, which means giving formal advice to the client. Thus, consultants need to take more initiative, do more research on the taxonomy's intended use, and make more decisions, and they may have to persuade the client that the taxonomy should be done a certain way. In compensation for this, of course, consultants get paid more than freelancers do. It is also more fulfilling to design an entire taxonomy and make the decisions about its structure. However, even consultants do not always get to design *new* taxonomies.

Increasingly, consulting projects involve reviewing existing taxonomies and making recommendations for improvements.

Following is a summary of what is expected of taxonomy consultants in contrast with taxonomy freelancers:

- Write up a proposal of what you intend to deliver (and then deliver it).

- Estimate how much time you will need (and then meet these deadlines).

- Set a pay rate as high as you dare without risking losing a bid to a competing consultant (and do not ask for more money later if it takes more time and effort than expected).

- Meet with the client face-to-face at the client's site, and possibly make several visits to conduct research for the taxonomy based on stakeholder interviews, card-sorting exercises, and test searching a system within a firewall.

- Deliver (PowerPoint) presentations to the client of what you intend to do and later what you have done, and what the issues are.

- Write up recommendations that will contribute to the taxonomy governance.

- Negotiate any differences of opinion on taxonomy design.

- Have your own thesaurus management software (with compatible export format options).

Consultants can work for distant clients, too, if they are willing to travel, and in the taxonomy field, most do. Recognizing the fact that there are relatively few qualified taxonomy consultants, a client does not necessarily expect to find a local consultant and will look nationally and reimburse travel expenses. Similarly, a consultant cannot expect to find all clients locally. A three-month project might involve three on-site visits of one to three days each, but a six-month project may not involve much more.

Working directly with a client on a taxonomy project, especially an enterprise taxonomy project, can be challenging, though. The client might have difficulty communicating the scope and requirements of the project or might not even know which makes it difficult for the consultant to know what is expected and what to deliver. Indeed some of the complaints taxonomists have about their work pertain specifically to consultant–client relationships. A survey response regarding the difficulties of taxonomy work in consulting stated: "The hardest part to taxonomy challenges is getting the full story from your clients. I work at an agency and often have to walk clients through our thinking."

A successful taxonomy project, though, can be very rewarding for the taxonomist.

Finally, consultants need to aggressively market themselves. This includes speaking at conferences and trade shows (commercial and industry shows, more so than librarian/indexer association events), publishing articles in trade journals, publishing a blog, participating in professional networking organizations, and actively contributing to discussion groups and social networking sites. The consultant should have a professional website, and the website should include all relevant informational resources (articles, presentations, etc.) and be optimized for search engines.

Working as a Freelancer

The work of a freelancer, on the other hand, may be less challenging than that of a consultant, but the diversity of projects usually keeps it stimulating. A freelancer typically works on only part of a taxonomy and does not get to see the bigger picture. The freelance taxonomist is usually immersed in terms, not in structure.

Following is a summary of what is expected of taxonomy freelancers in contrast with taxonomy consultants:

- Follow instructions, guidelines, and editorial policy provided by the client.

- Agree to work a set number of hours per week and/or complete a project by the client's deadline.

- Work with little or no contact with the taxonomy users.

- Accept any decisions that have already been made regarding the taxonomy design.

- Expect the client to provide any software that is not part of the standard Microsoft Office suite.

- Expect to do all or most work from home.

- Accept the hourly rate proposed by the client (with perhaps a little negotiation at the start).

In comparison with in-house taxonomist employees, freelance taxonomists do not usually get involved with full taxonomy and thesaurus development. A large thesaurus may be too complex and interrelated to be broken up into sections for freelancers, even if web-based thesaurus software permits remote access. Also, a project manager might feel that all taxonomists need to have broader overall knowledge of the thesaurus and favor former employees over new freelancers. An exception is work on named entities, whose relationships with other terms are generally not as complex. (Research regarding additional attributes for each name term might be a bigger part of the project.) A freelance taxonomist might not even be called a taxonomist but rather a *taxonomy editor*, with the implication that taxonomists design taxonomies. Freelance projects could include the following:

- Building term hierarchies for website taxonomies

- Building a top-level straw-man taxonomy

- Mapping nonpreferred search terms to taxonomy terms

- Researching, adding, and/or editing named entity terms

- Adding and editing additional attributes to terms (particularly named entities), involving research and data entry

- Providing training documents or writing term rules in support of auto-categorization

Freelance taxonomy work is paid on an hourly basis, and this could be frustrating for the freelancer who comes from an editing or indexing background and is accustomed to being paid per page or per database record. It is impossible to estimate how many terms one can create or edit per hour, because there are too many variables.

Freelance Opportunities

Freelance work is available for taxonomists, but unless you have a steady client, the work is quite sporadic, more so than book indexing or editorial freelance work. Thus, freelance taxonomists often combine this work with something else, such as consulting, teaching, indexing, or a part-time library job. Steady clients might be found among the few taxonomy vendors, information vendors, or software vendors mentioned in Chapter 2, but these opportunities are somewhat rare. Most of the freelance work offered by information vendors and publishers consists of indexing/tagging rather than taxonomy work. Sources of intermittent freelance taxonomy work include web/online advertisers and directories, search engines, ecommerce sites, and portals. Taxonomy consultancies are also a good source of work for freelance taxonomists, but their work is never steady or predictable, as it depends on when the consultants wins a contract with a client. Then on very short notice, there will be a substantial amount of work to take on. Thus freelancing requires flexibility.

Freelancers must also market and promote themselves, but not necessarily as publicly as consultants do. The best way for freelancers to get work is through networking, especially among taxonomy consultants and fellow freelancers. As taxonomy projects vary in size, often one project needs multiple part-time taxonomy editors. Thus, when one freelancer joins a project, the client may ask that freelancer to refer more taxonomy editors to help. In a more concerted effort to support freelance taxonomists in finding projects, the Taxonomies & Controlled Vocabularies Special Interest Group of the American Society for Indexing (ASI) has set up a directory of available freelance taxonomists on its website (www.taxonomies -sig.org/members.htm).

Taxonomists as Temporary Contract Employees
Finally, taxonomists on temporary assignment for a project could be hired as temporary contract employees, typically through a staffing agency to work at the staffing agency's client. They would be on the payroll of the staffing agency and treated as employees of the staffing agency for the duration of the project. This type of employment is quite common for short-term assignments in technology professions, and it is increasingly the case for the semitechnical role of a taxonomist.

The main difference from the previously described consultant and freelancer roles is that the contract employee is generally expected to work on-site full time for the duration of the project. Thus, contract work is typically only an option for taxonomists already living in major metropolitan areas. In other cases, they just might be very lucky to find something locally. Computer hardware and software will often be provided to the on-site contractor.

The nature of the temporary work may vary and could involve some level of responsibility and decision making, as is characteristic of the consultant, but it also could involve following more direction as is the case for the freelancer. It really depends on the level of expertise in taxonomy that the organization already has. A contract taxonomist, unlike a freelancer, may be the sole taxonomist on a project, so a certain degree of expertise and decision making may be expected, but their authority and flexibility is not as great as a consultant. The hourly pay rate is similar to freelancing, considerably less than consulting, but many more hours can be logged in a short period of time.

Education and Training

Taxonomy is still an accidental profession. Dedicated academic programs in the field are lacking. There are no majors, concentrations, or certificate programs and only a few courses on the subject. Thus, an aspiring professional cannot plan to become a taxonomist and take all the necessary university courses for it. Educational opportunities for learning how to create taxonomies, thesauri, controlled vocabularies, and so on consist of individual courses in library schools, continuing education workshops, professional organization online learning programs, consulting firm training programs, conference workshops and sessions, and online tutorials.

Information and Library Science Graduate Degree Courses

A review of the course catalogs on the websites for the 58 academic institutions with a graduate degree program in library/information science accredited by the American Libraries Association (ALA) in the United States and Canada, with instruction in English, reveals very few courses with the words *taxonomies*, *thesaurus*, or *ontology* in the titles. (There are no undergraduate courses in these fields.) Furthermore, some of these courses are only offered occasionally (not every year) or in the summer. In the 2015–2016 degree program course catalogs, there appeared to be only seven such courses:

- Indexing & Thesaurus Construction, University of California at Los Angeles

- Indexing, Abstracting, and Thesaurus Construction, Catholic University of America

- Knowledge Taxonomies, School of Information Studies, McGill University

- Taxonomies: Research and Evaluation, University of British Columbia

- Ontologies, Indiana University at Bloomington

- Ontology Development, University of Illinois at Urbana-Champaign

- Thesaurus Construction, University of Illinois at Urbana-Champaign

Courses that include coverage of various kinds of controlled vocabularies, while not dedicated exclusively to these topics, are greater in number. There are another 25 courses at ALA-accredited institutions that have various types of knowledge organization systems (controlled vocabularies, thesauri, taxonomies, or ontologies) mentioned in the course descriptions, as one of several topics covered. There are of course many other courses that may include a single class session on taxonomies but do not mention it in the brief, one- to three-sentence course description. Examples of courses with various kinds of knowledge organization systems mentioned in their description are as follows:

- Information Modeling, University of Illinois

- Introduction to Knowledge Organization, Long Island University

- Knowledge Management, University of Washington

- Managing Organizational Information Assets, University of Michigan

- Metadata & Access, McGill University

- Metadata and Resource Description, Drexel University

- Organization of Information, Dalhousie University

Graduate courses on knowledge organization or organization of information, however, tend to be surveys about the subject, rather than how to create knowledge organization systems. Sometimes the course is about organization of information just in libraries, such as Anglo-American Cataloging Rules, Dewey Decimal Classification, Library of Congress Classification, and Library of Congress Subject

Headings. But other times it covers various controlled vocabularies, such as taxonomies, thesauri, or ontologies.

Many library/information science programs include some instruction (perhaps only a class session) on thesaurus construction as part of a course on information management or indexing. Such literature retrieval thesauri, however, are only one kind of controlled vocabulary. A class session or project in creating an indexing thesaurus does not constitute sufficient training to start creating website or enterprise taxonomies. Nevertheless, even this instruction in the creation of traditional literature retrieval thesauri is not widespread in library school, compared with instruction in the cataloging of books.

Courses in cataloging and classification are taught in most library science programs, but the courses typically cover cataloguing standards, codes, and formats with respect to existing systems (Resource Description & Access (RDA), Dewey Decimal Classification (DDC), Library of Congress Subject Headings (LCSH), and Machine-Readable Cataloging (MARC21), rather than how to develop a new knowledge organization system.

Other courses of related interest are taught at schools of information science, without library science in the name, where the scope of study is broader. These courses include the following:

- Content Management Systems, University of Michigan

- Data Mining, McGill University

- Information Systems Design, Indiana University Bloomington

- Semantics-Based Knowledge Descriptions and Organization, University of Michigan

Although library and information science courses tend to be limited to students enrolled in a degree program, some graduate schools permit nondegree students to enroll in one or two regular courses if space is available. Such nondegree student options include the

Open Classes program at San Jose State University School of Information, the Nondegree/Community Credit program at the University of Illinois at Urbana-Champaign, and the Nondegree options
at St. Catherine University. The prerequisite is usually just a bache-
lor's degree. These courses may be online (as is the case for San Jose
State), making them accessible to anyone.

Information and Library Science Continuing Education Programs

"Continuing education" does not mean the same thing at every
institution. Many schools of library and information science offer
a form of continuing education, whereby someone who already
has the MLIS or equivalent degree can take individual courses, as
a nondegree student, selected from the regular course catalog. In
other cases, the only option to take courses as a nondegree student is to be enrolled in a post-master's certificate program, which
requires a minimum number of credits. Post-bachelor's certificate
programs are rare.

Only a few schools of library and information science offer a dedicated continuing education program or professional development
comprised of separate short classes or workshops available to anyone with no prerequisites. Such dedicated continuing education
classes or workshops are not for credit, are shorter than a regular
college course, and are less in-depth, but they do offer an interactive learning experience. They may be offered as single, full-day
on-site workshops or as online classes for just a few weeks. These
classes are an especially suitable source of instruction in new or hot
fields as they can be created and added on short notice and may
be taught by practicing professionals rather than academic faculty.
Such continuing education workshop programs are offered at the
following institutions:

- Kent State University, School of Library & Information
  Science (http://www.kent.edu/slis/continuing-study-
  courses-workshops)

- Simmons College, School of Library and Information Science (www.simmons.edu/academics/professional-education/slis-continuing-ed-workshops)

- University of Toronto, School of Continuing Studies and Faculty of Information (Classes are part of a certificate program in Information Management, but classes are shorter and less expensive than regular credit courses. Only some are online.) (learn.utoronto.ca/courses-programs/business-professionals/ischool)

- University of Wisconsin at Madison, School of Library and Information Science (www.slis.wisc.edu/continueed.htm)

At this time, only one of these continuing education programs offers an online workshop in taxonomies, and that is Simmons College, with a five-week workshop, "Taxonomies and Controlled Vocabularies." Other college continuing education programs could add a knowledge organization system class or workshop at any time.

Professional Association Programs

Several professional associations offer online taxonomy workshops and seminars, which are accessible globally. Examples of such programs are the following:

American Society for Indexing (ASI)

Part of ASI's Online Short Course program is "Practical Taxonomy Creation," a webinar series comprising three one-hour sessions, originally presented live and video-recorded in 2015. Handouts are also provided. Registrants have access to unlimited repeat viewings. Sessions are (1) Taxonomy types for different applications, (2) Gathering terms for a taxonomy, and (3) Thesaurus management software use with recorded demos (www.asindexing.org/online-learning/taxonomy-hedden).

AIIM (Association for Information and Image Management International)

"Taxonomy & Metadata Practitioner Course" is an online, self-paced course including an audio slide presentation. The topics are especially business-focused, including scoping a taxonomy project, developing a business case, selecting a taxonomy tool, and establishing a governance framework. There is one exam at the end of the course that must be passed in order to obtain a certificate. Once purchased, the course topics, supporting materials, and exams are accessible online and on demand from AIIM's training portal for six months. AIIM has also offered face-to-face workshops from time to time. Registration is 10 percent discounted for AIIM members (www.aiim.org/Training/Certificate-Courses/Taxonomy-and-Metadata).

SLA (Special Libraries Association)

SLA Taxonomy Division's Continuing Education program comprises one-hour live webinars on taxonomy-related topics presented several times a year. Registration is free for SLA Taxonomy Division members, and recordings are available at different rates for SLA members and non-SLA members (taxonomy.sla.org/category/ce).

American Libraries Association (ALA)

ALA-affiliated divisions may offer taxonomy-related webinars from time to time, as the Association of College and Research Libraries (www.ala.org/acrl) has in the past. In addition, the Association for Library Collections and Technical Services division of the ALA had codeveloped a full-day PowerPoint workshop for the Library of Congress Catalogers Learning Workshop/Cooperative Cataloging Training program called "Controlled Vocabulary & Thesaurus Design," intended to be taught by qualified instructors (www.loc.gov/catworkshop/courses/thesaurus).

Conference Workshops

If you prefer a live workshop with instructor interaction, then conference workshops might be your best option. A number of professional association and commercial conferences in the information management field include workshops on taxonomies. The exact programs and speakers will vary from year to year. In the case of professional organization conference workshops, nonmembers are typically permitted to attend at a slightly higher rate. If the program is offered as pre- or postconference workshop, either full day or half day, then there is a separate registration from the main conference with no obligation to register for the main conference. Sometimes taxonomy workshops of only two to three hours are offered as part of the main conference program.

Professional Organization Conference Workshops

Professional organization conferences with workshops include:

- The SLA Annual Conference (www.sla.org/attend) is usually held in June in different North American cities. There are both half-day and full-day preconference workshops called Continuing Education Courses with separate registrations, and typically there is a workshop on taxonomy creation. Some years there are even two taxonomy-related workshops. SLA chapters in different regions and countries also hold conferences and meetings, which may include taxonomy-related sessions.

- The American Society for Indexing (ASI) Annual Meeting (www.asindexing.org/conferences) is held every spring, usually in May, in different US cities. ASI typically offers a workshop on creating taxonomies and thesauri, either a half-day workshop as part of the regular two-day conference program or a full-day pre- or postconference workshop. Regional ASI chapters have also held taxonomy-related sessions and workshops.

- The Association for Information Science and Technology (ASIS&T) Annual Meeting (www.asist.org/events/annual-meeting), which is usually held in October or November in different North American cities, has two and half days of preconference workshops, and often there is a workshop on an aspect of knowledge organization systems. Although ASIS&T has the reputation of being more academic in its membership and in its regular conference sessions; its preconference workshops are very practical and are more often taught by practitioners than by academics.

- The Information Architecture (IA) Summit (www.iasummit.org), held in March or April in various North American cities and sponsored by ASIS&T, is a conference dedicated to information architecture. Most participants are not ASIS&T members but rather are practicing information architects. Often there is at least one taxonomy-related session among the numerous preconference workshops or regular sessions. Euro IA (www.euroia.org) is an affiliated English-language conference with a similar program that takes place on the European continent in September or October each year.

- The American Libraries Association (ALA) Midwinter Meeting in January and Annual Conference in June or July are held in different, major US cities every year (www.ala.org/ala/conferencesevents). Both of these annual events feature full-day and half-day preconference workshops, called Institutes, typically sponsored by ALA divisions. Considering that any topic related to libraries could be on the program, there often is not enough space to include a session on taxonomies, but occasionally a taxonomy-related workshop is included. ALA is very large, so its divisions are also large and have their own national, multiday conferences. These may also be venues for taxonomy-related workshops, especially the Association for Library Collections and Technical Services and the Library and Information Technology Association. Similarly, state and regional ALA chapters also hold conferences.

- The AIIM Conference (www.aiimevents.com) is held annually in March or April in different US cities. Its preconference workshops are some of the same as its certificate programs, which could include the Taxonomy & Metadata Practitioner Course described in the previous section, Professional Association Programs. In addition, the regular conference sessions typically include a session on a taxonomy topic. AIIM regional chapters also have conferences that may include half-day taxonomy workshops.

There are also several conferences pertaining to ontologies and the Semantic Web, which might be of interest, such as the International Semantic Web Conference (ISWC) (swsa.semanticweb.org/content/international-semantic-web-conference-iswc), but these conferences do not have workshops.

Commercial Conferences

Commercial conferences, some of which have workshops, include:

- Taxonomy Boot Camp (www.taxonomybootcamp.com), put on by Information Today, Inc., takes place every year in Washington, D.C., in late October or early November. It comprises two days of all taxonomy-related sessions. A taxonomy fundamentals workshop (1.5 hours) is often presented the first morning.

- KMWorld (www.kmworld.com/conference), a larger Information Today conference co-located and overlapping with Taxonomy Boot Camp (sharing the same exhibition and one keynote presentation), features sessions of related interest on knowledge management. KMWorld includes several half-day, preconference workshop options (with separate registration), which may be on taxonomy-related topics.

- Henry Stewart Conferences & Events hosts the DAM (Data Asset Management) Conference (www. henrystewartconferences.com) at different times of the year in Los Angeles, New York, Chicago, and London. Presentations often include a taxonomy topic, although the preconference workshops, called Tutorials, are usually not dedicated to taxonomies.

- SPTechCon (www.sptechcon.com) is one of several SharePoint conferences. It is usually held in Austin in winter, and San Francisco in spring, and Boston in late summer. The conference includes full-day and half-day Tutorials, although these are on various technical aspects of SharePoint, and not about developing taxonomies in SharePoint.

Organizations, Networking, and Resources

All kinds of taxonomists can benefit from networking, whether they are seeking jobs or clients or not. Employed taxonomists, too, feel a need for professional networking, perhaps because they are the only taxonomist in their organization or because new projects and technologies always bring new challenges. In addition, since it is often difficult for taxonomists to explain to others what they do, it is nice to get together, even if only virtually, with others in the same profession to exchange experiences.

Professional Associations

There is no professional association dedicated to taxonomists, but it is questionable whether there even should be one, since most taxonomists already belong to at least one, if not two or more, of the professional associations mentioned in the previous section. There is no shortage of conferences, and if a dedicated discussion forum is needed, a number of those already exist independently.

Two established professional associations have dedicated taxonomy subgroups. The American Society for Indexing (ASI) has had a Taxonomies and Controlled Vocabularies Special Interest Group (SIG) since 2008, and SLA has had a Taxonomy Division since 2009. There is some overlap in membership, but most of ASI's members are indexers, especially freelance back-of-the-book indexers, and most of SLA's Taxonomy Division members are corporate, special, or academic librarians.

ASI's Taxonomies and Controlled Vocabularies SIG (www.taxonomies-sig.org) is, according to its website, "for those in the indexing profession who are involved in creating or editing taxonomies, thesauri, or controlled vocabularies used for indexing." Some indexers may need to create controlled vocabularies for larger indexing projects, but others are simply attracted to thesaurus creation work due to its similarities with writing book indexes. Most of ASI's members are freelancers, and so are the members of the Taxonomies and Controlled Vocabularies SIG. The SIG's website thus serves the additional purpose of promoting members' freelance services. Membership in the SIG is open to members of ASI and affiliated indexing societies, such as the Indexing Society of Canada, the Society of Indexers (United Kingdom), and the Australia and New Zealand Society of Indexers.

The Taxonomy Division of SLA (taxonomy.sla.org) "offers a practical context for exploring issues and sharing experiences related to planning, creating and maintaining taxonomies, thesauri, authority files, and other controlled vocabularies and information structures," according to the SLA website. In contrast with ASI's group, the Taxonomy Division focuses more on conference program planning, educational webinars, and social networking applications. Although membership in the division is limited to SLA members,

SLA is an international organization with chapters and members throughout the world.

Other professional associations of possible interest to taxonomists include the IA Institute (www.iainstitute.org) for information architecture and ASIS&T (the Association of Information Science & Technology) (www.asist.org).

Networking

Well before these new professional organization subgroups were formed, taxonomists began actively networking through conference gatherings, discussion lists, and other social networking groups.

Conferences and Meetings

Taxonomy Boot Camp (www.taxonomybootcamp.com), sponsored by Information Today, Inc., is the only conference completely dedicated to taxonomies. As such, it is the best face-to-face networking event for taxonomists, whether employees or self-employed. In addition to those who already consider themselves taxonomists, many attendees simply want to learn more about taxonomies because of a project they are involved in. Taxonomy Boot Camp, usually held in late October or early November, first opened in New York in 2005 and took place in San Jose, California, for four years, but since 2010 it has been held in Washington, D.C. It is co-located with the KMWorld Conference and usually also Enterprise Search & Discovery and SharePoint Symposium, so all four conferences share the same exhibits and preconference workshops.

Local taxonomy gatherings are more difficult to arrange due to the relatively small numbers of taxonomists, but such events have occurred from time to time.

A growth in local face-to-face professional gatherings has been encouraged by the networking portal Meetup.com, founded in 2002, which facilitates the establishment and functioning of groups that meet regularly or periodically in locations around the world through hosted websites for event scheduling and attendee response. Although the field of taxonomy is probably too narrow for a dedicated meetup in any city, meetups in related fields, such as content management or information architecture, may include occasional taxonomy-focused events on their agendas.

In addition to the conferences mentioned in the previous section on Education and Training, other commercial conferences of potential interest with topics related to (if not about) taxonomies include Document Strategy Forum, CMSWire's DXSummit, the Gilbane Conference, and various text analytics conferences. Networking can be done at the exhibits and receptions without registering for the full conference.

Online Discussion and Social Networking Groups

Online discussion groups are a great way to both network and obtain advice or information. The platforms for the groups have been shifting. Originally they were just listserv mailing lists, then Yahoo! Groups became popular, and more recently LinkedIn is where most of the activity is. Taxonomy Community of Practice is the leading group. It started in 2005 and still exists as a Yahoo! Group (groups.yahoo.com/neo/groups/taxocop/info), where there are about 1,250 members, but discussion volume has dropped from over 100 messages per month in some of months of the early years to around 5–20 messages per month in recent years. As the name implies, most of the discussion centers around taxonomy development and maintenance practices. The corresponding LinkedIn group of the same name (www.linkedin.com/groups/1750) has 3,330 members as of fall 2015 and continues to grow. The LinkedIn group, however, tends to be used more for announcements than for topical discussions.

As a spin-off from Taxonomy Community of Practice, a live, Webex-based discussion group, called Real-World Taxonomy, was started in October 2015 by a taxonomist at Forrester Research, Marie Rodgers. It has periodic meetings, and discussion topics are proposed in advance via shared Google Docs. Topics of discussion have included taxonomy governance, taxonomy management and taxonomy management software, and integration with content management systems.

Other LinkedIn groups of related interest include ASI Taxonomies & Controlled Vocabularies SIG, Classification and Metadata for Information Governance, DAM Pros, Metadata Management, SLA Taxonomy Division, Semantic Technologies, Semantic Web, SharePoint Community Group, Text Analytics, Thesaurus Professionals, and User Experience.

Web Resources

Finally, there are a number of web resources on taxonomies. The following is only a sampling, and it also does not include the websites of the professional organizations previously mentioned in this chapter.

Online Tutorial:

- Construction of Controlled Vocabularies: A Primer, written by a member of the ANSI/NISO Z39.19 Standard Committee (marciazeng.slis.kent.edu/Z3919/index.htm)

Blogs:

- Accidental Taxonomist (accidental-taxonomist.blogspot .com)

- Earley & Associates Blog (www.earley.com/blog)

- Enterprise Knowledge (www.enterprise-knowledge.com/ category/blog)

- Green Chameleon (www.greenchameleon.com)

- Semantic Puzzle (blog.semantic-web.at)

- Synaptica Central (www.synapticacentral.com)

- TaxoDiary (taxodiary.com)

Resource-rich sites of consultants or vendors:

- Access Innovations (www.accessinn.com/media-library)

- Controlled Vocabulary (www.controlledvocabulary.com)

- Taxonomy Strategies (www.taxonomystrategies.com/ html/library.htm)

- Taxonomy Warehouse (www.taxonomywarehouse.com)

In addition to these web resources is, of course, the website of this book (www.accidental-taxonomist.com). The taxonomy profession is definitely an evolving one. New businesses and information needs of organizations and new technologies will impact the field. Taxonomists, too, can help define and direct the field through their professional organization activities, their writing (including blogging), and their speaking engagements. Individuals who are not afraid to try new things, such as taxonomy work, are also not likely to be afraid of changes and evolution within the field over time.

Endnote

1. John Magee, email to the author (rather than a survey response), October 23, 2015.

Survey of Taxonomists

Participant responses were gathered during the month of May 2015. A total of 150 people participated, although not all responded to all questions, with the number of respondents to each question varying from 132 to 150.

Participants in this survey were self-described taxonomists, who responded to a notice posted on various discussion groups and social media, including the following:

- Taxonomy Community of Practice (TaxoCoP) Yahoo group (finance.groups.yahoo.com/group)
- Taxonomies SIG Yahoo group (Taxonomies and Controlled Vocabularies Special Interest Group of the American Society for Indexing)
- SLA Taxonomy Division member mailing list

And the following LinkedIn groups were also posted:

- AIIM
- ASIS&T
- Content Management Professionals
- Content Strategy
- Controlled Vocabularies
- Information Architecture Institute
- KMWorld
- Knowledge Management Experts
- Metadata Management
- NFAIS

- Taxonomy Community of Practice (TaxoCoP)

- Thesaurus professionals

In addition, the notice was posted on The Accidental Taxonomy blog, the author's website, and the author's Twitter feed.

Attendees of the Content Strategy Seattle meetup of April 28, 2015, were also informed of the survey. To avoid bias, the author did not contact individuals directly. No effort was made, though, to track the media by which the respondents learned of the survey.

1. To what extent do you create and/or maintain taxonomies or other controlled vocabularies?

Answer Options	Percent	Count
My primary job responsibility	37.3%	56
One of my job responsibilities, but secondary	26.0%	39
Manage taxonomists or taxonomy projects, while also doing at least some taxonomy review work	14.0%	21
A special project, not in my job description or an originally expected responsibility	6.7%	10
Work done as contract/freelance often	8.0%	12
Work done as contract/freelance only occasionally	8.0%	12

2. How long have you been doing work on taxonomies or other controlled vocabularies?

Answer Options	Percent	Count
Less than 1 year	3.4%	5
1-2 years	8.8%	13
2-4 years	13.5%	20
4-6 years	15.5%	23
6-8 years	9.5%	14
8-10 years	12.8%	19
10-15 years	18.9%	28
15-20 years	5.4%	8
Over 20 years	12.2%	18

3. How long have you been doing work specifically called "taxonomy"?

Answer Options	Percent	Count
Less than 1 year	9.5%	14
1-2 years	14.2%	21
2-4 years	18.2%	27
4-6 years	10.8%	16
6-8 years	11.5%	17
8-10 years	13.5%	20
10-15 years	14.9%	22
15-20 years	6.1%	9
Over 20 years	1.4%	2

4. What is your current employment situation?

Answer Options	Percent	Count
Employee of an organization that uses taxonomies primarily internally, for its website, or in ecommerce	43.6%	65
Employee of an organization that incorporates taxonomies into an information product or information service, which it sells/offers	19.5%	29
Employee of a company or agency that provides taxonomy services or custom taxonomies to clients	12.1%	18
Independent contractor or freelancer (obtaining work primarily through subcontracting, agencies, other third parties, or as a temp employee)	6.7%	10
Consultant or business owner/partner (obtaining work primarily from direct clients)	18.1%	27

5. If you selected either the first or second response in question #4 (if you are an employee but not in consulting), where do you fit into your organization?

Answer Options	Percent	Count
Content management/content strategy	18.7%	17
Documentation/technical writing	2.2%	2

(Continued)

Editorial	2.2%	2
IT	19.8%	18
Knowledge management	12.1%	11
Library	9.9%	9
Marketing	3.3%	3
Operations	12.1%	11
Product development/product management	6.6%	6
Search	8.8%	8
User experience	4.4%	4

Other:
    Professor at University
    On a taxonomy team that supports our entire org.
    Institutional engagement
    Business Analysis
    Data Governance
    Data & Intelligence (within larger group Technology)
    Sales and Merchandising
    Engineering
    Entertainment
    Founder/Owner
    Technical Architecture team, which works with SOA architecture, metadata
        standards, and technical strategy
    Data Governance
    Browse Development

6. What is your job title?

Analytical Linguist
Associate Director Content
    Management
Associate Program Manager
Browse Developer & Taxonomist
Business Information Manager
CEO
Chief Taxonomy and Experience
    Officer
Clinical Data Analyst
Consultant (3)
Consultant/Sr. Analyst
Consultancy Director
Content Librarian

Content Manager XML Expert
Content Strategist (2)
Copy Editor
Corporate Archivist
Corporate Taxonomist
Creative Services Manager
DAM System Manager
Data Librarian
Developer/Documental Technology
    Director
Digital Asset Management Associate
Director (2)
Director of Product Development
Director of Taxonomy and Metadata

Director, Content Strategy
Director, Research & Knowledge
    Services
Document Management Specialist
Enterprise Information Architect
Enterprise Taxonomist (2)
Experience Architect
Founder
Founding Partner
Indexed Content Manager
Indexer and Taxonomist
Indexer/Lexicographer
Information Architect (5)
Information Architect /UX specialist
Information Life-Cycle and Context
    Manager
Information Management
    Consultant
Information Risk Management
    Consultant
Knowledge Architect
Knowledge Management Analyst
Knowledge Manager
Knowledge Sharing Business
    Analyst
Knowledge Sharing Strategy
    Specialist
Lead Consultant
Library Director & Taxonomist
Library Manager
Lifecycle Specialist
Linked Data Manager
Manager (2)
Manager, Content and Collaboration
    Services
Manager, Taxonomy and Metadata
    Services Group
Online Content Analyst
Ontologist (3)
Ontology Engineer
Owner and Principal Consultant
Partner, Metadata Management
    Associates
President
Principal
Principal Consultant (4)

Principal Program Manager
Product Manager
Product Ontology Linguist
Product Strategist
Professor (Information Science)
Program Manager
Project Manager
Records Management Analyst
Search Editor
Search Metadata Technical
    Specialist
Search Vocabulary Specialist
Semantic Analyst
Senior Consultant
Senior Experience Analyst
Senior Information Architect
Senior Knowledge Management
    Consultant
Senior Manager, Metadata
    Services
Senior Metadata Librarian
Senior Producer
Senior Solution Consultant
Senior Taxonomist (3)
Senior Taxonomy Analyst
Senior Taxonomy Specialist
Senior Usability Officer
Systems Librarian
Taxonomist (9)
Taxonomist/Browse Developer
Taxonomist/Human Factors
    Engineer
Taxonomist/Librarian
Taxonomy and Metadata Analyst
Taxonomy Development Manager
Taxonomy Manager (2)
Taxonomy Specialist (2)
Team Leader, Information
    Services
Technical Writing Supervisor
Terminologist, Linguistic
UX Consultant
UX Researcher
Vertical Domain Engineer
Web Architect for Technical
    Documentation

7. What degree(s) do you hold? (multiple responses permitted)

Answer Options	Percent	Count
Less than a BA/BS	4.7%	7
BA only (4 year college)	20.1%	30
BS only (4 year college)	8.7%	13
MA	15.4%	23
MS/M Eng.	8.7%	13
MLS/MLIS	54.4%	81
MBA	4.7%	7
PhD/doctorate	2.7%	4
Other advanced degree	5.4%	8

8. What is your study or training specifically in the field of taxonomy or classification? (multiple responses permitted)

Answer Options	Percent	Count
Concentration/specialty within a degree program	14.8%	22
Two or three college/university credit courses (but not a specialization)	16.1%	24
One college/university credit course	5.4%	8
Continuing education course or workshop	20.1%	30
Conference or professional seminar workshop	32.2%	48
On the job formal training	28.9%	43
On the job informal learning and experience	71.1%	106
Self-taught through reading	57.7%	86

9. Prior to your work in taxonomies, which best describes your professional background? (Multiple responses were not permitted, but additional responses could be added in an Other/comment field. If they corresponded to an existing option, they have since been added to the results.)

Answer Options	Percent	Count
Librarian	28.3%	41
Knowledge management	11%	16

Content management/Web content/Content strategy	11.7%	17
Document management	2.6%	4
Records management	4.1%	6
Project management	4.8%	7
User experience/Information architecture	6.9%	10
Software/IT	8.3%	12
Database design, development, or administration	1.4%	2
Indexing	6.2%	9
Writing, editing, or publishing	4.8%	7
Marketing/Sales	0.7%	1
None/Student	9%	13

Other (please specify):

Acting	Product management
Archivist	Program/Product Manager
Content architecture	Research in natural environment
Digital asset management (3)	Scientist
Engineering (2)	Systems Librarian
Film archive	Teacher (2)
Informal Education /Non-Profits	Text analytics and mining/
Linguist	computational linguistics

10. In your current position, what are your primary taxonomy-related activities? (multiple responses permitted)

Answer Options	Percent	Count
Design/model new taxonomies or other vocabularies, determining structure type and policies	72.8%	99
Based on an established model, develop and build out new taxonomies or other vocabularies	36.0%	49
Edit, update, or maintain taxonomies or other vocabularies	60.3%	82
Map (such as crosswalks), merge, integrate, or restructure existing taxonomies or other vocabularies	47.8%	65
Write auto-categorization rules for taxonomies or other vocabularies	22.8%	31

Comments:
    Just got an auto-classification/taxonomy management tool so will now be
        managing its governance and auto-categorization rules
    Software developer

(*Continued*)

Build & do outreach for a taxonomy creation, management and publication system

Use of taxonomies for metadata management

Manage the Open Metadata Registry with OMR developer

Design terminology servers

Building a graph-based ontology, with mappings to external linked data sources, and harvesting data from those sources

Software to perform these tasks

Manage the APIs & services, and serve as a product owner and evangelist for the taxonomy.

Advise clients on doing this work themselves; teach principles

Also product manager for search with filters/face ting based on taxonomy

Product dev is *missing* here. Integrating taxonomies into products etc.

11. What software do you primarily use to work on taxonomies or other controlled vocabularies?

Answer Options	Percent	Count
Commercial, dedicated thesaurus/taxonomy/ontology management software	22.7%	32
Open-source, dedicated thesaurus/taxonomy/ontology management software	9.2%	13
Commercial software, of which taxonomy management is a feature, module, or component	12.1%	17
An internally developed thesaurus/taxonomy management system	25.5%	36
Other commercial software not intended for taxonomies (such as a word processor, spreadsheet, or database management software)	30.5%	43

12. Which of the following describes the implementation and use of taxonomies or vocabularies you work on?

Answer Options	Percent	Count
For content organization, search/findability, and retrieval by internal users (employees)	20.4%	29
For content search/findability and retrieval by external users (customers, subscribers, members, partners, prospects, patrons, the public)	22.5%	32
For both internal users and external users	57.0%	81

13. What is the size of the controlled vocabularies you typically work on? (multiple responses permitted)

Answer Options	Percent	Count
Under 50 terms per vocabulary	5.8%	8
50-100 terms	9.4%	13
100-500 terms	17.4%	24
500-1500 terms	24.6%	34
1500-5000 terms	22.5%	31
5000-10,000 terms	13.8%	19
Over 10,000 terms	27.5%	38

Comments:
> Depends on the size of the client
> Controlled vocabularies vary in size from 4-5 to over 100
> I have worked on taxonomies of 100,000 terms
> We work on projects of all sizes, size, does not necessarily reflect the
> complexity of the project.
> Projects range from 14 to 57,000 terms
> Truly varies depending on intended use.
> Over 600,000 terms
> 190,000 total and counting

14. How are your current taxonomies/vocabularies linked to content?

Answer Options	Percent	Count
By manual tagging or indexing	38.7%	55
By auto-categorization/auto-indexing	11.3%	16
Some of each	47.2%	67
Don't know	2.8%	4

Comments:
> And synonyms via search solution
> I primary use DRUPAL and we define custom content models
> I also use CVs for search query enhancement, search type-aheads, and other
> application areas.

15. Are you familiar with and generally try to follow any of the following national or international standards: ANSI/NISO Z39.19 (2005) Guidelines for Construction, Format, and Management of Monolingual Controlled Vocabularies and ISO 25964 Information

and documentation—Thesauri and interoperability with other vocabularies?

Answer Options	Percent	Count
Don't know these standards and thus don't follow them.	19.0%	27
Have read at least some of these standards, but don't follow them.	23.2%	33
Generally keep these standards in mind and apply what is relevant, but not strictly.	45.1%	64
Attempt to follow these standards closely and refer to them as needed.	12.7%	18

16. What do you enjoy about taxonomy work?

The complete list of 90 responses is available on the book's website, www.accidental-taxonomist.com.

17. What are pain points or challenges in your taxonomy work?

The complete list of 89 responses is available on the book's website, www.accidental-taxonomist.com.

18. How did you first get started doing taxonomy work?

The complete list of 93 responses is available on the book's website, www.accidental-taxonomist.com.

Appendix B

Glossary

ANSI. American National Standards Institute. A private nonprofit organization that coordinates and oversees the creation and promoting of standards in various industries.

associative relationship. A relationship between two preferred terms, indicating that the terms are related to each other in some way that is not hierarchical. The generic associative relationship is usually called related term with the label RT and is a bidirectional symmetrical relationship.

asymmetrical relationship. A relationship between a pair of terms that is not the same in both directions. Asymmetrical relationships include hierarchical relationships (which point to a broader term in one direction and a narrower term in the opposite direction), equivalence relationships (which point to a preferred term in one direction and a nonpreferred term in the other direction), and sometimes associative relationships if they are customized/semantic.

authority file. Another name for a controlled vocabulary, especially if used just for named entities and restricted to a certain kind of entity (person names, company names, place names, etc.). As such, an authority file lacks the interterm relationships of a thesaurus but may have multiple nonpreferred terms for each preferred term. Also called an authority list.

authorized term. Another name for a preferred term, if nonpreferred terms are called unauthorized terms.

auto-categorization. A form of automated indexing that associates appropriate taxonomy terms with a document, based on one or more different technologies (such as rules or machine-learning) that automatically analyze the text and compare it with data stored with a given taxonomy term and possibly other data. Seeks to automatically discern what a document is about. Also called auto-classification or auto-tagging,

automated indexing. Any indexing done by software and not humans, which could include the indexing done by search engines and which may or may not involve taxonomies. It includes but is not limited to auto-categorization.

broader term. A preferred term that, in a hierarchical relationship to another term, is broader in meaning, more generic, or a larger whole with respect to its parts. Also called a parent term.

candidate term. A temporary term in a taxonomy, which cannot be used yet for indexing. Taxonomy or thesaurus software typically supports the creation of candidate terms that require an additional approval step before becoming approved terms. Also called a provisional term.

card sorting. A user-testing method for designing hierarchical taxonomies, whereby participants arrange cards of taxonomy terms into categories of their choice, using either physical cards or software to perform the task. There are two kinds: In a closed card sort, the categories are predefined, but in an open card sort, the participants must come up with and name their own categories.

cataloging. The process of both describing an item in a collection by various kinds of metadata and assigning it to an established classification system. Assigning subject terms is also often part of cataloging. Cataloging typically refers to physical items (books, periodicals, photos, music media, museum objects, etc.) but may apply to digitized collections of libraries and museums.

category. (1) Specifically in thesaurus management, any designated classification of terms that is distinct and that can be independent of the hierarchical relationships of the terms. (2) A relatively broad term used for classification of documents (on the whole, document level), rather than more granular indexing, and in particular for terms used in auto-categorization.

child term. Another name for a narrower term, a designation used more in hierarchical taxonomies than in thesauri. A broader term is then called a parent term.

classification. Assigning a class or a classification system code to an object (such as call numbers to a book) so that the object can be located by those who are familiar with the classification system. Classification is used for physical objects, and each can receive only a single classification.

closed indexing. Creating an index for back-of-the-book or a limited set of documents, for which the index project comes to a close once all the pages have been indexed, and publishing the index as part of the work. Closed indexing usually does not use a taxonomy. Contrasts with open indexing.

concept. A thing, idea, or shared understanding of something. It is what is meant by a set of synonymous terms. It is, therefore, the combination of both a preferred term and its various nonpreferred terms or of all the linked synonyms within a synonym ring. A concept is more than just a term.

content audit. A comprehensive survey of all representative content (not necessarily every piece of content) that will be indexed with an intended taxonomy, performed to both define the scope of the taxonomy and gather candidate terms.

content management system. Software used typically by an enterprise to manage the internal workflow of digital content through various phases of collaborative writing, commenting and revising, indexing, publishing (to an intranet or externally), search and retrieval, possibly translating, and archiving.

controlled vocabulary. A restricted list of words or terms for some specialized purpose, usually for indexing but sometimes also for writing. It may refer to any knowledge organization system (synonym ring, taxonomy, or thesaurus) but usually does not include the most complex systems of ontologies or topic maps.

cross-reference. An indication of the direction of a relationship from one term to another, such as *Use, See,* or *See also.* Cross-references exist in both taxonomies and indexes, but the term cross-reference is more often used in indexes.

CSV. Comma-separated values. A file format, used for storing structured data, whereby associated items are in the same line and separated by a comma, to correspond with rows and columns in a table. It is a multiplatform format useful for exporting data from one system and importing to another and thus serves interoperability.

descriptor. Another name for a preferred term, especially when nonpreferred terms are called nondescriptors.

enterprise taxonomy. A custom-developed taxonomy used within a large organization (an enterprise) as a common knowledge organization system for the entire organization, often implemented in an intranet or an enterprise content management system.

entity. Another name for a concept, which may have multiple equivalent terms, preferred and nonpreferred, to describe it.

entity extraction. A form of automated indexing that uses information extraction technologies to identify and index named entities (proper nouns) in documents.

entry term. Another name for a nonpreferred term.

equivalence relationship. A relationship between two terms that, for the sake of the taxonomy, have a close enough meaning to be treated as equal, with one being used for the other. The term that is used and displayed is the preferred term, and the term that points to the preferred term is called the nonpreferred term.

facet. A categorical grouping of terms in a taxonomy that cover a single dimension of a complex query for an item being searched. Multiple terms, one from each facet, are searched in combination to retrieve the most specific data records. A facet is typically its own hierarchy, but not all separate hierarchies are facets.

facet indicator. A term within a taxonomy that is not used itself for indexing or retrieval (thus a node label) but is rather used specifically to organize a significant number of narrower terms by type, or facet, of the narrower terms. Sometimes the word "by" is used preceding the facet indicator.

faceted search. A taxonomy structured and a user interface designed to permit the user to select multiple terms, one from each facet, to be searched in combination in order to retrieve the most specific data records that meet all the criteria. Faceted search works best with relatively uniform content records.

federated search. The simultaneous automated search of multiple online databases or web resources, each of which also has its own structure and search system/method and whose content would not otherwise be externally searchable. This may involve a metasearch engine, which is a search engine that sends user search requests to several other search engines and/or databases and aggregates the results. Taxonomies may or may not be involved in federated search.

fielded search. A type of end-user display that gives the searcher access to the taxonomy through multiple, labeled search box fields, which each might be distinct facets, various vocabulary categories, or other kinds of metadata. The user might be able to browse the taxonomy through drop-down scroll lists for each field, or there may be no browsable view of the taxonomy.

flat-format display. A common thesaurus display format, in which each term in the thesaurus is listed alphabetically and next to each term appear its details of immediate relationships to other terms and a scope note if any.

folksonomy. A collection of keyword terms or tags that have been assigned to content by multiple users (the creators of content and/

or the readers of content). These terms do not belong to any controlled vocabulary but are rather words of the users' own choosing.

governance. Policies and procedures to successfully manage a project and, for a taxonomy, its continual maintenance. These policies and procedures include roles and accountabilities, standards, process methodologies, and communication methods. Governance in project management also includes tasks of defining outcomes, controlling the project and its scope, monitoring the project, and measuring outputs.

granularity. Specificity in indexing and retrieval, both with respect to the specificity of the narrowest terms in a taxonomy and with respect to the unit of content being indexed, which could be as specific as a paragraph or sentence.

hierarchical relationship. A relationship between two preferred terms, in which one is broader, or superordinate, and one is narrower, or subordinate.

hierarchical taxonomy. A kind of controlled vocabulary in which each term has a designated broader term (unless it is the top-level term) and one or more narrower terms (unless it is a bottom-level term), and all the terms are connected together into a single large hierarchical structure.

hierarchy. Any collection of terms that are linked to each other by hierarchical relationships. Most controlled vocabularies of subjects contain multiple hierarchies that may be of various sizes.

homographs. Terms with the same name (same spelling) but different meanings. Homographs are typically distinguished from each other in a taxonomy by parenthetical qualifiers. (Homonyms are homographs, but homonyms must also be pronounced identically, whereas for homographs, identical pronunciation is not a requirement.)

index. The structured compilation of index terms associated with a body of content, whereby each index term points to a specific location in the content (document, page, paragraph, or embedded index notation), based on significant mention of that term's concept at that location. An index helps users find content corresponding to a chosen term. An index may be displayed to the user, typically alphabetically, for browsing, or it may be nondisplayed and merely searchable via a search box. The index terms may be restricted to taxonomy terms, or they could be any keywords. The index could be created by a human indexer, or it could be automatically generated.

indexing. The assignment of index terms (which may or may not come from a taxonomy) to content while simultaneously creating an index of terms, which users may then either browse or search to help locate identifiable content. Indexing can be a closed project for a single book or open and ongoing for accumulating content, and it can be manual or automated.

individual. A concept or object in an ontology.

information extraction. A method of automated indexing that uses natural language processing (based on computational linguistics and pattern recognition) to extract useful information, such as subject terms, from varied "unstructured" content. A common form of information extraction is entity extraction for names. Information extraction is also called data extraction.

instance. (1) Another name for an individual in an ontology. (2) A named entity as it relates to the topical term of which it is a narrower term, in an instance-type of broader/narrower relationship. (3) The most specific concept at the narrowest, bottom level of a taxonomy.

interoperability. The ability to use data, in different applications (implementations, software systems, such as a proprietary indexing system, or various proprietary search systems), in a commercial content management system, and on the web. Interoperability involves storing the data in a standard format.

intranet. A private network within an organization built on internet technology and protocols, with web-based content, organized as a large internal website with restricted access.

keyword. A word or phrase that is deemed significant to describe content for retrieval but is not usually part of a taxonomy. It can be assigned to content by an indexer or someone doing social tagging. Keyword may also refer to a word or phrases that an auto-categorization tool identifies within a text as significant. And keyword may also refer to a word that a searcher chooses to enter in a search.

KWIC. Keyword in Context. (1) A kind of permuted or rotated index display of a thesaurus whereby all the terms are sorted alphabetically not merely by their first word but by each of their constituent words (keywords, not prepositions or articles). The terms are indented to varying degrees so that the keyword of each term lines up with the others vertically, and each term is repeatedly mentioned on the occurrence of each of its keywords. The keywords are "in context" because they appear only within their full term phrases. (2) A search retrieval display in which an excerpted line of text is displayed for each returned record, showing where the keyword search term appears in context.

KWOC. Keyword Out of Context. A kind of permuted or rotated index display of a thesaurus whereby all the terms are sorted alphabetically not merely by their first word but by each of their constituent words (keywords, not prepositions or articles). The keywords from the terms appear as the alphabetized headwords in the display, and the terms appear under each of their constituent keywords. Thus, each term is repeatedly mentioned under the heading of each of its keywords. It is simply an index of words within terms. The keywords are "out of context" because they are listed alphabetically rather than in the context of how they appear in the terms.

linked data. A set of W3C specifications for web publishing that makes the data or content part of the Semantic Web, comprising URIs as names of things and HTTP URIs for looking up, using W3C standards (RDF and SPARQL) to describe the content, and links out to other content URIs.

localization. Translation into another language of software or online information plus other changes needed to adapt the displayed information to the target audience. This includes translating of content, menus, pop-ups, online help, and so on and supporting documentation. Additional adaptations include country-specific sorting and alphabetizing schemes, use of commas or decimals in numbers, date and time formats, and currency and other symbols.

machine learning. A method of auto-categorization whereby sample pre-indexed documents are submitted to the system, which then uses algorithms and performs statistical analysis to "learn" patterns of text content to determine what kind of text typically gets indexed with which taxonomy terms. This method is also known as catalog by example.

mapping. Combining two taxonomies (or one taxonomy and a set of keywords) on the same subject, so as to enable one taxonomy to be used for another while still retaining them both as continued distinct taxonomies. It involves individually matching terms from each taxonomy for equivalences.

merging. Combining two terms or two taxonomies deemed to be sufficiently equivalent, by using one of them in place for both, and the legacy terms not chosen to be used are then converted to non-preferred terms as appropriate.

metadata. Standardized data for a collection of resources/assets/ documents/files; sometimes referred to as "data about data," with defined fields, such as title, creator, date, location, audience, and subject. Values for some of the metadata fields, such as subject, can be managed with a controlled vocabulary.

named entities. Indexing terms for specific named people, places, organizations, events, creative works, products, laws, and so on, which generally correspond with proper nouns (with the possible addition of years or dates). Named entities in taxonomies are typically managed in distinct vocabulary files, categories, or facets.

narrower term. A preferred term that, in a hierarchical relationship to another term, is narrower in meaning, more specific, or a part with respect to a systematic whole. Also called a child term.

natural language processing. Technologies to automatically discern the meaning of text based on both linguistics and computer science, typically involving the parsing of text so that the grammar is also taken into consideration. Natural language processing technologies are often used in automated indexing.

NISO. National Information Standards Organization. A nonprofit association accredited by the American National Standards Institute that identifies, develops, maintains, and publishes technical standards pertaining to information management.

node. A concept within a hierarchical taxonomy. If a hierarchy is like a tree, then the nodes are the points where branches or leaves come out. A node may refer to the preferred term alone, especially if there are no nonpreferred terms, or to the preferred term plus its nonpreferred variants. But unlike the word *term*, a node is never used to refer to nonpreferred terms.

node label. A dummy term in a displayed hierarchical taxonomy; it holds the place to organize and label a category of narrower terms but is not used in indexing and retrieval itself. Node labels are often distinguished from indexing terms in a display by use of brackets or a different font style.

node name. Another name for a preferred term when the designation node is used for concepts. This is more often an internal, rather than an end-user, designation.

nondescriptor. Another name for a nonpreferred term, especially when preferred terms are called descriptors.

nonpreferred term. A variant term for a concept, for which a different term is preferred. A nonpreferred term points to a preferred term with a *Use* reference and is linked to a preferred term with an equivalence type of relationship. Nonpreferred terms are also sometimes called nondescriptors, nonpostable terms, alternate terms, or synonyms. A nonpreferred term serves as a synonym in a taxonomy but is not necessarily a linguistic synonym.

object. Another name for a concept, especially in an object-oriented database structure. An object also comprises any nonpreferred terms and their definition, notes, and any other attributes. The information on relationships to other terms/objects may also be considered part of an object.

ontology. A complex knowledge organization system that aims to describe a domain of knowledge. Relationships between concepts (also called individuals) in an ontology have various meanings and thus are called semantic relationships.

open indexing. Indexing of periodical or other accumulating content, whereby the index continually grows as content is added or revised. Open indexing usually relies on a taxonomy to maintain consistent use of index terms. Contrasts with closed or back-of-the-book indexing.

orphan term. A preferred term that has no broader terms and no narrower terms. Orphan terms should not exist in a hierarchical taxonomy, but they could be present in a thesaurus, although they are rare.

OWL. Web Ontology Language. Semantic markup language, built on the Resource Description Framework (RDF) for publishing and sharing ontologies on the web; supports Semantic Web applications. OWL is a set of guidelines supported by the World Wide Web Consortium.

parent term. Another name for a broader term, a designation used more in hierarchical taxonomies than in thesauri. A narrower term is then called a child term.

permuted index. A kind of alphabetical thesaurus display, more common in printed formats, whereby all the terms are sorted alphabetically, not by their first word but by each of their constituent words (keywords, not prepositions or articles) and thus repeated in the alphabetical list for each word. It is thus an index of words within terms. There are two variations, keyword in context (KWIC) and keyword out of context (KWOC). It is also called a rotated index.

polyhierarchy. A hierarchical structure in which a term has two or more broader terms; also called multiple broader terms (MBT).

postcoordination. The design or tendency of a taxonomy, its indexing, and its retrieval in which terms are kept simple, and usually a specific combination of terms is needed to describe a complex concept. Faceted search makes use of postcoordination, although postcoordination is not limited to faceted search. In any case, concepts are combined after indexing. The opposite taxonomy design approach is precoordinated terms.

precoordination. The design or tendency of a taxonomy to have complex specific terms, typically a noun phrase with multiple adjectives, which describe something that might otherwise be described by two separate terms. Another type of precoordination involves combining two terms, a main entry and subentry, both in indexing and at retrieval. In either case, concepts are combined prior to indexing and retrieval. The opposite taxonomy design is postcoordination.

preferred term. The displayed word or phrase for a concept, which a taxonomist has chosen as the best wording of the concept. Nonpreferred terms are the various synonyms, variants, or other sufficiently equivalent words or phrases used as cross-references pointing to the preferred term. Other names for a preferred term include descriptor, authorized term, and node name.

RDF. Resource Description Framework. A standard supported by the World Wide Web Consortium based on XML syntax for representing information about resources on the World Wide Web.

reciprocal relationships. All relationships between terms in a taxonomy are reciprocal because they function in both directions between a pair of terms, even if the relationship is not identical in both directions.

recursive retrieval. When a user selects a taxonomy term that has narrower terms, content will be retrieved not only for what was indexed with the selected term but also for what was indexed with each of its narrower terms. As a result, broader terms retrieve a greater number of results than narrower terms do.

regular expressions. Special text strings, in a prescribed syntax and scheme, for describing complex search pattern instructions, called regex for short. Regular expressions may be used to contribute to rules-based auto-categorization, among many other uses.

related term. A preferred term in an associative relationship with another term, which is also called a related term, since the relationship is symmetrical.

rotated index. Another name for a permuted index, a kind of alphabetical thesaurus display.

schema. A description of an XML document or set of documents that defines the tags and elements in the document. A schema is needed because XML tags are user-defined. The schema is a separate document, which can be considered as a model, template, or set of instructions.

scope note. A note attached to a preferred term in a thesaurus to clarify usage, such as by restricting the scope of the term. It is similar to but not the same as a definition of a term. Scope notes are used only as needed, not for all terms.

semantic relationships. Relationships between pairs of terms that have a more specific meaning than the generic relationships of broader term, narrower term, related term, and equivalent term. They are customized relationships defined and created by the taxonomist. Semantic relationships can describe any kind of relationship between a pair of concepts that are common among a number of concepts in the taxonomy, while still being based on either a hierarchical, associative, or equivalent relationship type.

sibling term. One of two or more terms that share the same immediate broader term (or parent).

SKOS. Simple Knowledge Organization System. A standard for XML representation specifically for knowledge organization systems, such as thesauri and taxonomies, built on the RDF to support interoperability for taxonomies.

social tagging. The assignment of tags or keywords by users to content in an unstructured manner without using a taxonomy, whereby anyone in an online community can both create tags and read others' tags, and the popularity of tags also takes on importance. The collection of such tags is called a folksonomy.

SPARQL. Stands for Simple Protocol and RDF Query Language, a standard query language and data access protocol for use with data in the Resource Description Framework (RDF), specified by the World Wide Web Consortium.

stakeholders. People who have a stake in a project, either an interest in it, a responsibility for it, or an influence over it, or who will be affected by it. Typically stakeholders include the taxonomy project manager, indexers, executives who control the taxonomy's funding, and key users or clients.

stemming. The stripping of grammatical endings to a word to obtain the root or stem word. The technique is often used in automated search-and-retrieval systems so that words that differ only in their grammatical endings (e.g., contractors, contracting, contracts) are treated as equivalent matches.

straw-man taxonomy. A first draft of a hierarchical taxonomy, with terms only in the higher levels but not necessarily all levels yet, which could be changed based on feedback. It is called straw-man because, like something built of straw, it can easily be torn down and reconstructed if feedback is critical.

structured indexing. A form of precoordination whereby an indexer assigns a main heading term and then a subdivision term to further narrow or qualify the heading term. For users' benefit, the results should be either a printed browsable alphabetical index or an online interface that permits the user to narrow main term search results by a choice of subdivisions. Structured indexing is standard in book indexing and sometimes used in open/database indexing.

subdivision. A term used in structured indexing to further qualify, narrow, or restrict the application of a main heading term. It may also be called a subheading. Use of subdivisions is a form of precoordination in indexing. Subdivisions may or may not be used in a controlled vocabulary. Subdivisions are similar to but not the same as subentries in book indexes.

subject heading. A preferred term or descriptor, especially in a controlled vocabulary used for human indexing; permits precoordinated or structured indexing by combining a subject heading with a subheading type of term.

symmetrical relationship. A relationship between a pair of terms that is the same in both directions. The only symmetrical relationships are generic associative relationships (related term) and equivalence relationships within a synonym ring.

synonym ring. A simple controlled vocabulary in which all equivalent terms (synonyms) of a concept have equal standing and no single term is designated as preferred. Another name is a synset. A synonym ring is thus not displayed to the end user, and usually there are no other relationships (hierarchical or associative) between concepts.

tagging. The assigning of terms to a content item, such as a file or a document, of either taxonomy terms or any keywords that the person doing the tagging thinks up.

taxonomy. (1) A hierarchically structured system of organizing names of concepts. (2) Any knowledge organization system, whether hierarchical or not, involving controlled names of concepts.

term. A label (word or phrase) for a concept. It is the most common, generic designation, which can be in any controlled vocabulary. It may be used to mean any kind of term, including both preferred terms and nonpreferred terms, but is sometimes used to refer to just the preferred term.

term record. The complete information regarding a term, especially as stored and displayed in taxonomy management or indexing software. It includes all of a term's relationships, notes, categories, and any additional attributes, along with administrative information, such as approval status, and creation and modification dates; in other words, the metadata for a single term. Not all these details need to be included, though, for it to be called a term record.

text mining. Automated methods of deriving high-quality or useful information from text. It could be based on various technologies, including, statistics, machine learning, computational linguistics, and/or pattern recognition. Text mining may be used to support automated indexing/auto-categorization, but it is not limited to such applications.

thesaurus. A structured type of controlled vocabulary that provides information about each term and its relationships to other terms within the same thesaurus. Typical relationships are equivalent, hierarchical, and associative, and term notes are a common feature. Published standards provide guidance on creating knowledge organization thesauri.

thesaurus software. Full-featured software for the design, creation, and management of thesauri or hierarchical taxonomies. Terms and their reciprocal relationships are maintained, and different displays or outputs are supported. Ideally such software supports creating terms and their relationships in accordance with standards, such as ANSI/NISO Z39.19.

top term. In a thesaurus or hierarchical taxonomy, a term that has no broader terms, only narrower terms. It is the top/highest term of its own hierarchy. A top term hierarchy is a display option, not only for hierarchical taxonomies but also for thesauri, in which case all the top terms are arranged alphabetically with their hierarchies of narrower terms displayed under each.

topic. Another name for a preferred term, specifically when it is a subject or common noun, not a named entity (proper noun).

topic map. A standard format for representing complex knowledge organization systems comprising topics (concepts), associations (relationships), and occurrences (either attributes or linked content). A topic map can be considered a kind of ontology or a representation of an ontology. It is a standard of the International Standards Organization: ISO 13250.

tuning. Human intervention adjustments to improve the automatic indexing results of machine-learning-based auto-categorization. It involves making changes to the types and numbers of training documents supplied to the auto-categorization system.

unauthorized term. Another name for a nonpreferred term, if preferred terms are called authorized terms.

upward posting. Treating narrower terms as equivalent, nonpreferred terms. A narrower term may be used as a nonpreferred term if users expect it but there is insufficient content. Upward posting is also done when editing a taxonomy to remove low-use terms or when mapping two taxonomies so that one is used for the other and the other taxonomy has a greater number of narrower terms.

weighting. In indexing, the assignment of degrees of strength of linkage between a document and a given index term. If implemented, there are typically only two or three levels of weight from which the indexer may choose. In automated indexing, weighting is usually called relevancy, and there can be various percentages of relevancies. In taxonomy design, there could also be the option of weights between relationships, but this is a level of complexity that is relatively rare.

World Wide Web Consortium. Abbreviated as W3C, the international standards organization for the World Wide Web, which has offices in various countries. It ensures compatibility for HTML, XML, RDF, OWL, and other coding schemes and their variations used for the web.

XML (eXtensible Markup Language). A general-purpose markup language for structuring, storing, and transporting data, which allows the user to define and label all of the tags, following only standard syntax conventions.

Zthes. A standard schema designed specifically for ANSI/NISO Z39.19-based thesauri, using XML syntax, to support interoperability of such thesauri.

Recommended Reading

Chapter 1

Abbas, June. *Structures for Organizing Knowledge: Exploring Taxonomies, Ontologies, and Other Schemas*. New York: Neal-Schuman, 2010.

Hlava, Marjorie M. K. *The Taxobook, Part 1: History, Theories, and Concepts of Knowledge Organization*. San Rafael, CA: Morgan & Claypool, 2014.

Hodge, Gale. *Systems of Knowledge Organization for Digital Libraries: Beyond Traditional Authority Files*. Washington, DC: The Digital Library Federation Council on Library and Information Resources, 2000. www.clir.org/pubs/reports/pub91/pub91.pdf.

Lambe, Patrick. "'Defining Our Terms' and 'Taxonomies Can Take Many Forms.'" In *Organising Knowledge: Taxonomies, Knowledge and Organisational Effectiveness*. Oxford: Chandos, 2007.

Chapter 2

Lambe, Patrick. "Taxonomists: Evolving or Extinct?" Presentation, Taxonomy Boot Camp conference, San Jose, CA, November 19, 2009. conferences.infotoday.com/documents/71/2818_Lambe.pdf.

Chapters 3 and 4

Aitchison, Jean, Alan Gilchrist, and David Bawden. "'Vocabulary Control,' 'Specificity and Compound Terms,' and 'Structure and Relationships.'" In *Thesaurus Construction and Use: A Practical Manual*. 4th ed. Chicago, IL: Fitzroy Dearborn, 2000.

Hlava, Marjorie M. K. *The Taxobook, Part 2: Principles and Practices of Taxonomy Construction.* San Rafael, CA: Morgan & Claypool, 2014.

Broughton, Vanda. *Essential Thesaurus Construction.* London: Facet, 2006.

National Institute of Standards Organization. ANSI/NISO Z39.19-2005 (R2010) *Guidelines for Construction, Format, and Management of Monolingual Controlled Vocabularies.* Bethesda, MD: NISO Press, 2010.

Zeng, Marcia Lei. "Construction of Controlled Vocabularies: A Primer." 2005. marciazeng.slis.kent.edu/Z3919.

Chapter 5

Hedden, Heather. "Taxonomy Software Trends." *The Accidental Taxonomist Blog,* January 31, 2015. accidental-taxonomist.blog-spot.com/2015/01/taxonomy-software-trends.html.

Pohs, Wendi. "Selecting a Taxonomy Management Tools." Presentation, SLA Annual Conference, San Diego, CA, June 2013. https:// www.sla.org/wp-content/uploads/2013/06/SelectingTool_Pohs .pdf.

Chapter 6

Bates, Marcia. "Indexing and Access for Digital Libraries and the Internet: Human, Database, and Domain Factors." Department of Information Studies, University of California, Los Angeles, 1996. www.gseis.ucla.edu/faculty/bates/articles/indexdlib.html.

Teridman, Daniel. "Folksonomies Tap People Power." *WIRED*, February, 2005. www.wired.com/2005/02/folksonomies-tap-people -power.

Chapter 7

Bedford, Denise A. D. "Ontologies, Taxonomies and Search." Presentation, Special Libraries Association conference, Baltimore,

MD, June 15, 2006. sla.dsoc.googlepages.com/Bedford2006 Ontologies.pdf.

Miller, Don. "Just the Facts: Auto-classification and Taxonomies." *Concept Searching,* 2014. www.conceptsearching.com/wp/ solutions-and-product-information.

Pohs, Wendi. "Building a Taxonomy for Auto-classification." *ASIS&T Bulletin.* Taxonomies in Practice Special Section, December 2012/January 2013. www.asis.org/Bulletin/Dec-12/DecJan13_ Pohs.html.

Reamy, Tom. *Enterprise Content Categorization—The Business Strategy for a Semantic Infrastructure.* SAS Institute, 2010. www .kapsgroup.com/presentations/ContentCategorization-Business %20Value.pdf.

Chapter 8

Quintarelli, E., A. Resmini, and L. Rosati. "FaceTag: Integrating Bottom-up and Top-down Classification in a Social Tagging System." *Bulletin of the American Society for Information Science & Technology* 33 (June/July 2007). www.asis.org/Bulletin/Jun-07/ quintarelli_et_al.html.

Tunkelang, Daniel. *Faceted Search.* San Rafael, CA: Morgan & Claypool, 2009.

Weinberger, David. *Everything Is Miscellaneous: The Power of the New Digital Disorder.* New York: Times Books, 2007.

Chapter 9

Blocks, Dorothee, Daniel Cunliffe, and Douglas Tudhope. "A Reference Model for User-System Interaction in Thesaurus-Based Searching." *Journal of the American Society for Information Science and Technology* 57, no. 12 (2006): 1655–65.

Gilchrist, Alan, and Barry Mahon, eds. *Information Architecture: Designing Information Environments for Purpose.* New York: Neal-Schuman, 2004.

Hlava, Marjorie M. K. *The Taxobook, Part 3: Applications, Implementation, and Integration in Search.* San Rafael, CA: Morgan & Claypool, 2014.

Louis Rosenfeld, Louis, Peter Morville, and Jorge Arango. *Information Architecture: For the Web and Beyond.* 4th ed. Sebastopol, CA: O'Reilly Media, 2015.

Morville, Peter, and Jefferey Callender. *Search Patterns.* Sebastopol, CA: O'Reilly Media, 2010.

Chapter 10

Busch, Joseph, and Zach Wahl. "Building an Intranet Governance Strategy Workshop." Presentation, KMWorld Conference, Washington, DC, November 15, 2010. www.taxonomystrategies.com/html/archive.htm.

Carlson, Gary. "Putting the Go in Governance." Presentation, Taxonomy Boot Camp Conference, Washington, DC, November 2, 2015. www.slideshare.net/garyecarlson/factor-presentation-for-taxonomy-bootcamp-governance-2015.

Daniel, Ron, Jr., and Joseph Busch. "Taxonomy Governance." Pre-conference workshop, Enterprise Search Summit, New York, May 16, 2005. www.taxonomystrategies.com/html/archive.htm.

Foulonneau, Muriel, and Jenn Riley. *Metadata for Digital Resources: Implementation, Systems Design, and Interoperability.* Oxford: Chandos, 2008.

Jansen, Bernard J. "Search Log Analysis: What It Is, What's Been Done, How to Do It." *Library & Information Science Research* 28, no. 3 (2006): 407–32.

Lambe, Patrick. "'Preparing for a Taxonomy Project,' 'Designing Your Taxonomy,' and 'Implementing Your Taxonomy.'" In *Organising Knowledge: Taxonomies, Knowledge and Organisational Effectiveness.* Oxford: Chandos, 2007.

Owens, Leslie. *How to Build a High-Octane Taxonomy for ECM and Enterprise Search Systems.* Cambridge, MA: Forrester Research, November 17, 2008.

Spencer, Donna. *Card Sorting: Designing Usable Categories*. New York: Rosenfeld Media, 2009.

Stewart, Darin L. "Preparations." In *Building Enterprise Taxonomies*. Portland, OR: Mokita Press, 2008.

Chapter 11

Allemang, Dean, and Jim Hendler. *Semantic Web for the Working Ontologist: Effective Modeling in RDFS and OWL*. 2nd ed. Waltham, MA: Morgan Kaufmann, 2011.

Dextre Clarke, Stella G., and Marcia Lei Zeng. "From ISO 2788 to ISO 25964: The Evolution of Thesaurus Standards Towards Interoperability and Data Modeling." *Information Standards Quarterly* 24, no. 1 (2012): 20–6. www.niso.org/publications/isq/2012/v24no1/clarke/.

ISO 25954-2 *Information and Documentation—Thesauri and Interoperability with Other Vocabularies—Part 2: Interoperability with Other Vocabularies*. Geneva: International Organization for Standardization, 2013.

Stewart, Darin L. "Interoperability." In *Building Enterprise Taxonomies*. Portland, OR: Mokita Press, 2008.

Sweeny, Jim, "Successfully Managing Multilingual Taxonomies." Presentation, Taxonomy Community of Practice, Washington, DC, November 5, 2013. http://www.slideshare.net/jws356/multi-lingual-tbc2013v4.

SKOS Primer. http://www.w3.org/TR/skos-primer/.

Will, Leonard. "The ISO 25964 Data Model for the Structure of an Information Retrieval Thesaurus. *Bulletin of the American Society for Information Science and Technology* 38, no. 4 (April/May 2012): 48–51. www.asis.org/Bulletin/Apr-12/AprMay12_Will.pdf.

Chapter 12

Hedden, Heather. "Opportunities in Freelance Taxonomy Work." *Key Words, The Bulletin of the American Society for Indexing* 22, no. 12 (December 2014): 165–167

Websites

Chapter 1

International Organization for Standardization (ISO), www.iso.
org/iso/catalogue_ics
National Information Standards Organization (NISO), www.niso.org
ANSI/NISO Z39.19 2005, www.niso.org/standards/z39-19-2005
Library of Congress Subject Headings, authorities.loc.gov
Medical Subject Headings, www.nlm.nih.gov/mesh/MBrowser.
html
ERIC Thesaurus, eric.ed.gov
Getty Research Institute Vocabularies, getty.edu/research/tools/
vocabularies
Verizon SuperPages, www.superpages.com/yellowpages
Amazon.com departments, www.amazon.com/gp/site-directory
Shoebuy.com advanced search, www.shoebuy.com
Microbial Life Education Resources, serc.carleton.edu/
microbelife/resources
Information Architecture Institute site map, iainstitute.org/en/
site-map.php
MyFlorida.com site map, www.myflorida.com/taxonomy
Taxonomy Warehouse, www.taxonomywarehouse.com
www.wand.com
www.photo-keywords.com/keywording-resources.php

Chapter 3

AlchemyAPI, www.aclchemyapi.com
TerMine, www.nactem.ac.uk/software/termine

Translated Labs, labs.translated.net/terminology-extraction
Term Extraction, fivefilters.org
Online Thesauri and Authority Files, American Society for
    Indexing, www.asindexing.org/about-indexing/thesauri/
    online-thesauri-and-authority-files

Chapter 5

Xmind, www.xmind.net
FreeMind, freemind.sourceforge.net/wiki
Cmap, cmap.ihmc.us
TheBrain, www.thebrain.com
MindManager, www.mindjet.com
VisiMap, www.visimap.com
TopBraid Composer, www.topquadrant.com/tools/modeling-
    topbraid-composer-standard-edition
Taxonomy Warehouse, www.taxonomywarehouse.com
TaxoBank resource website, http://www.taxobank.org/content/
    resources
MultiTes, www.multites.com
Coreon, www.coreon.com
Data Harmony Thesaurus Master, www.dataharmony.com
Mondeca Intelligent Topic Manager, www.mondeca.com
PoolParty, www.poolparty.biz
SAS Ontology Management, www.sas.com
Semaphore, www.smartlogic.com
STAR/Thesaurus from Cuadra Associates, lucidea.com
Synaptica, www.synaptica.com
TopQuadrant Enterprise Vocabulary Net, www.topquadrant.com
Wordmap, www.wordmap.com
TemaTres, www.vocabularyserver.com
VocBench, vocbench.uniroma2.it
ThManager, thmanager.sourceforge.net
Protégé, protege.stanford.edu

SKOS Editor Plug-in, code.google.com/p/skoseditor
SoutronTHESAURUS, www.soutronglobal.com
Adlib, www.adlibsoft.com
a.k.a. from Synercon, www.a-k-a.co
One-2-One from Active Classification Solutions, www.acs121.com

Chapter 6

Delicious, delicious.com
Pinterest, www.pinterest.com
Diigo, www.diigo.com
Flickr, www.flickr.com

Chapter 7

NetOwl, www.netowl.com
Rosette Entity Extractor, www.basistech.com/text-analytics/
    rosette/entity-extractor
Rosoka Extraction, www.rosoka.com/content/extraction
OpenCalais, www.clearforest.com/solutions.html
BA Insight, www.BAInsight.com
conceptSearching, www.conceptsearching.com
Cogito from Expert Systems, www.expertsystem.com
Data Harmony MAI, www.dataharmony.com
Mondeca Content Annotation Manager, www.mondeca.com
OpenText Content Analytics, www.opentext.com/what-we-do/
    products/discovery/information-access-platform/
    content-analytics
PoolParty Power Tagging, www.poolparty.biz/poolparty-power
    tagging
Semaphore Classification Server, www.smartlogic.com/what-we-
    do/products-overview/classification-server
SAS Enterprise Content Categorization, http://support.sas.com/
    software/products/ccs/index.html Synaptica, www.synaptica.com

Chapter 8

Job facets on Simply Hired, www.simplyhired.com/a/jobs/
  advanced-search
Recipe facets on Food.com, www.food.com/recipe
Car facets at Kelley Blue Book, www.kbb.com/cars-for-sale
Art object facets at the Carnegie Museum of Art, www.cmoa.org/
  collection-search
Shirt facets at Sears, www.sears.com

Chapter 9

USDA National Agriculture Library Thesaurus, agclass.nal.usda.gov
ERIC Thesaurus A-Z Browse display, eric.ed.gov
Dex Media Superpages yellow pages directory, www.superpages.
  com/yellowpages
USA Today Content Tree, content.usatoday.com/community/tags/
  topic-index.aspx
Lynda.com categories, www.Lynda.com
Amazon.com categories, www.amazon.com/gp/site-directory
Buzzillions facets, www.buzzillions.com
North Carolina State University Libraries facets, www.lib.ncsu.
  edu/catalog
Clinical Trials facets, www.clinicaltrials.gov/ct2/search/advanced

Chapter 10

ClickTale, www.clicktale.com
Clicky, www.getclicky.com
iWebTrack, www.iwebtrack.com
OptimalSort, www.optimalworkshop.com/optimalsort
User Zoom Card Sorting, www.userzoom.com/card-sorting
Measuring the User Experience, www.measuringux.com/
  CardSorting

Chapter 11

XML, www.w3.org/XML

Zthes, zthes.z3950.org

RDF, www.w3.org/RDF

OWL, www.w3.org/2001/sw/wiki/OWL

SKOS, www.w3.org/2004/02/skos

AGROVOC Thesaurus, http://aims.fao.org/vest-registry/vocabularies/
agrovoc-multilingual-agricultural-thesaurus

Chapter 12

Taxonomy Jobs Yahoo! list, *groups.yahoo.com/neo/groups/
taxonomy-jobs*

Taxonomies & Controlled Vocabularies SIG directory of available
freelance taxonomists, www.taxonomies-sig.org/members.htm

Kent State University, School of Library & Information Science,
www.kent.edu/slis/library-and-information-science-workshops

Simmons College, School of Library and Information Science,
www.simmons.edu/academics/professional-education/
slis-continuing-ed-workshops

University of Toronto, School of Continuing Studies and Faculty of
Information, learn.utoronto.ca/courses-programs/business-
professionals/ischool

University of Wisconsin at Madison, School of Library and
Information Science, www.slis.wisc.edu/continueed.htm

American Society for Indexing, "Practical Taxonomy Creation,"
www.asindexing.org/online-learning/taxonomy-hedden

AIIM, "Taxonomy & Metadata Practitioner Course," www.aiim.org/
Training/Certificate-Courses/Taxonomy-and-Metadata

SLA Taxonomy Division webinars, taxonomy.sla.org/category/ce

Association for Library Collections and Technical Services division
of the ALA, "Controlled Vocabulary & Thesaurus Design," www.
loc.gov/catworkshop/courses/thesaurus

SLA conferences, www.sla.org/attend

American Society for Indexing Annual Meeting, www.asindexing. org/conferences

Association for Information Science & Technology Annual Meeting, www.asist.org/events/annual-meeting

Information Architecture (IA) Summit, www.iasummit.org

Euro IA, www.euroia.org

American Library Association conferences, www.ala.org/ala/ conferencesevents

AIIM Conference, www.aiimevents.com

International Semantic Web Conference (ISWC), swsa.semanticweb.org/content/ international-semantic-web-conference-iswc

Taxonomy Boot Camp, www.taxonomybootcamp.com

KMWorld, www.kmworld.com/conference

Henry Stewart DAM, www.henrystewartconferences.com

SPTechCon, www.sptechcon.com

ASI Taxonomies & Controlled Vocabularies SIG, www.taxonomies-sig.org

SLA Taxonomy Division, taxonomy.sla.org

Information Architecture Institute, www.iainstitute.org

Association for Information Science & Technology, www.asist.org

Meetup.com, www.meetup.com

Taxonomy Community of Practice, groups.yahoo.com/neo/ groups/taxocop/info

Taxonomy Community of Practice from LinkedIn, www.linkedin. com/groups/1750

Construction of Controlled Vocabularies: A Primer, written by a member of the ANSI/NISO Z39.19 Standard Committee, marciazeng.slis.kent.edu/Z3919/index.htm

Accidental Taxonomist, accidental-taxonomist.blogspot.com

Earley & Associates Blog, www.earley.com/blog

Enterprise Knowledge, www.enterprise-knowledge.com/category/
   blog

Green Chameleon, by Patrick Lambe, www.greenchameleon.com

Semantic Puzzle, blog.semantic-web.at

Synaptica Central, www.synapticacentral.com

TaxoDiary, taxodiary.com

Access Innovations, www.accessinn.com/media-library

Controlled Vocabulary, www.controlledvocabulary.com

Taxonomy Strategies, www.taxonomystrategies.com/html/library.
   htm

Taxonomy Warehouse, www.taxonomywarehouse.com

About the Author

Heather Hedden has been active in developing and editing taxonomies since 1995. She has worked as an independent consultant (Hedden Information Management, www.hedden-information.com) and currently is a senior vocabulary editor at Cengage Learning. Heather is also an instructor of taxonomy development through the continuing education program of Simmons College School of Library and Information Science.

Heather began her taxonomy work as a controlled vocabulary editor at Cengage Learning's predecessor companies, Information Access Company, Gale Group, and Thomson Learning. Her work there included converting the controlled vocabularies into ANSI/NISO standard thesauri, updating and adding new taxonomy terms, communicating new terms and policies to indexers, mapping taxonomies, and creating new user interface taxonomies. Heather then worked as the information taxonomist at an enterprise search software startup, Viziant Corporation, where she was solely responsible for developing all taxonomies used with machine-learning-based auto-categorization. After that, she worked as the taxonomy manager at First Wind, where she developed taxonomies for search and navigation in the company's SharePoint intranet. Heather worked as a taxonomy consultant employee of Project Performance Company and then pursued full-time independent taxonomy consulting through Hedden Information Management. Over the years, Heather has also done freelance back-of-the-book indexing.

Heather is the author of *Indexing Specialties: Web Sites* (2007), the chapter "Controlled Vocabularies, Thesauri, and Taxonomies" in *Index It Right! Advice From the Experts* (Vol. 2, 2010), and the chapter "Indexing Arabic Names" in *Indexing Names* (2012), all of which are published by Information Today, Inc., on behalf of the American Society for Indexing (ASI). She has also published numerous articles in journals, such as *EContent, Intranets, Computers in Libraries, Journal of Digital Asset Management, The Indexer*, and *Key Words* (bulletin of ASI). Heather has given presentations and workshops nationally and internationally at conferences, including Taxonomy Boot Camp, Enterprise Search Summit, Gilbane Conference, Content Management Professionals, SLA, ASI, Indexing Society of Canada, Society of Indexers (UK), and Netherlands Society of Indexers.

Her professional association memberships include Special Libraries Association and its Taxonomy Division, the Information Architecture Institute, and ASI. Heather has served as president of the New England Chapter of ASI, manager of the Web Indexing special interest group of ASI, and founder/manager of the Taxonomies & Controlled Vocabularies special interest group of ASI. She is currently (2015–2018) a member of the board of the American Society for Indexing and a member (2015–2016) of the NISO working group "Development of Standards to Support Bibliographic Data Exchange."

Heather has a BA from Cornell University and an MA from Princeton University. She lives with her husband in Carlisle, Massachusetts.

Index